Sheffield Hallam University
Learning and IT Services
Collegiate Learning Centre
Collegiate Crescent Campus
Sheffield   S10 2BP

KT-451-473

Sheffield Hallam University
Learning and Information Services
Withdrawn From Stock

ONE WEEK LOAN

THE JUVENILE SEX OFFENDER

The Juvenile Sex Offender

SECOND EDITION

EDITED BY

Howard E. Barbaree
William L. Marshall

THE GUILFORD PRESS
New York   London

© 2006 The Guilford Press
A Division of Guilford Publications, Inc.
72 Spring Street, New York, NY 10012
www.guilford.com

All rights reserved

No part of this book may be reproduced, translated, stored in a retrieval
system, or transmitted, in any form or by any means, electronic, mechanical,
photocopying, microfilming, recording, or otherwise, without written
permission from the Publisher.

Printed in the United States of America

This book is printed on acid-free paper.

Last digit is print number: 9 8 7 6 5 4 3 2 1

Library of Congress Cataloging-in-Publication Data

The juvenile sex offender / edited by Howard E. Barbaree, William L.
Marshall.—2nd ed.
    p. cm.
Includes bibliographical references and index.
ISBN 1-59385-198-7 (cloth)
1. Teenage sex offenders. I. Barbaree, H. E. II. Marshall, William L.
RJ506.S48J88 2006
364.15′3′0835—dc22

                                            2005017006

In memory of Stephen M. Hudson
January 18, 1950–November 1, 2001

On the first day of November 2001, our esteemed coeditor and dear friend Steve Hudson died in his hometown of Christchurch, New Zealand. His death was a shock to those who knew his energetic and buoyant spirit and, of course, to those who loved him.

Steve spent his 1990 sabbatical leave in Ontario, Canada, in order to work with us. He proved to be a remarkably talented colleague whose theoretical, research, and clinical skills enhanced all aspects of our work. We were both richer for his time with us. Steve went on to publish extensively, and his work, along with that of his colleague Dr. Tony Ward, has exerted a profound influence on the field of sex offender research and treatment. His brilliance as a researcher was surpassed only by his skill as a clinician. All who knew him, either directly or indirectly, profited from the experience.

Steve will be sorely missed as a valuable colleague and friend. He leaves behind his wife, Karyn; son, Ben; and daughter, Chloe, each of whom he loved dearly.

HOWARD E. BARBAREE
WILLIAM L. MARSHALL

About the Editors

Howard E. Barbaree, PhD, is Professor and Head, Law and Mental Health Program in the Department of Psychiatry, University of Toronto, and Clinical Director, Law and Mental Health Program, Centre for Addiction and Mental Health, Toronto, Ontario, Canada. He has devoted much of his career to research, teaching, and clinical practice related to sexual aggression and sexual deviance. Dr. Barbaree has published numerous journal articles and book chapters and is coeditor of the *Handbook of Sexual Assault: Issues, Theories, and Treatment of the Offender* (1990) as well as of the first edition of *The Juvenile Sex Offender* (1993). He has served as a member of the National Institute of Mental Health Violence and Traumatic Stress Grant Review Committee and received the Significant Achievement Award from the Association for the Treatment of Sexual Abusers in 2000. In 2004 Dr. Barbaree began a 4-year term as editor of *Sexual Abuse: Research and Treatment.*

William L. Marshall, PhD, is Professor Emeritus of Psychology and Psychiatry at Queen's University and Director of Rockwood Psychological Services, Kingston, Ontario, Canada, which provides sex offender treatment in two Canadian federal penitentiaries. Dr. Marshall has 35 years of experience in assessment, treatment, and research with sex offenders and has over 300 publications, including 16 books. Along with Dr. Barbaree and the late Stephen M. Hudson, he served as coeditor of the first edition of *The Juvenile Sex Offender.* He was President of the Association for the Treatment of Sexual Abusers from 2000 to 2001 and received its Significant Achieve- ment Award in 1993. In 1999 Dr. Marshall received the Santiago Grisolia Prize from the Queen Sophia Centre in Spain for his worldwide contributions to the reduction of violence, and in 2000 he was elected a Fellow of the Royal Society of Canada. In 2003 Dr. Marshall was one of six invited experts who were asked to advise the Vatican on how best to deal with sexual abuse within the Catholic Church.

Contributors

Karen Bachar, PhD, Department of Psychology, University of Arizona, Tucson, Arizona

John Bancroft, PhD, (retired) The Kinsey Institute for Research in Sex, Gender, and Reproduction, Indiana University, Bloomington, Indiana

Howard E. Barbaree, PhD, Law and Mental Health Program, Centre for Addiction and Mental Health, University of Toronto, Toronto, Ontario, Canada

Judith V. Becker, PhD, Department of Psychology, University of Arizona, Tucson, Arizona

Ray Blanchard, PhD, Centre for Addiction and Mental Health, University of Toronto, Toronto, Ontario, Canada

John M. W. Bradford, MD, Division of Forensic Psychiatry, University of Ottawa, Ottawa, Ontario, Canada

David L. Burton, PhD, MSW, School for Social Work, Smith College, Northampton, Massachusetts

James M. Cantor, PhD, Centre for Addiction and Mental Health, University of Toronto, Toronto, Ontario, Canada

Alan Carr, PhD, Department of Psychology, University College Dublin, Dublin, Ireland

Paul Fedoroff, MD, Forensic Research Unit, University of Ottawa Institute of Mental Health Research, Ottawa, Ontario, Canada

Sarah Jane Frankel, MA, School of Social Work Joint Doctoral Program in Social Work and Developmental Psychology, University of Michigan, Ann Arbor, Michigan

C. Quince Hopkins, JD, School of Law, Washington and Lee University, Lexington, Virginia

John A. Hunter, PhD, Juvenile Justice Program, Louisiana State University Health Sciences Center, New Orleans, Louisiana

Kelly M. Kadlec, MA, Department of Psychology, University of North Carolina–Greensboro, Greensboro, North Carolina

Mary P. Koss, PhD, Arizona College of Public Health, University of Arizona, Tucson, Arizona

Martin L. Lalumière, PhD, Law and Mental Health Program, Centre for Addiction and Mental Health, University of Toronto, Toronto, Ontario, Canada

Calvin M. Langton, PhD, Law and Mental Health Program, Centre for Addiction and Mental Health, University of Toronto, Toronto, Ontario, Canada

Niklas Långström, PhD, Centre for Violence Prevention, Karolinska Institute, Stockholm, Sweden

Elizabeth J. Letourneau, PhD, Family Services Research Center, Medical University of South Carolina, Charleston, South Carolina

Lenard J. Lexier, MD, Alternative Behavioral Services, Portsmouth, Virginia

William L. Marshall, PhD, Rockwood Psychological Services, Kingston, Ontario, Canada

Gary O'Reilly, PhD, Department of Psychology, University College Dublin, Dublin, Ireland

Lori K. Robichaud, PhD, Centre for Addiction and Mental Health, University of Toronto, Toronto, Ontario, Canada

Stacy Sechrist, MA, Department of Psychology, University of North Carolina–Greensboro, Greensboro, North Carolina

Michael C. Seto, PhD, Centre for Addiction and Mental Health, University of Toronto, Toronto, Ontario, Canada

Stephen W. Smallbone, PhD, School of Criminology and Criminal Justice, Griffith University, Queensland, Australia

Joanne Smith-Darden, MA, School of Social Work Joint Doctoral Program in Social Work and Developmental Psychology, University of Michigan, Ann Arbor, Michigan

Jo Thakker, PhD, Department of Psychology, University of Waikato, Hamilton, New Zealand

Patrick Tidmarsh, PhD, Male Adolescent Program for Positive Sexuality, Adolescent Forensic Health Service, Melbourne, Australia

Tony Ward, PhD, School of Psychology, Victoria University of Wellington, Wellington, New Zealand

Jacquelyn W. White, PhD, Department of Psychology, University of North Carolina–Greensboro, Greensboro, North Carolina

James R. Worling, PhD, Sexual Abuse: Family Education & Treatment (SAFE-T) Program, Thistletown Regional Centre, Toronto, Ontario, Canada

Acknowledgments

The editors would like to sincerely thank Seymour Weingarten, editor-in-chief at The Guilford Press, for his unwavering support and enthusiasm for this project. Seymour assisted us over several hurdles and provided important impetus at critical junctures. Thanks as well to all of the staff at Guilford who contributed to various aspects of production and marketing, including Carolyn Graham, Jennifer DePrima, Katherine Lieber, and Paul Gordon.

We express deep gratitude to Karyn France, who encouraged us to continue with the project after the untimely death of Stephen M. Hudson, who served as coeditor on the first edition of this book. We missed Steve's friendly collegiality and his editorial contribution very much.

As editors, we wish to express our sincere thanks to the authors who have contributed chapters to the book. The chapters are of a uniformly high quality. We particularly appreciate those authors who submitted chapters early in the process and who have patiently accepted inevitable delays in completion of the volume.

Finally, we wish to acknowledge financial support provided by the Correctional Services of Canada and the Ontario Mental Health Foundation during our work on this project. In addition, Howard Barbaree completed much of his work on the book while on a sabbatical generously granted by the Centre for Addiction and Mental Health.

Preface

When we wrote the preface to the first edition of *The Juvenile Sex Offender* in 1993, we complained that, at the time, there was relatively little published empirical research on the topic, and what was available was of uneven quality. This lack of research on the juvenile sex offender stood in stark contrast to what we described as a veritable explosion of scholarly interest in the adult sex offender. By the early 1990s, a large, high-quality scientific literature was available and expanding on the psychological and biological factors underlying sexual aggression perpetrated by adult males. While the first edition provided a comprehensive review of what was known then about the juvenile sex offender, the fact was that we knew very little about this important subject.

Now, more than 10 years later, a modest but respectable scientific literature has emerged and is developing both in quantity and quality. As you will see, the authors who have contributed to the second edition of *The Juvenile Sex Offender* have relied heavily on the empirical data published in the peer-reviewed scientific literature. This edited volume does not contain everything we now know about the juvenile sex offender, but it describes most of the essential information.

Central concepts and terms are defined in the first chapter; following this, sexual crimes committed by the juvenile offender are set in the context of the normal development of sexuality in adolescence. Developmental factors contributing to sexual aggression are presented next; these comprise biological, social, and psychological determinants, including family background and the experience of child sexual abuse. Sexual aggression in the teen years is then discussed in the context of the development of heterosexual relationships and general criminal conduct. Later chapters describe what has been done to intervene with these offenders, including assessment of risk and factors that contribute to risk, and interventions such as cognitive-behavioral and pharmacological treatment. Special chapters are included on legal interventions, including the use of sex offender registries with juveniles and approaches to rehabilitation based on restorative justice.

We trust this book will serve as an important resource to students, researchers, and practitioners in the field and that it will promote future empirical research on the juvenile sex offender.

HOWARD E. BARBAREE
WILLIAM L. MARSHALL

Contents

THE JUVENILE SEX OFFENDER

CHAPTER 1

An Introduction to the Juvenile Sex Offender
Terms, Concepts, and Definitions

Howard E. Barbaree
William L. Marshall

Sexual assault is now recognized as one of the more significant problems in modern Western society, ranking as a societal ill with nonsexual crime, poverty, environmental damage, communicable and chronic disease, and substance abuse. The severity of the problem of sexual assault is the result of the number of individuals who are victimized and the degree of harm they suffer by their victimization. Large-scale surveys using stratified random samples of the general population have informed us of the prevalence of sexual assault. Approximately one half of adult women surveyed report having experienced some form of sexual victimization since the age of 14, and approximately one in six adult women have experienced penetrative rape (e.g., Koss, Gidycz, & Wisniewski, 1987). Similarly, approximately one in four adult female respondents and one in ten male respondents report that they were sexually abused prior to the age of 18 (e.g., Committee on Sex Offenders Against Children and Youth, 1984). The trauma associated with this victimization leads to both immediate and longer term negative effects in a number of domains of mental health outcomes, including depression, anxiety, substance abuse, and negative behavioral outcomes such as early pregnancy, suicide, and antisocial conduct (e.g., Kilpatrick et al., 2000, 2003).

Although the majority of sexual assaults are committed by adult men, a significant minority of sexual assaults, approximately 20%, are committed by juveniles. This chapter provides a general introduction to the understanding, assessment, and treatment of the juvenile sex offender. The chapter discusses terms and defines concepts relating to the offender and his or her criminal behavior. Additionally, the chapter provides important definitions for related concepts, including sexual deviance, sexual abuse, sexual consent, and sexual crime.

The Juvenile Sex Offender

Sex offenders are persons who have been convicted in a criminal court of a sexual crime. Sexual crimes include those that are nominally sexual (e.g., sexual assault, rape) and crimes that have some sexual intent or component (e.g., murder or attempted murder during the commission of a rape, simple assault pled down from rape). This definition excludes persons who are merely suspected of committing sexual offenses (charged but not convicted) and persons who display sexual behaviors that are socially undesirable or deviant but not criminal (e.g., extreme promiscuity). A more detailed definition of sexual crime is presented later in this chapter.

For our purposes in this chapter, we divide sex offenders into two broad age categories: adult and juvenile. The criminal justice system holds an adult sex offender fully responsible for their criminal behavior and subjects them to the full range of criminal sanctions available, including a prison sentence and, in some jurisdictions, the death penalty. The term "juvenile" is used here in the legal sense as describing "an individual who is under an age fixed by law at which he or she would be charged as an adult for a criminal act" (*Merriam-Webster Dictionary of Law*, 1996). In most Western jurisdictions, youthful offenders are provided with a juvenile criminal justice system that is separate from the adult system, in which the penalties are less severe and the emphasis is on rehabilitation rather than punishment. In the majority of U.S. states and in most other Western jurisdictions, a person is considered to be an adult when he or she reaches the age of 18. A small minority of U.S. states ($n = 10$) regard 17-year-olds as adults, and an even smaller number ($n = 3$) regard 16-year-olds as adults (Snyder, 2003).

The law makes an additional distinction between children and juveniles. In the criminal justice system, a person is considered to be a child when, by virtue of his or her immaturity, he or she cannot be held to be responsible for criminal behavior. In most Western jurisdictions, a person younger than 12 years of age is considered to be a child. By definition, then, children cannot be sex offenders because they have not been convicted of a sexual crime. Put a different way, if a person has been convicted of a sexual crime, the convicting court did not regard him or her as a child. When children engage in sexual behaviors that would be regarded as criminal when they are older, they are described as "children with sexual behavior problems" (Grey, Busconi, Houchens, & Pithers, 1997).

In the juvenile courts throughout the United States, from 1985 to 2000, 91.8% of accused persons standing trial for offenses against persons were between the ages of 12 and 17, whereas 6.5% were below the age of 12 and only 1.6% were above the age of 17 (Stahl, Finnegan, & Kang, 2003). Therefore, a juvenile sex offender is a person who has been convicted of a sexual offense and who is considered by law to be old enough to be held criminally responsible for the crime (generally by age 12), but not so old as to be subject to the full range of adult criminal sanctions (as would be the case after his or her 18th birthday).

An alternative age-related nomenclature is based on developmental processes and milestones, with the developmental categories being child, adolescent, and adult. These terms roughly coincide with the legally based terms described previously. Adolescence is defined as "the period of physical and psychological development from the onset of puberty to maturity" (*American Heritage Stedman's Medical Dictionary*, 2002). Puberty is defined as "the condition of being or the period of becoming first capable of reproducing sexually, marked by maturing of the sexual organs, development of secondary sex characteristics, and menstruation in the female . . . the age at which puberty occurs being typically between 13 and 16 years in boys and 11 and 14 in girls" (*Merriam-Webster Medical Dictionary*, 2002).

In the scientific literature, youthful sex offenders may be referred to as juvenile or adolescent sex offenders, these terms being somewhat interchangeable. Strictly speaking, however, these terms refer to different identifying features of the offenders. For example, an offender who is held to be criminally responsible for a sexual offense but who has not yet reached puberty would be a juvenile, not an adolescent, sex offender.

The Incidence and Prevalence of Sexual Crimes by Male Juveniles

Ageton (1983) estimated that 2–4% of adolescent males have reported committing sexually assaultive behavior. Although the prevalence of sexual assault among adolescents may be low, a substantial proportion of all sexual offenses can be attributed to adolescents. The best available estimates suggest that approximately 20% of all rapes and between 30 and 50% of child molestations are perpetrated by adolescent males (Becker, Kaplan, Cunningham-Rathner, & Kavoussi, 1986; Brown, Flanagan, & McLeod, 1984; Deisher, Wenet, Paperny, Clark, & Fehrenbach, 1982; Groth, Longo, & McFadin, 1982). The FBI Uniform Crime Report for 2002 (Federal Bureau of Investigation, 2002) presents arrest data for violent crimes, including murder, forcible rape, aggravated assault, and other sexual offenses. Persons under the age of 18 account for 16.7% of all forcible rapes and 20.61% of other sexual offenses, and these percentages are consistent with figures from 10 years ago. Nevertheless, there have been substantial reductions in the numbers of persons arrested for violent crimes over this same 10-year period, a decrease that is matched by reductions in child sexual victimization, a phenomenon that is at present not completely understood or explained (Finkelhor & Jones, 2004).

Sexual crimes committed by juveniles are sometimes difficult to distinguish from normal sexual activity in adolescence. For example, when a 15-year-old youth has sexual intercourse with his 13-year-old girlfriend, is it criminal sexual activity or normal adolescent sexual development? Of course, when a 30-year-old man has sexual relations with a 13-year-old girl, no one disputes that it is quite clearly classified as criminal behavior.

In order to inform our discussion of these issues, it is necessary to define a number of terms and concepts. The remainder of the chapter provides these definitions. Deviant sexual behavior in adolescence is discussed in terms of (1) the statistical prevalence of particular sexual behaviors in a specific population, (2) moral and religious condemnation of unusual sexual behaviors, (3) potential harmful effects of sexual behaviors, and (4) criminal sanctions. The purpose of the introduction is to compare and contrast three related concepts: sexual deviance, sexual abuse, and sexual crime.

Deviant Sexual Behavior

"Deviance" is a statistical term, denoting the tendency in a distribution of scores of any quantifiable variable for the values of individual observations to disperse from the average value, or midpoint. Accordingly, sexual behavior is said to be deviant when it is outside the "norm" for a particular population of individuals. We can determine whether or not a sexual behavior is deviant if we know the group membership of the individual who has engaged in the behavior and what sexual practices are usual for that group. For example, an unmarried 18-year old-girl engaging in sexual intercourse would be considered normative in modern Western society because such behavior is not unusual in her peer group

(Leitenberg & Saltzman, 2000, 2003). However, such behavior would be considered deviant in many parts of the world where such behavior is unusual in the local population.

Deviant Sexual Behavior in Children and Adolescents

High-quality scientific studies of sexual behavior in adolescents are few in number. The result is that we have very little objective information about the normal developmental course of sexual behavior. There have been many explanations offered to account for this lack of basic and fundamental knowledge. For example, it has been suggested that research on children's sexuality is discouraged by legal and ethical considerations where the mere act of observing or enquiring about sexual behavior in children could lay the experimenter open to charges of sexual abuse (Bancroft, 1989). And the development of sexual modesty and embarrassment from childhood to adolescence has frustrated the accumulation of reliable and accurate information on sexual behaviors in children and adolescents. Friedrich, Grambsch, Broughton, Kuiper, and Beilke (1991) surveyed mothers of 880 2- to 12-year-olds using a behavior checklist that included a number of sexual behaviors. These overt sexual behaviors decreased with age in this sample in both sexes. Money and Ehrhardt (1972) observed this same decline and suggested that as children get older they seek to conceal their sexual behavior in order to conform to society's rules on modesty and manners.

And, even when studies have been done, the observations made have led to widely different interpretations depending on culture and social climate (Vizard, Monck, & Misch, 1995). In Norway, for example, Gundersen, Melas, and Skar (1981) conducted individual interviews with 60 preschool teachers concerning their observations of sexual behavior of their pupils. Many of the teachers reported seeing children exploring their own bodies, manipulating their own genitals, exhibiting an interest in their fellow students' genitals, and behaviors they described as "coitus training." In the United States, Cantwell (1988) described the same behaviors in very young children but judged these preschool and school-age children as "perpetrators" of inappropriate sexual behavior and recommended an educational program of prevention (Vizard et al., 1995).

We do know that adolescents engage in many of the deviant sexual behaviors exhibited by adults, including child molestation, pedophilia, and fetishism (Zolondek, Abel, Northey, & Jordan, 2001). Perhaps ironically, we may know more about deviant than about normative sexual behavior in these age groups. Whereas research into normative sexual behavior of children and adolescents has been difficult and frustrating, research into deviant sexual behavior has become widespread. Upon disclosure, these sexual behaviors become the subject of intense investigation and scrutiny by the school authorities, child protective agencies, the police, the courts, and correctional authorities. These cases are often referred to clinical practitioners for evaluation and intervention. As a consequence, a large clinical and scientific literature now exists on deviant sexual behavior in adolescents. Because our scientific knowledge is based almost entirely on research with clinical cases, it likely suffers from what has been called external validity bias (Rind, Tromovitch, & Bauserman, 2001).

When considering whether or not a sexual behavior is deviant, the issue is complicated during adolescence by the fact that normative sexual behavior changes over age and between developmental stages. In the normal course of development from childhood through adolescence, sexual behavior becomes more frequent, extensive, and complex, following a developmental sequence from hugging and kissing in the earliest stages to fondling and touching of the breasts and genitals in later stages to more intimate interactions involving oral–genital contact and penetrative intercourse in the final stage (Smith & Udry, 1985). When the sexual behavior of an adolescent is consistent with sexual behavior exhibited by his or her peers in their own age group, such sexual behavior is considered to be normative.

However, when children engage in sexual behaviors that are unusual for their current age group, these behaviors are considered deviant even though these same behaviors may be normative later in development. Again, sexual intercourse in young girls provides an illustrative example. Leitenberg and Saltzman (2000) conducted a statewide survey of a representative sample of adolescent girls in grades 8–12 (n = 4,201) in Vermont. Participants were asked to report their age at first experience of consensual sexual intercourse. Prior to age 14, only 5% of surveyed girls reported that they had engaged in sexual intercourse. Therefore, to this stage in development, sexual intercourse is rare or unusual in the peer group, and such behavior might be said to be deviant. However, among the girls who were 18 years of age, 51% reported that they had engaged in sexual intercourse. At this level of prevalence, sexual intercourse would be considered a normative behavior. From a developmental perspective, when a sexual behavior appears earlier in the development sequence than usual in the population, we regard such sexual behavior as deviant.

If we restrict ourselves to the statistical definition of deviance, no value judgment of the sexual behavior is made or conveyed. But deviant sexual behaviors have been characterized in negative terms in a number of ways, including (1) as immoral as a result of religious or moral condemnation, (2) as pathological by diagnosis as a mental disorder, (3) by association as a correlate with negative outcomes, (4) as abusive when the deviant sexual behavior involves nonconsenting partners or children, and (5) as criminal when the behavior violates the criminal law.

Religious or Moral Condemnation of Deviant Sexual Behavior

In colloquial usage, the term "sexual deviance" has acquired a pejorative connotation and conveys at least a tone of moral disapproval, more often outright condemnation. It seems a prominent human trait and a pervasive aspect of human society that religious and moral judgments are readily made about all forms of sexual behavior, but particularly when the sexual behavior is unusual. For the obvious example, the world's religions have condemned homosexual behavior throughout history. But religious disapproval has not been restricted to less prevalent sexual behavior. Leaders in the early Christian church expressed disapproval of sexual intercourse between a husband and his wife even when performed for the purposes of procreation (Tannahill, 1992). A current example of moral condemnation of sex between adolescents is the prohibition by the Catholic Church and other fundamental Christians of premarital sex (e.g., Smith, 1996). In this chapter, we resist the human tendency to condemn sexual behaviors on moral or religious grounds, except, of course, as explained, in the case of sexual abuse, on the basis of its harmful effects on victims.

Resisting the general temptation to make moral judgments of deviant sexual behaviors is especially important when considering deviant sexual behavior in children and adolescents. Young children may not yet have an ability to appreciate that particular sexual behaviors are considered to be morally wrong, socially inappropriate, harmful, or illegal (Pithers & Gray, 1998). In addition, according to many authorities in this field, and as is discussed later, deviant sexual behaviors in adolescents are often the result of abusive experiences they have endured as children (e.g., Craissati, McClurg, & Browne, 2002), in which case moral or religious condemnation is akin to blaming the victim.

Diagnosis as a Mental Disorder

Sexual deviation is often used as a synonym for "sexual perversion" or "paraphilia" (Travin & Protter, 1993). When the object of sexual desire is unusual, an underlying pathology of sexual interest is inferred, and a mental health professional will make a diagnosis of paraphilia according to criteria set out in DSM-IV-TR (American Psychiatric Association, 2000). For example, when the objects of desire are children, women's undergarments, or animals, diagnoses of pedophilia, fetishism, and zoophilia, respectively, would be made.

Deviant Sexual Behavior and Associated Negative Outcomes

Deviant sexual behaviors may come to be viewed as undesirable because they are associated with less desirable circumstances or outcomes. We continue with the example of girls engaging in consenting sexual intercourse at an early age. Such girls exhibit more behavior problems and experience more negative outcomes than similar-age girls who are not yet sexually active (Irwin & Millstein, 1992; Jessor & Jessor, 1977); these behavior problems and negative outcomes include suicide, alcohol use, drug use, truancy, and pregnancy (Leitenberg & Saltzman, 2000). Later, in adulthood, these girls are more likely to endorse symptoms of psychological distress (Leitenberg & Saltzman, 2003). Girls who engage in sexual intercourse early in adolescence experience greater family conflict and exhibit less positive affect (McBride, Paikoff, & Holmbeck, 2003), are more likely to come from single-parent families (Wyatt, Durvasula, Guthrie, LeFranc, & Forge, 1999), and are less likely to achieve their educational goals (Hays, 1987). There are reasons to believe that the younger the girl is when she first has intercourse, the more likely she is to have had a much older partner. For example, Elo, King, and Furstenberg (1999) found that 45% of women who first had intercourse when they were 14 years of age or younger had partners 4 or more years older than themselves, compared with 18% who first had intercourse between ages 15 and 17. Lindberg, Sonenstein, Ku, and Martinez (1997) found that the youngest teenage mothers in their sample were the most likely to have had substantially older partners. These findings suggest that when a girl experiences first intercourse at a very young age, she may have been subject to the undue influence of a much older partner, even though she described the interaction as consenting.

It is not known whether early sexual intercourse causes these less desirable outcomes or whether early sexual intercourse is a result of these undesirable circumstances. Of course, early intercourse together with these outcomes may be a result of some other unknown determining factor (Billy, Lindale, Grady, & Zimmerle, 1988; Bingham & Crockett, 1996; Costa, Jessor, Donovan, & Fortenberry, 1995).

Sexual Abuse

A significant subset of deviant sexual behaviors are referred to as sexually abusive. In order to define sexual abuse properly, we must first define "consent" to sexual relations. Movies, television, and other popular media often portray the pleasurable aspects of sexual activity but place much less emphasis on the significant risks to participants. There are well-known health risks of sexual intercourse, including the acquisition of sexually transmitted diseases and HIV, with the potential for serious negative health outcomes. Girls have their own specific set of risks. Pregnancy and the subsequent birth of a child will present the teenage mother with difficult choices between abortion, giving the child up for adoption, or raising the child in very difficult circumstances. Parenthood leads to serious long-term lifestyle changes and financial challenges. Sexual relationships, particularly during adolescence, are associated with negative emotional states, including jealousy, rejection, and abandonment. Of course, sex can have a number of benefits as well, including increased psychological well-being, the solidification of human partnerships, the formation of family units, and procreation. Considering the potential risks and rewards of sexual relations, the decision to engage in sexual activity can be a critically important decision with long-term consequences for the individual.

There is now widespread recognition that adults have the right to make autonomous decisions concerning their participation in sexual relations (United Nations General Assembly, 1994) by weighing for themselves the balance between the potential risks and rewards of any sexual relationship. This recognition is the result of the long history of the emancipation of women and more recent feminist scholarship and activism (Brownmiller, 1975; Largen, 1985). The absolute right of women to refuse sexual relations has been articulated in the slogan "no means no" used in campaigns on college campuses over the past 15 years to raise awareness of this important principle (Monson, Langhinrichsen-Rohling, & Binderup, 2000). Perhaps the ultimate recognition of women's right to refuse sexual relations is contained in laws against rape in marriage that have been enacted over the past several years in many Western jurisdictions. Although the right to refuse sexual relations has been won largely by women for women, the resulting principle that consent is required to be obtained before sexual relations begin is now a benefit afforded to all persons.

When sexual interactions are forced against a nonconsenting person, the sexual interactions are, by definition, abusive. In these circumstances, the person (adult or juvenile) who forces sex is referred to as the "perpetrator" or as a "sexual abuser," and the nonconsenting person is recognized as a victim of sexual abuse. Though it has been argued that prevalence rates of sexual abuse are high (e.g., Koss et al., 1987), there is general agreement that sexual abuse is outside the norm in our society. Therefore, sexual abuse is a subset of deviant sexual behavior; not all deviant sexual behaviors are abusive, but all abusive sexual behaviors are considered to be deviant.

Considering the relationship between sexual abuse and consent to sexual relations, it follows that sex between an adult (or older adolescent) and a child is inherently abusive because children are unable to provide true consent (Finkelhor, 1979). Finkelhor articulated two preconditions to true consent: (1) full knowledge regarding what is being consented to and (2) absolute freedom to accept or decline. Young children have not yet developed the capacity to give consent to sexual relations because (1) they have not yet developed the intellectual ability or the knowledge to properly weigh the risks and rewards of sexual relations and (2) children are susceptible to influence by adults, who, by virtue of their maturity and greater experience, easily exert control over children (Ondersma et al., 2001). In short, children are neither knowledgeable nor autonomous beings, and as a consequence they are not able or free to make their own decisions regarding sexual relations. Over the past 25 years, the influence of the child protection, victim's rights, and women's movements have combined with emerging scientific research regarding the harmful effects of child sexual abuse, leading to a dramatic shift in public awareness and concern. Children have come to be viewed as potential victims of sexual exploitation by adults or adolescents, and as such, they deserve and require what protection society can provide (Ondersma et al., 2001; Myers, Diedrich, Lee, Fischer, & Stern, 1999).

An important distinction is to be made here between "willingness" and "consent." A child may be "willing" to engage in sexual interactions. He or she may express a desire for sexual interactions and may even seem to initiate sexual interactions. But however willing they may be, according to the argument just presented, children do not have the psychological capacity to give consent. Therefore, all sexual interactions between an adult and a child are, by definition, abusive to the child. Child sexual abuse has been used in the psychological literature to describe virtually all sexual interactions between children or adolescents and significantly older persons, as well as between same-age children or adolescents when coercion or a power imbalance is involved (Rind, Tromovitch, & Bauserman, 1998).

Sexual Crime

In all jurisdictions in modern Western society, criminal laws against sexual assault have been enacted to protect the individual's right to autonomy and self-determination in sexual relations. Although these laws contain language that varies from jurisdiction to jurisdiction, they all prohibit all forms of sexual behavior, including touching, kissing, and intercourse, when the prospective sexual partner does not give consent. Forcing another person of any age to engage in sexual relations of any kind is against the law in every modern Western society.

Additionally, in every jurisdiction in modern Western society, criminal laws specifically protect children from sexual victimization by adults and/or adolescents. When a child is unwilling and sexual interactions are forced upon him or her, the sexual crime is referred to as child rape, or simply as sexual assault. When the child is willing and agrees to sexual interactions with an adult, the sexual crime is sometimes referred to as "statutory rape" (Leitenberg & Saltzman, 2000, 2003; Oberman, 1994).

Laws against child sexual abuse require the establishment of an age below which the individual is considered to be unable to provide consent to sexual relations. This is often referred to as the "age of consent." According to Leitenberg and Saltzman (2003), in the United States, 15 states have established 18 years, six states have set 17 years, and 28 states have chosen 16 years as their age of consent. Only one American state has established age 14 as the age of consent (Donovan, 1997). In Europe, one half of the separate legal jurisdictions use 14 as the age of consent, whereas most of the remainder has set 15 or 16 as the age of consent (Graupner, 2000). In Canada, the age of consent is 14 years (Rodrigues, 2004).

The intent of these laws is to protect children from sexual victimization and exploitation by adults. In the same vein, very young children require protection from older children or adolescents who might take advantage of a very young child. However, it was not the original intent of these laws to criminalize sexual interactions between adolescent peers when such interactions are a normal part of adolescent development. Unfortunately, such criminalization does occur.

The Adolescent Male Sexual Partner: Boyfriend or Sexual Abuser?

Imagine the situation when two 13-year-old neighbors, one male and the other female, engage in sexual intercourse while their parents are at work. Because these two adolescents are of equal age and maturity, it would be inappropriate to label such interactions as abusive. At 13 years of age, the law would state that neither one of them has the psychological capacity to consent to sexual activity. But, because their interactions did not involve any force or violence or threats of violence, and there is no power imbalance between them, according to the definition of sexual abuse provided earlier, we would not be able to determine which of these individuals is the abuser and which the victim. If we agree that there has been no abuse in this situation, we should also agree that it would be inappropriate to subject either of these adolescents to criminal prosecution.

Now consider that these two adolescents are separated by several years in age. In this circumstance, we have to consider that the relationship was abusive, and that the older of the two was the "abuser." The question then arises: how much of an age difference is required before we regard this situation as either (1) abusive or (2) criminal? It seems reasonable to suggest that, when an older individual has sex with a child who is below the age of consent, it should not be considered abusive or criminal when the older individual's age is close to the age of the younger. In the research literature, child sexual abuse is said to occur when there is at least a 5-year difference between partners (Finkelhor, 1984). For the purposes of this chapter, child sexual abuse will be defined as sexual interactions between a child under the age of 14 years with a person more than 5 years older than the child.

According to Leitenberg and Saltzman (2003), in the United States, four states require a minimum of a 5-year age difference between partners in order for the sexual interaction to qualify as a statutory rape offense (Donovan, 1997). However, 29 states do not require any age discrepancy for these laws to be prosecuted. Among these states, some require more severe penalties based on the magnitude of the age discrepancy, the absolute age of the defendant (e.g., 20 and over), and whether or not the defendant is a repeat offender. However, in these states, when the "alleged (usually female) victim" is at all younger than the age of consent, her (usually male) sexual partner of any age can be charged with a criminal sexual offense (statutory rape; Leitenberg & Saltzman, 2003). With respect to the example of the male and female 13-year-olds given earlier, the male partner could be prosecuted and convicted of sexual assault in many U.S. states.

In the study described earlier by Leitenberg and Saltzman (2000), young girls were asked to report the age at which they first experienced sexual intercourse, and, in addition, they were asked to report the age of their partner during their first experience. For 11- to 12-year-old girls, only 37% reported that their partners were of similar age. Twenty-nine percent and 34% reported that their partners were 2 to 4.5 years older and more than 5 years older, respectively. For 13- to 15-year-olds, 45%, 43%, and 12% reported that their partners were of similar age, 2 to 4.5 years older, and more than 5 years older, respectively. This study confirmed the concern about the welfare of very young girls having much older partners. For girls who first had intercourse in early adolescence

(11–12), much older partners (+5 years) were associated with more suicide attempts, more alcohol and drug abuse, and a higher incidence of pregnancy. However, for older girls (13+ years), having much older partners (+5 years) did not lead to significantly more problems, except for truancy. Nevertheless, a large number of male adolescents not much older than their female partners have consensual sex with girls below the age of consent and would be subject to criminal proceedings in many states in the United States.

The following discussion illustrates how peer-to-peer sexual relations in adolescence have been accommodated in Canadian law (Rodrigues, 2004). When sexual relations involve a person under the age of consent (12–13 years of age) with a person who is the same age or only marginally older (12–15 years of age) and who has no other relationship with the underage person that would make the relationship a nonpeer relationship (teacher, coach, etc.), then the sexual relations would be viewed as an example of peer-to-peer relations. In this circumstance, the older adolescent would be allowed to offer the defense at trial that the alleged victim consented to sexual activity. In this case, the older adolescent would perhaps not be subject to successful criminal prosecution in Canada. However, when the alleged victim is below the age of consent, the alleged perpetrator cannot use the defense that the alleged victim consented to sexual activity when the alleged victim is less than 12 years of age or when the alleged perpetrator is over the age of 16.

The Canadian law also takes age into account in determining criminal sanctions in cases of sexual assault. As mentioned earlier in this chapter, in most Western jurisdictions, youthful offenders are provided with a criminal justice system that is separate from the adult system, in which the penalties are less severe and the emphasis is on rehabilitation rather than punishment. It is interesting to note here the different ways in which the law treats immaturity in the victim as compared with the perpetrator. For the victim below the age of consent, the law regards the individual to be "incapacitated" by her or his immaturity, lacking the psychological resources to make autonomous decisions regarding sexual behavior. In contrast, the perpetrator of the same age is not viewed as being incapacitated. He or she is held to be fully responsible for the criminal sexual behavior. In Canada, as in many other Western jurisdictions, when the perpetrator is older than 12 but below the age of consent (14), the law regards the individual to be incapable of consenting to sexual behavior yet fully responsible for criminal sexual behavior, though deserving of less severe punishment on account of his or her immaturity. Under the age of 12, in Canada, as in most Western jurisdictions, the alleged perpetrator is "exempt" from prosecution, and this may recognize the assumption that, below this age, the individual does not have the "capacity" to appreciate the fact that the behavior was illegal.

Summary and Conclusions

At the time of writing our first edition of this book (Barbaree, Marshall, & Hudson, 1993), we referred to a time in the not too distant past when juvenile sex offenders were not taken as seriously as is the case now.

> Prior to the early 1980s, the predominant view of the sexual offenses committed by [juveniles] was that they constituted a nuisance value only, reflecting a "boys-will-be-boys" attitude and a discounted estimate of the severity of harm produced. . . . the sexually offensive behavior was not seen as assaultive; instead, these acts were seen as examples of experimentation and therefore as innocent. (Barbaree, Hudson, & Seto, 1993, p. 10)

By the early 1990s, however, we reported that "the tendency to minimize the sexual crimes of juveniles has been reduced substantially over the past decade" (Barbaree et al., 1993, p. 10). Now, more than 10 years later, perhaps we could argue that the pendulum has continued to swing in this direction, and some would argue that it has swung too far. For example, in some U.S. states, juvenile sex offenders are subject to legislation on sexually violent predators that leads in some cases to lifetime detention in strict custody (Trivits & Reppucci, 2002).

The terms and concepts introduced in this chapter provide the basis for a more informed and sophisticated discussion of this issue. From our perspective, we would make the point that criminal prosecution or other onerous public safety interventions should not be brought to bear in the case of juveniles' sexual behavior simply because it was deviant or unusual. Nor would we agree to criminal prosecution being used to reinforce moral or religious condemnation of sexual activity in juveniles. In other words, criminal prosecution should not be used in cases in which the juvenile has been engaged in peer-to-peer sexual activity. Criminal sanctions and public safety interventions should be reserved for cases in which there has been actual sexual abuse and victimization, as these terms have been defined in this chapter.

Juveniles who face prosecution for sex offenses are often taken from their families and placed in custody or foster homes; ostracized by friends, family, community, and society; and suffer persecution and stigma that outlasts whatever temporal criminal sentence may be imposed. Such negative effects suffered by the juvenile offender may be justified in the interests of providing a concrete solution to sexual assault as a significant problem in our society. Such justification is based on (1) the need for specific deterrence of sexually abusive behavior in the individual offender, (2) the need for general deterrence in society, and (3) the need to protect the safety of the public. Nevertheless, we support attempts to minimize the negative effects on juvenile offenders of society's response to the problem of sexual abuse.

The remainder of this volume is intended to increase general understanding of sexual abuse committed by juvenile sex offenders, to increase our ability to discriminate between abusive and nonabusive sexual behavior in juveniles, to increase awareness of assessment methodology and treatment interventions that lead to a minimization of sexual abuse committed by juvenile sex offenders, and to promote interventions that minimize the negative effects for juvenile perpetrators in the course of society's response to this important societal ill.

References

Ageton, S. (1983). *Sexual assault among adolescents*. Lexington, MA: Lexington Books.

American Heritage Stedman's Medical Dictionary. (2002). New York: Houghton Mifflin.

American Psychiatric Association. (2000). *Diagnostic and statistical manual of mental disorders* (4th ed., text rev.). Washington, DC: Author.

Bancroft, J. (1989). *Human sexuality and its problems* (2nd ed.). Edinburgh, UK: Churchill Livingstone.

Barbaree, H. E., Hudson, S. M, & Seto, M. C. (1993). Sexual assault in society: The role of the juvenile offender. In H. E. Barbaree, W. L. Marshall, & S. M. Hudson (Eds.), *The juvenile sex offender* (pp. 1–24). New York: Guilford Press.

Barbaree, H. E., Marshall, W. L., & Hudson, S. M. (Eds.). (1993). *The juvenile sex offender*. New York: Guilford Press.

Becker, J. V., Kaplan, M. S., Cunningham-Rathner, J., & Kavoussi, R. J. (1986). Characteristics of adolescent incest sexual perpetrators: Preliminary findings. *Journal of Family Violence, 1*, 85–97.

Billy, J. O., Lindale, N. S., Grady, W. R., & Zimmerle, D. M. (1988). Effects of sexual activity on adolescent social and psychological development. *Social Psychology Quarterly, 51*, 190–212.

Bingham, C. R., & Crockett, L. J. (1996). Longitudinal adjustment of boys and girls experiencing early, middle, and late sexual intercourse. *Deviant Psychology, 32*, 647–658.

Brown, E. J., Flanagan, T. J., & McLeod, M. (Eds.). (1984). *Sourcebook of criminal justice statistics—1983*. Washington, DC: Bureau of Justice Statistics.

Brownmiller, S. (1975). *Against our will: Men, women and rape.* New York: Simon & Schuster.

Cantwell, H. B. (1988). Child sexual abuse: Very young perpetrators. *Child Abuse and Neglect, 13,* 65–75.

Committee on Sexual Offenses Against Children and Youth. (1984). *Sexual offenses against children.* Ottawa, Ontario, Canada: Canadian Goverment Publishing Centre.

Costa, F. M., Jessor, R., Donovan, J. F., & Fortenberry, J. D. (1995). Early initiation to sexual intercourse: The influence of psychosocial unconventionality. *Journal of Research on Adolescence, 5,* 93–121.

Craissati, J., McClurg, G., & Browne, K. (2002). Characteristics of perpetrators of child sexual abuse who have been sexually victimized as children. *Sexual Abuse: A Journal of Research and Treatment, 14,* 225–239.

Deisher, R. W., Wenet, G. A., Paperny, D. M., Clark, T. F., & Fehrenbach, P. A. (1982). Adolescent sexual offense behavior: The role of the physician. *Journal of Adolescent Health Care, 2,* 279–286.

Donovan, P. (1997). Can statutory rape laws be effective in preventing adolescent pregnancy? *Family Planning Perspectives, 29,* 30–34.

Elo, I. T., King, R. B., & Furstenberg, F. F. (1999). Adolescent females: Their sexual partners and the fathers of their children. *Journal of Marriage and the Family, 61,* 74–84.

Federal Bureau of Investigation. (2002). *Uniform crime report.* Washington, DC: Author.

Finkelhor, D. (1979). What's wrong with sex between adults and children? Ethics and the problem of sexual abuse. *American Journal of Orthopsychiatry, 49,* 692–697.

Finkelhor, D. (1984). *Child sexual abuse: New theory and research.* New York: Free Press.

Finkelhor, D., & Jones, L. M. (2004, January). Explanations for the decline in child sexual abuse cases. *Juvenile Justice Bulletin,* 1–12.

Friedrich, W. N., Grambsch, P., Broughton, D., Kuiper, J., & Beilke, R. J. (1991). Normative sexual behavior in children. *Pediatrics, 88,* 456–464.

Graupner, H. (2000). Sexual consent: The criminal law in Europe and overseas. *Archives of Sexual Behavior, 29,* 415–461.

Grey, A., Busconi, A., Houchens, P., & Pithers, W. D. (1997). Children with sexual behavior problems and their caregivers: Demographics, functioning, and clinical patterns. *Sexual Abuse: A Journal of Research and Treatment, 9,* 267–290.

Groth, A., Longo, R. E., & McFadin, J. (1982). Undetected recidivism among rapists and child molesters. *Crime and Delinquency, 28,* 450–458.

Gundersen, B. H., Melas, P. S., & Skar, J. E. (1981). Sexual behavior of preschool children: Teachers' observations. In L. L. Constantine & F. M. Martinson (Eds.), *Children and sex: New findings, new perspectives* (pp. 45–61). Boston: Little, Brown.

Hays, C. H. (1987). *Risking the future: Adolescent sexuality, pregnancy, and childbearing.* Washington, DC: National Academy Press.

Irwin, C. E., & Millstein, S. G. (1992). Risk-taking behaviors and biopsycholog-ical development during adolescence. In E. J. Sussman, T. V. Feagans, & W. J. Ray (Eds.), *Emotion, cognition, health and development in children and adolescents* (pp. 95–102). Hillsdale, NJ: Erlbaum.

Jessor, R., & Jessor, S. L. (1977). *Problem behavior and psychological development: A longitudinal study of youth.* New York: Academic Press.

Kilpatrick, D. G., Acierno, R., Schnurr, P. P., Saunders, B., Resnick, H. S., & Best, C. L. (2000). Risk factors for adolescent substance abuse and dependence: Data from a national sample. *Journal of Consulting and Clinical Psychology, 68,* 19–30.

Kilpatrick, D. G., Ruggiero, K. J., Acierno, R., Saunders, B. E., Resnick, H. S., & Best, C. L. (2003). Violence and risk of PTSD, major depression, substance abuse/dependence, and comorbidity: Results from the national survey of adolescents. *Journal of Consulting and Clinical Psychology, 71,* 692–700.

Koss, M. P., Gidycz, C. A., & Wisniewski, N. (1987). The scope of rape: Incidence and prevalence of sexual aggression and victimization in a national sample of higher education students. *Journal of Consulting and Clinical Psychology, 55,* 162–170.

Largen, M. A. (1985). The anti-rape movement: Past and present. In A. W. Burgess (Ed.), *Rape and sexual assault: A research handbook.* New York: Garland.

Leitenberg, H., & Saltzman, H. (2000). A statewide survey of age at first intercourse for adolescent females and age of their male partners: Relation to other risk behaviors and statutory rape implications. *Archives of Sexual Behavior, 29,* 203–215.

Leitenberg, H., & Saltzman, H. (2003). College women who had sexual intercourse when they were underage minors (13–15): Age of their male partners, relation to current adjustment, and statutory rape implications. *Sexual Abuse: A Journal of Research and Treatment, 15,* 135–147.

Lindberg, L. D., Sonenstein, F. L., Ku, L., & Martinez, G. (1997). Age differences between minors who give birth and their adult partners. *Family Planning Perspectives, 29,* 61–66.

McBride, C. K., Paikoff, R. L., & Holmbeck, G. N. (2003). Individual and familial influences on the onset of sexual intercourse among urban African American adolescents. *Journal of Consulting and Clinical Psychology, 71,* 159–167.

Merriam-Webster Dictionary of Law. (1996). New York: Merriam-Webster.

Merriam-Webster Medical Dictionary. (2002). New York: Merriam-Webster.

Money, J., & Ehrhardt, A. (1972). *Man and woman: Boy and girl.* Baltimore: Johns Hopkins University Press.

Monson, C. M., Langhinrichsen-Rohling, J., & Binderup, T. (2000). Does "no" really mean "no" after you say "yes"? *Journal of Interpersonal Violence, 15,* 1156–1175.

Myers, J. E. B., Diedrich, S., Lee, D., Fincher, K. M., & Stern, R. (1999). Professional writing on child sexual abuse from 1900 to 1975: Dominant themes and impact on prosecution. *Child Maltreatment, 4,* 201–216.

Oberman, M. (1994). Turning girls into women: Re-evaluating modern statutory rape law. *Journal of Criminal Law and Criminology, 85,* 15–79.

Ondersma, S. J., Chaffin, M., Berliner, L., Cordon, I., Goodman, G. S., & Barnett, D. (2001). Sex with children is abuse: Comment on Rind, Tromovitch, and Bauserman (1998). *Psychological Bulletin, 127,* 707–714.

Pithers, W. D., & Gray, A. (1998). The other half of the story: Children with sexual behavior problems. *Psychology, Public Policy, and Law, 4,* 200–217.

Rind, B., Tromovitch, P., & Bauserman, R. (1998). A meta-analytic examination of assumed properties of child sexual abuse using college samples. *Psychological Bulletin, 124,* 22–53.

Rind, B., Tromovitch, P., & Bauserman, R. (2001). The validity and appropriateness of methods, analyses, and conclusions in Rind et al. (1998): A rebuttal of victimological critique from Ondersma et al. (2001) and Dallam et al. (2001). *Psychological Bulletin, 127,* 734–758.

Rodrigues, G. P. (2004). *Pocket criminal code.* Toronto, Ontario, Canada: Thomson Carswell.

Smith, E. A., & Udry, J. R. (1985). Coital and non-coital sexual behaviours of white and black adolescents. *American Journal of Public Health, 75,* 1200–1203.

Smith, J. A. (1996). *The family in America.* Washington, DC: Culture of Life Foundation. Retrieved December 23, 2004, from www.christianity.com

Snyder, H. N. (2003). *Juvenile arrests 2001.* Retrieved December 23, 2004, from U.S. Department of Justice Web site: www.ojp.usdoj.gov/ojjdp

Stahl, A., Finnegan, T., & Kang, W. (2003). *Easy access to Juvenile Court statistics: 1985–2000.* Retrieved December 23, 2004, from ojjdp.ncjrs.org/ojstatbb/ezajcs/

Tannahill, R. (1992). *Sex in history.* Bath, UK: Scarborough House.

Travin, S., & Protter, B. (1993). *Sexual perversion: Integrative treatment approaches for the clinician.* New York: Plenum Press.

Trivits, L. C., & Reppucci, N. D. (2002). Application of Megan's Law to juveniles. *American Psychologist, 57,* 690–704.

United Nations General Assembly. (1994). *Declaration on the elimination of violence against women.* Geneva, Switzerland: Office of the United Nations High Commissioner for Human Rights.

Vizard, E., Monck, E., & Misch, P. (1995). Child and adolescent sex abuse perpetrators: A review of the research literature. *Journal of Child Psychology and Psychiatry, 56,* 731–756.

Wyatt, G., Durvasula, R. S., Guthrie, D., LeFranc, E., & Forge, N. (1999). Correlates of first intercourse among women in Jamaica. *Archives of Sexual Behavior, 28,* 139–157.

Zolondek, S. C., Abel, G. G., Northey, W. F., & Jordan, A. D. (2001). The self-reported behaviors of juvenile sexual offenders. *Journal of Interpersonal Violence, 16,* 73–85.

CHAPTER 2

Normal Sexual Development

John Bancroft

Given the fundamental and organizing impact that sexuality has on the lives of almost all of us, it is a striking fact that we understand little about normal sexual development. The prevailing need to regard the prepubertal child as asexual and any evidence of sexual expression in childhood as a symptom of child sexual abuse (CSA) has made research into normal sexual development during childhood even more difficult and, at times, hazardous. Although there has been a substantial amount of research on adolescent sexuality, most of it has focused on the dire consequences, such as unwanted pregnancy and sexually transmitted infections. The emphasis has been on restricting and, as far as possible, eliminating the sexuality of teenagers, rather than understanding the key aspects of sexual development that occur during adolescence that prepare us for the "legitimate" sexuality of adulthood.

This chapter, not surprisingly in these circumstances, raises more questions than answers. In 2001 the Kinsey Institute hosted a workshop on sexual development in childhood, which brought together many of the key researchers in the field of child and adolescent sexual development. The papers presented and the discussions following them have been published (Bancroft, 2003a), and this chapter draws extensively from the contents of that volume. Other relatively recent compilations of papers on this topic, to which I refer, are edited by Perry (1990) and by Sandfort and Rademakers (2000).

Much of this workshop was taken up with recognizing the extensive gaps in our knowledge of the sexuality of childhood. Participants acknowledged the varying impact of culture, across societies and through history, on what was regarded as "normal" for children, as well as on what constituted a "child." They also recognized the need to at least identify the boundaries of the normal range for different cultural groups, so that we could inform parents, child-care providers, and educators. It was clear that we needed theoretical models to facilitate our interpretation of the available evidence—much of it focused on the effects of CSA rather than on "normal" sexual development—and in the process guide our further research.

In this chapter, I first consider the limitations of the methods of research that are available to us in this field and the constraints they impose. This is followed by a review of what this limited research has so far told us; not an exhaustive review of the literature, but hopefully a representative one. The terms "child" and "childhood" are used to refer to the prepubertal phase of development, and "adolescence" as the phase of sexual development between puberty and the rather intangible onset of "early adulthood." Puberty is variably defined in the literature, involving a number of physiological and structural changes that tend to occur over a variable time period. In this chapter I use the most specific indicators—spermarche, or first ejaculation, in the male and menarche, or first menstruation, in the female.

Methodological Issues

The large majority of research on sexuality at any age relies on self-report, which is clearly limited by problems of recall error and bias, depending on the time period being recalled. When recalling, as adults, or even adolescents, our sexual experiences during childhood, there is the further problem of recalling events that occurred at a time in our development when the sexual significance of them may not have been apparent to us. Empirical studies of the validity and reliability of adults' recall of childhood sexual experiences are almost entirely confined to recall of CSA. This literature has been reviewed by Graham (2003). A number of studies have assessed the consistency of recall of CSA by asking adults on more than one occasion, finding variable degrees of inconsistency; other studies have asked adults who recalled such childhood experiences whether they had gone through phases of not remembering these experiences, and many had. Fortenberry and Aalsma (2003) found inconsistency among middle adolescents when they were asked, on two occasions 7 months apart, to recall CSA experienced before age 12. There have been two prospective studies in which individuals with previously documented histories of sexual abuse as children have been followed up in adulthood (Widom & Morris, 1997; Williams, 1994). These found from 32 to 60% underreporting of CSA at follow-up, depending on the particular measure of CSA. These findings have generated considerable debate about whether "repression" or simply forgetting was responsible. Overall, women have been found to be more likely to forget (or repress) earlier CSA experiences than men.

This restructuring of childhood by adult recall can also have a validating effect; attributing sexual meaning to a childhood experience with the wisdom of hindsight. Also, whether the sexual meaning is understood at the time or not, there are other developmental factors that may influence and possibly distort how a child or adolescent would report experiences, making later adult recall more valid. A good example of this was reported by Halpern, Joyner, Udry, and Suchindran (2000), who found that young adults recalled masturbation during early adolescence as substantially more frequent than was reported by those same adults 8 to 9 years earlier, when they were around age 13. Although it could be argued that the adults were overreporting this behavior (e.g., Tolman, 2003), it is more likely that the adolescents were reluctant to acknowledge this behavior and, hence, underreported it (e.g., Friedrich, 2003a). In support of this, Halpern et al. (2000) had shown that the underreporting was more likely in those with negative attitudes toward masturbation.

Use of parental reports is the next most widely used method, although this has mainly been used for parental observations of young preschool children. Most studies have used questionnaires or checklists completed by a parent (usually the mother; e.g., Sex Problem scale of the Child Behavior Checklist, Achenbach, 1991; Child Sexual Behavior Inventory, Friedrich, 2003b; Meyer-Bahlburg & Steel, 2003). There are two major limitations to this approach: first, its value is largely restricted to observations of children young enough not to have learned that sexuality-related behaviors are taboo and therefore not to be enacted in front of adults; second, there is scope for observation bias in the mothers (discussed later).

Another approach to parental observation involves training the parent to observe the child over a period of time (e.g., Schuhrke, 2000). This method has been used to a very limited extent, and although it has considerable potential value—partly because the parent is helped to interpret behaviors they might observe—it will always be limited by a participation-bias factor; it will not be the "average parent" who agrees to participate in such a study.

Obtaining information directly from the child has been tried to a limited extent, and the methodological issues involved are reviewed by O'Sullivan (2003). Most research of this kind has focused on the child's sexual knowledge and how this varies with his or her stage of cognitive development. The pioneering studies of Goldman and Goldman (1982), for example, used interviews in their study of children ages 5–15. Their questions were to some extent nested so that use of more advanced questions, about sexual behavior in particular, would depend on the child's answer to earlier questions. Kinsey and his colleagues interviewed 305 boys and 127 girls ages 4–14. The only report of this data is a brief account by Elias and Gebhard (1970). A detailed description of the method is given in Kinsey, Pomeroy, and Martin (1948). For children age 12 or older, the regular interview was adapted with appropriate vocabulary. For younger children, especially those under 8 years, a totally different approach was used. One parent was always present. The interviewer interacted with the child in a range of activities that children generally enjoy, involving toys, dolls, puzzles, romps, telling stories, getting the child to draw pictures, and so forth. Questions were inserted at appropriate points during these activities and followed no set sequence. Volbert (2000) interviewed children between the ages of 2 and 6, the interviews being carried out at the child's kindergarten school. Drawings were used to lead into discussions about various topics, including genital differences, gender identity, sexual body parts, pregnancy, birth, procreation, and sexual behavior of adults. In another recent study, Rademakers, Laan, and Straver (2003) used a semistructured interview with 8- and 9-year-old children. The children were asked to talk about "romping" (as a nonintimate form of physical contact), cuddling, and "being in love." The children were also invited to mark on a drawing of a same-sex child's body which parts they considered pleasant and which exciting and to tell stories in reaction to drawings portraying scenes such as "playing doctor" or having a bath with an adult. The children's reactions were compared with comments from their parents. Such projective methods with children are of interest, but their validity and meaning need further methodological research. O'Sullivan, Meyer-Bahlburg, and Wasserman (2000) interviewed boys ages 7–13. Although the boys were not upset by their participation, considerable reticence was expressed by some of them when responding to questions about sexual knowledge. This reaction seemed to be the result of both a limited sexual vocabulary and, in this group of inner-city, mainly African American and Hispanic boys, a clear taboo against talking openly about sex with adults. In an early study, Ramsey (1943) found that boys ages 10–12 years had a reasonable knowledge of sexual matters but very little socially acceptable vocabulary to communicate this knowledge. Schoof-Tams, Schlaegel, and Walczak (1976) studied the sexual attitudes, values, and meanings of schoolchildren ages 11–16. They used a questionnaire approach, in which three or four response options were presented in cartoon form. Other methods, which have appeared in the literature and are of interest, include direct observation of children through one-way screens (i.e., without the child's knowledge; e.g., Langfeldt, 1990) and using older children as "interviewers" (Borneman, 1990).

Studying normal sexual development in adolescence also presents methodological challenges. Recent studies have shown that adolescents are more likely to reveal sensitive information about their behavior to a computer than in a face-to-face interview or pencil-and-paper questionnaire (Turner, Miller, & Rogers, 1997) and that it may be more acceptable for a teenager to reveal delinquent behavior than a sexually sensitive behavior such as masturbation. Fortenberry and his colleagues (Fortenberry & Aalsma, 2003; Fortenberry, Cecil, Zimet, & Orr, 1997) have used daily diaries to explore the relationship between the sexual activity of male and female adolescents and such ongoing factors as interaction with the partner and mood, providing a rare example of research into what might be regarded as the basic fundamentals of adolescent sexual behavior.

The fundamental importance of longitudinal studies is fairly clear. As yet, no such study has been designed to look specifically at sexual development, but a number of studies (e.g., Bates, Alexander, Oberlander, Dodge, & Pettit, 2003; Caspi et al., 1997; Fergusson, Horwood, & Lynskey, 1997; Kagan & Moss, 1962) have included questions about sexual development in a more general developmental project.

Finkelhor (2003), who has had considerable experience of studies using retrospective recall of childhood, concluded that the methods most appropriate for studying a particular issue depend on the stage of development of knowledge about that issue. Thus, for most aspects of normal sexual development, about which we know little, the use of retrospective recall is warranted, as well as other methods described previously. In the case of CSA, on the other hand, in which a considerable amount of data based on retrospective recall has been collected, much of it inconsistent, Finkelhor emphasizes the serious validity problems with retrospective recall, and he no longer advocates use of those methods. Current social attitudes toward CSA are likely to influence how people recall such experiences, and the relatively recent social trend toward "survivor movements" is likely to influence how people interpret their childhoods when searching for explanations for their current problems.

Overall, there is no escaping the fact that those of us who seek to study normal sexual development in childhood and adolescence face substantial methodological challenges. The issues at stake, however, are sufficiently important that it must be hoped that research into improving relevant methods will be given high priority.

Theoretical Issues

Heiman, Verhulst, and Heard-Davison (2003) reviewed theoretical approaches to understanding the developmental sequence from childhood experience to adult sexuality. Such approaches emphasize the unfolding nature of the developmental process by which, at each stage, the child's experiences are given meaning and value by the family and sociocultural context. This also involves reviewing and reinterpreting earlier experiences in the light of more recent influences, a process that has received little research attention. Childhood sexual experiences are more likely to be incorporated into a learned sexual "script" if they originally involved intense emotional reactions, either positive or negative, and if they are repeated. Attachment theory (Bowlby, 1969, 1973, 1980) may be useful in conceptualizing early experiences with significant others, including physical closeness, touch, and learning emotional regulation, and how they might affect sexual development.

Normal sexual development can be seen as resulting from the integration of three developmental "strands": sexual responsiveness, gender identity, and the capacity for close dyadic relationships (Bancroft, 1989). The development of gender identity and the capacity for dyadic relationships are major topics that are only touched on in this chapter. But their relevance to sexual development is apparent at various points in the following overview, and this "three-strand" model is used at the end of the chapter to integrate the main findings reviewed.

Browning and Laumann (2003) discussed theoretical models of the impact of CSA. They contrasted "psychogenic" models, which have dominated the literature on the effects of CSA, with the "life course" approach, involving a cumulative series of behavioral transitions. Whereas the psychogenic approach sees the long-term consequences of CSA as the lingering presence of the initial traumatic effects, the life-course approach sees the sexual abuse as influencing the next stages of sexual and personal development, which in turn influence subsequent behavioral patterns. Thus if the CSA experience establishes a link between sexual feelings and negative mood, then this will influence how subsequent sexual relationships are negotiated, often with an early onset of sexual activity that leads to other consequences, including increased number of sexual partners, risk of sexually transmitted infections, and associations with relatively delinquent peer groups. In both the psychogenic and life-course approaches, it is recognized that the sexual outcomes can be polarized, in some cases leading to avoidance of sexual encounters and in others increased confrontation with sexual situations. The mediating mechanisms that determine which of these contrasting trajectories is followed remain obscure.

Finkelhor's (1988) traumagenic dynamics model does provide some degree of integration of psychogenic and life-course factors. The effects of child sexual abuse, according to this model, are affected by the presence or absence of four key factors; powerlessness, betrayal, traumatic sexualization, and stigmatization. In general it makes sense to pursue such integrative models, as Browning and Laumann (2003) acknowledge.

Sexual Development in the Prepubertal Child

The Development of "Sexual Meaning," "Sexual Behavior," and "Sexual Response"

The first conceptual step is to distinguish between the physiological responses that are the basis of a sexual experience and the "sexual" meanings attributed to such response patterns. It is conceivable, though as yet not demonstrated, that the impact of the physiological response may be altered, and possibly intensified, by the attribution of sexual meaning to it. It is also possible that the occurrence of an experience involving a sexual response may activate a child's need to seek and comprehend a "meaning" for this response. It is nevertheless appropriate to assume that the acquisition of "sexual meaning" and the experience of a response, such as orgasm or erotic sensation, which become central to the adult's sexual experience, can be disconnected during childhood. Furthermore, some children may develop concepts of sexual meaning before they have any physiological experiences that can be regarded as sexual, and vice versa. What evidence do we therefore have of the "normal" development of sexual meaning, on the one hand, and sexually relevant physiological response patterns on the other hand? And how do they interact to lead to a "sexual experience"?

Sexual Meanings

Goldman and Goldman (1982) interviewed children ages 5–15 in four countries: Australia, Britain, North America, and Sweden. Overall, sexual learning and understanding lagged behind other aspects of cognitive development, except for the Swedish children, who had received more sex education from an earlier age. Larger families, particularly those with opposite-sex siblings, were associated with more advanced sexual thinking, and to some extent boys were more advanced than girls. Boys attached more importance to companionship and girls to romantic love. Given the gradual progression of sexual thinking through the age range studied, Goldman and Goldman (1982) concluded that there was no support for the psychoanalytic concept of a latency period. However, their evidence also indicated the children's growing awareness of social taboos about sexuality, particularly in relation to the sexuality of their parents. They found that children perceived a special relationship between men and women early in development but took much longer to recognize or comprehend the sexuality of such relationships. The sexual taboos additionally compound children's delay in understanding sex by depriving them of an appropriate vocabulary.

Volbert (2000) interviewed 147 children ages 2–6. Although these children had knowledge of gender identity, genital differences, and sexual body parts, they had little understanding of pregnancy, birth, and procreation and almost no knowledge of adult sexual behavior. Whereas 73.5% mentioned kissing and cuddling, only 8% of 6-year-olds and 3% of 5-year-olds gave a description of adult sexual behavior. Rademakers et al. (2003), in a study of 8- and 9-year-old Dutch children (15 girls and 16 boys), asked the children to talk about cuddling and being in love. Not surprisingly, cuddling was familiar to almost all the children as a positive experience, though not one to which they appeared to attribute any sexual meaning. Falling in love, although familiar to most of them (and half of them said they were "in love" at that time or previously) was, interestingly, a cause of some embarrassment. Most regarded being in love as a positive experience, but one that made them vulnerable to teasing. Again, it was not apparent that this vulnerability was linked to any sexual meaning. Schoof-Tams et al. (1976) noted a shift from understanding sex as a means to procreate at age 11 to seeing it by middle adolescence as central to affectionate relationships. For many years, young children have been confronted with numerous scenarios of romantic love on movies and television. Although these are often based on traditional "fairytales" (e.g., "Cinderella" or "Beauty and the Beast"), the "love" component is conveyed more intensely and graphically than has been the case in traditional written versions. Yet there is typically an innocent quality to the romance, which does not require any sexual meaning to be conveyed beyond the fact that the love is between a man and a woman.

Gebhard (1977) asked young adults to recall the age at which they learned sexual meanings. He compared a small group of current students at his university with comparable data from Kinsey's original study, which had not been previously reported. This comparison showed a progression of knowledge about sexual behavior that accelerated around puberty and also earlier acquisition of such knowledge in his recent sample compared with the Kinsey sample interviewed about 25 years earlier.

The evidence is consistent in showing that children learn, first, about gender differences and body parts, somewhat later about procreation, and later still about sexual behavior. The earlier and more extensive knowledge shown by Swedish children in Goldman and Goldman's (1982) study, compared with Australian, British, and North American children—all of whom had received less sex education—plus Gebhard's (1977) evidence of earlier learning in children over a 25-year period during which both sex education and general dissemination of information about sex had increased, demonstrate that not only the stage of cognitive development but also the environment and culture determine the learning of sexual meaning, with such learning occurring earlier than in the past.

"Sexual" Behaviors and Taboos

A crucial and culturally determined phase in this learning process is when a child first learns that sexual issues are taboo, at least in the adult world. To begin with, taboos about sexual and excretory functions are somewhat linked (a linkage that doesn't always disappear), and the issue is one of "bathroom" language. What they have in common, apart from the challenging overlap of excretory and sexual anatomy, is the issue of privacy, and the need for the child to learn when and how to maintain privacy. With excretory function, the child may retain some embarrassment, not infrequently reflecting parental awkwardness with this topic, but at least there is a general acceptance that excretory function should happen in private. With sexual activities it's a different matter, although how different is, once again, determined by the family's cultural context and the parents' degree of comfort with the topic of sex. The child is either explicitly encouraged to keep sexual acts, such as touching one's genitals, private or concludes that this is necessary to avoid censure. Prior to the recognition of the sexual taboo many children display such behaviors as touching their own genitals and those of other people and, in some cases, overtly display pleasure from touching themselves. An important consequence of this recognition is that such behaviors either stop or are concealed from adult view—a stage of development mistakenly interpreted by psychoanalysts, at least until recently, as the "latency period."

Friedrich (2003b) came to the study of normative sexual behavior in childhood from his earlier studies of sexually abused children. Starting with the assumption that sexual behaviors in a child are indicative of previous sexual abuse, he was confronted by the fact that most such behaviors were ubiquitous from ages 2 through 12. Friedrich had first used the Child Behavior Checklist (Achenbach, 1991), which has six questions of sexual relevance and which was carefully reviewed by Meyer-Bahlburg and Steel (2003). Friedrich went on to develop the Child Sexual Behavior Inventory as a more comprehensive standardized method of asking parents about sexually relevant behaviors observed in their children. The most recent version has 38 items (Friedrich, 1997). Examples are "touches sex parts in public," "masturbates with a toy or object," "touches another child's sex parts," "rubs body against people or furniture," "puts objects in vagina or rectum," "pretends that dolls or stuffed animals are having sex," "talks about sexual acts," and "is very interested in the opposite sex." Parents are asked to indicate whether each behavior occurs "never" (0) to "at least once a week" (3). In order to show age relatedness of such behaviors, Friedrich identified behaviors endorsed by at least 20% of parents in each age group. These are listed in Table 2.1.

Many of the behaviors represented in the Child Sexual Behavior Inventory are endorsed by parents of children with no history of sexual abuse or behavioral problems. However, in a study comparing such children with a sample of sexually abused children and a sample of psychiatric outpatients, Friedrich found the behaviors most common in the sexually abused group. They were, however, also more common in the psychiatric outpatient children than in the nonclinical, nonabused group (Friedrich et al., 2001). Meyer-Bahlburg, Dolezal, and Sandberg (2000) used the Child Behavior Checklist of Achenbach (1991) with parents of 6- to 10-year-old children in a community sample. The data were collected from 1986 through 1988. Sexual behavior, as described in the Child Behavior Checklist, was reported by the parents of one in six boys and one in seven girls. An association with "externalizing" behaviors was found, particularly in boys.

Friedrich (2003b) also reviewed three studies in which cross-cultural comparisons of the Child Sexual Behavior Inventory were involved, comparing children from the United States with Dutch, Belgian, and Swedish children. In each study, the European children, most notably the Dutch, were reported as showing more of these sexual behaviors than the American children. These cultural differences may be to some extent explainable by more relaxed sexual attitudes in the European mothers, leaving us with the question of whether European children show more of such behaviors or whether their mothers are more comfortable reporting them—probably a combination of the two.

In general, therefore, evidence based on parental observations indicates sexually relevant behavior as most likely to be observed in younger children, confronting us with the older child's retreat as a reaction to sexual taboos. Whereas children clearly vary in the age at which this shift towards "concealed" sexuality occurs, it appears to occur somewhere between the ages of 6 and 10. Thereafter we have to depend to a large extent on recall by adults of their own childhood experiences.

Reynolds, Herbenick, and Bancroft (2003) recruited a sample of

TABLE 2.1. Developmentally Related Sexual Behaviors

Age group	Item	Endorsement %
2–5 boys	Stands too close to people.	29.3
	Touches sex parts when in public places.	26.5
	Touches or tries to touch their mother's or other women's breasts.	42.4
	Touches sex parts at home.	60.2
	Tries to look at people when they are nude or undressing.	26.8
2–5 girls	Stands too close to people.	25.8
	Touches or tries to touch their mother's or other women's breasts.	43.7
	Touches sex parts at home.	43.8
	Tries to look at people when they are nude or undressing.	26.9
6–9 boys	Touches sex parts at home.	39.8
	Tries to look at people when they are nude or undressing.	20.2
6–9 girls	Touches sex parts at home.	20.7
	Tries to look at people when they are nude or undressing.	20.5
10–12 boys	Is very interested in the opposite sex.	24.1
10–12 girls	Is very interested in the opposite sex.	28.7

Note. Table from Freidrich (2003b). Copyright 2003 by Indiana University Press. Reproduced by permission.

university students ages 18–22 years, 154 female and 149 male, who answered an extensive series of questions about sexual experiences during different stages of their childhoods, as well as questions about their current sexual adjustment. Data were collected during 1998 and 1999 using computer-assisted self-interviewing. A further age-matched and much larger sample of university students was taken from Kinsey's original study: 1,913 women and 1,770 men. Thus there were two samples studied approximately 50 years apart. Although there were limitations to direct comparison of the two data sets, some interesting comparisons were drawn. In the earlier sample, 68% of males and 42% of females had reported childhood sexual experiences with peers (CSEP). In the recent sample the percentages were 87% for males and 84% for females. This suggests not only an increase in CSEP over the past 50 years but also a much greater increase for the females, effectively eliminating the earlier gender difference. As expected, CSEP were more common during elementary school years than pre-elementary, and CSEP involving genital touching or more advanced sexual behaviors increased substantially with age, especially among the males. The most frequently stated reason for CSEP at each stage was curiosity about sexual matters. Physical or sexual pleasure as a reason was more common during junior high school, particularly for the boys.

Using the same two samples, Bancroft, Herbenick, and Reynolds (2003) reported on age at first masturbation. Here we found some striking similarities, as well as differences, over the 50 years. In the recent sample, 98% of men and 83% of women indicated that they had masturbated prior to the study, and 38% of men and 40% of women reported first masturbation before puberty. This compares with 95% of men and 39% of women who had masturbated in the earlier sample, with 27% and 13%, respectively, reporting a prepubertal onset. Thus we see relatively little change in masturbation histories for the males but a major change for the females. When those who had masturbated in each study were compared for the age of onset of masturbation in relation to the age at puberty, there was a striking similarity across the two samples both for males and for females (Figure 2.1). Eighty percent of the males had started to masturbate within 2 years either before or after the onset of puberty (i.e., spermarche). For women, the age of onset was much more widely spread, and in both samples, for those with a prepubertal onset, the females on average started 2 years earlier than the males. What this reflects is a relatively marked organizing effect of puberty on masturbation onset in males that is not apparent in females.

Both of these studies (Reynolds et al., 2003; Bancroft, Herbenick, et al., 2003) reported subtle relations between childhood experiences (CSEP and prepubertal masturbation) and earlier, more frequent, or more enjoyable sexual experiences during teenage years. This raises the crucial question of whether the childhood experiences, as postulated in the life-course perspective, influenced later sexual development or whether they indicated a greater inherent "sexuality" in those children that was also manifested in their adolescent development. A further explanation was suggested by DeLamater (2003); that is, that both childhood and adolescent patterns of sexual development were influenced by the family in a similar way.

In discussing these results, the need for caution in generalizing from these student studies to other socioeconomic and ethnic groups was emphasized (Fortenberry, 2003). A considerable amount of attention was given in the sexual development workshop to the importance of cultural factors (Frayser, 2003; Herdt, 2003). Thigpen, Pinkston, and

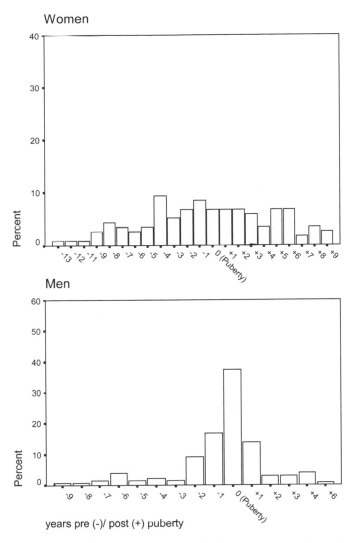

FIGURE 2.1a. Onset of masturbation in relation to age at puberty: Study A. Only participants with complete data and who had masturbated are included in these figures; 16% of women and 2% of men had not masturbated, and 5% of women and 1% of men had incomplete or missing data. Data from Bancroft, Herbenick, and Reynolds (2003).

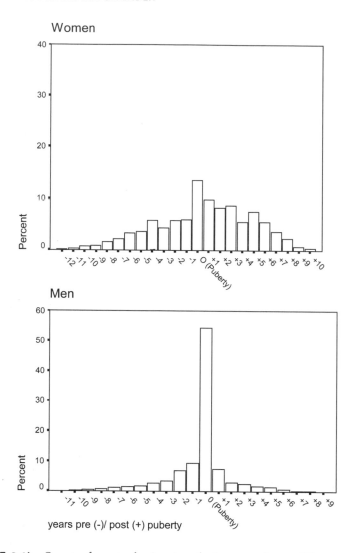

FIGURE 2.1b. Onset of masturbation in relation to puberty: Kinsey sample. Only participants with complete data and who had masturbated are included in these figures; 55% of women and 5% of men had not masturbated, and 10% of women and 2% of men had incomplete or missing data. Data from Bancroft, Herbenick, and Reynolds (2003).

Mayefsky (2003) reported the negative consequences of having even less normative data for African American than for white children. Their study was driven by concern that young African American children in foster care were being labeled as "sexually aggressive" because of sexual behaviors that may well have been within the norm for their age and culture. Their concerns reflect two potentially important aspects of sexual development—consistent and close parenting and the experience of privacy. The lack of both typifies the child brought up in foster care. Whether or not the lack of consistent, positive parenting directly influences behavioral development, it is likely that in such circumstances adult reactions to observed sexual behaviors of the child will be different, possibly with long-term adverse consequences. This underlines a fairly obvious but important point about sexual development during childhood: How parents or other adults react to a child's emerging sexuality can have major effects on that child's subsequent development, either positively or negatively.

Other examples of studies using adult recall of childhood sexual experiences include Finkelhor (1980), Green (1985), Haugaard and Tilly (1988), Kilpatrick (1992), Lamb and Coakley (1993), and Leitenberg, Greenwald, and Tarran (1989). Estimates of child sexual experiences with peers range from 39 to 85%, depending on two factors: how "childhood" is defined (e.g., prior to age 6, prior to age 13, inclusive of adolescence) and the type of memory elicited by the researchers (e.g., "sexual games" or "most memorable experience").

"Sexual" Response in Childhood

Penile erections occur in infants and children. Whether prepubertal boys vary in the likelihood of experiencing erections is not known, and we should not assume that all prepubertal boys are capable of erections. The relevance of erections during childhood to erectile function postpuberty is not clear; anatomically, the prepubertal penis is not fully developed, and the hormonal component of erectile function in the adult is not present before puberty.

An interesting "window" into the development of erectile function is nocturnal penile tumescence (NPT, or sleep erection). Although the evidence from prepubertal boys is limited, it suggests that NPT does occur before puberty but that the erections are less frequent and of shorter duration. Obviously the amount of tumescence will be smaller due to the smaller size of the penis, and I am not aware of any evidence relating to the rigidity of prepubertal NPT. The frequency, duration, and rigidity of NPT peak around the age of 13 and thereafter slowly decline with age (Karacan, Salis, Thornby, & Williams, 1976). This association between NPT and puberty is a good illustration of the role of testosterone in male sexual function. Adult men who are deficient in testosterone have NPT episodes, but they involve substantially less tumescence and rigidity and are of shorter duration than those in eugonadal men, a difference that is readily eliminated by testosterone replacement (Bancroft, 2003b). NPT in hypogonadal men is probably similar to that of prepubertal boys, although their comparability is limited by the developmental differences in size of the penis and erectile tissues.

Genital response in female children (i.e., vasocongestion of the vaginal wall, vulva, and clitoris) is obviously much less likely to be observed by adults if it occurs, and we consequently have little evidence of this. Some children, both boys and girls, do stimulate their genitalia in ways that indicate arousal and pleasure and sometimes orgasm. There are striking case reports in the literature of such masturbation in very young children, who, because of their age, are oblivious of being observed by their parents (e.g., Kinsey, Pomeroy, & Martin, 1948; Kinsey, Pomeroy, Martin, & Gebhard, 1953). We also have clear reports of young adults recalling orgasmic experiences prior to puberty, most often as a result of masturbation. In our recent study (Bancroft, Herbenick, et al., 2003) 12% of women and 13.5% of men reported their first orgasm before onset of puberty (i.e., menarche for females or spermarche for males). For women the mean age was 8.5 years, ranging from 4 to 13; for men, 9.6 years, ranging from 5 to 13).

In the adult female, multiple orgasms are possible, although they are not part of typical sexual experience for most women. Men are clearly different in having a postejaculatory refractory period in which sexual arousal and orgasm are inhibited for a period of time. It is possible that these refractory mechanisms in the male are established around puberty as part of the organizing effects of androgens (Sachs, 1995). This then raises the question of whether some boys (and girls) are capable of repeated orgasm before puberty, with boys losing this ability around puberty.

We can conclude that some children are capable of genital response and orgasm prior to puberty, possibly in infancy, but we have no idea of how many children have such capability. It is possible that the large majority of children have this capability, but only a few have the relevant experiences or circumstances to realize it. Alternatively, some children may be more sexually responsive and others relatively unresponsive prior to puberty. In either case, we are left uncertain of whether variability across children in either the capability or its expression depends on variable learning experiences or is genetically determined. Such genetic variability may be expressed as variable responsiveness to hormonal changes that occur at adrenarche (i.e., increase in adrenal androgens), as well as at puberty.

The issue of individual variability is particularly relevant to girls. As indicated earlier, data from both a recent study and Kinsey's original study (Bancroft, Herbenick, et al., 2003) show the age of onset of masturbation, which can be regarded as a useful marker of sexual development, to be close to the age at puberty in the large majority of boys, but not so in girls. One possible explanation of this greater variability in girls is greater individual variability in the behavioral effects of androgens from adrenarche onward (Bancroft, 2002). Thus those girls who are highly sensitive to the behavioral effects of androgens may experience onset of "sexual" interest and possibly masturbation in association with the increase in androgens at adrenarche.

With the male, the small proportion of boys who first experience orgasm and sexual arousal more than two years before puberty may be more responsive to androgens than normal, and hence they are activated by hormonal changes at adrenarche, at a time when they are unrestrained by the peripubertal development of refractory inhibition. At this stage of our knowledge, we can only speculate on such matters.

The Transition from Childhood to Adolescence

Sexually Relevant Behaviors

While the awareness of sexual taboos continues to contain most sexual activity of the child within his or her private nonadult world, there emerges a more open phase of interest, usually in the opposite sex, and the onset of dating behavior in a proportion of children. Here we see the impact of socially sanctioned scripts for interactions between boys and girls, acceptable providing that they retain a childlike innocence. It is quite possible that at this developmental stage, in the minds of many boys and girls, such scripts remain disconnected from their earlier or even current "childhood sexual experiences."

Table 2.2 shows findings from our recent study of young adults (Reynolds et al., 2003) in relation to first experience of sexual arousal, sexual attraction to another person, and sexual fantasy. Sexual arousal, comparable for boys and girls, first occurs before puberty for the majority, with an average age for the prepubertal onset group of around 9 years. First sexual attraction shows a gender difference, with the majority of boys reporting it occurring before puberty (average age 11) and a majority of girls reporting it postpuberty (average age 13.7 years). The

TABLE 2.2. Sex Differences in First Intrapsychic Sexual Experiences in Relation to Puberty Onset

	Prepubertal	Postpubertal
Sexual arousal		
Male	70%	30%
Female	63%	37%
Mean age		
Male	8.8 years	12.0 years
Female	9.2 years	13.6 years
Sexual attraction		
Male	67%[a]	33%[a]
Female	38%[b]	62%[b]
Mean age		
Male	11.0 years	12.1 years[a]
Female	10.2 years	13.7 years[b]
Sexual fantasy		
Male	55%[a]	45%[a]
Female	38%[b]	62%[b]
Mean age		
Male	10.8 years	12.6 years[a]
Female	10.5 years	14.4 years[b]

Note. Data from Reynolds, Herbenick, and Bancroft (2003).
[a]Significantly different from [b] for sex difference comparisons ($p < .05$).

onset of sexual fantasies shows the gender difference more strongly. To some extent this reflects the greater variability of timing of sexual development in girls, as discussed earlier in relation to onset of masturbation (Bancroft, Herbenick, et al., 2003). However, it also points to gender differences of wider relevance, which are as yet not well understood.

Dating

Kagan and Moss (1962), in a unique longitudinal study from birth to early adulthood, commented that although "dating" may start from age 10, "it is not until 11 or 12 years of age that interactions between boys and girls acquire a sexual connotation." They also found some interesting relations between early behavioral patterns and late adolescent and adult behaviors, although only in boys. Thus boys who did not adopt conventional masculine behaviors between the ages of 3 and 10 years were more likely to report high sexual anxiety, less likely to engage in early dating, and more likely to show avoidance of erotic behavior in adolescence. Boys who avoided dating between 10 and 14 years were less likely to establish intimate heterosexual relationships or engage in erotic activity during late adolescence and adulthood. Their inability to identify similar predictors in girls is noteworthy.

Broderick (1966) characterized three developmental phases. First, 10- to 11-year-olds showed predominantly same-sex social interactions but were expressing some heterosexual interest; around 25% had had their first date, and "kissing games" were common at parties. Second, 12- to 13-year-olds showed little inclination to form close attachments with the opposite sex, but they were increasingly likely to identify "objects of romantic attraction." Third, 14 to 15 years was "an age of transition," with increasing cross-gender social interactions, previously "secret loves" being more openly acknowledged, and dating increasingly popular. In Schofield's (1965) study of English teenagers, a quarter of the boys and nearly a third of the girls had their first date by the age of 13; this changed rapidly over the next 2 years of age, and by age 16, over 70% of boys and 85% of girls had experienced dating. Broderick (1966) regarded 10–13 years as a period of rehearsal of skills and feelings appropriate for later heterosexual relationships. Schoof-Tams et al. (1976) found that two thirds of 11-year-old German children reported having been in "in love," about half had kissed, and yet only 7–8% had experienced first ejaculation or menarche. One might have expected changes in these patterns over the past 40 years, but there is no clear evidence that that is the case.

Reynolds et al. (2003) found that the average age for experiencing a first "crush" was 8 to 9 years; having a first girlfriend or boyfriend, 12 to 13 years; and a first date, between 14 and 15 years. Phinney, Jensen, Olsen, and Cundick (1990), in a nationally representative sample of adolescent females, found that dating started, on average, 2.5 years after menarche. The average age at menarche in our study (Reynolds et al., 2003) was 12.6 years. According to Montgomery and Sorell (1998), dating typically progresses through a "group dating" phase before "couple dating" is established. They found more adolescent boys than girls saying that they were or had been "in love," although clearly an adolescent's concept of what being "in love" means evolves. Montgomery and Sorell (1998) comment, "adolescent girls, as well as boys, utilize adolescence (a time of sanctioned delay of adult functioning), to experiment with attracting and being attracted to others while continuing to sort who one is" (p. 686). Zimmer-Gembeck, Siebenbruner, and Collins (2001) reported on a longitudinal study in which development was compared at ages 12 and 16. The average age at initiation of dating and first romantic relationships was around 14 years. Adolescents who were "overinvolved" in dating at age 16 were more likely to have shown psychosocial and behavioral problems at age 12. However, dating, in what these authors regarded as more appropriate ways, was associated with positive consequences, including greater competence in the peer social domain.

Sexual Activity

An interesting and potentially important example of the void in our knowledge is the recent focus within the media on oral sex as an increasingly common substitute for vaginal intercourse among teenagers. According to Remez (2000), we have little clear evidence of whether such behavior has actually increased among teenagers. Remez (2000) attributes this to the barriers that exist to asking adolescents for details of their sexual experiences. She goes on to describe the impact of such barriers in the "abstinence only" movement, in which there is ongoing disagreement about whether educators should avoid going into details about what "having sex" actually means for fear of shattering the teenagers' innocence or whether they should be specific about which behaviors are covered by "abstention" (which usually means anything beyond perhaps kissing on the lips). Oral sex is an interesting issue. In earlier studies of adolescent sexual behavior, it was unusual for teenagers to have experienced oral sex before they had experienced vaginal intercourse, oral sex being seen, in some way, as a more advanced type of sexual activity (e.g., Kinsey et al., 1948, 1953; Schofield, 1965). Studies in the 1980s suggested that oral sex was more frequent among adolescents than previously but still experienced predominantly by those who had already experienced vaginal intercourse (Gagnon & Simon, 1986; Newcomer & Udry, 1985). More recently, Schwartz (1999) found that a majority of males and females had had experience of oral sex before intercourse, although this was a small convenience sample of students. The question of whether oral sex was an example of "having sex" became a public issue with the attempts to impeach President Clinton, and it was soon apparent that many students, like President Clinton, did not make the connection (Bogart, Cecil, Wagstaff, Pinkerton, & Abramson, 2000; Sanders & Reinisch, 1999). Teenagers in the United States are entitled to feel confused about what *is* acceptable for them to do with their romantic partners, particularly in an age when young people, as well as everyone else, are bombarded with sexual images and messages.

Keeping in mind that we know little about nonintercourse expressions of sexuality in adolescent relationships, what have we learned about sexual intercourse per se? Perhaps not surprisingly, there has been far more research on teenage girls than boys, reflecting not only the societal attachment to the double standard but also, according to Sonenstein, Ku, and Pleck (1997), the belief that teenage males are more difficult to survey. A number of surveys of adolescent females, starting in 1971 and repeated every few years (reviewed in Bancroft, 1989), showed a substantial increase in the proportion engaging in sexual intercourse and a reduction in age at first intercourse during the 1970s and early 1980s. This trend was accompanied by an increase in the average number of sexual partners. During the late 1980s and 1990s this pattern for teenage girls leveled out, although the *number* of girls with experience of sexual intercourse before age 15 has continued to increase (Abma & Sonenstein, 2001). The National Survey of Adolescent Males (NSAM), the first systematic survey to assess teenage males (ages 15–19), started in 1988 (Sonenstein, Pleck, & Ku, 1989). Santelli, Lindberg, Abma, McNeely, and Resnick (2000) compared four national surveys that had been repeated over time: the National Survey of Family Growth (NSFG), the NSAM, the Youth Risk Behavior Survey (YRSB), and the National Longitudinal Study of Adolescent Health (Add Health). All four surveys covered high school students ages 15–17 and between them covered the period from 1988 to 1997. There was a consistent finding across the surveys that the proportion of males who had ever experienced sexual intercourse had fallen significantly. Santelli et al. (2000) warned, however, that survey data on adolescent sexual behavior should be treated with caution. Other trends were not consistent across surveys, reminding us of the methodological difficulties of obtaining sensitive information from adolescents. Overall, however, male adolescents tend to initiate sexual experience earlier and to have more sexual partners than female adolescents. Given the emphasis that has been placed on age at first intercourse, we understand surprisingly little about how the timing of this seemingly pivotal event influences the developmental process (Graber, Brooks-Gunn, & Galen, 1998).

What Is "Appropriate" Sexual Development?

Distinguishing between and understanding the determinants of "appropriate" and "inappropriate" sexual development as the child enters and proceeds through adolescence presents us with a formidable challenge. We have at least three patterns of influence to consider. First, there is the emerging sexual responsiveness, which, as already discussed, may have a substantial hormonal basis, which needs to be incorporated into the young persons evolving sexual meanings, and which should be regarded as central to normal sexual development. Let us call this the "peripubertal" pattern. Although the timing of puberty can be affected by a variety of environmental factors, we are dealing here principally with individual variability relatively independent of the child's social and family context at this age.

Second, we need to recognize that adolescence involves a process of developing a "separate identity," which in part is achieved by rejecting, often transiently, some of the values or norms or expectations that one's parents uphold. This process has been amplified by the emergence of a "youth culture" (Hobsbawm, 1994). This relatively new social phenomenon thrives in many respects on modern technology, which allows music and television, for example, and the various messages conveyed by such media, to be shared widely among teenagers, often crossing cultural and geographic boundaries. Identification with a peer group therefore takes on an "institutionalized" form, at least for many teenagers. A substantial part of the "scripts" of such youth culture are sexual. Along with drug use and other behaviors that worry parents, sex is a vehicle, albeit a problematic one, for asserting one's emerging autonomy and independence. Schoof-Tams et al. (1976), in their study of German adolescents, commented that attitudes toward sexuality change dramatically between the ages of 11 and 16. Their 11-year-olds were representing a more traditional morality, presumably consistent with that of their parents, whereas by 16, attitudes and morals about sex were more permissive. These authors considered this a shift to more gender-equal roles in sexuality and "an abandonment of the double standard" (p. 369). There is evidence that in some parts of Europe, there has been a move toward a "single standard" (e.g., Haavio-Mannila & Kontula, 2003). In the United States, however, the double standard seems to remain very much alive (Crawford & Popp, 2003), particularly for adolescents, with teenage girls needing to guard their reputations in ways that do not apply to boys (Orenstein, 1994; Tolman, 2002). We therefore need to understand the balance between parental influences, which tend to predominate during prepubertal childhood, and peer group influences, which are increasingly important during adolescence. Let us call this the "parent versus peer group" pattern.

Third, and this overlaps with the second, we see sexual behavior as one of the adolescent "externalizing" behaviors that are often part of a pattern of maladaptive behavior beginning in childhood and associated with a range of negative developmental influences. Sexual "acting out" gets added to the list of such behaviors as the child enters adolescence; let us call this the "maladaptive pattern."

The peripubertal pattern is thus intrinsically about normal sexual development, although individuals will clearly vary in how they experience this process, to a considerable extent because of biological factors. The parent-versus-peer-group pattern involves a normative developmental process, but one that is very susceptible to sociocultural influences, with the youth culture being, in various respects, reactive to the current adult world. Here the outcomes are uncertain. For most adolescents, this period of "rebellion" is formative in the long term; for others, particularly where sex is concerned, the consequences can be disastrous, so inevitably the adult world looks on with apprehension. The maladaptive pattern, by definition, recognizes certain types of adolescent sexual behavior as symptoms of a more long-standing problematic development in which other forms of acting out may be equally or more disastrous in their long-term effects. The challenge is to distinguish between these three patterns.

What have we learned from the research that has been done about the peripubertal and parent-versus-peer-group patterns of development in adolescents? A few pieces of the jigsaw puzzle are beginning to emerge.

The Peripubertal Pattern

The changes that occur in association with puberty represent probably the most discontinuous phase in human development. There are major changes in body shape and function. It is not simply a matter of growing more or more quickly. Body shape changes, particularly for females, who also have to contend with the onset of menstruation. Males grow hair where they didn't have it before, their voices change substantially, and they have to come to terms with an associated increase in genital responsiveness. All of these changes have an impact on the individual's gender identity, requiring reestablishment and revalidation. Alongside these major individually oriented shifts, the young person's social scripts change, with sexual scripts taking on a new importance.

The challenge in understanding the peripubertal pattern, which clearly shows considerable individual variability in timing, is to assess the relative importance of cognitive development, the availability of social scripts, and the impact of hormonal changes. McClintock and Herdt (1996; Herdt, 2000) point to evidence that in both gay and heterosexual males, sexual attraction starts around age 10, and they link this to the hormonal changes associated with adrenarche. This developmental stage in adrenal function, which is associated with an increase in adrenal androgens in both boys and girls, occurs, on average, around 8 years. The extent to which adrenal androgens can account for this stage of development in both boys and girls is questionable. The principal adrenal androgen is DHEA, and although a small amount of this steroid is converted into testosterone, the levels are very low compared with those associated with puberty in the male. It is conceivable that boys are more responsive to androgens when adrenarche begins and become less responsive as the levels increase dramatically with puberty, whereas girls' responsivity to androgens might remain unchanged. But apart from the fact that males are exposed to androgens in utero whereas females are not, there is a substantial rise in testosterone for a period of 2 to 3 months shortly after birth in the male but not in the female (Forest, Deperetti, & Bertrand, 1976). I have postulated elsewhere that early exposure to androgens desensitizes the male to the central nervous system effects of testosterone, so that when puberty occurs, high levels of androgens necessary for the peripheral secondary sexual differentiation of the male can occur without overstimulation of the brain (Bancroft, 2002). Females, on the other hand, remain, in general, much more sensitive to the behavioral effects of testosterone, although substantial interindividual variability in this responsiveness exists, quite possibly across different stages of the reproductive life span. As discussed earlier, the substantial difference between males and females in age of onset of masturbation, which can be regarded as a useful marker of sexual development, suggests on the one hand that male sexuality is substantially organized around, as well as activated by, pubertal changes, whereas the impact of puberty—and here we should also consider adrenarche—will be much less predictable in the female. Those women who are highly responsive to androgens may be activated at adrenarche, with those who have lower responsiveness showing an onset around puberty or even much later. In other words, the impact of hormonal changes on sexual development in preadolescence and adolescence will be variable in males but substantially more variable in females.

Little research has looked directly at the relation between hormonal changes and behavioral change in early adolescence, and most of the research that has been done has been by Udry and his colleagues. Their earlier studies were cross-sectional. From a study of 102 boys in 9th or 10th grades, using questionnaires and blood sampling, they concluded that free testosterone was a strong predictor of sexual motivation, with stage of pubertal development otherwise having little effect (Udry, Billy, Morris, Groff, & Raj, 1985). In a later longitudinal study of boys over a 3-year period, they were unable to replicate these findings; stage of pubertal development was now a much stronger predictor of sexual interest and behavior (Halpern, Udry, Campbell, & Suchindran. 1993). In a cross-sectional study of white girls in 8th, 9th, or 10th grades, testosterone level was correlated with sexual interest and frequency of masturbation but was not predictive of sexual intercourse, which seemed to be more determined by peer group influences (Udry, Talbert, & Morris, 1986). In a later longitudinal study, testosterone levels were related to transition to first sexual intercourse, but not to sexual interest or masturbation (Halpern, Udry, & Suchindran, 1997). It is difficult to understand these conflicting results, although I have discussed the possible implications more fully elsewhere (Bancroft, 2003b). Clearly, more research is needed on these issues, but we should not expect the interaction between biological factors, cognitive development, and sociocultural influences to be simple.

The Parent versus Peer Group Pattern

There is limited evidence that directly addresses the relative importance of parents and peers on adolescent development. Kinsman, Romer, Furstenberg, and Schwartz (1998) assessed 1,389 sixth graders, with a mean age of 11.7 years, at the beginning (Time 1) and at the end (Time 2) of the school year. At Time 1, 30% had already experienced sexual intercourse; 5% had first experience between Time 1 and Time 2. These "initiators" were more likely to be male, African American, attending poor schools, and living in an area with many single-parent families. The strongest predictor of "initiation" was the belief that most friends had already experienced sexual intercourse, indicating a significant peer group effect. Ramirez-Valles, Zimmerman, and Newcomb (1998) found, in their predominantly African American high school students, that those engaging in risky sexual behavior were more likely to live in poor neighborhoods and less likely to engage in "prosocial activities" (e.g., church programs, youth programs, organized sports).

Several studies have looked at parental influences, mainly those of mothers. Parental communication about sex and birth control is seen as important for reducing adolescent sexual risk behavior (Jaccard & Dittus, 1991; Jaccard, Dittus, & Gordon, 2000). Perceived maternal disapproval of sexual intercourse in mother–child relationships that are characterized by high levels of warmth and closeness may be important protective factors related to delay of first sexual intercourse (Sieving, McNeely, & Blum 2000), although the mother's values and beliefs appear to influence daughters more than sons (McNeely et al., 2002).

The impact of religion on the sexual experiences of 3,356 adolescent girls (mean age 16 years) in the Add Health study was reported by Miller and Gur (2002). Personal devotion (i.e., a sense of personal connection to God) and frequent attendance at church activities was associated with greater sexual responsibility; these girls were less likely to have partners outside of a romantic, loving relationship and more likely to use contraception within such relationships. "Personal conservatism," which meant a rigid adherence to one's religious creed, was associated with more exposure to unprotected sex, including forced sex, and greater tendency to leave birth control to their male partners. This religious "personality style" was regarded as leading to fewer coping resources in sexual situations.

Bearman and Brückner (2001) found that "pledging virginity" was associated with a substantial delay in initiating sexual intercourse, but this effect was not apparent at all ages of adolescence and was more effective when the pledge was not the norm for one's group. They concluded that the pledge worked because it was part of establishing one's identity, for which pledging needed to be at least partially nonnormative. Pledgers who "broke their promise" were less likely to use contraception at first sexual intercourse.

Halpern, Joyner, Udry, and Suchindran (2000) used data from the Add Health study, in which 100 white boys were assessed over 3 years and 200 white and black girls over 2 years. Controlling for age, physical maturity and mother's education, they found a curvilinear relationship between intelligence and experience of sexual intercourse; the upper and lower ends of the intelligence range were less likely to have experienced sexual intercourse. Furthermore, those with higher intelligence were more likely to have postponed initiation of the full range of partnered sexual activities. It was postulated that intelligence might be associated with a greater ability to consider the consequences of sexual activity and to weigh up the "pros and cons." However, it was acknowledged that further research was needed to fully understand this effect of intelligence.

These and other studies reinforce the idea that adolescents who feel positive about their future, who look forward to successful careers, or who have relatively high self-esteem are more likely to delay sexual intercourse. It might be that such positive self-esteem factors make the adolescent less dependent on peer group influences.

What is strikingly missing in the modern discourse on adolescent sexuality is the idea of helping teenagers to become more responsible in this emerging part of their lives, which, if only because of the potential for creating new life, carries huge responsibilities from the time they are fertile. These responsibilities are, or should be, as great for the teenage boy as for the girl. The policy of advocating sexual abstinence until marriage, with no consideration of how to implement abstinence at the stage of life when, at least for boys, sexual arousability is at its maximum, is a disturbing form of denial. How the young adolescent negotiates this developmental phase to move toward a stable and rewarding sexual life as an adult receives scant attention.[1]

The Maladaptive Pattern

There is now an extensive literature showing that during adolescence, sexual behavior, particularly in terms of early age at first sexual intercourse, number of sexual partners, and sexual risk taking, is associated with other types of maladaptive or "delinquent" behavior, such as drug and alcohol use. There is much more limited evidence from longitudinal studies that indicate that maladaptive behavior in childhood is predictive of later sexual patterns in adolescence. Thus Caspi et al. (1997) found that "undercontrolled" behavior at age 3 predicted high "negative emotionality" and low "constraint" on the Tellegen Personality Profile at age 18, which in turn predicted a range of high-risk behaviors, including sexual behavior, at the age of 21. Bates et al. (2003) showed that personality factors, such as a tendency to "externalizing behavior" in kindergarten-age children, are predictive of number of sexual partners in late adolescence.

There is also an extensive literature on the relationship between CSA and maladaptive patterns of sexual behavior and function in adolescence and adulthood. This is covered elsewhere in this book (see Barbaree & Langton, Chapter 3, this volume). Also relevant to the main theme of this volume is the potential relationship between "maladaptive" patterns of sexual development and the emergence of antisocial patterns of sexual behavior, including sexual offenses. These are also dealt with elsewhere in this book (see Seto & Lalumière, Chapter 8, and O'Reilly & Carr, Chapter 9, this volume).

There is one particular aspect of the "maladaptive" pattern that warrants closer scrutiny: the relation between negative mood and sexuality. It is conventional wisdom that in states of negative mood, such as depression or anxiety, the sexual interest and responsiveness of most people declines. Yet comorbidity of affective disorders with maladaptive "sexual compulsions" or "sexual addictions" has been reported (Black, Kehrberg, Flumerfelt, & Schlosser, 1997). Our recent research has shown that a substantial minority of heterosexual men (Bancroft, Janssen, Strong, Vukadinovic, & Long, 2003) and women (Lykins, Janssen, & Graham, in press) and gay men (Bancroft, Janssen, Strong, & Vukadinovic, 2003) report that they typically experience an increase in sexual interest when in negative mood states and that this pattern is predictive of some aspects of high-risk sexual behavior in both straight and gay men (Bancroft, Janssen, Strong, Carnes, & Long, 2003; Bancroft, Janssen, Strong, Goodrich, & Long, 2004). This pattern is also strongly apparent in self-identified "sex addicts" (Bancroft & Vukadinovic, 2004). Furthermore, at least in heterosexual men and women, we have found that this paradoxical increase in sexual interest during negative mood states is more likely in younger adults, raising the question of when this pattern, which may lessen as one gets older, first becomes established. Is it in childhood or around the peripubertal transition? Could there be a stage of sexual development at which the arousing effects of negative mood, such as anxiety, become associated with the arousal response to sexual stimuli, at least in some people—what might be described as age-dependent "excitation transfer" (Zillman, 1983)? This brings to mind Ramsey's (1943b) early study in which boys ages 10 to 12 reported erections occurring to a variety of "arousing" but nonsexual situations, such as being chased by a policeman, flying in an airplane, or wrestling with a friend. This transitional phase of nonspecific genital responsiveness soon gave way, at least in most of the boys Ramsey interviewed, to a more discriminatory sexual response pattern. Could that type of sexual learning process be disrupted by the effects of CSA and lead to the establishment of a paradoxical relation between negative mood and sexual interest and response? To what extent is this paradoxical pattern evident in the "juvenile sex offender"? These are researchable questions.

Sexual Preferences and the Development of "Sexual Identity"

As the three strands—sexual responsiveness, gender identity, and dyadic relationships—start to integrate in this transitional stage between childhood and adolescence, a key element among the evolving sexual meanings is an emerging "sexual identity"—initially, "What part does sex play in the person that I am?" and subsequently, "What kind of sexual person am I?" Obviously an important component of sexual identity is sexual orientation. If we know little about normal heterosexual development, we know even less about normal homosexual development (Savin-Williams, 1995). It is not clear when sexual orientation becomes established in the developmental sequence. It is reasonable to assume that the basic developmental mechanisms will be the same for those with heterosexual and with homosexual orientations. We can consider a "prelabeling" stage, when childhood and early adolescent sexual experiences occur, including feelings of attraction, without the need to categorize them as either heterosexual or homosexual. At some stage, which is likely to be socially determined, the individual asks the question, "Am I straight or gay?" This is the "self-labeling" stage. Later the social world starts asking the same questions about the individual; this is the "social labeling" stage. These stages typically reinforce the idea that "you are either one thing or the other" (Bancroft, 1989). However, the "normalizing" influence of the social labeling process, particularly as it is expressed through the peer group, is going to have very different effects on the adolescent who is experiencing cross-gender attraction and who will progress, almost without consideration, into a heterosexual identity. In contrast, one who is experiencing same-gender attraction will be either struggling in a sociocultural vacuum or, more likely, experiencing the impact of social stigmatization. It is therefore to be expected that the integration of our three developmental strands will take substantially longer in those who emerge with a homosexual identity, rendering them more psychologically vulnerable in the process. An interesting example of how sociocultural influences appear to have changed over the past 50 years is in the prevalence of male–male sexual interactions in early adolescence. Gagnon and Simon (1973) clarified the original Kinsey data to show that most of the 37% of men who had experienced orgasm in a sexual encounter with another male were referring to early adolescent experience. Although we lack good evidence of how this pattern may have changed over time in the United States, Schmidt, Klusmann, Zeitzschel, and Lange (1994) have shown that this type of early adolescent same-sex interaction declined substantially in Germany between 1970 and 1990. Although this may in part reflect increased opportunities for sexual interaction with girls at this age, it is also likely that early adolescents are now much more aware of the "identity implications" of such behavior and hence avoid it.

It is beyond the scope of this chapter to give full consideration to the determinants of sexual orientation. (For recent discussions, see Bem, 2000; Herdt, 2000; and Meyer-Bahlburg, 2000.) Biological factors, both genetic and prenatal hormonal, are likely to play an important role, probably more so in males than in females (see Mustanski, Chivers, & Bailey, 2002, for recent review). There are also good grounds for concluding that "sexual identity," in terms of sexual orientation, is socially constructed, reflecting the ways that different societies at different historical periods have made sense of variability in sexual preference. The challenge is to understand how biological and sociocultural factors interact to influence the development of first sexual preferences and subsequent sexual orientation and identity. Extensive evidence suggests a link between gender identity during childhood and subsequent sexual orientation. An association between gender nonconformity in male children and subsequent homosexual orientation is one of the most robust findings in developmental psychology (Mustanski et al., 2002). However, gender nonconformity is not a necessary prerequisite for homosexual orientation, and we remain uncertain whether the impact of biological or genetic factors is more direct on gender identity and secondary on sexual orientation, or whether both are manifestations of a common biological basis.

Beyond sexual orientation, we also need to consider the extraordi-nary individual variability in more specific sexual preferences. Again we have more questions than answers. The "normalizing" effect of the peer group is likely to be important, with unusual sexual preferences, includ-ing most of the paraphilias, being more likely to become established in those relatively isolated from a "normalizing" peer group. The seminal study of Ramsey (1943a, 1943b), discussed earlier, which has long awaited replication, suggests, at least in males, a phase of relatively indiscriminate sexual arousability, which then becomes focused, by dis-criminatory learning, into more specifically sexual response patterns. Given the almost exclusive restriction of fetishes to males, it may well be that erectile response plays a crucial role in this discriminatory learning process. Genital responses in females are, at least for the majority, much less obvious. Hence other markers of sexuality are required for the sex-ual learning process in females. There is a further aspect of sexual learn-ing, particularly in male sexuality, which has been largely ignored in the research literature: the issue of specificity. Some individuals develop response patterns to very specific sexual stimuli, which remain central to their sexual preferences. In contrast, others require novelty in order to maintain sexual responsiveness. Most individuals come somewhere in between. However, no attempt has yet been made to explain what deter-mines these contrasting patterns. Nor is it clear when in the developmen-tal sequence this learning takes place, though it is reasonable to assume, at least in boys, that it will be associated with the increased arousability around puberty. This chapter is about normal sexual development, but it may be relevant that some abnormal types of sexual learning, particu-larly the more bizarre fetishes, are sometimes associated with abnormal brain function, such as temporal lobe epilepsy (Bancroft, 1989). This might indicate that there are specific mechanisms in the brain relevant to sexual learning that, although fundamental to normal sexual develop-ment, sometimes go wrong.

Summary and Conclusions

I return to the "three-strand" model of sexual development (Bancroft, 1989) to help organize the conclusions to this chapter. The three strands—(1) gender identity, (2) dyadic relationships, and (3) sexual response—are relatively independent during childhood. Thus the factors that influence a child's emerging sense of gender identity have relatively little effect on the emerging ability to establish and maintain close dyadic relationships, and vice versa. Although the child's gender identity may influence whether peer relationships are with the same sex or not, important learning, relevant to the dyadic strand, is occurring in interactions with both mother and father and with older siblings, relatives, and friends. Both gender identity and the capacity for close dyadic relationships are fundamental to childhood development in a more general sense. In contrast, the sexual-response strand has a much more variable role during childhood, with some children having clear sexual awareness and associated experiences, such as masturbation, and others remaining relatively unaware. We remain uncertain of the extent to which these individual differences result from early learning and family environment or are genetically or prenatally determined. As the child approaches adolescence, however, all three strands become increasingly interactive and interdependent. Gender identity is thrown into a transient state of confusion; although the prepubertal child is likely to have established a secure understanding of what it means to be a boy or a girl, the physical changes that occur around puberty produce a new phase of considerable uncertainty. "What shape am I going to end up?" "How much like a 'normal male' (or female) am I going to be?" and, as a relatively new concern, "How sexually attractive am I going to be?" (Bancroft, 1989). Hierarchies of relationships between peers can be disrupted. Previously dominant boys and girls can find themselves left behind by the earlier pubertal development of their peers. In turn, the newly organizing sense of masculinity or femininity will influence how dyadic relationships, both sexual and nonsexual, are formed and experienced. The emerging adolescent "scripts" for male and female behavior will now have a clearer sexual component, and sexual response will affect new relationships, leading to an emerging distinction between sexual and nonsexual relationships. The sexual-response strand may make an early entry in the developmental process for some and a late entry for others, neither having clear implications for eventual normal sexual development. We have considered how the key biological factors associated with adrenarche and puberty interact with the cognitive processes of acquired meanings, with the crucial shift from predominantly parental influence early in this integrative process to a greater peer group influence during adolescence. We have also considered various ways in which this integrative developmental process can be derailed, either as a result of early negative sexual experiences or because of the establishment of nonsexual maladaptive patterns during childhood that evolve into adolescent maladaptive patterns, including sexual "acting out." In addition, problems in relating to the peer group may result in a relatively isolated stage of discriminative sexual learning, when inappropriate or paraphilic response patterns are more likely to become established. At a later stage, problems in establishing intimate dyadic relationships may present a further barrier to the development of a "mature" sexuality, in which we incorporate our sexuality into the primary relationship in our lives, leading typically to new family formation.

However, there are many gaps in our knowledge and understanding of these processes and significant methodological, as well as political, constraints on our ability to fill them. We must hope for more substantial progress in the future.

Note

1. Many interesting and informative narratives by young adults of their adolescent sexual development can be found in Martinson (1994).

References

Abma, J. C., & Sonenstein, F. L. (2001). Sexual activity and contraceptive practices among teenagers in the United States, 1988 and 1995 (DHHS Publication No. 2001-1997). Washington, DC: Government Printing Office.

Achenbach, T. M. (1991). *Manual for the Child Behavior Checklist/4–18 and 1991 Profile.* Burlington: University of Vermont, Department of Psychiatry.

Bancroft, J. (1989). *Human sexuality and its problems* (2nd ed.). Edinburgh, UK: Churchill Livingstone.

Bancroft, J. (2002). Sexual effects of androgens in women: Some theoretical considerations. *Fertility and Sterility, 77*(Suppl. 4), S55–S59.

Bancroft, J. (Ed.). (2003a). *Sexual development in childhood.* Bloomington: Indiana University Press.

Bancroft, J. (2003b). Androgens and sexual function in men and women. In C. J. Bagatell & W. J. Bremner (Eds.), *Androgens in health and disease* (pp. 259–290). Totowa, NJ: Humana.

Bancroft, J., Herbenick, D., & Reynolds, M. (2003). Masturbation as a marker of sexual development. In J. Bancroft (Ed.), *Sexual development in childhood* (pp. 156–185). Bloomington: Indiana University Press.

Bancroft, J., Janssen, E., Carnes, L., Strong, D. A., Goodrich, D., & Long, J. S. (2004). Sexual activity and risk taking in young heterosexual men: The relevance of personality factors. *Journal of Sex Research. 41,* 181–192.

Bancroft, J., Janssen, E., Strong, D., Carnes, L., & Long J. S. (2003). Sexual risk taking in gay men: The relevance of sexual arousability, mood, and sensation seeking. *Archives of Sexual Behavior, 32*(6), 555–572.

Bancroft, J., Janssen, E., Strong, D., & Vukadinovic, Z. (2003). The relation between mood and sexuality in gay men. *Archives of Sexual Behavior, 32,* 231–242.

Bancroft, J., Janssen, E., Strong, D., Vukadinovic, Z., & Long, J. S. (2003). The relation between mood and sexuality in heterosexual men. *Archives of Sexual Behavior, 32,* 217–230.

Bancroft, J., & Vukadinovic, Z. (2004). Sexual addiction, sexual compulsivity, sexual impulse disorder or what? Towards a theoretical model. *Journal of Sex Research, 41*, 225–234

Bates, J. E., Alexander, D. B., Oberlander, S. E., Dodge, K. A., & Pettit, G. S. (2003). Antecedents of sexual activity at ages 16 and 17 in a community sample followed from age 5. In J. Bancroft (Ed.), *Sexual development in childhood* (pp. 206–238). Bloomington: Indiana University Press.

Bearman, P. S., & Brückner, H. (2001). Promising the future: Virginity pledges and first intercourse. *American Journal of Sociology, 106*, 859–912.

Bem, D. (2000). The exotic-becomes-erotic theory of sexual orientation. In J. Bancroft (Ed.), *The role of theory in sex research* (pp. 67–80). Bloomington: Indiana University Press.

Black, D. W., Kehrberg, L. L. D., Flumerfelt, D. L., & Schlosser, S. S. (1997). Characteristics of 36 subjects reporting compulsive sexual behavior. *American Journal of Psychiatry, 154*(2), 243–249.

Bogart, L. M., Cecil, H., Wagstaff, D. A., Pinkerton, S. D., & Abramson, P. R. (2000). Is it "sex"? College students' interpretations of sexual behavior terminology. *Journal of Sex Research, 37*(2), 108–116.

Borneman, E. (1990). Progress in empirical research on children's sexuality. In J. Money & H. Musaph (Series Eds.) & M. E. Perry (Vol. Ed.), *Handbook of sexology: Vol. 7. Childhood and adolescent sexology* (pp. 201–210). Amsterdam: Elsevier.

Bowlby, J. (1969). *Attachment and loss: Vol. 1. Attachment.* New York: Basic Books.

Bowlby, J. (1973). *Attachment and loss: Vol. 2. Separation.* London: Hogarth Press.

Bowlby, J. (1980). *Attachment and loss: Vol 3. Loss, sadness and depression.* New York: Basic Books.

Broderick, C. B. (1966). Socio-sexual development in a suburban community. *Journal of Sex Research, 2*(1), 1–24.

Browning, C. R., & Laumann, E. O. (2003). The social context of adaptation to childhood sexual maltreatment: A life course perspective. In J. Bancroft (Ed.), *Sexual development in childhood* (pp. 383–403). Bloomington: Indiana University Press.

Caspi, A., Begg, D., Dickson, N., Harrington, H. L., Langley, J., Moffitt, T. E., & Silva, P.A. (1997). Personality differences predict health-risk behaviors in young adulthood: Evidence from a longitudinal study. *Journal of Personality and Social Psychology, 73*, 1052–1063.

Crawford, M., & Popp, D. (2003). Sexual double standards: A review and methodological critique of two decades of research. *Journal of Sex Research, 40*, 27–35.

DeLamater, J. D. (2003). [Discussion paper]. In J. Bancroft (Ed.), *Sexual development in childhood* (pp. 186–191). Bloomington: Indiana University Press.

Elias, J., & Gebhard, P. (1970). Sexuality and sexual learning in childhood. In D. L. Taylor (Ed.), *Human sexual development: Perspectives in sex education* (pp. 16–27). Philadelphia: Davis.

Fergusson, D. M., Horwood, L. J., & Lynskey, M. (1997). Childhood sexual abuse, adolescent sexual behaviors, and sexual revictimization. *Child Abuse and Neglect, 21,* 789–803.

Finkelhor, D. (1980). Sex among siblings: A survey on prevalence, variety, and effects. *Archives of Sexual Behavior, 9*(3), 171–194.

Finkelhor, D. (1988). The trauma of child sexual abuse: Two models. In G. Wyatt & E. Powell (Eds.), *Lasting effects of child sexual abuse* (pp. 61–84). Newbury Park, CA: Sage.

Finkelhor, D. (2003). [Discussant]. In J. Bancroft (Ed.), *Sexual development in childhood* (pp. 98–99). Bloomington: Indiana University Press

Forest, H. G., Deperetti, E., & Bertrand, J. (1976). Hypothalamic–pituitary–gonadal relationships from birth to puberty. *Clinical Endocrinology, 5,* 551–569.

Fortenberry, J. D. (2003). [Discussant]. In J. Bancroft (Ed.), *Sexual development in childhood* (pp. 202–203). Bloomington: Indiana University Press.

Fortenberry, J. D., & Aalsma, M. C. (2003). Abusive sexual experiences before age 12 and adolescent sexual behaviors. In J. Bancroft (Ed.), Sexual development in childhood (pp. 359–369). Bloomington: Indiana University Press.

Fortenberry, J. D., Cecil, H., Zimet, G. D., & Orr, D. P. (1997). Concordance between self-report questionnaires and coital diaries for sexual behaviors of adolescent women with sexually transmitted infections. In J. Bancroft (Ed.), *Researching sexual behavior: Methodological issues* (pp. 237–249). Bloomington: Indiana University Press.

Frayser, S. G. (2003). Cultural dimensions of childhood sexuality in the United States. In J. Bancroft (Ed.), *Sexual development in childhood* (pp. 255–273). Bloomington: Indiana University Press.

Friedrich, W. N. (1997). *Child Sexual Behavior Inventory: Professional manual.* Odessa, FL: Psychological Assessment Resources.

Friedrich, W. N. (2003a). [Discussant]. In J. Bancroft (Ed.), *Sexual development in childhood* (p. 100). Bloomington: Indiana University Press.

Friedrich, W. N. (2003b). Studies of sexuality of nonabused children. In J. Bancroft (Ed.), *Sexual development in childhood* (pp. 107–120). Bloomington: Indiana University Press.

Friedrich, W. N., Fisher, J., Dittner, C. A., Acton, R., Berliner, L., Butler, J., et al. (2001). Child Sexual Behavior Inventory: Normative, psychiatric, and sexual abuse comparisons. *Child Maltreatment, 6,* 37–49.

Gagnon, J., & Simon, W. (1973). *Sexual conduct: The social sources of human sexuality.* Chicago: Aldine.

Gagnon, J. H., & Simon, W. (1987). The scripting of oral–genital conduct. *Archives of Sexual Behavior, 16,* 1–25.

Gebhard, P. H. (1977). The acquisition of basic sex information. *Journal of Sex Research, 13,* 148–169.

Goldman, R., & Goldman, J. (1982). *Children's sexual thinking: A comparative study of children aged 5 to 15 years in Australia, North America, Britain and Sweden.* London: Routledge & Kegan Paul.

Graber, J. A., Brooks-Gunn, J., & Galen, B. R. (1998). Betwixt and between: Sexuality in the context of adolescent transitions. In R. Jessor (Ed.), *New perspectives on adolescent risk behavior* (pp. 270–316). Cambridge, UK: Cambridge University Press.

Graham, C. A. (2003). Methodological issues involved in adult recall of childhood sexual experiences. In J. Bancroft (Ed.), *Sexual development in childhood* (pp. 67–76). Bloomington: Indiana University Press.

Green, V. (1985). Experiential factors in childhood and adolescent sexual behavior: Family interactions and previous sexual experiences. *Journal of Sex Research, 21,* 157–182.

Haavio-Mannila, E., & Kontula, O. (2003) Single and double standards in Finland, Estonia and St. Petersburg. *Journal of Sex Research, 40,* 36–49.

Halpern, C. J. T., Joyner, K., Udry, R., & Suchindran, C. (2000). Smart teens don't have sex (or kiss much either). *Journal of Adolescent Health, 26,* 213–225.

Halpern, C. J. T., Udry, R., Campbell, B., & Suchindran, C. (1993). Testosterone and pubertal development as predictors of sexual activity: A panel analysis of adolescent males. *Psychosomatic Medicine, 55,* 436–447.

Halpern, C. J. T., Udry, J. R., & Suchindran, C. (1997). Testosterone predicts initiation of coitus in adolescent females. *Psychosomatic Medicine, 59,* 161–171.

Haugaard, J. J., & Tilly, C. (1988). Characteristics predicting children's responses to sexual encounters with other children. *Child Abuse and Neglect, 12,* 209–218.

Heiman, J. R., Verhulst, J., & Heard-Davison, A. R. (2003). Childhood sexuality and adult sexual relationships: How are they connected by data and by theory? In J. Bancroft (Ed.), *Sexual development in childhood* (pp. 404–420). Bloomington: Indiana University Press.

Herdt, G. (2000). Why the Sambia initiate boys before age 10. In J. Bancroft (Ed.), *The role of theory in sex research* (pp. 82–104). Bloomington: Indiana University Press.

Herdt, G. (2003). [Discussion paper]. In J. Bancroft (Ed.), *Sexual development in childhood* (pp. 274–279). Bloomington: Indiana University Press.

Hobsbawm, E. (1994). *Age of extremes: The short twentieth century 1914–1991.* London: Abacus.

Jaccard, J., & Dittus, P. J. (1991). *Parent–teen communication: Toward the prevention of unintended pregnancies.* New York: Springer-Verlag.

Jaccard, J., Dittus, P. J., & Gordon, V. V. (2000). Parent–teen communication about premarital sex: Factors associated with the extent of communication. *Journal of Adolescent Research, 15*(2), 187–208.

Kagan, J., & Moss, H. A. (1962). *Birth to maturity: A study in psychological development.* New York: Wiley.

Karacan, I., Salis, P. J., Thornby, J. I., & Williams, R. L. (1976). The ontogeny of nocturnal penile tumescence. *Waking and Sleeping, 1,* 27–44.

Kilpatrick, A. (1992). *Long-range effects of child and adolescent sexual experiences: Myths, mores, menaces.* Hillsdale, NJ: Erlbaum.

Kinsey, A. C., Pomeroy, W. B., & Martin, C. E. (1948). *Sexual behavior in the human male*. Philadelphia: Saunders.

Kinsey, A. C., Pomeroy, W. B., Martin, C. E., & Gebhard, P. H. (1953). *Sexual behavior in the human female*. Philadelphia: Saunders.

Kinsman, S. B., Romer, D., Furstenberg, F., & Schwartz, D. F. (1998). Early sexual initiation: The role of peer norms. *Pediatrics, 102*(5), 1185–1192.

Lamb, S., & Coakley, M. (1993). "Normal" childhood sexual play and games: Differentiating play from abuse. *Child Abuse and Neglect, 17*, 515–526.

Langfeldt, T. (1990). Early childhood and juvenile sexuality, development and problems. In J. Money & H. Musaph (Series Eds.), & M. E. Perry (Vol. Ed.), *Handbook of sexology: Vol. 7. Childhood and adolescent sexology* (pp. 179–200). Amsterdam: Elsevier.

Leitenberg, H., Greenwald, E., & Tarran, M. (1989). The relation between sexual activity among children during preadolescence and/or early adolescence and sexual behavior and sexual adjustment in young adulthood. *Archives of Sexual Behavior, 18*, 299–313.

Lykins, A., Janssen, E., & Graham, C. (in press). The relationship between negative mood and sexuality in heterosexual college women. *Journal of Sex Research*.

Martinson, F. M. (1994). *The sexual life of children*. Westport, CT: Bergin & Garvey.

McClintock, M., & Herdt, G. (1996). Rethinking puberty: The development of sexual attraction. *Current Directions in Psychological Science, 5*, 178–183.

McNeely, C., Shew, M. L., Beuhring, T., Sieving, R., Miller, B. C., & Blum, R. W. (2002). Mothers' influence on the timing of first sex among 14- and 15-year-olds. *Journal of Adolescent Health, 31*, 256–265.

Meyer-Bahlburg, H. F. L. (2000). Sexual orientation: Discussion of Bem and Herdt from a psychobiological perspective. In J. Bancroft (Ed.), *The role of theory in sex research* (pp. 110–124). Bloomington: Indiana University Press.

Meyer-Bahlburg, H. F. L., Dolezal, C., & Sandberg, D. E. (2000). The association of sexual behavior with externalizing behaviors in a community sample of prepubertal children. In T. G. M. Sandfort & J. Rademakers (Eds.), *Childhood sexuality: Normal sexual behavior and development* (pp. 61–79). New York: Haworth.

Meyer-Bahlburg, H. F. L., & Steel, J. L. (2003). Using the parents as a source of information about the child with special emphasis on the sex problems scale of the Child Behavior Checklist. In J. Bancroft (Ed.), *Sexual development in childhood* (pp. 34–53). Bloomington: Indiana University Press.

Miller, L., & Gur, M. (2002). Religiousness and sexual responsibility in adolescent girls. *Journal of Adolescent Health, 31*, 401–406.

Montgomery, M. J., & Sorell, G. T. (1998). Love and dating experience in early and middle adolescence: Grade and gender comparisons. *Journal of Adolescence, 21*, 677–689.

Mustanski, B. S., Chivers, M. L., & Bailey, J. M. (2002). A critical review of recent biological research on human sexual orientation. *Annual Review of Sex Research, 13*, 89–140.

Newcomer, S. F., & Udry, J. R. (1985). Oral sex in an adolescent population. *Archives of Sexual Behavior, 14,* 41–46.

Orenstein, P. (1994). *School girls: Young women, self-esteem, and the confidence gap.* New York: Doubleday.

O'Sullivan, L. F. (2003). Methodological issues associated with studies of child sexual behavior. In J. Bancroft (Ed.), *Sexual development in childhood* (pp. 23–33). Bloomington: Indiana University Press.

O'Sullivan, L. F., Meyer-Bahlburg, H. F. L., & Wasserman, G. (2000). Reactions of inner-city boys and their mothers to research interviews about sex. In T. G. M. Sandfort & J. Rademakers (Eds.), *Childhood sexuality: Normal sexual behavior and development* (pp. 81–103). New York: Haworth.

Perry, M. E. (Vol. Ed). (1990). *Handbook of sexology: Vol. 7. Childhood and adolescent sexology.* Amsterdam: Elsevier.

Phinney, V. G., Jensen, L. C., Olsen, J. A., & Cundick, B. (1990). The relationship between early development and psychosexual behaviors in adolescent females. *Adolescence, 25,* 321–332.

Rademakers, J., Laan, M. J. C., & Straver, C. J. (2003). Body awareness and physical intimacy: An exploratory study. In J. Bancroft (Ed.), *Sexual development in childhood* (pp. 121–125). Bloomington: Indiana University Press.

Ramirez-Valles, J., Zimmerman, M. A., & Newcomb, M. D. (1998). Sexual risk behavior among youth: Modeling the influence of pro-social activities and socioeconomic factors. *Journal of Health and Social Behavior, 39,* 237–253.

Ramsey, G. V. (1943a). The sex information of younger boys. *American Journal of Orthopsychiatry, 8*(2), 347–352.

Ramsey, G. V. (1943b). The sexual development of boys. *American Journal of Psychology, 56*(2), 217–234.

Remez, L. (2000). Oral sex among adolescents: Is it sex or is it abstinence? *Family Planning Perspectives, 32*(6), 298–304.

Reynolds, M. A., Herbenick, D. L., & Bancroft, J. (2003). The nature of childhood sexual experiences: Two studies 50 years apart. In J. Bancroft (Ed.), *Sexual development in childhood* (pp. 134–155). Bloomington: Indiana University Press.

Sachs, B. D. (1995). In J. Bancroft (Ed.), *The pharmacology of sexual function and dysfunction* (p. 130). Amsterdam: Excerpta Medica.

Sanders, S. A., & Reinisch, J. M. (1999). Would you say you "had sex" if . . . ? *Journal of the American Medical Association, 281,* 275–277.

Sandfort, T. G. M., & Rademakers, J. (Eds.). (2000). *Childhood sexuality: Normal sexual behavior and development.* New York: Haworth.

Santelli, J., Lindberg, L. D., Abma, J., McNeely, C. S., & Resnick, M. (2000). Adolescent sexual behavior: Estimates and trends from four nationally representative surveys. *Family Planning Perspectives, 32*(4), 156–166.

Savin-Williams, R. C. (1995). An exploratory study of pubertal maturation timing and self-esteem among gay and bisexual male youths. *Developmental Psychology, 31*(1), 56–64.

Schmidt, G., Klusmann, D., Zeitzschel, U., & Lange, C. (1994). Changes in adolescents' sexuality between 1970 and 1990 in West Germany. *Archives of Sexual Behavior, 23*(5), 489–513.

Schofield, M. (1965). *The sexual behaviour of young people.* Boston: Little, Brown.

Schoof-Tams, K., Schlaegel, J., & Walczak, L. (1976). Differentiation of sexual morality between 11 and 16 years. *Archives of Sexual Behavior, 5,* 353–370.

Schuhrke, B. (2000). Young children's curiosity about other people's genitals. In T. G. M. Sandfort & J. Rademakers (Eds.), *Childhood sexuality: Normal sexual behavior and development* (pp. 27–48). New York: Haworth.

Schwartz, I. M. (1999). Sexual activity prior to coital initiation: A comparison between males and females. *Archives of Sexual Behavior, 28*(1), 63–69.

Sieving, R., McNeely, C. S., & Blum, R. W. (2000). Maternal expectations, mother–child connectedness, and adolescent sexual debut. *Archives of Pediatrics and Adolescent Medicine, 154*(8), 809–816.

Sonenstein, F. L., Ku, L., & Pleck, J. H. (1997). Measuring sexual behavior among teenage males in the United States. In J. Bancroft (Ed.), *Researching sexual behavior: Methodological issues* (pp. 87–105). Bloomington: Indiana University Press.

Sonenstein, F. L., Pleck, J. H., & Ku, L. C. (1989). Sexual activity, condom use, and AIDS awareness among adolescent males. *Family Planning Perspectives, 21,* 152.

Thigpen, J. W., Pinkston, E. M., & Mayefsky, J. H. (2003). Normative sexual behavior of African American children: Preliminary findings. In J. Bancroft (Ed.), *Sexual development in childhood* (pp. 241–254). Bloomington: Indiana University Press.

Tolman, D. L. (2002). *Dilemmas of desire: Teenage girls talk about sexuality.* Cambridge, MA: Harvard University Press.

Tolman, D. L. (2003). [Discussant]. In J. Bancroft (Ed.), *Sexual development in childhood* (p. 100). Bloomington: Indiana University Press.

Turner, C. F., Miller, H. G., & Rogers, S. M. (1997). Survey measurement of sexual behavior: Problems and progress. In J. Bancroft (Ed.), *Researching sexual behavior: Methodological issues* (pp. 37–60). Bloomington: Indiana University Press.

Udry, J. R., Billy, J. O. G., Morris, N. M., Groff, T. R., & Raj, M. H. (1985). Serum androgenic hormones motivate sexual behavior in adolescent boys. *Fertility and Sterility, 43*(1), 90–94.

Udry, J. R., Talbert, L. M., & Morris, N. M. (1986). Biosocial foundations of adolescent female sexuality. *Demography, 23*(2), 217–229.

Volbert, R. (2000). Sexual knowledge of preschool children. In T. G. M. Sandfort & J. Rademakers (Eds.), *Childhood sexuality: Normal sexual behavior and development* (pp. 5–26). New York: Haworth.

Widom, C. S., & Morris, S. (1997). Accuracy of adult recollections of childhood victimization: 2. Childhood sexual abuse. *Psychological Assessment, 9,* 34–46.

Williams, L. M. (1994). Recall of childhood trauma: A prospective study of women's memories of child sexual abuse. *Journal of Consulting and Clinical Psychology, 62,* 1166–1176.

Zillman, D. (1983). Transfer of excitation in emotional behavior. In J. T. Cacioppo & R. E. Petty (Eds.), *Social psychophysiology: A sourcebook* (pp. 215–240). New York: Guilford Press.

Zimmer-Gembeck, M. J., Siebenbruner, J., & Collins, W. A. (2001). Diverse aspects of dating: Associations with psychosocial functioning from early to middle adolescence. *Journal of Adolescence, 24,* 313–336.

CHAPTER 3

The Effects of Child Sexual Abuse and Family Environment

Howard E. Barbaree
Calvin M. Langton

Abusive sexual behavior in juveniles is strongly influenced by the youngsters' family environment and their early sexual experiences, particularly the experience of child sexual abuse. Additionally, sexual behavior "problems" exhibited by the child lay a foundation for later sexually abusive behavior in the juvenile. Of course, not all adolescents who display abusive sexual behavior have experienced child sexual abuse, nor have they all grown up in families that allow or promote the development of these behaviors. But, as will be seen, empirical data confirm the clinical impressions of professionals in the field that family context, early sexual behavior, and the experience of child sexual abuse are important contributory factors in the development of abusive sexual behavior in juveniles.

Sexual Behavior Problems in Children

Children naturally engage in a wide range of sexual behaviors (Friedrich, Grambsch, Broughton, Kuiper, & Beilke, 1991). However, sexually abused children exhibit a higher frequency of sexual behaviors than nonabused children (Berliner, 1991; Gale, Thompson, Moran, & Sack, 1988). In a review of the literature on the effects of childhood maltreatment, Kendall-Tackett, Williams, and Finkelhor (1993) found that 13 of 45 studies examining these effects reported the occurrence of sexual behaviors earlier in development than expected. Twenty-eight percent of 1,353 maltreated children had engaged in sexual behaviors, but these studies showed a large range in the proportion of children showing premature sexual behaviors (i.e., 7–90%). Although most maltreated children may not exhibit highly sexualized behaviors, the available data suggest that sexual behaviors may occur earlier than expected in development in approximately one quarter of all maltreated children. These premature sexual behaviors are some of the most distinguishing consequences of childhood sexual victimization (Pithers & Gray, 1998).

The Child Sexual Behavior Inventory (CSBI) is a 36-item checklist completed by the child's caregiver, who rates behaviors manifested over the previous 6 months on a scale from 0 to 4, reflecting the frequency of problematic sexual behaviors (Freidrich, Grambsch, Damon, & Hewitt, 1985). The CSBI was developed on sexually abused and abuse-free children ages 2–12. The inventory has shown discriminant validity in the sense that it shows significant differences in the frequency of sexual behaviors between children referred to clinical services subsequent to their experience of child sexual abuse and nonreferred children. Problematic sexual behavior exhibited by the children who had experienced child sexual abuse include touching the sex parts of another child, touching animals' sex parts, asking others to engage in sex, rubbing sex parts against other people, inserting objects in vagina or rectum, and trying to undress other children. These problematic sexual behaviors were extremely rare in the nonreferred sample.

Gray, Busconi, Houchens, and Pithers (1997) reported on a sample of children with sexual behavior problems. This sample comprised 65% boys and 35% girls. Mental health practitioners, child protective agencies, and the courts referred these children for treatment after they had been identified as a result of their own victimization. Gray et al. (1997) defined children with sexual behavior problems as 6- to 12-year-olds who had engaged in sexual behaviors that were (1) repetitive; (2) unresponsive to adult intervention and supervision; (3) equivalent to a criminal violation, if performed by an adult; (4) pervasive, occurring across time and situations; or (5) a diverse array of sexual acts.

Although the sample of children with sexual behavior problems had experienced all recognized forms of child maltreatment, sexual victimization predominated. Sexual victimization occurred in 95% of the 66 children for whom data could be collected. All of the females in this study were sexually abused, as were 93% of the males. Physical abuse was the second most common type of victimization, experienced by 48% of the entire sample, with 52% of the males and 42% of the females being affected. One third of all the children had been emotionally abused. More than half of the children with sexual behavior problems were victims of multiple forms of abuse, with the most frequent combination being sexual and physical abuse. Considering all forms of abuse, the average number of perpetrators per child was 2.5. Most of the children's abusers were male (73.2%). Other children and adolescents were responsible for nearly 40% of abuse to these children, with 16.7% of the perpetrating children being 5–10 years old and 22.7% being 11–18. Young adults ages 19–25 represented 6.1% of the children's abusers, and older adults accounted for 33% of their abusers. The average age of these children at the time of their own maltreatment was 3.4 years.

It is important to recognize, particularly in the context of this chapter on the influence of child sexual abuse and family environment in the lives of juvenile sex offenders, that not only are sexual behavior problems in childhood precursors to abusive sexual behavior in adolescence, but also the more serious and harmful juvenile sex offenders report having engaged in problematic sexual behavior as children. Burton (2000) compared three groups of incarcerated adolescents who admitted to sexual offending in an anonymous survey project on measures of trauma, sexual offending, and the relationship between trauma and sexual offending. Burton divided his sample into those who admitted to offending before the age of 12 only, those who admitted to offending after the age of 12 only, and those who offended before and after the age of 12. Approximately half of the total sample who reported any sexually aggressive behavior reported having begun their aggressive behavior prior to the age of 12. Further, the severity and complexity of the sexual aggression was greater for adolescents who reported continuous sexual aggression (both before and after the age of 12).

The Contribution of Family Environment

As has been reported for the adult sex offender (Barbaree, Hudson, & Seto, 1993), the families of adolescent sexual abusers are characterized by frequent violence, family instability, and disorganization (Awad, Saunders, & Levene, 1984; Deisher, Wenet, Paperny, Clark, & Fehrenbach, 1982; Fehrenbach, Smith, Monastersky, & Deisher, 1986; Lewis, Shankok, & Pincus, 1979; Longo, 1982; Smith, 1988). Although these same family characteristics and backgrounds may be said to apply to persons who later exhibit a wide variety of dysfunctional behaviors (e.g., criminal behavior, substance abuse), the families that particularly seem to produce sexually abusive behavior are characterized by (1) instability and lack of resources; (2) the failure to promote or establish strong emotional bonds particularly between parent and child; (3) early exposure to sexual material and behavior; (4) an environment in which the child is at high risk for sexual abuse or sexual exploitation by an adult; and (5) lack of resources to cope with the effects of child sexual abuse after it has been disclosed.

Families of children with sexual behavior problems are characterized as being unstable with few resources. In a study of children with sexual behavior problems, Gray et al. (1997) found that half of the caregivers were single parents. Although most caregivers in this sample had completed high school, their annual family incomes were low, with 38% of these families falling below the U.S. federal poverty level. Poverty has been shown to be highly associated with all forms of child maltreatment (Coulton, Korbin, Su, & Chow, 1995; Garbarino & Sherman, 1980; Gelles, 1992; Tzeng & Schwarzin, 1990; Zuravin, 1989). The Third National Incidence Study of Child Abuse and Neglect (Sedlak & Broadhurst, 1996) compared families with incomes over $30,000 with families with incomes under $15,000. The poorer families had 12–16 times the incidence of physical abuse and 18 times the incidence of child sexual abuse (Sedlack & Broadhurst, 1996).

Second, these families fail to establish strong emotional bonds (Blaske, Borduin, Henggeler, & Mann, 1989). In recent years, the etiological significance of insecure childhood attachment among sexual offenders has received theoretical consideration (Marshall, 1989; Ward, Hudson, Marshall, & Siegert, 1995) and tentative empirical support (Smallbone & Dadds, 1998; 2000; Ward, Hudson, & Marshall, 1996). Childhood attachment insecurity among sexual offenders has been proposed to lead to disruptions in empathy and to the failure to achieve intimacy in adolescence and adulthood (Marshall, 1989; Ward et al., 1995), contributing to sexually abusive behaviors (Smallbone & McCabe, 2003).

The families of children with sexual behavior problems were described as involving parent–child conflict, inadequate parental monitoring of children, and lack of positive involvement between parent and child (Pithers & Gray, 1998). Parents of children with sexual behavior problems indicated that they had difficulty fulfilling their parental role as a result of qualities in their children that they found undesirable or disappointing (Pithers & Gray, 1998). They considered their children to be overreactive to changes in routine, difficult to calm when upset, and excessively demanding. The parents regarded interactions with their children as generally unrewarding. Further, parents of children with sexual behavior problems reported feeling emotionally distant from their children, suggesting an impaired parent–child attachment (Pithers & Gray, 1998).

Third, these families promote or allow early exposure to sexual material and behavior. Friedrich et al. (1991) surveyed mothers of 2- to

12-year-olds (n = 880) using a behavior checklist that included a number of sexual behaviors. These authors report that increased overt sexual behavior in children was positively related to family nudity and general behavior problems. Ford and Linney (1995) compared adolescent sex offenders, violent nonsexual offenders, and nonviolent offenders. The content of early childhood memories and exposure to pornographic material differed among the groups. Forty-two percent of the sex offenders reported exposure to hard-core sex magazines, compared with 29% of the violent and nonviolent offenders. Post hoc comparisons indicated that the sex offenders were exposed to pornographic magazines at the youngest ages, between 5 and 8 years old, with child molesters being the most frequently exposed.

Fourth, these families allow an environment to exist in which the child is at high risk for both sexual and physical abuse (Awad & Saunders, 1989; Becker, Cunningham-Rathner, & Kaplan, 1986; Becker, Kaplan, Cunningham-Rathner, & Kavoussi, 1986; Fehrenbach et al., 1986; Lewis et al., 1979; Longo, 1982; Robertson, 1990; Smith, 1988; Van Ness, 1984). In the Ford and Linney (1995) study cited earlier, adolescent child molesters were found to have experienced more physical and sexual abuse than violent nonsexual and nonviolent offender groups. Some of these families include an adult perpetrator of child sexual abuse. In families of children with sexual behavior problems, Gray et al. (1997) found that, excluding the sexual abuse perpetrated by the child who had been referred for sexual behavior problems, 62% of the families contained at least one additional person who had performed a sexually abusive act. In the 72 families involved in the study, there were a total of 87 additional perpetrators, an average of 1.3 additional sexual abusers per family. Further, sexual abuse perpetrators within the family tended to act against other family members, with 94% of the victims being within the extended family and 84.8% of the abuse occurring within the abuser's or victim's own home.

But, even when the family does not contain another perpetrator of child sexual abuse, some of these families fail their children by allowing the child to be sexually abused by perpetrators outside the family, through neglect, ignorance, or incompetence. Hummel, Thomke, Oldenburger, and Specht (2000) compared adolescent child molesters with and without a history of sexual abuse. Adolescent child molesters who had a history of sexual abuse reported more frequent absence of the parent from the family home.

Finally, these families do not have the resources required to cope effectively with the effects of child sexual abuse once it has occurred. Friedrich and Luecke (1988) observed than after child sexual abuse, appropriate parenting is the exception, rather than the rule, and this further exacerbated the trauma of sexual abuse. Whereas highly skilled, nurturing parents may assist children to overcome difficulties early in life, a rejecting parental response will worsen behavior problems (Henggeler, 1989; McCord, 1979; Patterson & Stouthamer-Loeber, 1984). Parental incompetence and parents' relative detachment from their children both predispose their child to maltreatment and also reduce the moderating effect of the parental relationship on subsequent behavior problems (Pithers & Gray, 1998). The fact that these families fail to cope effectively with the effects of child sexual abuse makes it even more likely that the child victim will engage later in aggressive and/ or deviant sexual behavior (Pithers & Gray, 1998).

The Effects of Child Sexual Abuse

It is not universally accepted that child sexual abuse has entirely negative effects on children. In a 1998 article, Rind, Tromovitch, and Bauserman presented the results of a meta-analysis of 59 studies of the effects of child sexual abuse among college students. According to these authors, the prevalent view among the general public and among prominent governmental authorities and policy makers is that child sexual abuse causes intense psychological effects; that the psychological effects are pervasive, affecting all individuals who had experienced child sexual abuse; and that the effects are equivalent between genders. Based on the results of the meta-analysis, the authors challenged those views in their conclusions that: (1) there was no evidence in the literature that child sexual abuse "causes" psychological disturbance or other effects, particularly when the confounding effects of family environment were taken into account; (2) the effects of child sexual abuse were not pervasive; (3) the intensity of the effects of child sexual abuse were low overall but variable, ranging from "pronounced deleterious effects" seen in a small number of individuals to weak or neutral effects seen in the majority of participants; and (4) that the effects were much less serious in boys than girls. Most relevant to the focus of discussion in this chapter, these authors took the position that the effects of child sexual abuse in boys are often benign and that boys sometimes experience sexual interactions with adults as positive, even pleasurable (Rind, 2001). These authors proposed that terminology related to child sexual abuse that implies a moral judgment should be abandoned.

As would be expected, the publication of the Rind et al. (1998) article set off a firestorm of controversy (Dallam et al., 2001; Ondersma et al., 2001). The scientific community responded with strongly worded rejoinders. Dallam et al. (2001) criticized the authors on the basis of their methodology, citing numerous problems with the study that minimized the relationships between child sexual abuse and the psychological effects studied, including the use of a healthy sample, an overly broad definition of child sexual abuse, failure to correct for statistical attenuation, and misreporting of original data. Ondersma et al. (2001) criticized Rind and colleagues for the way they had presented their findings as a direct contradiction of current governmental policy on child sexual abuse and for implying that scientific or empirical data could invalidate what was essentially a consensual moral position. Rind et al. (2001) struck back with a detailed defense of their original article, admitting none of the weaknesses raised by the scientific critics.

Outside scientific circles, the article attracted staunch proponents and engendered bitter opposition. The article was hailed on websites of organizations devoted to the legalization of adult–child sex (e.g., North American Man/Boy Love Association) as representing scientific endorsement of their views (Riegel, 2000). The article became the subject of discussion on radio talk shows, where it elicited outrage (Saunders, 1999) directed at both the authors and the publisher of the article. Debate ensued in the Congress and Senate of the United States, resulting in a formal unanimous denouncement of the article and its findings. Apparently, this was the first time in U.S. history that any legislative body has formally repudiated a scientific study (Dallam et al., 2001). The American Psychological Association acknowledged that it had not given sufficient attention to the implications for public policy and admitted that the article included expressions of opinions by the authors that were inconsistent with official APA policy. APA's defensive response in turn set off a secondary firestorm of controversy over issues of scientific freedom, the relation between scientific inquiry and societal values, and the independence of editorial authority (Ondersma et al., 2001).

We support a full and frank discussion of such disagreements, especially when scientific data and public policy appear to disagree. Many of the objections to Rind and colleagues' work appear to us to be valid, but some of the authors' points appear to be valuable as well. We are particularly concerned that no reasonable inferences from valid scientific data should be suppressed.

We agree with Rind et al. (2001) that the current data do not allow a clear causal inference between child sexual abuse and observed negative effects. The data are correlational (not causal) in nature, and there are numerous confounding variables (family environment included) that could be causally related to both child sexual abuse and the putative negative effects of child sexual abuse. As indicated earlier, we regard child sexual abuse as being an integral part of the family environment that leads to the later development of deviant sexual behavior, and we believe that the distinctive effects of sexual abuse cannot be disentangled from those of other factors.

Additionally, we think that it is clear that the extreme negative effects of child sexual abuse are not universal; not all victims of child sexual abuse will manifest serious debilitating negative effects, and the effects of child sexual abuse may seem to be benign or neutral in some cases. However, the explanation for the lack of a traumatic outcome may have more to do with the ability of the victim to cope with the event and with his or her family supports than with the nature of the traumatic event itself. It is a well-established and accepted psychological principle that the effects of any traumatic event may be reduced substantially when appropriate personal resources are available and external support enhances the ability to cope with the trauma (see discussion of resiliency in Mahoney, 1991, pp. 158–162).

Having made these concessions to Rind and colleagues (1998), it would be important to emphasize that, in accordance with the definition of sexual abuse presented by Barbaree and Marshall in Chapter 1 of this volume, sexual interactions between an adult and child are always abusive. It is important here to make a clear distinction between the nature of the abusive act and its consequences. Although the severity of the harm done to the victim may seem to vary in intensity from victim to victim, the act is abusive by definition. The fact that the effects of the abusive experience seem to be benign or neutral in an individual case does not justify the view that the act was benign or neutral or nonabusive. The effects of child sexual abuse are intense and serious in many individuals who experience child sexual abuse, and the intensity of the effect is not predictable for any individual victim.

We endorse the criticisms of Rind et al. (1998) by Dallam et al. (2001) concerning the methodological aspects of their meta-analysis that may have restricted the magnitude of the observed child sexual abuse effects. First, Rind and colleagues confined the participant pool to college students (who might have greater resources and support), with the consequence that more seriously affected victims of child sexual abuse may not have been included in the sample. Second, by studying these individuals in their early adulthood, in many cases several years after the sexual abuse experience, the chronic effects observed may not have been reflective of the severity of the acute effects immediately after the child's sexual abuse experience.

More recent research addresses these concerns. Using a large ($n = 4,023$) nationwide (U.S.) probability sample of adolescents ages 12–17, Kilpatrick and his colleagues (Kilpatrick et al., 2000, 2003) surveyed symptoms of posttraumatic stress disorder (PTSD), major depression, and substance abuse and dependence. A significant minority of this representative sample of adolescents (15.5% of boys and 19.3% of girls) met diagnostic criteria for at least one of these DSM-IV diagnoses. Adolescents who reported experiencing sexual assault were 2.4 times more likely to have comorbid PTSD and a major depressive episode, 6.73 times more likely to have comorbid PTSD and substance abuse/dependence, and 4.43 times more likely to have comorbid major depressive episode and substance abuse/dependence (Kilpatrick et al., 2003). Similarly, adolescents who reported being victims of sexual assault were 2.4 times more likely to abuse alcohol or to be alcohol dependent and more than 2.5 times more likely to abuse hard drugs (Kilpatrick et al., 2000). Although psychological harm might not be the experience of every victim of sexual assault, and although some minors may report positive experiences in their sexual interactions with adults (e.g., Rind, 2001), the risk for psychological harm is high, particularly in childhood and adolescence.

Some children may report that their experience of sex with adults was a positive, even pleasurable, experience. However, some of the boys and men who report that sex with adults was perceived by them to be a positive experience may have been affected in negative ways that they do not recognize or understand. A number of well-known psychological processes might interfere with a victim's ability to judge whether the effects of the experience were positive, negative, or neutral, including cognitive dissonance, rationalization, identification with the perpetrator, and responses to demands or social pressure from the perpetrator. Moreover, a victim who judges the experience of abuse to be neutral or positive at a particular point in time may change his or her judgment to negative in the future.

With respect to the issue of equivalence of effects in girls and boys, Rind et al. (1998) entertain only two possible results: either equivalence of effects or less severe effects in boys than in girls. However, empirical data reviewed subsequently, suggest that the effects are different in boys than in girls and that these differences are highly relevant to the issue of central focus in this chapter, namely, the development of abusive sexual behavior. Although girls may express the negative effects of child sexual abuse emotionally, as evident in internalizing factors (psychological effects such as depression and reduced self-esteem), boys are more likely to show the negative effects of child sexual abuse behaviorally, as evident in externalizing factors (such as antisocial behavior and suicidality).

As pointed out in Dallam et al.'s (2001) critique of Rind et al. (1998), numerous nonclinical studies of high school students have reported that child sexual abuse is associated with a wide variety of high-risk behaviors, including antisocial behavior, conduct disorders, self-destructive behavior, substance abuse, younger age at first coitus, more frequent and risky sexual activity, not using condoms or birth control, sexually transmitted diseases, increased HIV risk, and teen pregnancy (Bensley, Spieker, Van Eenwyk, & Schoder, 1999; Bensley, Van Eenwik, Spieker, & Schoder, 1999; Fiscella, Kitzman, Cole, Sidora, & Olds, 1998; Harrison, Fulkerson, & Beebe, 1997; Hibbard, Brack, Rauch, & Orr, 1988; Hibbard, Ingersoll, & Orr, 1990; Nagy, DiClemente, & Adcock, 1995; Stock, Bell, Boyer, & Connell, 1997). Moreover, studies of high school students have reported that sexual abuse has a particularly negative impact on the behavior of adolescent males (e.g., Chandy, Blum, & Resnick, 1996; Garnefski & Arends, 1998; Hibbard et al., 1990). Chandy et al. (1996) examined gender-specific outcomes for 370 abused boys and 2,681 abused girls who were identified in a study of more than 36,000 students in grades 7 to 12. Compared with their female counterparts, male adolescents who acknowledged experiencing child sexual abuse were at significantly higher risk for poor school performance, delinquent activities, sexual risk taking, and dropping out of high school. These results suggest that, by restricting their analysis to longer term psychological effects in college samples, Rind et al. (1998) may have missed some of the most harmful effects associated with child sexual abuse, namely, the negative behavioral effects on boys.

The Experience of Child Sexual Abuse among Juvenile Sex Offenders

A long-standing and prevalent clinical assumption regarding both adult and adolescent sex offenders has been that many have been sexually abused as children and, therefore, that sexually deviant behavior somehow stems from early sexual victimization (e.g., Breer, 1987; McCormack, Rokous, Hazelwood, & Burgess, 1992). By 1990, numerous authorities in the field had reported that a significant minority (19–49%) of youthful sex offenders had experienced child sexual abuse (Becker, Cunningham-Rathner, & Kaplan,1986; Becker, Kaplan, et al., 1986; Fehrenbach et al., 1986; Longo, 1982; Pierce & Pierce, 1987). Before 1990, clinical experience suggested that even higher rates were to be found in specific subgroups of sex offenders (e.g., male adolescents who molest younger boys; Davis & Leitenberg, 1987). Some specific samples had been reported to show rates of child sexual abuse of as high as 75% (a sample of incarcerated child molesters who had offended against boys; Robertson, 1990; a sample of children younger than 6 who had engaged in sexual abuse; Johnson, 1988).

Johnson (1988), studying 47 boys between ages 4 and 13 who had engaged in sexually abusive behaviors, found an inverse relationship between the children's own sexual victimization and the age at which their sexual behavior problems began. Of the children who began their sexually abusive behavior when they were 6 or younger, 72% reported having been sexually abused themselves, whereas 42% of the children who began their sexually abusive behaviors between ages 7 and 11 were victims of sexual abuse. In children who began sexually abusing between ages 11 and 12, 35% had acknowledged having been sexually abused. Other reports went beyond simply recording whether or not abuse had occurred. Friedrich and Luecke (1988) studied a group of school-age children (4–11 years; M = 7.3 years) who had engaged in genital contact involving coercion and found that the sexual abuse these children had experienced had been more severe than that found for a comparison group of sexually abused children.

By the mid-1990s, research on child sexual abuse in juvenile sex offenders was becoming more systematic. Worling (1995) reviewed the extant literature on child sexual abuse in juvenile sex offenders and reported that of the 1,268 adolescent male sex offenders in these samples, 31% reported some form of sexual abuse, approximately triple the rate typically reported in studies of men in the general population (Peters, Wyatt, & Finkelhor, 1986). Although the rates of child sexual abuse varied widely in these studies (19–55%), Worling reported that the rates differed between studies that had been based on data collected at pretreatment (22%) and studies that collected data after substantial treatment had been completed (52%). Worling speculated that this result was a reflection of clinical reports indicating that many adolescent sex offenders acknowledge sexual victimization only after they have formed a trusting relationship with a therapist (Becker, 1988; Kahn & Lafond, 1988). These data would argue that the reported rates of child sexual abuse experienced in sex offenders may be underestimates because most studies collected data at pretreatment or in circumstances in which there was no treatment involvement.

An alternative perspective is that at least some offenders claim to have been sexually abused as children in order to mitigate the responsibility for their own abusive behavior, perhaps once they recognize that child sexual abuse represents a clinical focus in treatment. Research on the effects of polygraph testing on sexual offenders' self-reported history of personal victimization indicates that overreporting does occur (Hindman & Peters, 2001). Clearly, the methodological limitations inherent in studies that rely on self-report data, as well as those that utilize polygraph testing, restrict current understanding of the etiological role of child sexual abuse in later sexual offending behavior.

From the data that have been reported, the rates of child sexual abuse seem to vary across groups of adolescent sex offenders subdivided according to aspects of their offense history. For example, more adolescent sex offenders against children report a history of child sexual abuse than do adolescents who offend against peers or adults (Awad & Saunders, 1991; O'Brien, 1991), and offenders who assault a male child are more likely to report sexual victimization than those who offended exclusively against female children (Hanson & Slater, 1988). However, Worling (1995) has pointed out that in these studies, age and gender of victim are confounded; although youthful sex offenders victimize females of all ages, they do not offend against adult males. Therefore, when the research findings suggest that child sexual abuse rates are higher among offenders against children, it may be that this finding is entirely due to the fact that all male victims are children.

Benoit and Kennedy (1992) examined institution records of adolescent offenders who assaulted only children, thereby eliminating the confound. Offenders who assaulted both male and female children were combined with those who assaulted only male children, and it was found that 36% of adolescents who assaulted even one male child disclosed a history of sexual abuse. Conversely, only 16% of those who offended against female children reported sexual victimization.

Similar findings were reported by Worling (1995). He collected data from 87 adolescent male sex offenders between the ages of 12 and 19 years. Initial victimization and offending histories were collected by therapists during regular clinical interactions with the adolescents, which ranged in duration from 2 to 50 months with a mean of 13 months. Sexual victimization was recorded and corroborated by reports from child welfare or probation agencies. The sample of participants was divided into four groups: offenders against female adolescents and adults ($n = 27$); offenders against female children ($n = 29$); offenders against only male children ($n = 12$); and offenders against both male and female children ($n = 19$). Overall, 43% of the participants reported sexual victimization. When the four groups were compared in terms of the frequency of sexual victimization, the four groups were significantly different, and the overall statistical significance was attributable to the finding that 75% of adolescents who had ever assaulted a male child disclosed a history of childhood sexual abuse, in comparison to only 25% who had only assaulted females (of any age).

In summary, the literature indicates that most offenders who assault even one male child report a history of sexual abuse. This finding corroborates clinical observations (Breer, 1987; Davis & Leitenberg, 1987) and the results of investigations of adolescent offenders (Becker & Stein, 1991; Benoit & Kennedy, 1992). Furthermore, it is similar to the results reported for adult offenders against children (Hanson & Slater, 1988).

Models of the Effects of Child Sexual Abuse

According to Worling (1995), there are a number of possible explanations for these results. The first is based on learning, or a conditioning process in which physiological arousal is seen as a component of the experience of victimization. Sexual abuse often involves sexual stimulation of the victim (Breer, 1987; Wheeler & Berliner, 1988). If some boys subsequently masturbate to fantasies that include aspects of their own abuse (namely, an image of the sexual abuse of a young boy), they may be conditioning their sexual arousal to cues of young boys (Becker & Stein, 1991; Laws & Marshall, 1990; McGuire, Carlysle, & Young, 1965). The second possible explanation is that sexual victimization may raise questions of sexual orientation for a male child; in particular, a male victim may wonder whether he is homosexual because of sexual arousal experienced during the assault (Gilgun & Reiser, 1990). The adolescent offenders' subsequent sexual offenses against male children may represent some form of "recapitulation" of the victimization incident, whereby the offender attempts to regain a sense of control and mastery over homosexual conflicts (Breer, 1987; Watkins & Bentovim, 1992). Perhaps the most parsimonious explanation is based on social learning principles. Quite simply, it is possible that some male child victims will model the behavior of their offender (Laws & Marshall, 1990).

The following study provides some support for the conditioning and modeling theories of child sexual abuse's role in the development of deviant sexual behavior. Veneziano, Veneziano, and LeGrande (2000) studied 74 adolescent male sex abusers who had been referred or court ordered to a residential treatment facility. Of the 74 participants, 92% had been sexually abused, as documented by the family, the criminal justice system, or the referral source. After eliminating those participants who had no experience of child sexual abuse, data analysis indicated that the participants who were themselves first sexually abused when they were younger than the age of 5 were twice as likely to victimize someone younger than the age of 5. Similarly, they were twice as likely to have sexually abused males if they had been so abused by males. If they were victimized by a relative, it was 1.5 times more likely that they would victimize a relative. The boys who had been subjected to anal intercourse were 15 times more likely to abuse their victims in this fashion. If they had been fondled, they were 7 times more likely to fondle their victims, and if their sexual abuse had involved fellatio, they were twice as likely to have engaged in fellatio with their victims. This suggests that sexual abuse of children by some adolescent sex offenders may be a reenactment of their own sexual abuse or a learned behavior pattern (Burton, 2003; Longo, 1982; McCormack et al., 1992, Ryan, Miyoshi, Metzner, Krugman, & Fryer, 1996).

The following study provides further support for the conditioning model. Lambie, Seymour, Lee, and Adams (2002) examined the moderating factors that may prevent a victim of male sexual abuse from entering the "victim–offender cycle." Two groups were interviewed as part of the study: a resilient group ($n = 47$), who had experience with sexual victimization but no history of perpetration, and a victim–offender group ($n = 41$). Compared with the offender group, the resilient group was less likely to have fantasized and masturbated about the abuse, less likely to report deriving pleasure from the abuse, more likely to have had frequent social contact with adolescent peers, and more likely to have had more family and nonfamily support during childhood.

Although these findings provide general support for the role of child sexual abuse in the development of deviant sexual behavior, it is important and worthwhile to note that child sexual abuse is neither necessary nor sufficient for later abusive sexual behavior. Most male victims of sexual abuse do not become sex offenders (Finkelhor, 1986), and 25% of the offenders against male children in Worling's (1995) study did not report a history of sexual abuse.

Summary and Conclusions

The family environments that promote the development of problem sexual behavior in children and abusive sexual behavior in juveniles are characterized by the following: parent–child conflict, lack of positive involvement between parent and child, failure to promote or establish strong emotional bonds between parent and child, early exposure to sexual material, an environment in which the child is at high risk for child sexual abuse, and lack of resources to deal effectively with child sexual abuse once it has been disclosed.

Child sexual abuse has many diverse negative effects in numerous mental health domains. These effects can be described as acute or immediate, or chronic and long-lasting. Of particular interest in the context of the development of abusive sexual behavior in juveniles is that, whereas the effect of child sexual abuse is described as being primarily psychological in girls (depression, anxiety), the effects are described as more behavioral (antisocial) in boys. A high proportion of juvenile sex offenders report a history of child sexual victimization, and it is likely that victims of child sexual abuse who later engage in abusive sexual behavior are modeling the behavior of their perpetrators.

References

Awad, G. A., & Saunders, E. (1989). Adolescent child molesters: Clinical observations. *Child Psychiatry and Human Development, 19,* 195–206.

Awad, G. A., & Saunders, E. (1991). Male adolescent sexual assaulters: Clinical observations. *Journal of Interpersonal Violence, 6,* 446–460.

Awad, G. A., Saunders, E., & Levene, J. (1984). A clinical study of male adolescent sex offenders. *International Journal of Offender Therapy and Comparative Criminology, 28,* 105–116.

Barbaree, H. E., Hudson, S. M, & Seto, M. C. (1993). Sexual assault in society: The role of the juvenile offender. In H. E. Barbaree, W. L. Marshall, & S. M. Hudson (Eds.), *The juvenile sex offender* (pp. 1–24). New York: Guilford Press.

Becker, J. V. (1988). The effects of child sexual abuse on adolescent sexual offenders. In G. E. Wyatt & G. J. Powell (Eds.), *Lasting effects of child sexual abuse* (pp. 193–207). Newbury Park, CA: Sage.

Becker, J. V., Cunningham-Rathner, J., & Kaplan, M. S. (1986). Adolescent sexual offenders: Demographics, criminal and sexual histories, and recommendations for reducing future offenses. *Journal of Interpersonal Violence, 1,* 431–445.

Becker, J. V., Kaplan, M. S., Cunningham-Rathner, J., & Kavoussi, R. J. (1986). Characteristics of adolescent incest sexual perpetrators: Preliminary findings. *Journal of Family Violence, 1,* 85–97.

Becker, J. V., & Stein, M. (1991). Is sexual erotica associated with sexual deviance in adolescent males? *International Journal of Law and Psychiatry, 14,* 85–95.

Benoit, J. L., & Kennedy, W. A. (1992). The abuse of male adolescent sex offenders. *Journal of Interpersonal Violence, 7,* 543–548.

Bensley, L. S., Spieker, S. J., Van Eenwyk, J., & Schoder, J. (1999). Self-reported abuse history and adolescent problem behaviors: 2. Alcohol and drug use. *Journal of Adolescent Health, 24,* 173–180.

Bensley, L. S., Van Eenwyk, J., Spieker, S. J., & Shoder, J. (1999). Self-reported abuse history and adolescent problem behaviors: I. Anti-social and suicidal behaviors. *Journal of Adolescent Health, 24,* 163–172.

Berliner, L. (1991, June). Effects of sexual abuse on children. *Violence Update, 1,* 10–11.

Blaske, D. M., Borduin, C. M., Hengeler, S. W., & Mann, B. J. (1989). Individual, family, and peer characteristics of adolescent sex offenders and assaultive offenders. *Developmental Psychology, 25,* 846–855.

Breer, W. (1987). *The adolescent molester.* Springfield, IL: Thomas.

Burton, D. L. (2000). Were adolescent sexual offenders children with sexual behavior problems? *Sexual Abuse: A Journal of Research and Treatment, 12,* 37–48.

Burton, D. L. (2003). Male adolescents: Sexual victimization and subsequent sexual abuse. *Child and Adolescent Social Work Journal, 20,* 277–296.

Chandy, J. M., Blum, R. W., & Resnick, M. D. (1996). Gender-specific outcomes for sexually abused adolescents. *Child Abuse and Neglect, 20,* 1219–1231.

Coulton, C., Korbin, J., Su, M., & Chow, J. (1995). Community level factors and child maltreatment rates. *Child Development, 66,* 1262–1276.

Dallam, S. J., Gleaves, D. H., Cepeda-Benito, A., Silberg, J. L., Kaemer, H. C., & Spiegel, D. (2001). The effects of child abuse: Comment on Rind, Tromovitch, and Bauserman (1998). *Psychological Bulletin, 127,* 715–733.

Davis, G. E., & Leitenberg, H. (1987). Adolescent sex offenders. *Psychological Bulletin, 101,* 417–427.

Deisher, R. W., Wenet, G. A., Paperny, D. M., Clark, T. F., & Fehrenbach, P. A. (1982). Adolescent sexual offense behavior: The role of the physician. *Journal of Adolescent Health Care, 2,* 279–286.

Fehrenbach, P. A., Smith, W., Monastersky, C., & Deisher, R. W. (1986). Adolescent sexual offenders: Offender and offense characteristics. *American Journal of Orthopsychiatry, 56,* 225–233.

Finkelhor, D. (1986). Abusers: Special topics. In D. Finkelhor (Ed.), *A sourcebook on child sexual abuse* (pp. 119–142). Newbury Park, CA: Sage.

Fiscella, K., Kitzman, H. J., Cole, R. E., Sidora, K. J., & Olds, D. (1998). Does child abuse predict adolescent pregnancy? *Pediatrics, 101*(4, Pt. 1), 620–624.

Ford, M. E., & Linney, J. A. (1995). Comparative analysis of juvenile sex offenders, violent nonsexual offenders, and status offenders. *Journal of Interpersonal Violence, 10,* 56–70.

Friedrich, W. N., Grambsch, P., Broughton, D., Kuiper, J., & Beilke, R. J. (1991). Normative sexual behavior in children. *Pediatrics, 88,* 456–464.

Friedrich, W. N., Grambsch, P., Damon, L., & Hewitt, S. (1985). Child Sexual Behavior Inventory: Normative and clinical comparisons. *Psychological Assessment, 4,* 303–311.

Friedrich, W. N., & Luecke, W. J. (1988). Young school-age sexually aggressive children. *Professional Psychology Research and Practice, 19,* 155–164.

Gale, J., Thompson, R. J., Moran, T., & Sack, W. H. (1988). Sexual abuse in young children. *Journal of Pediatric Psychology, 11,* 47–57.

Garbarino, J., & Sherman, D. (1980). High-risk neighborhoods and high-risk families: The human ecology of child maltreatment. *Child Development, 51,* 188–198.

Garnefski, N., & Arends, E. (1998). Sexual abuse and adolescent maladjustment: Differences between male and female victims. *Journal of Adolescence, 21,* 99–107.

Gelles, R. (1992). Poverty and violence towards children. *American Behavioral Scientist, 35,* 258–274.

Gilgun, J. F., & Reiser, E. (1990). The development of sexual identity among men sexually abused as children. *Families in Society: The Journal of Contemporary Human Services, 71,* 515–523.

Gray, A., Busconi, A., Houchens, P., & Pithers, W. D. (1997). Children with sexual behavior problems and their caregivers: Demographics, functioning, and clinical patterns. *Sexual Abuse: A Journal of Research and Treatment, 9,* 267–290.

Hanson, R. K., & Slater, S. (1988). Reactions to motivational accounts of child molesters. *Journal of Child Sexual Abuse, 2,* 43–59.

Harrison, P. A., Fulkerson, J. A., & Beebe, T. J. (1997). Multiple substance use among adolescent physical and sexual abuse victims. *Child Abuse and Neglect, 21,* 529–539.

Henggeler, S. (1989). *Delinquency in adolescence.* Newbury Park, CA: Sage.

Hibbard, R. A., Brack, C. J., Rauch, S., & Orr, D. P. (1988). Abuse, feelings, and health behaviors in a student population. *American Journal of Diseases of Childhood, 142,* 326–330.

Hibbard, R. A., Ingersoll, G. M., & Orr, D. P. (1990). Behavioral risk, emotional risk, and child abuse among adolescents in a nonclinical setting. *Pediatrics, 86,* 896–901.

Hindman, J., & Peters, J. M. (2001). Polygraph testing leads to better understanding adult and juvenile sex offenders. *Federal Probation, 65,* 8–15.

Hummel, P., Thomke, V., Oldenburger, H. A., & Specht, F. (2000). Male adolescent sex offenders against children: Similarities and differences between those offenders with and those without a history of sexual abuse. *Journal of Adolescence, 23,* 305–317.

Johnson, T. C. (1988). Child perpetrators: Children who molest other children: Preliminary findings. *Child Abuse and Neglect, 12,* 219–229.

Kahn, T. J., & Lafond, M. A. (1988). Treatment of adolescent sexual offenders. *Child and Adolescent Social Work, 5,* 135–148.

Kendall-Tackett, K. A., Williams, L. M., & Finkelhor, D. (1993). Impact of sexual abuse on children: A review and synthesis of recent empirical studies. *Psychological Bulletin, 113,* 164–180.

Kilpatrick, D. G., Acierno, R., Schnurr, P. P., Saunders, B., Resnick, H. S., & Best, C. L. (2000). Risk factors for adolescent substance abuse and dependence: Data from a national sample. *Journal of Consulting and Clinical Psychology, 68,* 19–30.

Kilpatrick, D. G., Ruggiero, K. J., Acierno, R., Saunders, B. E., Resnick, H. S., & Best, C. L. (2003). Violence and risk of PTSD, major depression, substance abuse/dependence, and comorbidity: Results from the national survey of adolescents. *Journal of Consulting and Clinical Psychology, 71,* 692–700.

Lambie, I., Seymour, F., Lee, A., & Adams, P. (2002). Resiliency in victim-offender cycle in male sexual abuse. *Sexual Abuse: A Journal of Research and Treatment, 14,* 31–48.

Laws, D. R., & Marshall, W. L. (1990). A conditioning theory of the etiology and maintenance of deviant sexual preferences and behavior. In W. L. Marshall, D. R. Laws, & H. E. Barbaree (Eds.), *Handbook of sexual assault: Issues, theories, and treatment of the offender* (pp. 209–229). New York: Plenum Press.

Lewis, D. O., Shankok, S. S., & Pincus, J. H. (1979). Juvenile male sexual assaulters. *American Journal of Psychiatry, 136,* 1194–1196.

Longo, R. E. (1982). Sexual learning and experience among adolescent sexual offenders. *International Journal of Offender Therapy and Comparative Criminology, 26,* 235–241.

Mahoney, M. J. (1991). *Human change processes: The scientific foundations of psychotherapy.* New York: Basic Books.

Marshall, W. L. (1989). Intimacy, loneliness, and sexual offenders. *Behaviour Research and Therapy, 27,* 491–503.

McCord, J. (1979). Some child-rearing antecedents of criminal behavior in adult men. *Journal of Personality and Social Psychology, 8,* 1477–1486.

McCormack, A., Rokous, F. E., Hazelwood, R. R., & Burgess, A. W. (1992). An exploration of incest in the childhood development of serial rapists. *Journal of Family Violence, 7,* 219–228.

McGuire, R., Carlysle, J., & Young, B. (1965). Sexual deviation as conditioned behavior: A hypothesis. *Behaviour Research and Therapy, 2,* 185–190.

Nagy, S., DiClemente, R., & Adcock, A. G. (1995). Adverse factors associated with forced sex among southern adolescent girls. *Pediatrics, 96*(5, Pt. 1), 944–946.

O'Brien, M. J. (1991). Taking sibling incest seriously. In M. Q. Patton (Ed.), *Family sexual abuse: Frontline research and evaluation* (pp. 75–92). Newbury Park, CA: Sage.

Ondersma, S. J., Chaffin, M., Berliner, L., Cordon, I., Goodman, G. S., & Barnett, D. (2001). Sex with children is abuse: Comment on Rind, Tromovitch, and Bauserman (1998). *Psychological Bulletin, 127,* 707–714.

Patterson, G. R., & Stouthamer-Loeber, M. (1984). The correlation of family management practices and delinquency. *Child Development, 55,* 1299–1307.

Peters, S. D., Wyatt, G. E., & Finkelhor, D. (1986). Prevalence. In D. Finkelhor (Ed.), *A sourcebook on child sexual abuse* (pp. 15–59). Newbury Park, CA: Sage.

Pierce, J. H., & Pierce, R. L. (1987). Incestuous victimization by juvenile sex offenders. *Journal of Family Violence, 2,* 351–364.

Pithers, W. D., & Gray, A. (1998). The other half of the story: Children with sexual behavior problems. *Psychology, Public Policy, and Law, 4,* 200–217.

Riegel, D. (2000). *Understanding loved boys and boy lovers.* Philidelphia: Safe-Haven Foundation Press.

Rind, B. (2001). Gay and bisexual adolescent boys' sexual experiences with men: An empirical examination of psychological correlates in a nonclinical sample. *Archives of Sexual Behavior, 30,* 345–368.

Rind, B., Tromovitch, P., & Bauserman, R. (1998). A meta-analytic examination of assumed properties of child sexual abuse using college samples. *Psychological Bulletin, 124,* 22–53.

Rind, B., Tromovitch, P., & Bauserman, R. (2001). The validity and appropriateness of methods, analyses, and conclusions in Rind et al. (1998): A rebuttal of victimological critique from Ondersma et al. (2001) and Dallam et al. (2001). *Psychological Bulletin, 127,* 734–758.

Robertson, J. M. (1990). Group counseling and the high risk offender. *Federal Probation, 54,* 48–51.

Ryan, G., Miyoshi, T. J., Metzner, J. L., Krugman, R. D., & Fryer, G. E. (1996). Trends in a national sample of sexually abusive youths. *Journal of the American Academy of Child and Adolescent Psychiatry, 33,* 17–25.

Saundero, D. J. (1999, March 28). Lolita nation. *San Francisco Chronicle,* p. 7.

Sedlak, A. J., & Broadhurst, D. D. (1996). *Executive summary: Third National Incidence Study of Child Abuse and Neglect.* Washington, DC: Department of Health and Human Services.

Smallbone, S. W., & Dadds, M. R. (1998). Childhood attachment and adult attachment in incarcerated adult male sex offenders. *Journal of Interpersonal Violence, 13,* 555–557.

Smallbone, S. W., & Dadds, M. R. (2000). Attachment and coercive sexual behavior. *Sexual Abuse: A Journal of Research and Treatment, 12,* 3–15.

Smallbone, S. W., & McCabe, B. (2003) Childhood attachment, childhood sexual abuse, and onset of masturbation among adult sexual offenders. *Sexual Abuse: A Journal of Research and Treatment, 15,* 1–9.

Smith, W. R. (1988). Delinquency and abuse among juvenile sexual offenders. *Journal of Interpersonal Violence, 3,* 400–413.

Stock, J. L., Bell, M. A., Boyer, D. K., & Connell, F. A. (1997). Adolescent pregnancy and sexual risk-taking among sexually abused girls. *Family Planning Perspective, 29,* 200–203, 227.

Tzeng, O., & Schwarzin, H. (1990). Gender and race differences in child sexual abuse correlates. *International Journal of Intercultural Relations, 14,* 135–161.

Van Ness, S. R. (1984). Rape as instrumental violence: A study of youth offenders. *Journal of Offender Counseling, Services and Rehabilitation, 9,* 161–170.

Veneziano, C., Veneziano, L., & LeGrande, S. (2000). The relationship between adolescent sex offender behaviors and victim characteristics with prior victimization. *Journal of Interpersonal Violence, 15,* 363–374.

Ward, T., Hudson, S. M., & Marshall, W. L. (1996). Atachment style in sex offenders: A preliminary study. *Journal of Sex Research, 33,* 17–26.

Ward, T., Hudson, S. M., Marshall, W. L., & Siegert, R. J. (1995). Attachment style and intimacy deficits in sexual offenders: A theoretical framework. *Sexual Abuse: A Journal of Research and Treatment, 7,* 317–335.

Watkins, B., & Bentovim, A. (1992). The sexual abuse of male children and adolescents: A review of current research. *Journal of Child Psychology and Psychiatry, 33,* 197–248.

Wheeler, J. R., & Berliner, L. (1988). Treating the effects of sexual abuse on children. In G. E. Wyatt & G. J. Powell (Eds.), *Lasting effects of child sexual abuse* (pp. 227–247). Newbury Park, CA: Sage.

Worling, J. R. (1995). Sexual abuse histories of adolescent male sex offenders: Differences on the basis of the age and gender of their victims. *Journal of Abnormal Psychology, 104,* 610–613.

Zuravin, S. (1989). The ecology of child abuse and neglect: Review of the literature and presentation of data. *Victims and Violence, 4,* 101–120.

CHAPTER 4

Biological Factors in the Development of Sexual Deviance and Aggression in Males

Ray Blanchard
James M. Cantor
Lori K. Robichaud

For the last 150 years, clinicians and researchers have theorized that biological factors contribute to the development of paraphilias and other characteristics that increase a male's propensity to commit sexual offenses. The amount of hard evidence for such factors must be described as scanty, despite the decades it has had in which to accumulate. There are both general and special reasons for this. The general reasons are those that plague many immature research areas, for example, small sample sizes, poorly defined groups, and invalid or unreliable behavioral measures.

The special reasons include the secretive nature of paraphilias. This problem may be illustrated with the example of pedophilia. The great majority of pedophiles seen by clinicians are referred for evaluation because they have been accused or convicted of child molestation, not because they have come forward spontaneously complaining of sexual attraction to children. The majority of these deny erotic interest in children, even in the face of sexual histories that make a diagnosis of pedophilia relatively likely. This problem is bad enough in areas of research that require only a diagnosis of the individual. It becomes almost insurmountable in genetic research that requires diagnoses of the individual's relatives also. Pedophilic patients are unlikely, given their general tendency to deny that they themselves have this disorder, to produce the information that one or more of their close relatives has it; and, indeed, the patient's own father, brother, or son may have successfully concealed his pedophilia from the patient, as well as from the rest of the world. Thus the basic information needed for genetic linkage analyses or pedigree studies is virtually unobtainable.

This chapter summarizes the available evidence for biological influences on paraphilias and other factors affecting men's risk of sexual offending. It focuses on evidence that deviant sexual behaviors may be the result of pathogenic phenomena that disrupt the course of normal psychosexual development. It does not review evolutionary (or adaptationist) theories of sexual deviance, which seek to explain the incidence of such behaviors in terms of their reproductive advantage or in terms of their relation to other behaviors that confer a reproductive advantage. Such theories represent a completely separate class of biological explanations and would require a whole chapter to themselves. Our goals were to present the few conclusions about pathogenic biological factors that do appear to be justified by the available data and to highlight the various theoretical and empirical questions that remain to be answered.

IQ Studies

The biologically relevant trait most commonly assessed in sexual offenders is IQ, the first studies of which appeared in the 1930s (e.g., Frank, 1931). The mean IQs of samples of sexual offenders have ranged from 60 to 114 (cf. Rau, 1991; Selling, 1939), but fall typically in the low 90s (i.e., lower than the population mean of 100, but within the range classified as "average intelligence"). A recent meta-analysis compared the grand means of 100 samples of adult sexual offenders (representing 5,647 individuals) with that of 53 control samples (16,222 nonsexual offenders) and found that the sexual offenders scored significantly lower in IQ (Cantor, Blanchard, Robichaud, & Christensen, in press). The meta-analysis also demonstrated that the mean IQs of samples of sexual offenders against children were related to how stringently the sample was composed: The mean IQs from samples of men who offended against children age 13 or younger were lower than the IQs from samples of men who offended against children age 17 or younger.

The most comprehensive individual investigation of IQ among sexual offenders examined the scores of 454 men undergoing assessment for deviant sexual interests in relation to several variables, including the subjects' phallometric test results, their numbers of consenting sexual partners, and their numbers of victims in each of several age groups (Cantor et al., 2004). Analyses revealed lower IQ scores to be strongly related to greater numbers of child victims, and higher IQ scores to be related to greater numbers of consenting, adult sexual partners. Similarly, lower IQ scores were associated with greater phallometric responses to sexual stimuli involving children, and higher IQ scores were associated with greater responses to stimuli involving adults. The subjects also demonstrated significant group differences in IQ when trichotomized on the basis of their phallometric test results into pedophiles, hebephiles (men most attracted to pubescents), and teleiophiles (men most attracted to physically mature persons). The mean IQs of these groups were 89.5, 93.7, and 97.8, respectively.

These investigations suggest that IQ relates to the propensity to commit a sexual offense against children in general, but it remains unknown to what extent IQ might relate to the propensities to commit such offenses against male children versus female children, or against children from within the offender's family versus children from outside the family. Cantor et al. (2004) treated extrafamilial and intrafamilial offenses equivalently and did not directly compare offenders on the basis of the sex of their victims. Too few investigations providing samples of each type of sex offender were available to the aforementioned meta-analysis to resolve this problem. Further studies using more homogeneous samples of sexual offenders would be needed to address it.

Handedness

If IQ test scores were the only data available, it might be possible to explain the relatively low intelligence of pedophiles as an artifact of ascertainment bias. According to this explanation, less intelligent pedophiles are more likely to be apprehended (or unable to afford the best lawyers); therefore, convicted pedophiles will have lower mean IQs. One additional finding, however, argues against this interpretation. Bogaert (2001) found evidence that child molestation is related to left-handedness. Cantor et al. (2004) confirmed this relation in phallometrically diagnosed pedophiles and showed that it remained significant after controlling for age and IQ. One might plausibly argue that less intelligent pedophiles are more likely to be apprehended, but one cannot plausibly argue that left-handed pedophiles are more likely to be apprehended. It therefore appears that some other explanation is needed, one that can account for the association of pedophilia with left-handedness, as well as with below-average IQ.

Both low IQ and left-handedness are nonspecific indicators of per-turbations in prenatal neurodevelopment (see review in Blanchard et al., 2002). Thus the finding that pedophilia is associated with left-handed-ness and with poor cognitive functioning—two variables that are caus-ally related to neurodevelopment—suggests that pedophilia may also be causally related to neurodevelopment. It is possible, in other words, that associations exist among pedophilia, left-handedness, and poor cogni-tive functioning, because neurodevelopmental problems during prenatal life predispose a male to develop all three.

Neuropsychological Test Results

The evidence for neurodevelopmental perturbations in sexual offenders invites questions about whether those differences manifest generally, across cognitive abilities, or only with regard to specific cognitive func-tions. The identification of specificity could provide clues to etiology; for example, memory deficits associated with the hippocampus could sug-gest an etiological contribution of the limbic system, and deficits restricted to executive functioning could suggest behavioral disinhibition as a factor. Employing instruments that target individual cognitive func-tions, researchers have attempted to measure sexual offenders' abilities in reasoning, executive, memory, language, achievement, visuospatial, and motor domains. Table 4.1 summarizes the results of these investiga-tions, noting which ones identified significant differences between sexual offender samples and control groups (or published test norms, for the uncontrolled studies).

Of the cognitive domains tested, researchers have most frequently focused on executive function tasks, seeking evidence of an inability among sexual offenders to suppress sexual urges. In the most explicit test of this idea, Stone and Thompson (2001) anticipated that sexual offenders suffer from an impairment in the frontal lobes of the brain that produces a loss of self-control. The investigators assessed a heteroge-neous sample of sexual offenders with a battery of tests, sometimes called frontal lobe tests, and found that their sample scored significantly below published norms. Although they concluded that the offenders did indeed suffer from frontal lobe or executive function impairment, that conclusion seems somewhat unwarranted. The sample may have appeared to suffer from executive dysfunction only because the neuro-psychological battery consisted primarily of executive function tasks. One may reasonably hypothesize that these researchers would have actu-ally identified a broader deficit had they administered a broader battery.

Taken as a whole, the current literature has not identified any reli-

TABLE 4.1. Performance of Sexual Offenders on Selected Neuropsychological Tests Relative to Controls or Test Norms

Study	Participants	Reasoning				Executive							Memory								Language					Achievement		Visuospatial				Motor	
		MMMS	Raven's	SILS-T	SILS-A	COWA	CCPT	Maze	Stroop	Trails-A	Trails-B	WCST	BVMT	CVLT	FRT	HVLT	CFT	WMS	WNVI	WVL	ADA	NART	AST	SILS-V	WRM	PIA	WRAT	Bender	HVOT	JLO	PPV	Finger	Purdue
Abracen, O'Carroll, & Ladha (1991)	12 sexual offenders against children; 12 nonsexual nonviolent offenders; 13 healthy controls		ns								ns									ns		ns											
Baker (1985)	23 exhibitionists; 91 controls																		ns														ns
Bowden (1987)	39 pedophiles									ns	<									<													
Cantor et al. (2004)	47 pedophiles; 161 hebephiles; 94 teleiophiles (43, 138, and 79, respectively for BVMT-R)															<																	
Cohen et al. (2002)	22 heterosexual, nonincestuous, nonexclusive pedophiles; 24 healthy controls					ns			ns	ns	ns	ns	<																				
Dolan, Millington, & Park (2002)	20 violent sexual offenders; 27 violent nonsexual offenders; 13 arsonists					ns			ns	ns	ns	<[a]						ns				ns											
Gillespie & Mckenzie (2000)	8 heterogeneous sexual offenders; 8 nonsexual offenders		ns			ns			ns	ns					ns							ns								ns			
Jacobs (1998)	72 pedophiles; 40 sexual offenders against peers; 27 sexual offenders against both peers and younger victims																										ns						
Jacobs, Kennedy, & Meyer (1997)	78 heterogeneous sexual offenders; 78 nonsexual offenders																										ns						

(cont.)

TABLE 4.1. *(cont.)*

Study	Participants	Reasoning				Executive							Memory								Language					Achievement		Visuospatial				Motor	
		MMMS	Raven's	SILS-T	SILS-A	COWA	CCPT	Maze	Stroop	Trails-A	Trails-B	WCST	BVMT	CVLT	FRT	HVLT	CFT	WMS	WNVL	WVL	KDA	NART	AST	SILS-V	WRM	PIA	WRAT	Bender	HVOT	JLO	PPV	Finger	Purdue
Knox-Jones (1994)	23 violent sexual offenders; 23 violent nonsexual offenders			∨	ns	ns				ns	ns							∨						∨					∨			∨	
Knox-Jones (1994)	18 nonviolent sexual offenders; 24 nonviolent nonsexual offenders			∧	ns	ns				ns	ns							∧						∧					∧			∧	
Langevin, Lang, Wortzman, Frenzel, & Wright (1989)	13 exhibitionists; 14 nonviolent nonsexual offenders									∨	ns												∨									ns	
Langevin, Wortzman, et al. (1989)	39 pedophiles; 48 incest offenders; 27 sexual offenders against adult women																	ns															
Lewis, Shankok, & Pincus (1979)	17 heterogeneous sexual offenders; 61 violent nonsexual offenders											ns																					
Miller (1997)	50 undescribed sexual offenders; 50 nonsexual offender controls																				ns				ns			ns					
O'Carroll (1989)	11 heterogeneous sexual offenders; 11 clinical controls (anxiety); 11 healthy controls	ns	ns			ns		ns		ns	ns	ns						ns		ns	ns	ns											
Rubenstein (1992)	25 pedophiles; 25 community controls													∨			∨																
Stone & Thompson (2001)	63 heterogeneous sexual offenders	∨				∨			∨	∨	∨	∨																					

(cont.)

TABLE 4.1. (cont.)

Study	Participants	Reasoning				Executive							Memory								Language					Achievement		Visuospatial				Motor	
		MMMS	Raven's	SILS-T	SILS-A	COWA	CCPT	Maze	Stroop	Trails-A	Trails-B	WCST	BVMT	CVLT	FRT	HVLT	CFT	WMS	WNVL	WVL	KDA	NART	AST	SILS-V	WRM	PIA	WRAT	Bender	HVOT	JLO	PPV	Finger	Purdue
Tarter, Hegedus, Alterman, & Katz-Garris (1983)	14 heterogeneous sexual offenders; 28 nonviolent nonsexual offenders; 31 violent nonsexual offenders	ns								ns	ns							ns					ns			ns					ns	ns	ns
Valliant, Gauthier, Pottier, & Kosmyna (2000)	34 heterogeneous sexual offenders; 20 nonsexual offenders							<																									
Westergren (2002)	96 heterogeneous sexual offenders					ns	ns					ns																					
Yeudall, Fedora, Schopflocher, Reddon, & Hyatt (1986; as cited in Flor-Henry, 1987)[b]	109 heterogeneous sexual offenders		<			<				<	<	<							ns	<			<				<					ns	ns

Note. All versions of a test appear under a single heading (e.g., results from the WMS, WMS-R, and WMS-III all appear under WMS). Less-than signs indicate inferior performance of sexual offenders on one or more subtests of the instrument; greater-than signs indicate superior performance on one or more subtests; "ns" indicates no significant group differences on any subtest between sexual offenders and control groups or available norms. MMS, Mini-Mental State; Raven's, Raven's Progressive or Coloured Matrices; SILS-T, Shipley Institute of Living Scale (total); SILS-A, Shipley Institute of Living Scale (abstraction subtest); COWA, Controlled Oral Word Association Test; CCPT, Conners' Continuous Performance Test; Maze, Porteus Maze Test; Stroop, Stroop Color and Word Test; Trails-A, Trail Making Test (form A); Trails-B, Trail Making Test (form B); WCST, Wisconsin Card Sorting Test; BVMT, Brief Visuospatial Memory Test; CVLT, California Verbal Learning Test; FRT, Facial Recognition Test; HVLT, Hopkins Verbal Learning Test; CFT, Rey Complex Figure Test; WMS, Wechsler Memory Scales; WNVL, Williams' Non-Verbal Learning Test; WVL, Williams' Verbal Learning Test; KDA, Keymath Diagnostic Arithmetic; NART, National Adult Reading Test; AST, Aphasia Screening Test (including Reitan Aphasia Test); SILS-V, Shipley Institute of Living Scale (vocabulary subtest); WRM, Woodcock Reading Mastery; PIA, Peabody Individual Achievement; WRAT, Wide Range Achievement Test; Bender, Bender Visual–Motor Gestalt Test; HVOT, Hooper Visual Organization Test; JLO, Judgment of Line Orientation; PPV, Peabody Picture Vocabulary Test; Finger, Finger Tapping Test; Purdue, Purdue Pegboard Test.
[a]Sex offenders scored significantly better than arsonists on WCST perseverative errors only. No other significant differences.
[b]Flor-Henry (1987) did not provide statistical tests, instead describing scores as differences in group means, expressed in standard deviations of difference. The table indicates an inferior performance of the sexual offenders only when Flor-Henry (1987) indicated the group to score in excess of one standard deviation below normal.

able support for this *frontal/dysexecutive hypothesis* of sexual offending; failures to replicate far outnumber the studies claiming positive findings. In fact, the literature provides little evidence for any specific neuropsychological profile; it suggests instead a methodological artifact. With one partial exception (Knox-Jones, 1994), offenders' performances were either normal on nearly every test of the battery employed (e.g., Cohen et al., 2002; Gillespie & Mckenzie, 2000; Tarter et al., 1983) or subnormal on nearly every test of the battery employed (e.g., Yeudall, Fedora, Schopflocher, Reddon, & Hyatt, 1986, as cited in Flor-Henry, 1987; Stone & Thompson, 2001). The latter studies employed the largest samples; they had greater power with which to detect differences. It would thus appear that any deficits among sexual offenders are broad in nature and that studies powerful enough to find any of them find all of them; whereas studies lacking the statistical power to find any of them find none of them.

It remains alternatively possible that specific cognitive deficits among sexual offenders do, in fact, exist but that only specific subtypes of sexual offenders exhibit them and that investigations using heterogeneous groups have obscured their detection. That is, combining different types of offenders created the semblance of broader yet less severe deficits. Arguing against this alternative interpretation is that the few attempts to analyze homogeneous subtypes found no group differences, although this failure could also have resulted from inadequate sample sizes. Therefore, it remains to be seen whether additional studies, employing adequate power and well-characterized and relatively homogeneous samples, can detect any specific neuropsychological deficits. Until then, these tests have provided little information beyond that provided by the IQ studies.

Halstead–Reitan and Luria–Nebraska Neuropsychological Batteries

Several investigators, primarily in the 1980s, have attempted to detect evidence of brain impairment with neuropsychological batteries composed of fixed sets of tests, the Halstead–Reitan Battery (HRB) and the Luria–Nebraska Neuropsychological Battery (LNNB). On the HRB, participants receive scores for each of the subtests administered (e.g., the Category Test, Tactual Performance Test, etc.). On the LNNB, participants' performance on 269 items is summarized in scales that reflect either a particular cognitive function or the brain area with which the test developers associated it. Both batteries also provide a summary score indicating whether the participant's performance indicates brain impairment. On the HRB, the ratio of subtests on which an individual shows below-criterion performance constitutes an Impairment Index (an index exceeding 0.5 indicating brain impairment). On the LNNB, scoring below a criterion value on two or more clinical scales indicates brain impairment.

Unfortunately, investigations of sexual offenders that employed these batteries have provided quite inconsistent results, likely due, at least in part, to psychometric problems with the batteries themselves. Neuropsychologists have generally concluded that the batteries reliably distinguish persons with organic brain impairment from persons with intact brains but that (1) the batteries do not distinguish brain impairment from psychiatric disorders as successfully, (2) many of the findings have failed to replicate the results when attempted by researchers other than the batteries' developers, and (3) neither battery has been shown reliably to localize brain dysfunction (for review, see Lezak, 1995).

The earliest reports with these batteries indicated that over 90% of sexual offenders showed brain impairment (Yeudall, 1977; Yeudall & Fromm-Auch, 1979). This appears to be an extreme overestimate; none of the subsequent investigations found levels nearly so high (Table 4.2). Excluding these outliers, the remaining investigations vary widely nonetheless, estimating rates of impairment from 8 to 55%.

There exist other uncertainties in the interpretation of these investigations. Langevin and Hucker and colleagues examined phallometrically diagnosed pedophiles in an initial and then subsequently expanded sample (Hucker et al., 1986; Langevin, Wortzman, Wright, & Handy, 1989). Both reports provided only equivocal results, however; in both cases, the pedophiles showed higher mean impairment scores than controls but did not differ in terms of the proportions of the sample scoring in the impaired range. Although the contradiction was not discussed in depth in either report, such a discrepancy would occur if the data were unduly influenced by outliers—such data points would disproportionately inflate mean scores without influencing the proportions lying above the cutoff for impairment. Unfortunately, neither report included variance statistics, which would have permitted examination of this possibility. Incest offenders examined by this research group also showed no significant differences from controls with regard either to mean impairment scores or to rates of impairment (Langevin, Wortzman, Dickey, et al., 1988).

Evidence of impairment using these batteries with sexual offenders against adults remains similarly inconsistent. Sexual offenders against adult women showed higher levels of impairment than controls in one report (Hucker et al., 1988) but showed no differences in another report by the same research group (Langevin, Ben-Aron, Wright, Marchese, &

TABLE 4.2. Studies of Sexual Offenders with the Halstead–Reitan Battery or Luria–Nebraska Neuropsychological Battery

Study	Measure	Participants	Results/conclusions
Galski, Thornton, & Shumsky (1990)	LNNB	35 heterogeneous sexual offenders	49% met criteria for impairment.
Graber et al. (1982)	LNNB	6 heterogeneous sexual offenders	50% met criteria for impairment.
Hucker et al. (1986)	HRB	37 pedophiles; 14 nonsexual offenders	Pedophiles showed significantly higher mean impairment index score, but showed no significant difference in proportions meeting criteria for impairment (23% and 0%, respectively).[a]
Hucker et al. (1986)	LNNB	37 pedophiles; 13 nonsexual offenders	Pedophiles had significantly more LNNB subtests in impaired range, but showed no significant difference in proportions showing none of their scores in the impaired range (54% and 83%, respectively).[b]
Hucker et al. (1988)	LNNB	12 sadistic offenders against women; 10 nonsadistic offenders against women; 12 nonsexual offenders	Nonsadists had significantly more subtests in impaired range than sadists and controls, but there were no significant differences in proportions meeting criteria for impairment (17%, 60%, and 17%, respectively).
Langevin, Ben-Aron, et al. (1985)	HRB	6 sadistic sexual offenders; 11 nonsadistic sexual offenders; 17 controls	Sadists had significantly higher mean impairment index than nonsadists and controls, but there were no significant differences in proportions meeting criteria for impairment (33%, 8%, and 18%, respectively).
Langevin, Ben-Aron, et al. (1988)	HRB	10 sexual killers; 11 sexual aggressors against women; 8 nonsexual killers	No significant differences in proportions meeting criteria for impairment (20%, 18%, and 13%, respectively).

Langevin, Ben-Aron, et al. (1988)	LNNB	6 sexual killers; 8 nonsexual killers	No significant differences in proportions meeting criteria for impairment (17% and 13%, respectively).
Langevin, Lang, et al. (1989)	HRB	15 exhibitionists; 14 controls	No significant differences in mean impairment index or proportions meeting criteria for impairment (10% and 0%, respectively).
Langevin, Wortzman, et al. (1988)	HRB	83 incest offenders; 14 controls	No significant differences in mean impairment index or proportions meeting criteria for impairment (13.3% and 0%, respectively).
Langevin, Wortzman, et al. (1989)	HRB	48 heterosexual pedophiles; 17 bisexual pedophiles; 49 homosexual pedophiles; 31 controls	Heterosexual and bisexual pedophiles showed higher mean impairment indices than controls, but no significant group differences in proportions meeting criteria for impairment (27.1%, 17.6%, 14.3%, and 9.7%, respectively).
Scott et al. (1984)	LNNB	22 sexual offenders against adults; 14 sexual offenders against children; 31 controls	55% of offenders against adults and 36% of offenders against children met criteria for impairment (rate among controls not reported).[c]
Yeudall (1977)	HRB	20 rapists	100% met criteria for impairment.
Yeudall & Fromm-Auch (1979)	HRB	24 heterogeneous sexual offenders	96% met criteria for impairment.

[a]The authors indicated, "More pedophiles than controls were impaired [on the HRB]" (p. 443), but reanalysis showed no significant group difference, Yates-corrected χ^2 (1, n = 51) = 2.63, p = .11.

[b]The authors wrote that LNNB differences "diminished with age and sex corrections, but nevertheless remain statistically significant" (p. 444), but reanalysis indicated no such significant difference, Yates-corrected χ^2 (1, n = 50) = 2.63, p = .11.

[c]Although the offenders against children scored more poorly on each of the 14 subtests of the LNNB, it was the offenders against adults who more frequently scored in the cognitively impaired range overall. This paradox received no discussion in the article and may represent a reporting error.

Handy, 1988). Furthermore, sadistic sexual offenders showed significantly greater levels of brain impairment than nonsadistic sexual offenders in one report (Langevin, Ben-Aron, et al., 1985), whereas another report showed exactly the opposite (Hucker et al., 1988).

Regarding localization of impairment, the LNNB and HRB studies have variously concluded that sexual offending results from impairment to the left hemisphere (Galski, Thornton, & Shumsky, 1990; Langevin, Wortzman, et al., 1989), to the right hemisphere (Scott, Cole, McKay, Golden, & Liggett, 1984), to temporal and frontal lobes (Graber, Hartmann, Coffman, Huey, & Golden, 1982), to the left temporal and frontal lobes only (Yeudall & Fromm-Auch, 1979), to the left temporal and parietal lobes only (Hucker et al., 1986), or to the whole cortex globally (Hucker et al., 1988). Thus, taken together, HRB and LNNB testing has provided few, if any, reliable findings. Given that these investigations have not provided any reasonably consistent estimate of rates of overall brain impairment, their claims regarding localization of that impairment are moot. Indeed, one could support theories of nearly any type of damage by selectively citing different subsets of this literature.

Brain Imaging

Brain imaging technology has provided the opportunity to visualize, in vivo, abnormalities associated with some gross neurological disorders. This technology might thus provide an opportunity to confirm whether sexual offending relates to neuropathy and to identify which specific brain area(s), if any, might be linked to it. Caution must be employed, however, both in the design and interpretation of such investigations. In addition to all the aforementioned methodological issues, imaging research with sexual offenders remains highly exploratory, with several parameters of myriad brain areas potentially available for measurement. Conducting large numbers of atheoretical analyses capitalizes on chance, inflating Type I error.

To the extent to which they have been hypothesis-driven, investigations have concentrated on two broad cerebral areas. First, the aforementioned frontal/dysexecutive hypothesis of sexual offending predicts anatomical brain abnormalities to occur in the frontal lobes of the cortex, producing an inability to inhibit sexual urges. This same idea provided the impetus for the previously reviewed studies using neuropsychological tests of functions associated with the frontal lobes. Second, researchers have pursued *temporal/limbic hypotheses,* predicting sexual offending to relate to deep temporal lobe structures involved in the regulation of sexual behavior. These latter hypotheses arise from previous research detecting an association of atypical sexual behavior with temporal lobe epilepsy (e.g., Kolársky, Freund, Machek, & Polák, 1967) and with temporal lobe lesions in Klüver–Bucy syndrome. Some researchers have hypothesized temporal lobe abnormalities among sexual offenders, not because of any role in abnormal sexual behavior per se, but because of a putative role in behavioral disinhibition (e.g., Graber et al., 1982).

Despite its potential to test these and other hypotheses, the body of research employing imaging techniques with sexual offenders remains quite impoverished. Magnetic resonance imaging (MRI) studies on groups of sexual offenders have not yet been published; imaging investigations have thus far been limited to computerized tomography (CT) scans (Table 4.3). Of the eleven published reports providing imaging data, eight came from the same researchers, and those eight employed overlapping samples of participants, included overlapping control groups, and compared their samples on very large numbers of other variables (cf. Tables 4.1–4.3). In more than one imaging study, the number of comparisons actually exceeded the number of participants in the study.

Although five CT studies included a sample of sexual offenders against children, none clearly revealed greater rates of neuropathology among them relative to controls. Comparisons indicated either no significant difference, only a trend toward significance when applying liberal α levels, or inconsistencies among the multiple dependent measures employed (i.e., brain density measures vs. brain areas and ventricular sizes). None of the CT studies that included a group of nonsadistic sexual offenders against adults found a significant difference between the sexual offenders and controls. Two investigations compared sadistic with nonsadistic sexual offenders, finding no significant group differences in overall numbers of CT abnormalities; however, the sadists showed significantly more abnormalities when analyses were restricted to the right temporal horns.

It remains possible that some types of sexual offenders do indeed manifest differences in brain structure and that such differences might be detected by larger samples; more than one of the investigations in Table 4.3 identified significant group differences after combining subsamples into larger, albeit heterogeneous, samples. This suggests the need to repeat these types of investigations with larger samples and with the more powerful imaging techniques currently available.

Researchers have also assessed brain functioning (as opposed to brain structure) with imaging techniques, employing either positron emission tomography (PET) or regional cerebral blood flow (rCBF) measures. Two of three such studies indicated that sexual offenders against

TABLE 4.3. Studies of Sexual Offenders with Neuroimaging

Study	Measure(s)	Participants	Results/conclusions
Cohen et al. (2002)	PET	7 heterosexual pedophiles; 7 controls	Univariate comparisons of 40 regions of interest under each of three conditions showed no significant group differences at adjusted α of .0125.
Graber et al. (1982)	CT; rCBF	3 sexual offenders against children; 3 sexual offenders against women	Groups not statistically compared. Three offenders showed low cerebral densities on CT, but two of those had comorbid conditions (head injury, hallucinations). rCBF scores of offenders were within 1 s.d. of normal, except for one with a known head injury. Offenders against children showed lower global rCBF than offenders against adults.
Hendricks et al. (1988)	CT	12 sexual offenders against children; 10 radiology patients with negative findings (3 female, 7 male; Control Group I); 3 female and 7 male university students and employees (Control Group II)	Offenders against children showed significantly lower average brain density, but no differences in brain area or ventricular area. Authors attributed much of the group differences to skull-thickness differences. No significant differences between left and right hemispheres or between anterior and posterior portions of the brain. Sex differences not controlled.
Hendricks et al. (1988)	rCBF	16 sexual offenders against children; 2 female and 14 male university staff	Lower rCBF in offenders relative to controls. Sex differences not controlled.
Hucker et al. (1986)	CT	29 pedophiles; 12 nonsexual offenders	Rates of any abnormality marginally different (one-tailed p = .0395). Authors reported a significant group difference for "left and bilateral temporal" areas, and no significant differences for left temporal, right temporal, or right and bilateral temporal areas. Other areas, such as frontal lobes, were not described.
Hucker et al. (1988)	CT	22 sadistic sexual offenders against adult females; 21 nonsadistic sexual offenders against adult females; 36 controls	No significant group differences for proportions of samples showing any abnormality. Sadists showed significantly more abnormalities in right temporal horn than nonsadists.

Study	Method	Sample	Findings
Langevin, Ben-Aron, et al. (1985)	CT	9 sexual sadists; 11 nonsadistic sexual offenders; 18 controls	No significant group differences between sexual offenders and controls in overall presence of abnormalities or in the temporal lobes. No significant group difference between sadistic and nonsadistic sexual offenders in overall presence of abnormalities. Authors reported greater proportion of sadistic offenders to show abnormality of the temporal lobe and described this typically to be right temporal horn dilation.
Langevin, Ben-Aron, et al. (1988)	CT	10 sexual killers (against female children and adults); 10 sexual aggressors (against females, youngest victims age 15); 10 nonsexual killers (against female children and adults)	No significant group differences between sex killers and sexual aggressors. Sexual offender groups (combined) showed more overall abnormalities than nonsexual killers. Sexual offender groups (combined) marginally showed significantly more abnormalities ($p < .10$) in right temporal horn than nonsexual killers. Other brain areas not described.
Langevin, Lang, et al. (1989)	CT	15 exhibitionists; 36 nonsexual offenders	No significant differences in abnormalities in general or in the temporal lobes. Other brain areas not described.
Langevin, Wortzman, et al. (1988)	CT	68 incest offenders; 36 nonsexual offenders	No significant differences in abnormalities in general or in the temporal lobes. Other brain areas not described.
Langevin, Wortzman, et al. (1989)	CT	39 heterosexual pedophiles; 9 bisexual pedophiles; 36 homosexual pedophiles; 32 nonsexual offenders	No significant differences in abnormalities in general or in the temporal lobes. Other brain areas not described.
Wright, Nobrega, Langevin, & Wortzman (1990)	CT	34 sexual offenders against women; 18 pedophiles; 12 incest offenders; 12 nonsexual offenders	No significant group differences in brain area or optical density. Sexual offender samples (combined) showed significantly less anterior left hemisphere area, left hemisphere area, overall brain area, and left:right symmetry (left smaller than right). No significant group differences in right hemisphere area or in optical density in any brain region. Significant differences occurred in brain width, but not length, with the combined set of sexual offenders having decreased width relative to controls.

children demonstrate less overall brain activity than do nonoffenders or offenders against adults. This finding is consistent with the previously reviewed pattern among the IQ studies in that it is both nonspecific and found predominantly among sexual offenders against children and not offenders against adults. Electroencephalographic (EEG) studies of brain activity in sexual offenders have been inconsistent, however. Investigations have found either no significant difference between sexual offenders and controls (e.g., Lewis et al., 1979), global differences in functioning but no significant differences in any individual brain area between sexual offenders and controls (Baker, 1985), or abnormal functioning in 100% of the sexual offenders tested (Corley, Corley, Walker, & Walker, 1994). Such discrepancies in findings may be at least partially attributable to how well such studies control for comorbid characteristics of the samples. This last study compared controls who were free of head injury history, developmental abnormality, learning problems, and psychological problems with 24 heterogeneous sexual offenders who frequently had chemical dependence (50%), ADHD or learning disability (29%), or a history of head injury (67%).

As a group, imaging studies of sexual offenders provide some, but only some, data supporting the general conclusion that sexual offenders against children may show elevated rates of neuropathology. This portion of the literature, in itself, says little regarding other types of sexual offenders. Furthermore, claims regarding any localization of brain dysfunction must be evaluated with skepticism when the areas are quite large. For example, although some investigators have implicated dysfunction in, for example, the left hemisphere and bilateral temporal lobes (Hucker et al., 1986), this describes nearly two-thirds of the cortex. Conclusions that sexual offending relates to dysfunction in a region so broad cannot be meaningfully said to be localized at all. Indeed, because of the small samples, one might reasonably argue that, with larger samples, researchers would have identified abnormalities in the remaining third of the cortex, as well.

Hormones

Research that has examined hormone levels in sexual offenders and paraphilics shows methodological problems similar to those in other areas of research on this population. In addition to common methodological flaws, hormonal studies have used different assay techniques (cf. Aromäki, Lindman, & Eriksson, 2002; Haake et al., 2003) and different types of hormone samples, including serum (e.g., Bain, Langevin, Hucker, et al., 1988), plasma (e.g., Bradford & McLean, 1984), and saliva (e.g., Aromäki et al., 2002). Despite well-documented fluctuations in hormone levels, many studies included a single sample rather than repeated, pooled samples (e.g., Brooks & Reddon, 1996), and some took samples at different times of day (cf. Giotakos, Markianos, Vaidakis, & Christodoulou, 2003; Rada, Laws, Kellner, Stivastava, & Peake, 1983). Furthermore, two investigations used multiple laboratories to conduct their assays (Gurnani & Dwyer, 1986; Seim & Dwyer, 1988); the latter investigation employed one laboratory to assay its experimental group but an altogether different laboratory to assay its controls. Finally, the majority of these studies lacked a priori hypotheses, leading to the investigation of numerous hormones, frequently with no statistical adjustment for multiple comparisons.

The foregoing problems make it difficult to draw firm conclusions. There are perhaps two possible trends involving hormone levels in relation to sexually violent acts and to pedophilia. Various studies have attempted to link sexual aggression to hormone levels, citing previous research that has found a relationship between testosterone and aggression as their rationale. The studies of testosterone and sexual aggression have yielded either nonsignificant results (Aromäki et al., 2002; Bain, Langevin, Dickey, Hucker, & Wright, 1988; Bradford & McLean, 1984; Brooks & Reddon, 1996; Langevin, Ben-Aron, et al., 1988; Langevin, Bain, et al., 1985; Rada et al., 1983; see Table 4.4) or have found that groups with more sexual violence show higher levels of testosterone than do groups with less sexual violence or than do controls (Giotakos et al., 2003; Rada, Laws, & Kellner, 1976). Unlike studies on sexual aggression and testosterone, studies on pedophilia and testosterone have lacked a priori hypotheses. These have found either nonsignificant results (Aromäki et al., 2002; Gaffney & Berlin, 1984; Lang, Flor-Henry, & Frenzel, 1990; Rada et al., 1976, 1983) or that pedophiles have lower levels of testosterone compared with controls or nonviolent nonsexual offenders (Bain, Langevin, Hucker, Dickey, et al., 1988; Gurnani & Dwyer, 1986; Seim & Dwyer, 1988). In summary, the available results suggest that both sexually violent offenders and pedophiles may differ in testosterone level from controls, but in opposite directions. Investigations of other hormones (e.g., androstenedione and cortisol) have been too few and the findings too mixed to draw even tentative conclusions.

Comorbidity with Other Disorders

It is sometimes possible to find clues to the nature of a disorder in the phenomena with which it is associated. Raymond, Coleman, Ohlerking, Christenson, and Miner (1999) conducted a systematic study of major

TABLE 4.4. Studies of Sexual Offenders and Paraphilics with Hormone Assessments

Study	Participants	Results/conclusions
Aromäki et al. (2002)	10 sexual offenders against women; 10 child molesters; 31 controls (offenses not described)	No significant group differences in T.[a]
Bain, Langevin, Dickey, et al. (1988; Study 1)	20 sadistic sexual offenders; 14 nonsadistic sexual aggressors; 15 nonviolent nonsexual offenders	No significant group differences in A, C, DHEA-S, E, FSH, LH, Prl, SHBG, or T.[b]
Bain, Langevin, Dickey, et al. (1988; Study 2)	15 sadistic sexual offenders; 8 nonsadistic sexual offenders; 20 controls (nonviolent nonsexual offenders and university students; no history of sexual anomaly)	No significant group differences in C.[b] Sadistic and nonsadistic sexual offenders showed significantly less DHEA-S than controls.
Bain, Langevin, Hucker, et al. (1988; Study 1)	26 pedophiles; 16 nonviolent nonsexual offenders	Pedophiles showed significantly more FSH and LH.[a] Pedophiles showed significantly less T. No significant group differences in C, DHEA-S, or E.
Bain, Langevin, Hucker, et al. (1988; Study 2)	26 pedophiles (from Study 1); 14 healthy community controls	No significant group differences in FSH or LH.[a] No significant differences in A, C, DHEA-S, Prl, or T. LH increased significantly more in pedophiles than controls in response to GnRH injection.
Bradford & McLean (1984)	17 exhibitionists; 13 low-violence sexual offenders; 20 high-violence sexual offenders	No significant group differences in T.[d]
Brooks & Reddon (1996)	17 juvenile sexual offenders (offenses not described); 102 juvenile, nonviolent nonsexual offenders; 75 juvenile, violent nonsexual offenders	Violent nonsexual offenders showed significantly more T relative to both the nonviolent nonsexual and sexual offender groups, but there were no significant group differences between the sexual offenders and nonviolent nonsexual offenders.[d]
Gaffney & Berlin (1984)	7 pedophiles; 5 nonpedophilic paraphilics; 5 controls (hospital employees, medical students, or relatives of employees; all without paraphilia)	No significant group differences in FSH, LH, or T.[b] Pedophiles showed significantly more hypersecretion of LH in response to LHRH administration than did nonpedophilic paraphilics and controls.

Study	Sample	Findings
Giotakos et al. (2003)	52 sexual offenders against women; 25 controls (hospital staff; no information on offense history)	Sexual offenders showed significantly more DHT, FAI, LH, and T[a] and significantly less 5-HIAA. No significant group differences in SHBG or FSH.
Gurnani & Dwyer (1986)	23 incest offenders against children; 16 clinical controls (psychogenic erectile dysfunction)	Offenders showed significantly less T.[b]
Haake et al. (2003)	10 sexual offenders with high sex drive; 10 healthy controls with average sex drive	No significant differences in C, FSH, LH, Prl, or T.[a]
Lang et al. (1990)	55 heterosexual pedophiles; 27 homosexual pedophiles; 88 nonincestuous pedophiles; 45 incestuous pedophiles; 44 nonoffender community controls	Incestuous pedophiles showed significantly more E than nonincestuous pedophiles.[a] Pedophiles showed significantly more A, C, and Prl than controls, and incestuous pedophiles showed significantly more A, C, and Prl than nonincestuous pedophiles. No significant group differences in DHEA-S, FAI, FSH, LH, SHBG, or T.
Lang, Langevin, Bain, Frenzel, & Wright (1989)	16 exhibitionists; 15 nonviolent nonsexual offenders	Exhibitionists showed significantly less E, FAI, and total T.[b] Exhibitionists showed significantly more free T. No significant group differences in C, DHEA-S, FSH, LH, Prl, or SHBG.
Langevin, Ben-Aron, et al. (1988)	7 sexual killers; 7 nonsexual killers; 6 nonhomicidal sexual aggressors	No significant group differences in A, C, DHEA-S, FAI, FSH, LH, Prl, SHBG, or T.[b]
Langevin et al. (1979)	96 exhibitionists; 54 controls; 141 men with multiple but unspecified sexual anomalies; 135 heterogeneous sexually atypical participants (exhibitionists, androphiles, pedophiles, multiple and miscellaneous deviants, and controls)	No significant group differences in T.[a]
Langevin, Bain, et al. (1985)	6 sadistic sexual aggressors; 9 nonsadistic sexual aggressors; 16 nonviolent nonsexual offenders	No significant group differences in A, C, FSH, LH, Prl, or total T.[a] Nonsadistic sexual aggressors showed significantly more DHEA-S than controls; the sadistic sexual aggressors did not differ significantly from either of the other two groups.
Maes et al. (2001)	8 pedophiles; 11 healthy controls	Pedophiles showed significantly less C and Prl.[b] Pedophiles showed prolonged increase in C in response to mCPP.

cont.

TABLE 4.4. *cont.*

Study	Participants	Results/conclusions
Rada et al. (1976)	13 rapists using verbal threats only; 12 rapists in possession of a weapon; 22 rapists who used physical force but did not inflict physical injury; 5 violent rapists who inflicted physical injury; 12 nonviolent child molesters; 48 healthy controls (employees)	Violent rapists showed significantly more T than all other groups.[d]
Rada et al. (1983)	9 violent rapists; 9 nonviolent rapists (verbal threats only); 6 violent child molesters; 20 nonviolent child molesters (verbal threats only); 11 controls (volunteers from treatment staff)	No significant group differences in DHT, LH, or T.[c]
Seim & Dwyer (1988)[e]	57 nonviolent sexual offenders (majority were pedophiles); 50 clinical controls (psychogenic erectile dysfunction)	No significant group differences in LH.[b] Nonviolent sexual offenders showed significantly less T; however, when the groups were divided on the basis of age range, this was significant only for the 19–29-year age group.

Note. DHT, 5α-dihydrotestosterone; 5-HIAA, 5-hydroxyindolacetic acid; A, androstenedione; C, cortisol; DHEA-S, dehydroepiandrosterone sulfate; DHT, dihydrotestosterone; E, estradiol; FSH, follicle-stimulating hormone; FAI, free-androgen index; GnRH, gonadotropin releasing hormone; LH, luteinizing hormone; LHRH, luteinizing hormone-releasing hormone; mCPP, meta-chlorophenylpiperazine; PrI, prolactin; SHBG, sex hormone-binding globulin; T, testosterone.
[a]Age was included as a covariate in the analyses or the groups were age-matched.
[b]Between-groups differences in age were not significant.
[c]Between-groups differences in age were significant, but age was not included as a covariate, and the groups were not age-matched.
[d]Between-groups differences in age were not reported.
[e]The serum samples for each group were assayed at different laboratories.

psychiatric disorders and personality disorders in a group of 45 male pedophiles. All but 3 of the participants would have met the diagnostic criteria for some major psychiatric disorder besides pedophilia at some point during their lives. The majority of lifetime diagnoses were anxiety and mood disorders, especially major depression. The clinical implication of this finding is that clinicians who treat sexual offenders should be careful to look for and treat comorbid psychiatric problems (Raymond et al., 1999).

The theoretical implications are not so clear. Do particular genes or noxious factors in the prenatal environment predispose a male to develop both affective disorders and pedophilia, or do the frustration, danger, and isolation engendered by unacceptable sexual desires—or their occasional furtive satisfaction—lead to anxiety and despair? The finding of Blanchard et al. (2002) that pedophiles are relatively likely to report that their mothers have undergone psychiatric treatment seems to support the genetic possibility. That was a preliminary finding, however, which has never been followed up.

Retrospective Self-Report Studies of Head Injury

Blanchard et al. (2002) investigated whether head injuries in childhood might increase the risk of pedophilia in males. The participants were two samples of 902 and 304 patients referred to a clinical sexology service for assessment of their erotic preferences. These samples were drawn from archival data stored in the computer files of that service. There was no systematic difference between the samples in terms of presenting complaint or final diagnosis; the second sample was simply used to confirm the results obtained with the first. Participants in both samples were classified, on the basis of phallometric test results, as pedophilic or nonpedophilic. Information regarding early head injuries had been collected with self-administered questionnaires. In both samples, pedophilic individuals were significantly more likely than nonpedophilic individuals to report childhood accidents that resulted in unconsciousness before age 13.

The data analyzed by Blanchard and colleagues (2002) did not include any information on head injuries that occurred after the patients' 13th birthdays. Therefore, Blanchard et al. (2003) studied 685 participants who represented all patients with usable data from a consecutive series of men subsequently referred to the same clinical sexology service. In addition to phallometric testing, these individuals were administered structured interviews, which included questions on lifetime history of head injury. The results again showed that the pedophilic patients reported significantly more head injuries before age 13 than did the nonpedophilic patients, but the pedophilic patients did not report more head injuries after age 13.

Between these two studies, the association between pedophilia and childhood head injuries has now been shown in three nonoverlapping samples, totaling 1,891 individuals. Thus the reliability of the correlation between pedophilia and childhood head injuries appears to be settled; however, its exact interpretation is not. Blanchard et al. (2002) argued that this correlation could mean either that (1) subtle brain damage after birth increases a boy's risk of pedophilia or (2) neurodevelopmental problems before birth increase a boy's accident-proneness, along with his risk of pedophilia. Blanchard et al. (2003) suggested that the choice of interpretation might be made by investigating whether pedophiles are more likely to report other kinds of childhood accidents—accidents not involving the head, such as broken arms or legs, cuts requiring stitches, or burns requiring clinical attention. If childhood head injuries cause pedophilia, then pedophiles should report more head injuries than comparison participants, but not more accidents involving other parts of the body. If prenatal neurodevelopmental problems cause both pedophilia and accident-proneness, then pedophiles should report more childhood accidents of all types. It should be noted that both interpretations imply that neurodevelopmental perturbations increase a male's risk of pedophilia. They differ primarily in the timing of the perturbation and the exact role played by childhood head injuries.

Head Injury and Late-Onset Sexual Offending or Paraphilia

A scattering of reports have documented instances in which a head injury in adult life was followed by a patient's first known sexual offense or first self-reported paraphilic interest (e.g., Simpson, Blaszczynski, & Hodgkinson, 1999). Such case reports do not appear to be consistent with the retrospective data on head injuries and pedophilia; this suggests that the time window in which brain damage might influence the establishment of true erotic preferences is during childhood when neurodevelopment of the brain is still incomplete (see review in Blanchard et al., 2002). It is therefore desirable to consider alternatives to the notion that brain damage in an adult can induce previously nonexistent paraphilias. One explanation is that the patient is using his head injury as a way of diminishing responsibility for his later sexual misconduct; another is that the head injury has disinhibited the patient, causing either indiscriminate, randomly directed sexual behavior or a loss of control over previously suppressed paraphilic impulses.

Genetics

Familial aggregation—the tendency for a given trait to run in certain families—is one indication that inherited genes increase an individual's likelihood of developing that trait. Familial aggregation does not necessarily implicate genes, because many other factors can cause a trait to cluster in families—for example, a shared diet, a common lifestyle, and exposure to the same environmental pathogens. Establishing the presence or absence of a familial pattern of occurrence is, nevertheless, an important preliminary step in identifying the etiology of a disorder.

Gaffney, Lurie, and Berlin (1984) conducted a chart review of inpatients to look for evidence of familial transmission of pedophilia. Their participants comprised three groups: 33 pedophiles, 21 nonpedophilic paraphiles (e.g., exhibitionists, sadists), and 33 psychiatric controls (men diagnosed with depression). The results showed higher rates of pedophilia in the first-degree relatives of pedophiles and higher rates of nonpedophilic paraphilias in the first-degree relatives of nonpedophilic paraphiles. The authors concluded that the presence of pedophilia in one member of a family increases the likelihood of pedophilia in other members of that family but does not increase the likelihood of other kinds of paraphilias. This reinforces the possibility that one or more genes make a relatively specific contribution to a male's risk of pedophilia.

A replication of this study with a much larger number of participants would be highly desirable. The prospects of that are dim, however, because the widespread enactment of mandatory reporting legislation and the increasing tendency of examining clinicians to warn patients in advance about professionals' reporting obligations make it even less likely that the pedophilic patient will want to volunteer any more information about his own or his relatives' pedophilic activities than is already known to the authorities.

Summary and Conclusions

The available data suggest that anomalous neurodevelopment, whether of genetic or environmental origin, does increase a male's risk of problematic sexual behavior, especially pedophilia. More detailed conclusions are difficult to justify. It may well be that specific brain structures or functions are implicated in erotic pathology, but this has not yet been convincingly demonstrated by neuropsychological testing or brain imaging techniques.

This single, provisional, general conclusion may seem a rather meager yield from the many studies that have been conducted; however, this does not appear so true in context. For many decades, anomalous sexual behavior has been widely viewed as the product of anything but anomalous brain development: classical conditioning, operant conditioning, psychodynamic processes, sexual politics, deficient social skills, reenactment of childhood traumas, and so on. In this context, the simple proposition that abnormal brains may produce abnormal sexual behavior is a relatively radical one, with the potential to energize a whole new generation of more sophisticated and more powerful research studies.

References

Abracen, J., O'Carroll, R., & Ladha, N. (1991). Neuropsychological dysfunction in sex offenders? *Journal of Forensic Psychiatry, 2,* 167–177.

Aromäki, A. S., Lindman, R. E., & Eriksson, C. J. P. (2002). Testosterone, sexuality, and antisocial personality in rapists and child molesters: A pilot study. *Psychiatry Research, 110,* 239–247.

Bain, J., Langevin, R., Dickey, R., Hucker, S., & Wright, P. (1988). Hormones in sexually aggressive men: I. Baseline values for eight sex hormones. II. The ACTH test. *Annals of Sex Research, 1,* 63–78.

Bain, J., Langevin, R., Hucker, S., Dickey, R., Wright, P., & Schonberg, C. (1988). Sex hormones in pedophiles: I. Baseline values of six hormones. II. The gonadotropin releasing hormone test. *Annals of Sex Research, 1,* 443–454.

Baker, L. (1985). *Neuropsychological and power spectral EEG characteristics of exhibitionists: A cerebral model of sexual deviation.* Unpublished doctoral dissertation, University of Alberta.

Blanchard, R., Christensen, B. K., Strong, S. M., Cantor, J. M., Kuban, M. E., Klassen, P., et al. (2002). Retrospective self-reports of childhood accidents causing unconsciousness in phallometrically diagnosed pedophiles. *Archives of Sexual Behavior, 31,* 511–526.

Blanchard, R., Kuban, M. E., Klassen, P., Dickey, R., Christensen, B. K., Cantor, J. M., et al. (2003). Self-reported head injuries before and after age 13 in pedophilic and nonpedophilic men referred for clinical assessment. *Archives of Sexual Behavior, 32,* 573–581.

Bogaert, A. F. (2001). Handedness, criminality, and sexual offending. *Neuropsychologia, 39,* 465–469.

Bowden, C. (1987). Plethysmographic assessment of sexual arousal in pedophiles: The relationship between intelligence, as measured by the WAIS-R and arousal (Doctoral dissertation, Simon Fraser University, 1987). *Dissertation Abstracts International, 50,* 900.

Bradford, J. M. W., & McLean, D. (1984). Sexual offenders, violence, and testosterone: A clinical study. *Canadian Journal of Psychiatry, 29,* 335–343.

Brooks, J. H., & Reddon, J. R. (1996). Serum testosterone in violent and nonviolent young offenders. *Journal of Clinical Psychology, 52,* 475–483.

Cantor, J. M., Blanchard, R., Christensen, B. K., Dickey, R., Klassen, P. E., Beckstead, A. L., et al. (2004). Intelligence, memory, and handedness in pedophilia. *Neuropsychology, 18,* 3–14.

Cantor, J. M., Blanchard, R., Robichaud, L. K., & Christensen, B. K. (in press). Quantitative reanalysis of aggregate data on IQ in sexual offenders. *Psychological Bulletin.*

Cohen, L. J., Nikiforov, K., Gans, S., Poznansky, O., McGeoch, P., Weaver, C., et al. (2002). Heterosexual male perpetrators of childhood sexual abuse: A preliminary neuropsychiatric model. *Psychiatric Quarterly, 73,* 313–336.

Corley, A. R., Corley, M. D., Walker, J., & Walker, S. (1994). The possibility of organic left posterior hemisphere dysfunction as a contributing factor in sex-offending behavior. *Sexual Addiction and Compulsivity, 1,* 337–346.

Dolan, M., Millington, J., & Park, I. (2002). Personality and neuropsychological function in violent, sexual, and arson offenders. *Medicine, Science and the Law, 42,* 34–43.

Flor-Henry, P. (1987). Cerebral aspects of sexual deviation. In G. D. Wilson (Ed.), *Variant sexuality research and theory* (pp. 49–83). London: Croom Helm.

Frank, B. (1931). Mental level as factor in crime. *Journal of Juvenile Research, 15,* 192–197.

Gaffney, G. R., & Berlin, F. S. (1984). Is there hypothalamic–pituitary–gonadal dysfunction in paedophilia? A pilot study. *British Journal of Psychiatry, 145,* 657–660.

Gaffney, G. R., Lurie, S. F., & Berlin, F. S. (1984). Is there familial transmission of pedophilia? *Journal of Nervous and Mental Disease, 172,* 546–548.

Galski, T., Thornton, K. E., & Shumsky, D. (1990). Brain dysfunction in sex offenders. *Journal of Offender Rehabilitation, 16,* 65–80.

Gillespie, N. K., & Mckenzie, K. (2000). An examination of the role of neuropsychological deficits in mentally disordered sex offenders. *Journal of Sexual Aggression, 5,* 21–29.

Giotakos, O., Markianos, M., Vaidakis, N., & Christodoulou, G. N. (2003). Aggression, impulsivity, plasma sex hormones, and biogenic amine turnover in a forensic population of rapists. *Journal of Sex and Marital Therapy, 29,* 215–225.

Graber, B., Hartmann, K., Coffman, J. A., Huey, C. J., & Golden, C. J. (1982). Brain damage among mentally disordered sex offenders. *Journal of Forensic Sciences, 27,* 125–134.

Gurnani, P. D., & Dwyer, M. (1986). Serum testosterone levels in sex offenders. *Journal of Offender Counseling, Services, and Rehabilitation, 11,* 39–45.

Haake, P., Schedlowski, M., Exton, M. S., Giepen, C., Hartmann, U., Osterheider, M., et al. (2003). Acute neuroendocrine response to sexual stimulation in sexual offenders. *Canadian Journal of Psychiatry, 48,* 265–271.

Hendricks, S. E., Fitzpatrick, D. F., Hartmann, K., Quaife, M. A., Stratbucker, R. A., & Graber, B. (1988). Brain structure and function in sexual molesters of children and adolescents. *Journal of Clinical Psychiatry, 49,* 108–111.

Hucker, S., Langevin, R., Wortzman, G., Bain, J., Handy, L., Chambers, J., & Wright, S. (1986). Neuropsychological impairment in pedophiles. *Canadian Journal of Behavioural Science, 18,* 440–448.

Hucker, S., Langevin, R., Wortzman, G., Dickey, R., Bain, J., Handy, L., et al. (1988). Cerebral damage and dysfunction in sexually aggressive men. *Annals of Sex Research, 1,* 33–47.

Jacobs, W. L. (1998). The utilization of offense characteristics in the classification of male adolescent sexual offenders (Doctoral dissertation, Florida State University, 1998). *Dissertation Abstracts International, 59,* 4466.

Jacobs, W. L., Kennedy, W. A., & Meyer, J. B. (1997). Juvenile delinquents: A between-group comparison study of sexual and nonsexual offenders. *Sexual Abuse: Journal of Research & Treatment, 9,* 201–217.

Knox-Jones, P. A. (1994). Neuropsychological functioning among violent and nonviolent sex offenders. (Doctoral dissertation, Virginia Consortium for Professional Psychology, 1994). *Dissertation Abstracts International, 56,* 2332.

Kolársky, A., Freund, K., Machek, J., & Polák, O. (1967). Male sexual deviation: Association with early temporal lobe damage. *Archives of General Psychiatry, 17,* 735–743.

Lang, R. A., Flor-Henry, P., & Frenzel, R. R. (1990). Sex hormone profiles in pedophilic and incestuous men. *Annals of Sex Research, 3,* 59–74.

Lang, R. A., Langevin, R., Bain, J., Frenzel, R. R., & Wright, P. (1989). An examination of sex hormones in genital exhibitionists. *Annals of Sex Research, 2,* 67–75.

Langevin, R., Bain, J., Ben-Aron, M. H., Coulthard, R., Day, D., Handy, L., et al. (1985). Sexual aggression: Constructing a prediction equation. A controlled pilot study. In R. Langevin (Ed.), *Erotic preference, gender identity, and aggression in men: New research studies* (pp. 39–76). Hillsdale, NJ: Erlbaum.

Langevin, R., Ben-Aron, M. H., Wright, P., Marchese, V., & Handy, L. (1988). The sex killer. *Annals of Sex Research, 1,* 263–301.

Langevin, R., Hucker, S. J., Handy, L., Purins, J. E., Russon, A. E., & Hook, H. J. (1985). Erotic preference and aggression in pedophilia: A comparison of heterosexual, homosexual, and bisexual types. In R. Langevin (Ed.), *Erotic preference, gender identity, and aggression in men: New research studies* (pp. 137–159). Hillsdale, NJ: Erlbaum.

Langevin, R., Lang, R. A., Wortzman, G., Frenzel, R. R., & Wright, P. (1989). An examination of brain damage and dysfunction in genital exhibitionists. *Annals of Sex Research, 2,* 77–87.

Langevin, R., Paitich, D., Ramsay, G., Anderson, C., Kamrad, J., Pope, S., et al. (1979). Experimental studies of the etiology of genital exhibitionism. *Archives of Sexual Behavior, 8,* 307–331.

Langevin, R., Wortzman, G., Dickey, R., Wright, P., & Handy, L. (1988). Neuropsychological impairment in incest offenders. *Annals of Sex Research, 1,* 401–415.

Langevin, R., Wortzman, G., Wright, P., & Handy, L. (1989). Studies of brain damage and dysfunction in sex offenders. *Annals of Sex Research, 2,* 163–179.

Lewis, D. O., Shankok, S. S., & Pincus, J. H. (1979). Juvenile male sexual assaulters. *American Journal of Psychiatry, 136,* 1194–1196.

Lezak, M. D. (1995). *Neuropsychological assessment* (3rd ed.). New York: Oxford University Press.

Maes, M., van West, D., De Vos, N., Westenberg, H., Van Hunsel, F., Hendriks, D., et al. (2001). Lower baseline plasma cortisol and prolactin together with increased body temperature and higher mCPP-induced cortisol responses in men with pedophilia. *Neuropsychopharmacology, 24,* 37–46.

Miller, A. D. (1997). *Executive functions deficits in incarcerated adolescent sexual offenders as measured by the Wisconsin Card Sorting Test (WCST).* Unpublished doctoral dissertation, Adler School of Professional Psychology, Chicago.

O'Carroll, R. (1989). A neuropsychological study of sexual deviation. *Sexual and Marital Therapy, 4,* 59–63.

Rada, R. T., Laws, D. R., & Kellner, R. (1976). Plasma testosterone levels in the rapist. *Psychosomatic Medicine, 38,* 257–268.

Rada, R. T., Laws, D. R., Kellner, R., Stivastava, L., & Peake, G. (1983). Plasma androgens in violent and non-violent sex offenders. *Bulletin of the American Academy of Psychiatry and the Law, 11,* 149–158.

Raymond, N. C., Coleman, E., Ohlerking, F., Christenson, G. A., & Miner, M. (1999). Psychiatric comorbidity in pedophilic sex offenders. *American Journal of Psychiatry, 156,* 786–788.

Rau, T. J. (1991). Cluster analytically derived MMPI profile types of outpatient child molesters (Doctoral dissertation, University of Arkansas, 1991). *Dissertation Abstracts International, 52,* 6094.

Rubenstein, J. A. (1992). *Neuropsychological and personality differences between controls and pedophiles.* Unpublished doctoral dissertation, University of New Mexico, Albuquerque.

Scott, M. L., Cole, J. K., McKay, S. E., Golden, C. J., & Liggett, K. R. (1984). Neuropsychological performance of sexual assaulters and pedophiles. *Journal of Forensic Sciences, 29,* 1114–1118.

Seim, H. C., & Dwyer, M. A. (1988). Evaluation of serum testosterone and luteinizing hormone levels in sex offenders. *Family Practice Research Journal, 7,* 175–180.

Selling, L. S. (1939). Types of behavior manifested by feeble-minded sex offenders. *Proceedings of the American Association on Mental Deficiency, 44,* 178–186.

Simpson, G., Blaszczynski, A., & Hodgkinson, A. (1999). Sex offending as a psychosocial sequela of traumatic brain injury. *Journal of Head Trauma Rehabilitation, 14,* 567–580.

Stone, M. H., & Thompson, E. H. (2001). Executive function impairment in sexual offenders. *Journal of Individual Psychology, 57,* 51–59.

Tarter, R. E., Hegedus, A. M., Alterman, A. I., & Katz-Garris, L. (1983). Cognitive capacities of juvenile violent, nonviolent, and sexual offenders. *Journal of Nervous and Mental Disease, 171,* 564–567.

Valliant, P. M., Gauthier, T., Pottier, D., & Kosmyna, R. (2000). Moral reasoning, interpersonal skills, and cognition of rapists, child molesters, and incest offenders. *Psychological Reports, 86,* 67–75.

Westergren, A. (2002). *Impulsivity, compulsivity, and obsessive compulsive disorder among various sex offender groups.* Unpublished doctoral dissertation, Auburn University, Auburn, Alabama.

Wright, P., Nobrega, J., Langevin, R., & Wortzman, G. (1990). Brain density and symmetry in pedophilic and sexually aggressive offenders. *Annals of Sex Research, 3,* 319–328.

Yeudall, L. T. (1977). Neuropsychological assessment of forensic disorders. *Canada's Mental Health, 25,* 7–15.

Yeudall, L. T., & Fromm-Auch, D. (1979). Neuropsychological impairments in various psychopathological populations. In J. Gruzzelier & P. Flor-Henry (Eds.), *Hemisphere asymmetries of function in psychopathology* (pp. 401–428). Elsevier: Biomedical Press.

CHAPTER 5

Social and Psychological Factors in the Development of Delinquency and Sexual Deviance

Stephen W. Smallbone

Criminological inquiry rests on the assertion that the phenomena of delinquency and crime are sufficiently coherent and observable to be studied in their own right. Criminology is an interdisciplinary enterprise involving, among other approaches, sociological, psychological, legal, and economic inquiry. Some of the most significant contributions to understanding those who engage in delinquency and crime have been made through the application of psychological concepts and methods. In particular, the field of developmental criminology has produced a substantial body of theoretical and empirical knowledge concerning risk and protective factors (Farrington, 1989; Lipsey & Derzon, 1998), antecedent developmental pathways (Loeber & Hay, 1994; Tolan & Gorman-Smith, 1998), the social ecology (Henggeler, Schoenwald, Borduin, Rowland, & Cunningham, 1998), and developmental trajectories (Elliot, Dunford, & Huizinga, 1987; Moffit, 1993), associated with delinquency and crime. Loeber and Farrington's (1998, p. xx) assertion that it is "never too early, never too late" to intervene successfully in serious and violent crime reflects a growing confidence in the knowledge base underpinning applied efforts in crime prevention, early intervention, and offender rehabilitation.

Criminological approaches have generally not conceived of sexual crime as a special class of delinquent or criminal behavior. In the main, the more specialized approaches to sexual crime have instead derived from a psychiatric and clinical psychology tradition. Although it has long been known that sexual offenders, like other offenders, are often versatile in their criminal behavior, psychiatric approaches have historically construed sexual crime principally in terms of the construct of sexual deviance (see Simon, 2000, for a critical analysis of clinical perspectives of sexual crime). A sexual deviance perspective emphasizes the sexual aspects of sexual crime and thereby explicitly or implicitly maintains conceptual links between sexual crime and legally tolerated sexual deviations. Perhaps because sexual deviance in children and adolescents is less amenable to empirical inquiry, much less is known about the development of sexual deviance than is known about the development of delinquency.

This chapter aims to integrate criminological and clinical concepts and knowledge in a developmental analysis of sexual crime. First, I offer a simple, rational definition of sexual crime in terms of its three key defining features—sexual behavior, criminal behavior, and interpersonal transgression—and distinguish the legal construct of sexual crime from the psychiatric construct of sexual deviance. This is followed by a brief commentary on two controversial assumptions concerning juvenile sex offenders that are of critical importance to a developmental analysis of the problem: that juvenile sex offenders are a distinct delinquent population and that without effective intervention juvenile sex offenders are likely to proceed to commit many new sexual offenses as adults. I then proceed to a somewhat more detailed examination of social and psychological factors in the development of delinquency and sexual deviance.

Defining Sexual Crime

Sexual crime, regardless of whether it is committed by adults or by young people, is a legal and not a psychiatric phenomenon. One becomes a sexual offender not by satisfying certain diagnostic criteria (e.g., for pedophilia or sexual sadism) but by satisfying tests of legal principles and definitions. This is more than a moot point. It is one that raises fundamental questions about the application of psychological concepts and knowledge to legally defined phenomena.

There are three key defining features of sexual crime. First, sexual crime involves sexual *behavior*. It is not sufficient to experience deviant sexual fantasies or urges, regardless of how repeated, intense, or sexually arousing these may be. Fantasies and urges may of course be etiologically or clinically relevant, but a sexual offense itself requires action. There may be important individual differences between those who experience deviant sexual impulses but who exercise restraint over those impulses and those who commit sexual offenses.

Second, the behavior must satisfy legally defined criteria. These are usually described in the criminal codes of the jurisdiction in which the alleged offense has occurred. Sexual offenses are typically defined in terms of the specific kinds of sexual behavior involved (e.g., actual or attempted vaginal or anal penetration), of whether the victim has provided (or is considered able to provide) consent, and of the degree of force used by the perpetrator (e.g., whether a weapon was used). Some sexual offenses require the nature of the relationship between the victim and perpetrator to be specified (e.g., whether the victim is biologically related to the perpetrator, as in the case of incest).

Because in many jurisdictions it is possible to construct a legal defense on the basis of mental incapacity, an offense also usually requires an assumption or test of mental competence and, in particular, the capacity to form intent (the principle of *mens rea*—literally, the guilty mind). The related principle of *doli incapax* (literally, not having the capacity for fraudulent conduct) is also applied in various ways and at various ages in different jurisdictions, and it is of particular relevance to juvenile offending. Children under 10 years of age cannot usually be prosecuted, and in many jurisdictions *doli incapax* may be contested up to 14 years of age. The sex offender, then, is assumed to have knowingly engaged in criminal behavior.

Third, sexual crime is virtually exclusively an interpersonal phenomenon. Even when a sexual offense does not involve direct physical contact with a victim (e.g., public masturbation, possession of child pornography), it is concerns about the exploitation of or harm to another person that underpin the legal response.

There are many forms of sexual deviance that do not satisfy these three criteria and that therefore do not constitute a criminal offense in most Western jurisdictions. In terms of formal diagnostic criteria, for example, almost half of the individual paraphilias noted in the current Diagnostic and Statistical Manual of Mental Disorders (DSM-IV-TR; American Psychiatric Association, 2000; fetishism, sexual masochism, transvestic fetishism, partialism, coprophilia, klismaphilia, and urophilia) would not by themselves normally lead to criminal investigation. If any of these paraphilias *were* the subject of criminal investigation, it would be because legal questions (e.g., concerning consent) were raised, not because they are statistically unusual practices or because the person him- or herself suffers distress or interpersonal difficulty. Indeed, it is the problem of interpersonal transgression that defines the other paraphilias (exhibitionism, frotteurism, pedophilia, sexual sadism, voyeurism, telephone scatalogia, necrophilia, and perhaps zoophilia) as illegal, and even then of course only when the paraphilic interest is acted upon.

A developmental analysis of sexual crime, then, requires consideration not only of developmental factors associated with sexual deviance but also, perhaps even more important, of developmental factors associated with antisocial and delinquent behavior. Indeed, as we will see, much more is known about developmental pathways to delinquency and crime than is known about the etiology of sexual deviance per se. The interpersonal context in which sexual crime occurs suggests that a developmental analysis must give particular attention to the interpersonal context of individual development.

Are Juvenile Sex Offenders a Distinct Delinquent Population?

The specialization of applied and research efforts with respect to both juvenile and adult sex offenders implies that sexual offenses are a rather unique phenomenon, or at least that sexual offending may need to be thought about differently from other kinds of offending behavior (Simon, 2000). The question of whether juvenile sex offenders constitute a distinct delinquent population has a significant bearing on whether developmental research on general delinquency is of direct relevance to the more specialized area of juvenile sexual offending. To the extent that young sex offenders are a distinct group, knowledge about delinquency may have limited validity for understanding juvenile sex offenders. Conversely, there may be much to be learned about juvenile sex offenders from the broader criminology knowledge base.

Many years of research on delinquency and crime have led to a broad consensus that offending patterns of both juvenile and adult offenders tend to be very versatile. Indeed, from a developmental perspective, there is strong evidence that similar developmental risk factors are associated with a broad array of problems, including delinquent and criminal behavior, sexual promiscuity, substance misuse, school problems, mental health problems, conflict with authority, and personal victimization (Huizinga & Jakob-Chien, 1998). Gottfredson and Hirschi's (1990) general theory of crime goes so far as to suggest that a single common mechanism—essentially the failure to exercise restraint over self-serving impulses—can account not only for most delinquent and criminal behavior but also for a broad range of irresponsible and risk-taking behavior.

It is well known that the great majority of youths who engage in delinquent conduct do not go on to become persistent offenders, despite the risks of "entrapment" through school failure, teenage pregnancy, negative self-labeling, and/or incarceration (Moffit, 1993). Indeed, some limited involvement in delinquent behavior during adolescence is considered by many to be almost universal (Elliot, Huizinga, & Morse, 1985; Farrington, 1987). For the relatively few persistent offenders, though, evidence shows that as the seriousness and frequency of criminal behavior increase, less serious infractions and offenses continue to be committed at much the same rates, creating a cumulative rather than a linear progression from less serious to more serious offending (Loeber & Farrington, 1998). It is thus generally, but of course not always, the case that as the frequency of offending behavior increases, so too does its diversity.

Although many sexual offenses (e.g., child molestation, exhibitionism) have been given surprisingly little attention in the developmental criminology literature, rape is generally included as one of a cluster of serious and violent offenses (see, e.g., Loeber & Farrington, 1998). This approach not only assumes the developmental antecedents to rape to be much the same as those leading to other serious offenses (e.g., homicide, armed robbery, serious assault), but it also suggests that rape committed by juveniles is often but one aspect of a versatile pattern of serious delinquent behavior. Indeed, rape is often seen as the *culmination* of a developmental pathway involving progression from less serious to more serious delinquent conduct (Loeber & Farrington, 1998).

Criminal versatility among juvenile sex offenders is perhaps most clearly seen in recidivism studies. Notwithstanding differences between sexual and nonsexual offenses in terms of reporting, clear-up (i.e., solved crimes), and prosecution rates, recidivism data show that juvenile sex offenders are between two and four times more likely to be reconvicted for new nonsexual offenses than they are to be reconvicted for new sexual offenses (Hagan, King, & Patros, 1994; Kahn & Chambers, 1991; Rubenstein, Yeager, Goldstein, & Lewis, 1993). A recent Australian study showed that juvenile sex offenders were up to 10 times more likely to become a "person of interest" to police for new nonsexual offense matters than for new sexual offense matters (Nisbet, Wilson, & Smallbone, 2004). Although relatively few adult nonsexual offenders are thought to recidivate with sexual offenses (Hanson & Bussiere, 1998), up to 10% of juvenile nonsexual offenders have been observed to recidivate with sexual offenses (Rubenstein et al., 1993).

The available evidence clearly does not support a conception of juvenile sexual offending as a distinct and specialized area of delinquent activity. However, it is possible, of course, that the picture is rather more complex than this. For example, nonsexual offending by sexual offenders may to some extent conceal sexual offense motivations (e.g., receiving a conviction for burglary when the intention was to rape). This is a critical theoretical question, but unfortunately it is one that has received little direct attention, and as yet there is no empirical foundation to support this view. It may also be the case that reporting rates for sexual offenses are so low as to grossly underrepresent the true rate of sexual recidivism, thereby leading to serious underestimates of the extent of sexual offending relative to nonsexual offending. Although there is indeed evidence that sexual offenses are underreported, so too are many nonsexual offenses. For example, although according to the 1996 U.S. National Crime Victimization Survey only 31% of all rapes and sexual assaults were reported to police, aggravated assaults (55%), burglaries (51%), simple assaults (37%), and theft (excluding motor vehicle theft; 28%) were also significantly underreported (Bureau of Justice Statistics, 1997). As with other offenses against the person, more serious sex offenses are more likely to be reported. A report of the 1989 International Crime Survey (van Dyck, Mayhew, & Killias, 1991) indicated that within the 14 participating industrialized countries, whereas only 24% of the combined rapes, attempted rapes, and indecent assaults were reported to police, completed rapes were twice as likely (48%) to be reported. Criminal versatility among juvenile (and adult) sex offenders cannot therefore be easily dismissed. Nor can criminal versatility be easily accounted for by a "sexual deviance" conception of sexual crime.

Progression from Juvenile to Adult Sex Offending

Another of the popular assumptions about juvenile sex offenders is that, without successful intervention, they are likely to proceed to careers as adult sex offenders. This assumption raises important empirical questions about the developmental trajectories of juvenile sexual offending and about the applicability of retrospective studies of adult sex offenders to understanding juvenile sex offenders. If adult sex offenders generally begin offending in adolescence, and if juvenile sex offenders generally go on to commit sexual offenses as adults, the more extensive knowledge base on adult sex offenders would have direct relevance to understanding juvenile sex offending.

Early studies of adult sex offenders indicated that adolescent onset of sexual offending was common (Groth, 1977; Longo & Groth, 1983). Perhaps the most widely cited evidence to support the early-onset hypothesis is Abel and his colleagues' confidential self-report study that showed that some 58% of nonincarcerated "paraphiliacs" reported onset of deviant sexual interests prior to age 18 (Abel & Osborn, 1992). Leaving aside the confusion that immediately arises when the constructs of deviant sexual interests, paraphilias, and sexual offenses are not clearly distinguished, almost half (42%) of Abel and Osborne's (1992) sample by extension reported the onset of deviant sexual interests *after* 18 years of age. This is a very substantial proportion for whom an early-onset hypothesis would not apply. Indeed, Abel and Osborne's (1992) data show that, apart from "nonincestuous pedophilia against boys," the average self-reported age of onset for those "paraphilias" most commonly seen in forensic settings (incestuous pedophilia, nonincestuous pedophilia against girls, and rape) was not in adolescence at all, but instead ranged from 22 to 27 years.

Other researchers employing similar confidential self-report methods have found that late onset is at least as common as early onset. In their more homogenous sample of adult males serving sentences for sexual offenses against children, Smallbone and Wortley (2004) found that both the mean and median self-reported age at first sexual contact with a child was 31 years, with a range from adolescence to as late as the seventh decade. This suggests that although some adult sex offenders begin offending in adolescence, most do not.

Finally, as we have already seen, juvenile sex offender recidivism studies clearly show that relatively few go on to be reconvicted of a new sexual offense as adults.

In summary, there is little convincing evidence that juvenile sex offenders constitute a distinct and specialized delinquent population, and there is mixed evidence concerning the progression from juvenile to adult sexual offending. This indicates that knowledge about delinquency may have direct relevance for understanding juvenile sex offenders but that we should perhaps be more cautious about relying on the findings of adult sex offender research to understand juvenile sex offenders. However, aggregated data, especially from heterogeneous samples, may well mask important individual or subgroup differences. It is likely, for example, that a relatively small (but very important) subgroup of juvenile sex offenders *are* at significant risk to go on to become persistent sexual offenders. Integrating developmental criminology and sexual deviance perspectives, we may conceive of these young people as being early on a developmental pathway to paraphilic offending. Our own estimations, based on 150 adjudicated juvenile sex offenders thus far assessed in our Griffith University project (see Nisbet, 2000), are that this group may constitute as few as 10% of the youths we see (Smallbone, Nisbet, Rayment, & Shumack, 2005). Concepts related to sexual deviance may be especially relevant for understanding this group. Perhaps a rather larger group will be at significant risk of going on to become persistent general offenders. These young people may be thought of as being on an early developmental pathway to serious and/

or violent offending. If juvenile sexual offending conforms to general delinquency trajectories, as in many respects it appears to, we would expect the majority to be adolescence-limited offenders (Moffit, 1993) and to desist from crime altogether. This is not to suggest that interventions with juvenile sex offenders are unimportant. On the contrary, even the adolescence-limited offenders may continue to commit sexual and other offenses in the period prior to desistence, and the need for intervention with the more persistent offenders is self-evident. What is not so clear is the relative extent to which interventions should be based on knowledge of general delinquency or more specifically on knowledge of sexual deviance.

Development of Delinquency

The major empirical sources for the identification of developmental risk factors associated with delinquency and crime have been several large-scale prospective longitudinal studies, the results of which have been progressively reported over the past several decades. These include, among others, the Concordia Longitudinal High Risk Project (Serbin, Schwartzman, Moskowitz, & Ledingham, 1991), the Dunedin Multidisciplinary Study (Moffit, 1990), the Newcastle Thousand Families Study (Kolvin, Miller, Fleeting, and Kolvin, 1988), and the Cambridge Study of Delinquent Development (Farrington, 1995). Prospective longitudinal data have not only provided a basis for the discovery of risk factors but have also been able to clarify the direction of relationships between many key variables. For example, marital conflict is more likely to precede than to follow the emergence of conduct problems and delinquency (McCord, 1979; West & Farrington, 1973).

Longitudinal data have been complemented by clinical experimental findings (e.g., Bank, Patterson, & Reid, 1987) and evaluation outcomes of community-based developmental prevention programs (e.g., the Perry Preschool Program; Weikhart & Schweinhart, 1992). The former have been concerned with the critical task of identifying causal relationships between variables of interest; the latter have demonstrated the long-term impact of intervening early in developmental pathways. Experimentally controlled interventions that reduce marital conflict, for example, have been shown to produce sustained reductions in conduct problems (Dadds, 1997), suggesting that marital conflict is causally related to delinquency. Underscoring Loeber and Farrington's (1999) "never too early" principle, the remarkable reductions in both official and self-reported delinquent conduct in the children of vulnerable young mothers some 15 years after a perinatal home visitation program (Olds, 2002) suggest that it is possible to reduce the influence of family risk factors even before a child is born.

There are quite clear themes with respect to the kinds of developmental risk factors associated with delinquency and crime. One popular conceptual scheme has been to identify clusters of risk factors according to the different aspects of the developing person's social ecology. Key individual risk factors include low intelligence (Hirschi & Hindelang, 1977; West & Farrington, 1973), poor concentration and restlessness (Farrington, 1994), impulsivity (Farrington, Loeber, & Van Kamman, 1990), sensation seeking (White, Labouvie, & Bates, 1985), and low autonomic arousal (Venables & Raine, 1987). Key family risk factors include parental divorce and separation (Kolvin et al., 1988), parental conflict (McCord, 1979; West & Farrington, 1973), erratic and/or harsh parental discipline (Loeber, 1990; Patterson, 1986), poor parental monitoring and supervision (Robins, 1979; Wilson, 1980), low levels of parental (and especially paternal) involvement in the child's activities (West & Farrington, 1973; Farrington & Hawkins, 1991), and parental rejection (Loeber & Stouthamer-Loeber, 1986). Key school factors include academic failure (Maguin & Loeber, 1996) and truancy and school dropout (Farrington, 1989); and broader community features include socioeconomic disadvantage (Elliot, Huizinga, & Menard, 1989), neighborhood disorganization (Maguin et al., 1995), and neighborhood violence and crime (Paschall, 1996). Immediate situational predictors include the presence of a weapon, drug or alcohol intoxication, bystander behavior, the relationship between the potential offender and victim, and the behavior of the victim him- or herself (Hawkins et al., 1998).

Different risk factors are thought to exert different kinds of influences at different stages of individual development. For example, association with antisocial peers is a relatively strong predictor of delinquency for 12- to 14-year-olds but a weak predictor for 6- to 11-year-olds (Lipsey & Derzon, 1998). The influence of deviant peer associations may thus be more relevant for older youths who are more dependent on their peers and more subject to pressure to conform to peer norms than are their younger counterparts. A reverse pattern has been found with substance use, which is a strong predictor for 6- to 11-year-olds but a relatively weak predictor for 12- to 14-year-olds (Lipsey & Derzon, 1998). Whereas substance use in adolescence may be normative, substance use during middle childhood may be more indicative of a proclivity to engage in serious norm violations.

As work has progressed on understanding the complex empirical relationships between risk factors and behavioral outcomes and between the numerous risk factors themselves, theoretical and applied efforts have in recent years shifted toward constructing developmental pathway models based on the concepts of developmental phases and transitions. The concept of developmental phase transitions is particularly important, as it is thought that risk factors exert their most important influence at these transition points. Transition points may therefore also provide critical windows of opportunity for effective early intervention. The concept of "early intervention" thus has two distinct meanings for developmental criminologists: early in life and early in a developmental phase.

Developmental phases are periods of life during which individuals are typically presented with certain critical social and psychological challenges. Although these challenges are often new in the sense that they were not directly encountered in previous developmental phases, the successful transition from one phase to the next is often dependent on having successfully met the challenges of previous developmental phases. According to the Developmental Crime Prevention Consortium (1999), the significance of developmental phases "lies in the way society expects that people . . . will be engaged in some types of activities rather than others, will spend their time in the company of some people rather than others, or will be subject to particular sources of authority" (p. 131). For example, the transition to preschool will involve exposure to new learning and play activities, lengthy periods of absence from parents, spending much more time in peer interaction, being subject to new social rules, and developing a relationship with a new authority figure—the teacher.

From a developmental criminology perspective, the key developmental phases are the perinatal period, infancy, preschool, school, adolescence, and adulthood (Developmental Crime Prevention Consortium, 1999). The key transition points, then, are those that mark the emergence from one life phase to the next. Table 5.1 sets out the key developmental phases and transitions, together with their associated developmental tasks and risk factors, as summarized by the Developmental Crime Prevention Consortium (1999). As is suggested by Table 5.1, the concepts of developmental pathways and transitions take account of the complementary aspects of parent–child relationships and the intergenerational aspects of delinquency. Thus, for example, teenage pregnancy is identified as a risk factor simultaneously for both the teenager and the unborn child.

Over the course of development, an individual is likely to accrue a series of successes and/or failures in the achievement of social and psychological tasks. The net result for the great majority of youths is to emerge into adulthood more or less appropriately prepared to take on the responsibilities of gainful employment, long-term intimate relation-

TABLE 5.1. Developmental Phases, Transitions, Developmental Tasks, and Risk Factors Associated with Delinquency Outcomes

Developmental phase	Developmental tasks	Risk factors
Perinatal	Physical and neurological development	Parental substance abuse Adolescent pregnancy Inadequate perinatal care Birth injury
	Transition to being parented	
Infancy	Affect regulation Attachment Developing autonomy Sense of self	Disturbances of attachment Social isolation Inappropriate parenting
	Transition to preschool	
Preschool	Separation from mother Preparation for school Peer socialization	Inappropriate parenting Behavioral problems Peer difficulties Impulsivity and inattention
	Transition to school	
School	Adaptation to school Peer relationships Experiences of success and failure	School failure Lack of parental monitoring Inconsistent discipline Peer rejection
	Transition to high school	
Adolescence	Defining identity Growth of autonomy in the context of peer conformity Developing value system Intimate relationships	Teenage pregnancy Risk-taking behavior Unemployment Antisocial peers Lack of parental support

Note. Adapted from Developmental Crime Prevention Consortium (1999). Copyright 1999 by the Commonwealth of Australia. Adapted by permission.

ships, and parenting. Because the ultimate social goal is to find one's place within the complex of human society, the implications of adverse developmental pathways for antisocial behavior are self-evident. Some of the most fundamental and important goals of individual development are to emerge into adulthood with a stable sexual identity and, ultimately, to establish a satisfying sexual lifestyle (DeLamater & Friedrich, 2002).

Development of Sexual Deviance

Although the profound biological and psychosocial upheaval typically experienced during adolescence presents important new developmental challenges, adolescent sexual behavior does not itself emerge entirely anew and should be seen both in terms of antecedent developmental experiences and in terms of its significance for subsequent developmental phases. To the extent that healthy adolescent sexual behavior involves negotiating complex interpersonal interactions, prior attachment experiences and social cognitive development are likely provide a developmental basis for this new developmental challenge. Thus the cognitive, affective, and behavioral repertoire already established through prior experience with parents, siblings, peers, teachers, and so on that already constitutes a general template for interpersonal behavior is likely to be extended to the domain of adolescent sexual behavior. If one is inclined toward coercive rather than cooperative strategies for influencing others, is familiar with themes of exploitation at the hands of others, and/or has had limited exposure to models of mutual, committed, and enduring intimate relationships, early attempts to engage others for sexual contact are likely to be based on coercive, exploitative, self-serving, and/or opportunistic strategies. Although in their more extreme forms these features are definitive of sexual crime, studies of nonoffender populations show that sexual harassment and coercion are in fact very common among adolescents and young adults (Koss, Gidycz, & Wisniewski, 1987; Malamuth, 1984; Russell, 1984).

DeLamater and Friedrich (2002) have described a number of key developmental tasks necessary for achieving and maintaining sexual health. These include the formation of stable gender and sexual identities, managing physical and emotional intimacy, establishing a sexual lifestyle, and achieving sexual satisfaction. It is the formation of a sexual identity and the associated task of learning to manage intimacy that are the key developmental challenges of adolescence. Establishing a healthy sexual lifestyle and achieving sexual satisfaction, although they are themselves of course partially dependent on the developmental successes and failures of childhood and adolescence, are essentially challenges for adulthood, and I do not address these directly here.

Gender identity is an individual's sense of him- or herself as male or female and is thought to emerge as early as 3 years of age (DeLamater & Friedrich, 2002). The formation of gender identity is subject to socialization processes, in particular to pressures to conform to social norms concerning gender-role behavior (Bussey & Bandura, 1999). Concepts of marriage or committed relationships are typically formed by school age, by which time many children begin to engage in sexual play with their peers (Goldman & Goldman, 1982). Sexual thinking and behavior become increasingly covert to the extent that children discover that sexual talk and behavior are discouraged by adults, and by middle childhood the chief source of information about sex and sexuality is (usually same-gender) peers (DeLamater & Friedrich, 2002). This encouragement to keep sex and sexuality hidden during middle and late childhood may allow any emerging sexual deviance to go largely undetected. In particular, the effects of sexual abuse, or emerging patterns of sexual anxiety, preoccupation, or coercion, may be effectively allowed to proceed unmonitored.

The formation of a stable sexual identity is one of the key challenges for adolescence. Sexual identity refers to the sense of oneself in terms of one's sexual preferences and the prospects for engaging others in sexual contact. This involves both a sense of whether one is sexually attracted to same-gender or opposite-gender peers, for example, and a sense of whether one is likely to be attractive to these preferred sexual partners (DeLamater & Friedrich, 2002). The formation of sexual identity, as already discussed, is likely to depend in part on prior experiences of close interpersonal relationships. Childhood attachment experiences may be especially relevant, as these are thought to lead to relatively stable cognitive schemas—the so-called "internal working model of self and other" (Bowlby, 1969)—that involve expectations about the availability and responsiveness of others and the deservedness of oneself with respect to achieving intimate relations. With relatively few exceptions (e.g., aspiration to celibacy), sexual identity involves orientation to sexual partnership. The associated developmental challenge of learning how to manage physical and emotional intimacy is therefore almost universal.

There are two kinds of human relationships in which physical and emotional intimacy typically arise: attachment/caregiving relationships and sexual relationships. Whereas attachment and caregiving behavior are typically a feature of relationships both between parents and their children and between intimate partners, sexual behavior is typically restricted to peer interactions and in many cases is expressed more or less exclusively within intimate partner relationships. Thus we would expect the manifestation of developmental problems that affect the experience and expression of intimacy, and therefore perhaps also of sexuality, to be concentrated in the contexts of parental caregiving and intimate peer relations. It is unlikely to be mere coincidence that most sexual offenses occur within these contexts. Indeed, the smaller proportion of sexual offenses that involve no prior relationship between the victim and offender may be conceived of as extreme examples of sexual engagement in the absence of emotional intimacy.

Bowlby (1969) argued that the effective functioning of the attach-ment, caregiving, and sexual behavior systems is, in evolutionary terms, of fundamental importance for species survival. What may be effective for species survival may not, however, necessarily be effective or adap-tive in particular contemporary social environments. Belsky, Steinberg, and Draper (1991) have argued that childhood attachment experiences signal the availability and predictability of resources required for suc-cessful reproduction. In developmental environments in which resources are readily available (e.g., close relationships are seen as reliable and enduring), reproductive effort is likely to be directed toward establishing and maintaining few high-quality sexual pair bonds and toward high levels of parental investment. Conversely, in environments in which resources are scarce (e.g., close relationships appear to be self-serving and unreliable), reproductive effort is likely to be biased toward sexual promiscuity and low parental investment. Thus insecure childhood attachment is theoretically linked with opportunistic sexual behavior, short-term unstable pair bonds, and limited parental investment. We are thus biologically prepared for diversity of sexual expression. The process of positive socialization, on the other hand, constrains this potential and instead effectively serves the opposite purpose of conformity of sexual expression.

Marshall's and others' theoretical and empirical work on intimacy and attachment in sex offenders (Marshall, 1989, 1993; Marshall, Hud-son, & Hodkinson, 1993; Smallbone & Dadds, 1998, 2000, 2001; Smallbone & McCabe, 2003; Ward, Hudson, & Marshall, 1996; Ward, Hudson, Marshall, & Siegert, 1995) has highlighted the problems with sexual and emotional intimacy experienced by many juvenile and adult sex offenders. Smallbone and colleagues (Smallbone, 1999; Smallbone & Dadds, 1998, 2000, 2001; Smallbone & McCabe, 2003) have sug-gested that attachment theory may provide a useful conceptual frame-work for understanding both developmental and immediate situational influences on sexual crime. From a developmental perspective, attach-ment insecurity may reduce potential for emotional regulation, empathy, and perspective taking, the capacity for social problem solving, and courtship and parenting skills. From a situational perspective, reduced functional separation of the adult attachment, caregiving, and sexual behavior systems may result in sexual behavior being precipitated by cues that would otherwise trigger attachment (e.g., seeking comfort) and/or caregiving behavior (e.g., providing comfort). Examples are the activation of the sexual behavior system by subjective distress or by physical and/or emotional proximity to children.

The tension between the biological demands for diversity of sexual expression and the social demands for conformity of sexual expression is likely to be at its most pressing during adolescence. On the one hand, powerful sexual impulses are relatively new and may be at their most urgent during this developmental phase. On the other hand, social conformity is arguably at its weakest point, because stable social and sexual identities and sexual lifestyle are not yet fully established. We would therefore in normal circumstances expect adolescent sexual behavior to be highly experimental and somewhat disorganized. For adolescents already at risk for delinquency, a great potential thus exists for patterns of coercive, rule-breaking, sensation-seeking, self-serving, undercontrolled, and opportunistic behavior to be extended to the domain of sexual attitudes and behavior.

As we have already seen, research on the characteristics of juvenile sex offenders confirms that these young people are more similar than they are dissimilar to juvenile non-sex-offenders. Many juvenile sex offenders have engaged in prior delinquent and/or aggressive conduct (Righthand & Welch, 2001; Van Ness, 1984), and many proceed to engage further in nonsexual delinquency and aggression (Hagan, King, & Patros, 1994; Kahn & Chambers, 1991; Nisbet et al., 2004; Rubenstein et al., 1993). From a developmental perspective, many juvenile sex offenders, like juvenile non-sex-offenders, have backgrounds characterized by neuropsychiatric problems, behavioral problems, family environment problems, low socioeconomic family environments, absent-father homes, and family violence (Boyd, Hagan, & Cho, 2000). When differences between juvenile sex and non-sex-offenders are observed, the differences tend to be of degree rather than of kind. For example, some researchers have observed more troubled family relationships (Vizard, Monck, & Misch, 1995), greater levels of parental violence (Ford & Linney, 1995), and more exposure to physical abuse (Spaccarelli, Bowden, Coatsworth, & Kim, 1997) in the backgrounds of juvenile sex offenders. The greater severity of developmental problems in many juvenile sex offenders may to some extent reflect the greater seriousness of their offending. In any case, juvenile sexual offending, as has been observed in adult sexual offending (Hanson & Bussiere, 1998), clearly seems to involve an interaction of general antisocial and sexual deviance factors. So as to avoid further confusion by failing to distinguish between the legal construct of sexual offending and the psychiatric construct of sexual deviance, it may be helpful, in closing, to briefly consider what is known about developmental antecedents to sexual deviance per se.

As with sex offender research, the study of developmental factors associated with legally tolerated paraphilias is limited by its almost exclusive reliance on retrospective designs. Moreover, much of the research on legally tolerated paraphilias has relied on clinical case studies, and the relative dominance of psychoanalytic inquiry in this field appears to have resulted in greater attention being given to the subjective experience of the "paraphiliac" rather than to his or her social learning environment. Nonetheless, when compared with the findings of sex offender research, themes of parental conflict, parental rejection, harsh and erratic punishment regimes, and so on are much less prominent. For example, although Zucker and Bradley (1995) have suggested that devaluation or hostility directed toward the mother was not uncommon among transvestic fetishists, researchers have tended to concentrate on early exposure to women's clothing, either through forced (Stoller, 1968) or accidental (Person & Ovesey, 1978; Zucker & Blanchard, 1997) circumstances. Similarly, although some researchers have speculated about the role of paternal absence and maternal overprotection in the development of fetishism (Gosselin & Wilson, 1980), it is the circumstances in which the fetish object was first encountered that has been the principal focus of concern (Mason, 1997). The rarity of many of the other recognized paraphilias, and perhaps the historical dominance of psychoanalytic conceptions of these phenomena, has resulted in a rather poorly developed empirical knowledge base. In short, we know a great deal less about developmental factors associated with legally tolerated sexual deviations than we do about those associated with sexual crime. The limited knowledge base suggests that developmental factors associated with sexual crime are much more similar to those associated with nonsexual crime than they are to those associated with legally tolerated sexual deviations.

Summary and Conclusions

The empirical and theoretical knowledge base on juvenile sexual offending is still very limited. Juvenile sex offenders do not appear to constitute a distinct delinquent population, and questions about the progression from juvenile to adult sexual offending remain largely unresolved. It is therefore not clear to what extent we can rely on the larger and better established knowledge base on adult sex offenders to inform our thinking about juvenile sex offenders. Even if we were to look to the findings from adult sex offender research for guidance, knowledge about developmental pathways to sexual offending would be restricted by the retrospective methods that are almost exclusively employed in that research.

Prospective longitudinal studies have provided a strong empirical base for the identification of developmental risk factors associated with delinquency and crime, and important theoretical developments arising from this research have furthered our understanding and, in turn, led to significant preventative interventions. Unfortunately, prospective delinquency studies have not reported outcomes separately for sexual and nonsexual crime, and so it is not possible at this stage to conclude that the developmental pathways that lead to delinquency and crime are the same as those that lead more specifically to sexual offending. Cross-sectional studies, though, consistently find very similar developmental risk factors in juvenile sex offenders and juvenile non-sex-offenders. Moreover, diversity of delinquent behavior is consistently observed in both juvenile sex and non-sex-offenders. Developmental criminology thinking and research may therefore have considerable potential application to the more specialized field of juvenile sex offender research. The concepts of developmental phases and transitions may be particularly important for extending applied efforts beyond tertiary prevention (e.g., offender treatment) to primary and secondary prevention of juvenile sex offending. For example, developmental crime prevention programs, which typically aim to limit the development of criminal potential in at-risk individuals, may be equally effective in reducing the potential to commit sexual offenses.

Studies of normal sexual development have led to the identification of several key developmental challenges that need to be met in order to establish and maintain a healthy adult sexual lifestyle. Key challenges in adolescence are the establishment of a stable sexual identity and managing physical and emotional intimacy. The biological and psychosocial upheaval typically experienced during adolescence provides a context in which, perhaps unsurprisingly, many young people engage in or are subjected to sexual harassment and coercion. It is easy to see how those already at risk for delinquent conduct are likely to be among the first to join the ranks of the harassers and coercers.

Less normative forms of sexual impropriety, such as the sexual exploitation of younger children, may not be so easily explained. Nevertheless, some level of explanation may be found for those offenders who have emerged into adolescence with a lifetime experience of coercive, exploitative, self-serving, and opportunistic interpersonal relationships. When early attachment relationships have been disrupted or disorganized, the adolescent may be even less well equipped to maintain functional separation of attachment, caregiving, and sexual behavior. The insecure adolescent may therefore not only have fewer personal resources available to negotiate the complex interpersonal interactions needed for successful courtship but may also be susceptible to responding sexually in socially inappropriate circumstances.

Finally, theoretical and empirical research on intimacy and attachment problems in adult sex offenders, although not yet well advanced, shows some promise in developing our understanding of the interactions between delinquent or criminal potential and sexuality. In particular, attachment theory may provide a coherent conceptual framework within which to consider how patterns of both sexual and nonsexual offending behavior may be linked to earlier adverse attachment experiences. It is perhaps worth remembering in this regard that Bowlby's first work on attachment theory arose from his professional interest in delinquent behavior (Bowlby, 1944). Development of coercive versus cooperative relations, the regulation of negative affect, the capacity for empathy and perspective-taking, and expectations about the reliability of others and the worthiness of oneself are key developmental outcomes linked to the earliest attachment experiences. Indeed, if there is no other "real life" lesson to be taken from a developmental analysis of delinquency and crime, and perhaps especially of sexual crime, the obvious fact remains that we should be doing what we can to ensure that we maximize opportunities for children to establish and maintain secure attachment relationships. Among other things, this could help to protect children from becoming victims of sexual abuse and at the same time reduce the number of children at risk of joining the next generation of sexual abusers.

References

Abel, G. G., & Osborn, C. (1992). The paraphilias: The extent and nature of sexually deviant and criminal behavior. *Clinical Forensic Psychiatry, 15,* 675–687.

American Psychiatric Association. (2000). *Diagnostic and statistical manual of mental disorders* (4th ed. rev.). Washington, DC: Author.

Bank, L., Patterson, G. R., & Reid, J. B. (1987). Delinquency prevention through training parents in family management. *Behavior Analyst, 10,* 75–82.

Bowlby, J. (1944). Forty-four juvenile thieves: Their characters and home life. *International Journal of Psycho Analysis, 25,* 19–53.

Bowlby, J. (1969). *Attachment and loss: Vol. 1. Attachment.* New York: Basic Books.

Boyd, N. J., Hagan, M., & Cho, M. E. (2000). Characteristics of adolescent sex offenders: A review of the research. *Aggression and Violent Behavior, 5,* 137–146.

Bureau of Justice Statistics. (1997). *National Crime Victimization Survey.* Washington, DC: U.S. Department of Justice, Office of Justice Programs.

Bussey, K., & Bandura, A. (1999). Social cognitive theory of gender development and differentiation. *Psychological Review, 106,* 676–716.

Dadds, M. R. (1997). Conduct disorder. In R. T. Ammerman & M. Hersen (Eds.), *Handbook of prevention and treatment with children and adolescents* (pp. 521–550). New York: Wiley.

DeLamater, J., & Friedrich, W. N. (2002). Human sexual development. *Journal of Sex Research, 39,* 1–14.

Developmental Crime Prevention Consortium. (1999). *Pathways to prevention.* Canberra, Australia: Commonwealth Government.

Elliot, D. S., Dunford, F. W., & Huizinga, D. (1987). The identification and prediction of career offenders utilizing self-reported and official data. In J. D. Burchard & S. N. Burchard (Eds.), *Prevention of delinquent behavior* (pp. 90–121). Newbury Park, CA: Sage.

Elliot, D. S., Huizinga, D., & Menard, S. (1989). *Multiple problem youth: Delinquency, substance use and mental health problems.* New York: Springer-Verlag.

Elliot, D. S., Huizinga, D., & Morse, B. J. (1985). *The dynamics of deviant behavior: A national survey progress report.* Boulder, CO: Behavioral Research Institute.

Farrington, D. P. (1987). Epidemiology. In H. C. Quay (Ed.), *Handbook of juvenile delinquency* (pp. 33–61). New York: Wiley.

Farrington, D. P. (1989). Early predictors of adolescent aggression and adult violence. *Violence and Victims, 4,* 79–100.

Farrington, D. P. (1994). Early developmental prevention of juvenile delinquency. *Criminal Behaviour and Mental Health, 4,* 209–227.

Farrington, D. P. (1995). The development of offending and antisocial behaviour from childhood: Key findings from the Cambridge study in delinquent development. *Journal of Child Psychology and Psychiatry, 36,* 929–964.

Farrington, D. P., & Hawkins, J. D. (1991). Predicting participation, early onset and later persistence in officially recorded offending. *Criminal Behavior and Mental Health, 1,* 1–33.

Farrington, D. P., Loeber, R., & Van Kammen, W. B. (1990). Long-term criminal outcomes of hyperactivity-impulsivity-attention deficit and conduct problems in childhood. In L. Robins & M. Rutter (Eds.), *Straight and devious pathways from childhood to adulthood* (pp. 62–81). New York: Cambridge University Press.

Ford, M. E., & Linney, J. A. (1995). Comparative analysis of juvenile sexual offenders, violent nonsexual offenders, and status offenders. *Journal of Interpersonal Violence, 10,* 56–70.

Goldman, R., & Goldman, J. (1982). *Children's sexual thinking.* London: Routledge & Kegan Paul.

Gosselin, C., & Wilson, G. (1980). *Sexual variations.* London: Faber & Faber.

Gottfredson, M., & Hirschi, R. (1990). *A general theory of crime.* Stanford, CA: Stanford University Press.

Groth, A. N. (1977). The adolescent sexual offender and his prey. *International Journal of Offender Therapy and Comparative Criminology, 21,* 249–254.

Hagan, M. P., King, R. P., & Patros, R. L. (1994). Recidivism among adolescent perpetrators of sexual assault against children. *Journal of Offender Rehabilitation, 21,* 127–137.

Hanson, R. K., & Bussiere, M. T. (1998). Predicting relapse: A meta-analysis of sexual offender recidivism studies. *Journal of Consulting and Clinical Psychology, 66,* 348–362.

Hawkins, J. D., Herrenkohl, T., Farrington, D. P., Brewer, D., Catalano, R. F., & Harachi, T. W. (1998). A review of predictors of youth violence. In R. Loeber & D. P. Farrington (Eds.), *Serious and violent juvenile offenders: Risk factors and successful interventions* (pp. 106–146). Thousand Oaks, CA: Sage.

Henggeler, S. W., Schoenwald, S. K., Borduin, C. M., Rowland, M. D., & Cunningham, P. B. (1998). *Multisystemic treatment of antisocial behavior in children and adolescents.* New York: Guilford Press.

Hirschi, T., & Hindelang, M. J. (1977). Intelligence and delinquency: A revisionist review. *American Sociological Review, 42,* 521–587.

Huizinga, D., & Jakob-Chien, C. (1998). The contemporaneous co-occurrence of serious violent juvenile offending and other problem behaviors. In R. Loeber & D. P. Farrington (Eds.), *Serious and violent juvenile offenders: Risk factors and successful interventions* (pp. 47–67). Thousand Oaks, CA: Sage.

Kahn, T. J., & Chambers, H. J. (1991). Assessing reoffense risk with juvenile sexual offenders. *Child Welfare, 70,* 333–345.

Kolvin, I., Miller, J. W., Fleeting, M., & Kolvin, P. A. (1988). Social and parenting factors affecting criminal-offence rates: Findings from the Newcastle thousand family study (1947–1980). *British Journal of Psychiatry, 152,* 80–90.

Koss, M. P., Gidycz, C., & Wisniewski, N. (1987). The scope of rape: Incidence and prevalence of sexual aggression in a national sample of higher education students. *Journal of Consulting and Clinical Psychology, 55,* 162–170.

Lipsey, M. W., & Derzon, J. H. (1998). Predictors of violent or serious delinquency in adolescence and early adulthood: A synthesis of longitudinal research. In R. Loeber & D. P. Farrington (Eds.), *Serious and violent juvenile offenders: Risk factors and successful interventions* (pp. 86–105). Thousand Oaks, CA: Sage.

Loeber, R. (1990). Development and risk factors of juvenile antisocial behaviour and delinquency. *Clinical Psychology Review, 10,* 1–41.

Loeber, R., & Farrington, D. P. (1998). (Eds.). *Serious and violent juvenile offenders: Risk factors and successful interventions.* Thousand Oaks, CA: Sage.

Loeber, R., & Hay, D. F. (1994). Developmental approaches to aggression and conduct problems. In M. Rutter & D. F. Hays (Eds.), *Development through life: A handbook for clinicians* (pp. 488–515). Oxford, UK: Blackwell Scientific.

Loeber, R., & Stouthamer-Loeber, M. (1986). Family factors as correlates and predictors of juvenile conduct problems and delinquency. In M. Tonry & N. Morris (Eds.), *Crime and justice: An annual review of research* (Vol. 7, pp. 219–339). Chicago: University of Chicago Press.

Longo, R. E., & Groth, A. N. (1983). Juvenile sexual offenses in the histories of adult rapists and child molesters. *International Journal of Offender Therapy and Comparative Criminology, 27,* 150–155.

Maguin, E., Hawkins, J. D., Catalano, R. F., Hill, K., Abbott, R., & Herrenkohl, T. (1995, November). *Risk factors measured at three ages for violence at age 17–18.* Paper presented at the meeting of the American Society of Criminology, Boston.

Maguin, E., & Loeber, R. (1996). Academic performance and delinquency. In M. Tonry (Ed.), *Crime and justice: A review of research* (Vol 20, pp. 145–264). Chicago: University of Chicago Press.

Malamuth, N. M. (1984). Aggression against women: Cultural and individual causes. In N. M. Malamuth & E. Donnerstein (Eds.), *Pornography and sexual aggression* (pp. 19–52). Orlando, FL: Academic Press.

Marshall, W. L. (1989). Intimacy, loneliness and sexual offenders [Invited essay]. *Behaviour Research and Therapy, 27,* 491–503.

Marshall, W. L. (1993). The treatment of sex offenders: What does the outcome data tell us? A reply to Quinsey, Harris, Rice and Lalumière. *Journal of Interpersonal Violence, 8,* 524–530.

Marshall, W. L., Hudson, S. M., & Hodkinson, S. (1993). The importance of attachment bonds in the development of juvenile sex offending. In H. E. Barbaree, W. L. Marshall, & S. M. Hudson (Eds.), *The juvenile sex offender* (pp. 164–181). New York: Guilford Press.

Mason, F. L. (1997). Fetishism: Psychopathology and theory. In D. R. Laws & W. O'Donohue (Eds.), *Sexual deviance: Theory, assessment, and treatment* (pp. 75–91). New York: Guilford Press.

McCord, J. (1979). Some child-rearing antecedents of criminal behavior in adult men. *Journal of Personality and Social Psychology, 37,* 1477–1486.

Moffit, T. (1990). Juvenile delinquency and attention deficit disorder: Boys' developmental trajectories from age 3 to age 15. *Child Development, 61,* 893–910.

Moffit, T. (1993). Adolescence-limited and life course-persistent antisocial behavior: A developmental taxonomy. *Psychological Review, 100*(4), 674–701.

Nisbet, I. A. (2000). Responding to adolescents who sexually offend in Queensland. *Australian Educational and Developmental Psychologist, 17,* 135–139.

Nisbet, I., Wilson, P., & Smallbone, S. (2004). A prospective longitudinal study of sexual recidivism among adolescent sexual offenders. *Sexual Abuse: A Journal of Research and Treatment, 16,* 223–234.

Olds, D. L. (2002). Prenatal and infancy home visiting by nurses: From randomized trials to community replication. *Prevention Science, 3,* 153–172.

Paschall, M. J. (1996, June) . *Exposure to violence and the onset of violent behavior and substance use among black male youth: An assessment of independent effects and psychosocial mediators.* Paper presented at the meeting of the Society for Prevention Research, San Juan, Puerto Rico.

Patterson, G. R. (1986). Performance models for antisocial boys. *American Psychologist, 41,* 432–444.

Person, E., & Ovesey, L. (1978). Transvestism: New perspectives. *Journal of the American Academy of Psychoanalysis, 6,* 301–323.

Righthand, S., & Welch, C. (2001). *Juveniles who have sexually offended: A review of the professional literature.* Rockville, MD: Office of Juvenile Justice and Delinquency Prevention.

Robins, L. N. (1979). Sturdy childhood predictors of adult outcomes: Replications from longitudinal studies. In J. E. Barrett, R. M. Rose, & G. L. Klerman (Eds.), *Stress and mental disorder* (pp. 219–235). New York: Raven Press.

Rubenstein, M., Yeager, C. A., Goldstein, C., & Lewis, D. O. (1993). Sexually assaultive male juveniles: A follow-up. *American Journal of Psychiatry, 150,* 262–265.

Russell, D. E. H. (1984). *Sexual exploitation.* Beverly Hills, CA: Sage.

Serbin, L. A., Schwartzman, A. E., Moskowitz, D. S., & Ledingham, J. E. (1991). Aggressive, withdrawn and aggressive/withdrawn children in adolescence: Into the next generation. In D. J. Pepler & K. H. Rubin (Eds.), *The development and treatment of childhood aggression* (pp. 55–70). Hillsdale, NJ: Erlbaum.

Simon, L. (2000). An examination of the assumptions of specialization, mental disorder, and dangerousness in sex offenders. *Behavioral Sciences and the Law, 18,* 275–308.

Smallbone, S. W. (1999). *The role of attachment security in the development of sexual offending behaviour.* Unpublished doctoral dissertation, Griffith University, Queensland, Australia.

Smallbone, S. W., & Dadds, M. R. (1998). Childhood attachment and adult attachment in incarcerated adult male sex offenders. *Journal of Interpersonal Violence, 13,* 555–573.

Smallbone, S. W., & Dadds, M. R. (2000). Attachment and coercive behavior. *Sexual Abuse: Journal of Research and Treatment, 12,* 3–15.

Smallbone, S. W., & Dadds, M. R. (2001). Further evidence for a relationship between attachment insecurity and coercive sexual behavior in nonoffenders. *Journal of Interpersonal Violence, 16,* 22–35.

Smallbone, S. W., & McCabe, B. A. (2003). Childhood attachment, childhood sexual abuse and onset of masturbation among adult sexual offenders. *Sexual Abuse: Journal of Research and Treatment, 15,* 1–10.

Smallbone, S. W., Nisbet, I., Rayment, S., & Shumack, D. (2005). Unpublished clinical data, Griffith Adolescent Forensic Assessment and Treatment Centre, Queensland, Australia.

Smallbone, S. W., & Wortley, R. K. (2004). Criminal versatility and paraphilic interests among adult males convicted of sexual offenses against children. *International Journal of Offender Therapy and Comparative Criminology, 48,* 175–188.

Spaccarelli, S., Bowden, B., Coatsworth, J. D., & Kim, S. (1997). Psychosocial correlates of male sexual aggression in a chronic delinquent sample. *Criminal Justice and Behavior, 24,* 71–95.

Stoller, R. J. (1968). *Sex and gender: Volume 1. The development of masculinity and femininity.* New York: Aronson.

Tolan, P. H., & Gorman-Smith, D. (1998). Development of serious and violent offending careers. In R. Loeber & D. P. Farrington (Eds.), *Serious and violent juvenile offenders: Risk factors and successful interventions* (pp. 68–85). Thousand Oaks, CA: Sage.

van Dyck, J. J. M., Mayhew, P., & Killias, M. (1991). *Experiences of crime across the world: Key findings from the 1989 International Crime Survey.* Deventer, The Netherlands: Kluwer.

Van Ness, S. R. (1984). Rape as instrumental violence: A study of youth offenders. *Journal of Offender Counselling, Services and Rehabilitation, 9,* 161–170.

Venables, V. H., & Raine, A. (1987). Biological theory. In B. J. McGurk, D. Thornton, & M. Williams (Eds.), *Applying psychology to imprisonment: Theory and practice* (pp. 3–27). London: HM Stationery Office.

Vizard, E., Monck, E., & Misch, P. (1995). Child and adolescent sex abuse perpetrators: A review of the research literature. *Journal of Child Psychology and Psychiatry and Allied Disciplines, 36,* 731–756.

Ward, T., Hudson, S. M., & Marshall, W. L. (1996). Attachment style in sex offenders: A preliminary study. *Journal of Sex Research, 33,* 17–26.

Ward, T., Hudson, S. M., Marshall, W. L., & Seigert, R. (1995). Attachment style and intimacy deficits in sex offenders: A theoretical framework. *Sexual Abuse: A Journal of Research and Treatment, 7,* 317–335.

Weikhart, D. P., & Schweinhart, L. J. (1992). High/Scope preschool program outcomes. In J. McCord & R. E. Tremblay (Eds.), *Preventing antisocial behavior: Interventions from birth through adolescence.* New York: Guilford Press.

West, D. J., & Farrington, D. P. (1973). *Who becomes delinquent? Second report of the Cambridge Study in Delinquent Development.* London: Heinemann.

White, H. R., Labouvie, E. W., & Bates, M. E. (1985). The relationship between sensation seeking and delinquency: A longitudinal analysis. *Journal of Research of Crime and Delinquency, 22,* 197–211.

Wilson, H. (1980). Parental supervision: A neglected aspect of delinquency. *British Journal of Criminology, 20,* 203–235.

Zucker, K. J., & Bradley, S. J. (1995). *Gender identity disorder and psychosexual problems in children and adolescents.* New York: Guilford Press.

Zucker, K. J., & Blanchard, R. (1997). Transvestic fetishism: Psychopathology and theory. In D. R. Laws & W. O'Donohue (Eds.), *Sexual deviance: Theory, assessment, and treatment* (pp. 253–279). New York: Guilford Press.

CHAPTER 6

Adolescent Sexual Aggression within Heterosexual Relationships

Jacquelyn W. White
Kelly M. Kadlec
Stacy Sechrist

Juvenile sex offenders are a heterogeneous group, ranging from child molesters to exhibitionists to acquaintance sexual offenders (Barbaree, Hudson, & Seto, 1993). This chapter focuses specifically on acquaintance sexual offenders, that is, young men who engage in sexually coercive or abusive behavior directed toward an acquaintance of similar age. Many of these offenses occur in the context of a date or other casual social encounter. Following a discussion of definitions of acquaintance sexual offending in the first section, we present data on the incidence and prevalence of this form of sexual aggression in the second section. The third section concludes the chapter by providing a model for understanding the acquaintance sexual offender. The model examines various facets of a youthful offender's social ecology from a developmental perspective.

Definitions

In the literature the terms "sexual coercion," "sexual aggression," "sexual assault," "sexual offense," and "sexual perpetration" are often used interchangeably to refer to a continuum of sexual behaviors in which one person, the *perpetrator*, engages in behavior against the will of another, the *victim*. These terms include a range of behaviors from unwanted contact, such as touching, fondling, and kissing, to completed rape, which includes penetrating the victim orally, anally, or vaginally with the penis or other objects. To engage in these behaviors with an unwilling partner, perpetrators rely on various tactics, including psychological pressure (i.e., threatening to end the relationship; saying things they do not mean, such as falsely professing love), verbal pressure (i.e., overwhelming a person with continual arguments), using a position of authority, giving drugs or alcohol, taking advantage of an intoxicated person, threatening or using physical force (e.g., holding down, pushing, slapping, beating, choking), and displaying a weapon (Cleveland, Koss, & Lyons, 1999).

The criminal justice system distinguishes rape from less severe forms of sexual coercion. The Uniform Crime Reports (Federal Bureau of Investigation [FBI], 2000) defines forcible rape as "the carnal knowledge of a female forcibly and against her will. Assaults or attempts to commit rape by force or threat of force are also included; however, statutory rape (without force) and other sex offenses are excluded" (p. 29). The definition of rape varies by jurisdiction and specific elements of the definition; gaining carnal knowledge, threatening or using force, and lack of consent are included in most legal definitions of rape. This seemingly straightforward definition of rape has proven problematic for the legal system when prosecuting offenders and for social scientists studying rape. People's judgments of "force" and "will" often differ, making it difficult to reach a common understanding of the event. Goodchilds, Zellman, Johnson, and Giarrusso (1988) found that several variables affect whether instances of forced sex will be labeled rape, leading to the conclusion that rape is socially constructed and vulnerable to inconsistent interpretations (Burkhart & Bohmer, 1990).

Although legal definitions of rape do not encompass the lesser forms of sexual coercion, this chapter broadens the focus to include a continuum of sexual coercion, from unwanted sexual contact to rape, via tactics from verbal pressure to physical force. There are three primary reasons to consider a continuum of sexually coercive behaviors. First, even the less severe acts of sexual coercion "have a powerful, insidious effect upon women in our society" (Muehlenhard & Schrag, 1991, p. 115). Second, by conceptualizing rape as an extreme form of sexually coercive behavior, the similarities between men who commit one type of sexual coercion and those who commit others are enhanced. Third, men who commit acts of rape often have also perpetrated other forms of sexual coercion (White & Smith, 2004).

Incidence and Prevalence

Four sources of data provide indices of incidence and prevalence of sex-ual aggression among adolescent males: the FBI's Uniform Crime Reports, which is supplemented by the National Incident-Based Reporting System (FBI, 2000, 2001), the Bureau of Justice's National Crime Victimization Survey (Office of Juvenile Justice and Delinquency Prevention, 1999), self-reports based on national samples, and self-reports based on convenience samples.

The Uniform Crime Reports and National Incident-Based Reporting System reflect only instances of *reported* forcible rape and other sexual offenses and report only the most serious offense charged to a perpetrator. Approximately 45.4% of arrests for forcible rape in 2001 were of persons under 25 years of age (FBI, 2001). Of all men arrested for forcible rape, 12.4% were juveniles under the age of 18; for other sexual offenses the comparable figure was 18.6% in 2000 (FBI, 2000). Although juvenile arrests for rape have been declining in recent years, for juveniles age 13 years and younger, the trend has increased, from 4% in 1980 to 12% by 1997 (Office of Juvenile Justice and Delinquency Prevention, 1999).

The National Incident-Based Reporting System collects detailed information on crimes reported to law enforcement agencies, but rela-tively few law enforcement agencies report these data. In years 1991–1996, the data included information from only 12 states, but data were given on more than 1.1 million incidents of violence (Office of Juvenile Justice and Delinquency Prevention, 1999). Based on these data, juve-niles age 17 years and younger were charged with 43% of all rapes of victims 6 years and younger, 34% of all rapes of victims between the ages of 7 and 11, 24% of all rapes of victims between the ages of 12 and 17, 7% of all rapes of victims ages 18–25, and 5% of all rapes of victims age 25 and older.

The Uniform Crime Reports and National Incident-Based Report-ing System figures do not reflect unreported instances of sexual assault, and rape is known to be the least reported and prosecuted crime (Feild & Bienen, 1980). Data from the National Crime Victimization Survey (Office of Juvenile Justice and Delinquency Prevention, 1999), intended to estimate the true magnitude of crimes, are based on interviews with a random sample of the population age 12 years and older. The National Crime Victimization Survey is taken from the perspective of the victim, so characteristics of the perpetrators are based on the victim's perception of the perpetrator. The Office of Juvenile Justice and Delinquency Pre-vention (1999) provided a thorough summary of juvenile crime rates based on data from the survey. This summary reported the following findings: Only 51% of sexual assaults committed by juveniles were ever reported to law enforcement; juveniles under the age of 18 committed 14% of all sexual assaults; and the percentage of all criminal juveniles who were perpetrators of sexual assault declined from 45% in 1993 to 37% in 1997.

Using offender self-report methodology, Ageton (1983) conducted a longitudinal study using a national probability sample of boys ages 11–17 years. Boys were classified as sexually assaultive if they responded positively to questions dealing with the use of pressure, threat, or force to get women to do something sexual that they did not want to. The percentage of boys who reported engaging in sexually assaultive behaviors was 3.8% in 1978, 2.9% in 1979, and 2.2% in 1980. These data led to estimated sexual assault rates per 100,000 of 3,800 in 1978, 2,900 in 1979, and 2,200 in 1980.

Among college men the best estimates of self-reported sexual aggression have been reported by Koss, Gidycz, and Wisniewski (1987). In an anonymous paper-and-pencil survey of more than 3,000 men sampled from 32 institutions nationwide, Koss et al. found that 24.5% of men admitted that they had engaged in some form of sexually aggressive behavior since age 14. Of the total sample, 4.6% admitted to behaviors that meet the legal definition of rape; this translates to a rate of 4,600 rapes per 100,000 college males. An additional 3.2% of the total sample admitted to at least one attempted rape; 6.9% reported using verbal pressure to coerce a woman into sexual intercourse; and 9.8% reported using force or threat of force to obtain sexual contact, such as kissing and fondling.

Other surveys of college men have reported figures comparable to or higher than those of Koss et al. (1987), with rape estimates consistently ranging from 4 to 7% (Abbey, McAuslan, Zawacki, Clinton, & Buck, 2001; White & Smith, 2004), with estimates of attempted rape averaging 4% (White & Smith, 2004). Recently, Wheeler, George, and Dahl (2002) obtained a higher estimate when they found that 9% of the men in their sample reported sexual aggression that would meet most legal definitions of rape. Furthermore, White and Smith (2004) found that, of the 34.5% of men who had committed at least one form of sexual assault by the end of their fourth year in college, 22% had committed their first sexual assault while in high school.

Few studies other than Ageton (1983) have examined self-reported sexual assault among adolescents. Lundberg-Love and Geffner (1989) cited unpublished studies in which 2% of adolescents surveyed admitted to initiating forced sexual contact. Lodico, Gruber, and DiClemente (1996) sampled 10% of all 9th and 12th graders in a Midwestern state and found that sexual abuse history increased the likelihood of young men in the sample to be sexually assaultive. In this sample, 13.4% of abused boys forced someone else into sexual acts, whereas 3% of nonabused boys forced sexual acts on someone else. Also, 19.6% of abused boys had both forced someone else into sexual acts and had been forced into sexual acts themselves. The similar figure for nonabused boys was 1.3%.

Integrative Contextual Developmental Model

This chapter suggests that adolescent acquaintance sexual offending is rooted in childhood experiences. The following review of the literature describes the adolescent sexual offender and is organized based on the integrative contextual developmental (ICD) perspective of White and Kowalski (1998). The model presents a metatheoretical framework for categorizing variables at the sociocultural, social network, dyadic, situational, and individual levels. The model assumes an embedded perspective (see also Dutton, 1988; Lerner, 1991). The model assumes that in patriarchal societies men are accorded higher value than women and are expected to dominate in politics, economics, and the social world, including family life and interpersonal relationships. The historical and sociocultural climate defines patterns of ideas and beliefs passed down from generation to generation that shape the social networks in which children learn rules and expectations for behavior in family, peer, and intimate relationships. Furthermore, these social and cultural contexts are gendered, providing scripts for enacting power dynamics in intimate relationships. One result is the internalization of gendered values, expectations, and behaviors.

Sociocultural Level

At the sociocultural level sexual violence is viewed as a manifestation of gender inequality and as a mechanism for the subordination of women, both of which have a deep-rooted history. History serves as a means of transmitting sociocultural attitudes and beliefs regarding gender and rape. Sexual violence is perpetuated insofar as cultural traditions are reproduced and transmitted from generation to generation.

Macro-level research, especially in the sociological tradition, has documented the role that sociocultural factors play in sexual aggression (Rozee, 1993; Scully & Marolla, 2001). Cultures inundated with pervasive legitimate violence are more conducive to sexual violence (Baron & Straus, 1989). Acceptance of general violence, combined with other sociocultural influences that support sexual objectification of women, can contribute to rape and sexual aggression (Muehlenhard & Schrag,

1991). Acceptance of violence is reflected in many culturally sanctioned activities, such as violence within the mass media, violent sports, violent video games, and music, as well as government-supported policies such as the death penalty and war.

In interviews with incarcerated rapists, Scully and Marolla (2001) found that some men rape because in American culture they have learned that sexual violence is rewarding. Rape rates have been correlated with policies controlling gun ownership and hunting and with subscription rates for pornographic magazines (Baron & Straus, 1989). The relationship between pornography consumption and sexual violence is well established (Clark & Lewis, 1977; Malamuth, Addison, & Koss, 2000), but the causal direction is not clear; it has been argued that men who are already predisposed to sexual aggression are the most likely to show any and the strongest effects from pornography exposure (Seto, Maric, & Barbaree, 2001). The average age of young men's first exposure to pornography is 11 (Johnson, 1997). Additionally, sex offenders are more likely to have been exposed to pornography before the age of 10 than nonoffenders (Goldstein & Kant, 1973).

Other sociocultural factors that perpetuate the acceptance of sexual aggression include sexual inequalities sustained via gender role prescriptions (including dating and sexual scripts) and cultural norms and myths about women, men, children, family, sex, and violence. These cultural norms include scripts for enacting relationships. Appropriate roles for men and women are communicated through various institutionalized practices of society, including those of the legal system, the faith community, schools, media, politics, and the military. Each of these social communities can contribute to cultural myths that perpetuate male violence against women. Important to the emergence of sexual aggression in adolescence is the fact that young men and women are pressured to conform to traditional gender role expectations. Violence in adolescence may be due, in part, to the overall structure and meaning of maleness in our culture. Boys are encouraged to feel entitled to power at any cost. Scripts, that is, rules to follow, for being male and female are well defined and have not changed much over time. Dating and sexual scripts afford men greater power relative to women (Rose & Frieze, 1993). Women are assumed to be responsible for "how far things go," in a sense, to be sexual gatekeepers. And, if things "get out of hand," it is their own fault. Other sexual scripts that support sexual aggression include those that deprive the woman of her right to say no to further sexual advances and encourage the man to be a sexual stalker and the woman his prey. Also, many young men are taught to believe that women will offer token resistance to sexual advances when they really mean "yes." Thus, if he persists long enough, she will give in, or, because she really means "yes," then he has the right to proceed against her protests. In sum, sexual scripts socialize young men to believe in "male sexual access rights" (Mahoney, Shively, & Traw, 1986).

Cultures in which fewer traditional gender roles are prescribed and in which male dominance and female subordination are not encouraged show less male violence against women, supporting the idea of sociocultural contributions to sexual violence (Rozee, 1993). Although all men in a given culture are typically exposed to the same sociocultural pressures to behave in accordance with their assigned gender role, not all men are violent, nor do they rape. One reason not all men are violent lies in the multiply determined nature of violence. Embedded within one's culture are social, dyadic, situational, and individual influences that may either increase or mitigate the likelihood of violence.

Social Network Level

The social network level of analysis focuses on one's history of personal experiences within various social institutions—family, peers, school, faith community, and work settings. The gendered expectations that contribute to violence are transmitted through these institutions. Witnessing and experiencing violence in the family of origin alters the likelihood of later involvement in violent episodes; the effects of family violence have been reported, through meta-analysis, to be stronger for males than females (Stith et al., 2000). Men who either witnessed or experienced violence as children are more likely to be delinquent, as well as sexually (Forbes, 2001; White & Smith, 2004) and physically aggressive in dating situations (Kalmuss, 1984). Significant correlations have been found between rape-supportive attitudes and family functioning factors such as conflict, enmeshment, and authoritarian family styles (Aberle & Littlefield, 2001). In fact, gender roles and the sexual scripts discussed earlier are often facilitated within the family. Ross (1977) suggested that parents socialize sons to initiate sexual activity and daughters to resist sexual advances. Sexually aggressive behavior in sons has been linked to fathers' attitudes about sexual aggression (Kanin, 1985), and correlations have been found between college men's reports of sexual aggression and reports of their fathers' coerced sexual behavior against their mothers (White & Shuntich, 1991). The gender-related patterns learned in childhood are played out in adolescent dating and committed relationships. Dating and courtship offer opportunities for companionship, status, sexual experimentation, and conflict resolution. However, for men, courtship emphasizes "staying in control," and for women, "dependence on the relationship" (Lloyd, 1991). Violence is one of the tactics used to gain control in relationships, as is discussed in the following section.

Boys' early sexual experiences, including sexual victimization, have been found to predict sexual aggression (White & Smith, 2004). Early sexual experiences, especially abusive ones, may shape a young man's notion of normal sex. Furthermore, psychological consequences of abuse may include lowered self-esteem, another factor predictive of sexual assault (White & Humphrey, 1990). In addition, earlier sexual experiences increase the opportunity for a sexual assault to occur. Exposure to a greater number of sex partners provides more opportunity for sexually coercive incidents (White & Humphrey, 1990).

As with the family unit, other social networks may promote a system of values that reflects sociocultural understandings of gender inequality. Within these networks, the acceptance of interpersonal violence may be encouraged or rewarded. For example, exposure to delinquent peer groups, whether at school or in the community at large, has been shown to be related to delinquency in general (Ellickson & McGuigan, 2000), as well as to dating violence and sexual assault (Ageton, 1983). Other social network-level factors associated with sexual aggression include a weak commitment to conventional school values (Ageton, 1983) and low religious commitment (White & Humphrey, 1990). In general, low commitment to social norms and conventional ties may increase the risk of sexual aggression, whereas high commitment to social norms and conventional ties can decrease the risk.

Dyadic Level

The dyadic level features the specific relationship between the perpetrator and the victim of sexual coercion. According to crime statistics, it is much more likely for a perpetrator to assault an acquaintance than a stranger. Approximately 85% of sexually coercive experiences occur between a victim and a perpetrator who know each other at least casually. It has been observed that 61% of rapes occur on a date (Koss, 1988) and that 57% of sexual assaults occur between romantic partners (Koss, 1990). Data from the Office of Juvenile Justice and Delinquency Prevention (1999) reported that nearly half of all perpetrators who sexually assaulted victims between the ages of 12 and 17 were acquaintances of the victims and that these perpetrators were ages 12–24.

Analyses indicate that sexual assaults are more likely to occur between serious rather than casual dating partners (Abbey, McAuslan, et al., 2001). Muehlenhard and Linton (1987) found that men were more likely to be sexually coercive when they initiated, paid all expenses toward, and drove on a date, suggesting that men may feel entitled or justified to rape a woman after making such investments.

Researchers speculate that assaults occurring in developing relationships serve different functions than assaults that take place in established relationships. Sexual coercion manifesting in newer relationships may be a method of "testing the relative safety of a relationship before movement to greater commitment is risked" (Billingham, 1987, p. 288) or a strategy for engaging in sexual intercourse (Shotland, 1992). In steadier relationships, however, rape may emerge as an assumed legitimate means of conflict resolution (Billingham, 1987) or because the established patterns of intimacy do not satisfy the man's sexual desires, causing anger and frustration (Shotland, 1992).

Sexual coercion is more likely in relationships plagued with problems. Conflicts that young people report most frequently include jealousy, fighting, interference from friends, lack of time together, breakdown of the relationship, and problems outside the relationship (Riggs, 1993), as well as disagreements about drinking and sexual denial (Roscoe & Kelsey, 1986).

Nonverbal and verbal communication patterns between the members of the dyad may set the stage for violent interactions, especially when men and women perceive behaviors differently. According to a study by Koss (1988), there is a great discrepancy between men's and women's perceptions of consent. Whereas 75% of the men who had raped reported that the victim's nonconsent was "not at all clear," most victims perceived their nonconsent to be "extremely clear." These miscommunications may take the form of viewing women's behavior as more sexualized than intended (Kowalski, 1993), not taking verbal protestations seriously (Check & Malamuth, 1983), and perceiving sexual rejection as a threat to one's manhood (Beneke, 1982).

Situational Level

The situational level of analysis focuses on situational variables that increase or decrease the likelihood of interpersonal violence. Characteristics of the situation influence the likelihood that sexual coercion will occur by providing the opportunity (i.e., isolated locations and minimal detection) and/or by contributing to the ambiguity of the situation (White & Koss, 1993). Situational variables commonly identified include time of occurrence (i.e., daytime or nighttime), location (e.g., home, car, party), and the presence of social inhibitors and disinhibitors (i.e., the presence of others or the presence of alcohol and drugs).

The routine-activities model of crime emphasizes the role of opportunity, an essential element for completing an assault (Cohen & Felson,

1979). Although women's rates of violent crime victimization are higher during the daytime (57%) than at night, almost two thirds of rapes and sexual assaults take place during the nighttime (between 6 P.M. and 6 A.M.; U.S. Department of Justice, 2001). The peak time for sexual assault to occur among adolescents was immediately after school, with more than 1 in 7 sexual assaults perpetrated by juveniles occurring between 3 P.M. and 4 P.M. On non-school days, the prime hour for sexual assault to occur was between noon and 1 P.M. In addition, sexual assaults are most likely to occur during the weekend (Olday & Wesley, 1983), and acquaintance rapes are most likely during the summer season (Belknap, 1989). Most assaults take place in isolated (Abbey, McAuslan, et al., 2001), private settings (Roscoe & Kelsey, 1986) such as private homes and vehicles.

The use of drugs and alcohol is also related to incidents of sexual coercion (Abbey, Zawacki, Buck, Clinton, & McAuslan, 2001). In a review of the literature, Testa (2002) reported that 60–65% of perpetrators from community samples, with similar estimates from college samples, used drugs or drank alcohol during an assault. Alcohol can act as a disinhibitor for the man, as an excuse for the rape after it has occurred, and as a means of reducing the victim's resistance (Richardson & Hammock, 1991). A perpetrator's alcohol and/or drug intoxication can easily lead to misperceptions of the environment. A woman's alcohol consumption may be misinterpreted as sexual availability or viewed as an indicator that she will be less likely to resist an assault (Hammock & Richardson, 1997).

Individual Level

The individual level is concerned with a person's attitudes and beliefs, personality and behavioral characteristics, and motivations. From an embedded perspective, there is a dynamic interplay between the various levels of analysis, providing a context for the process of sexual coercion to occur. For instance, the underpinnings of rape-supportive attitudes are typically established through socialization within a family that considers violence normative. The extent to which individual variables influence the incidence of sexual coercion depends on the degree to which cultural norms and social groups affect individual perceptions of the situation and their relationship with the victim. The enactment of sexual scripts can be seen in men who endorse traditional scripts; these men are likely to perceive force and coercion as acceptable means of obtaining desired outcomes regardless of the circumstances (Goodchilds et al., 1988). Likewise, men's sense of sexual entitlement has been found to be an important mediator between masculinity and rape-related attitudes and behaviors (Hill & Fischer, 2001). Many date rapists report that they did not even realize the wrongdoing of their actions (Warshaw, 1988). It has also been found that although men will endorse survey items about their own behavior that meets legal definitions of rape, they do not endorse an item that asks them straightforwardly if they have raped a woman (Wheeler et al., 2002). Evidence of this nature lends support to the notion that sexual aggressors may feel that their means of obtaining sex is entitled; therefore, it is not wrong.

Sexually coercive young men more strongly subscribe to traditional sex-role and gender stereotypes, are more likely to accept rape-supportive myths, accept interpersonal violence as a strategy for resolving conflicts, and show hostility toward women (Lanier, 2001; Malamuth, 1998). These attitudes contribute to sexually coercive men's reluctance to view forced sexual relations on a date as rape. They are more likely to perceive a rape victim as seductive and desiring sexual relations, and thus more blameworthy. In addition, they are more likely to judge rape to be justifiable under various circumstances (Koss & Dinero, 1989).

In addition to attitudes, various other inhibitory and disinhibitory factors, such as personality characteristics, needs, motives, and situational features are operating. A sexually coercive man will likely have the appearance of a "normal" guy. However, he may show signs of psychopathy-related traits, which include the callous and remorseless exploitation of others and an impulsive, unstable, antisocial lifestyle (Kosson, Kelly, & White, 1997). Dean and Malamuth (1997) found sexually aggressive men to be higher in self-centeredness and dominance, relative to sensitivity to others, than sexually nonaggressive men. Sexually coercive men are attracted to sexual aggression (Calhoun, Bernat, Clum, & Frame, 1997) and find a wider range of behaviors to be indicative of sexual interest than do noncoercive men (Bondurant & Donat, 1999).

In addition to specific personality attributes, sexual coercion also has been associated with involvement in a delinquent peer group (Calhoun et al., 1997), being sexually promiscuous (Malamuth, 1998), and using alcohol and drugs (Abbey, Zawicki, et al., 2001; Wilson, Calhoun, & McNair, 2002). Sexual coercion has also been associated with membership in a fraternity and collegiate athletic affiliation (Frintner & Rubinson, 1993; Koss & Gaines, 1993). However, the research has not always been consistent. In a recent study, fraternity and athletic groups' parties were classified as high or low risk; those conducive to sexual assault were labeled "high risk." Results revealed that sexual coercion was related only to membership in high-risk fraternity and athletic groups (Humphrey & Kahn, 2000).

Several motives have been implicated in sexual aggression, including fulfillment of a sexual urge (Ellis, 1989), power and anger (Lisak & Roth, 1988), and a need to dominate and control (see Palmer, 1988). Related to the desire for power is the appetite for dominance. One laboratory study involving a 5-minute get-to-know-you conversation with a confederate revealed that sexually coercive men used more "one up" messages aimed at "gaining control of the exchange" with female than with male confederates (Malamuth & Thornhill, 1994). It is possible that sexually coercive men are verbally domineering in conversations to identify vulnerable targets that are indicating submissiveness. Sexually aggressive men also endorse dominance as a reason for sexual activity more strongly than their sexually nonaggressive peers (Malamuth, 1986).

Finally, a discussion of motives for sexual assault at the intrapersonal level would be incomplete without consideration of potential biological factors. Taking a sociobiological perspective, Ellis (1989) has argued that only men whose sex drive and need to control others surpass some threshold have any likelihood of committing sexually aggressive acts. Once that biological threshold is surpassed, the actual commission of the acts will be influenced by the strength of the drive and by various environmental factors, including opportunity and societal sanctions. The stronger the drives, the less effective environmental restraints will be.

Some theories have suggested that men who perpetrate violent acts against women have some underlying deviant physiological arousal pattern or intrapsychic pathology. For instance, researchers have found that sexually coercive men display more penile tumescence than sexually noncoercive men when exposed to audiotape and slide presentations depicting forced sex (Lohr, Adams, & Davis, 1997) and when asked to read a story about a rape (Malamuth, 1986). However, other researchers find more similarities than differences between sexual perpetrators and nonperpetrators. For example, no single "typical" profile of sex offenders has been found (Duthic & McIvor, 1990), and incestuous and pedophilic men resemble community volunteers in levels of some, although not all, sex hormones (Lang, Flor-Henry, & Frenzel, 1990). Similarly, arousal patterns to rape depictions only inconsistently distinguish college-age men who perpetrate acquaintance rape from those who do not (Rapaport & Posey, 1991).

Summary and Conclusions

Juvenile sex offenders are a heterogeneous group. The focus of this chapter has been on one particular subset of an array of juvenile sex offenders: those likely to offend against similar-age female peers whom they know.

The integrative contextual developmental model (ICD; White & Kowalski, 1998) was used to organize a review of studies describing adolescent acquaintance sexual offending. The model adopts an ecological framework and emphasizes the developmental and multiply determined nature of sexual aggression. The ecological approach posits that five levels or systems are at work in determining behavior. Smaller systems, such as families, are influenced by larger systems, such as communities and neighborhoods. Systems are viewed as layers, with larger ones influencing smaller ones. The ontogeny of behavior exists in the childhood of the individual and is influenced by the home environment, which exists in a broader system of cultural values and beliefs.

The *sociocultural level* represents the theme of sexual inequality, which penetrates the fibers of society through cultural myths about women, men, sex, and violence, as well as scripts for enacting relationships. Male dominance, in combination with our cultural subscription to the belief that aggression is used to control the weak, creates a context conducive to violence against women. Family, peers, schools, faith communities, and work groups are situated at the *social network level*. Through these social groups, gendered norms are introduced and reinforced. For example, children who witness domestic violence or experience parental punishment are more likely to engage in sexual coercion as adolescents and adults than their counterparts who were not exposed to family violence. Power and status differences between the victim and perpetrator are addressed at the *dyadic level* of analysis. Relationship characteristics such as degree of acquaintanceship, prior sexual relations, communication patterns, and relationship distress predict the likelihood of coercion. However, coercion is not likely to occur if the situation is not conducive to sexual violence. At the *situational level*, the time and location of the incident are examined, as well as the presence of social inhibitors and disinhibitors, such as the use of alcohol and drugs. Finally, there is evidence that attitudes and beliefs, personality and behavioral characteristics, and motivations operating at the *individual level* contribute to males' acts of violence against women. Sexually coercive men are likely to exhibit traditional gender-role stereotypes, acceptance of cultural myths about violence, self-centeredness without empathy for others, and a need for power, dominance, and control over women.

Thus the ICD model suggests that sexual coercion occurs at the intersection of perpetrator, victim, and situational variables. We find complementary theorizing and empirical evidence for the notion that the interplay between factors predicts sexual coercion against women in the work of Malamuth and his colleagues. In a series of studies, sexual aggression was most successfully predicted by the interaction of motivational, inhibition-reducing, and opportunity factors. Specifically, the interaction of five variables—tumescent arousal to rape, dominance as a motive, attitudes of hostility toward women, acceptance of interpersonal violence, and sexual experience—predict sexual coercion among college-age men (Malamuth, 1986). Malamuth's (1998) findings suggest that high levels of sexual aggression are unlikely when only one variable is present. Malamuth, Sockloskie, Koss, and Tanaka (1991) synthesized their findings into the confluence model of sexual aggression. In both cross-sectional and longitudinal analyses, Malamuth has found support for the two pathways hypothesized in his model. Both the impersonal sex pathway, consisting of childhood experiences with family violence, involvement with delinquent peers, and sexual promiscuity, and the attitudinal pathway, consisting of hostile attitudes toward women, predict an increased likelihood of sexual aggression, especially in men who are self-centered and low in empathy (Dean & Malamuth, 1997). Three additional studies have found support for the confluence model (Johnson & Knight, 2000; Sechrist & White, 2003; Wheeler et al., 2002). Johnson and Knight's (2000) is the only study to examine the model with adolescent sex offenders, and Sechrist and White's (2003) is the only study to take a truly longitudinal approach in testing the model. Clearly, more theory-driven research is needed, along with longitudinal work to identify risk factors and sustain causal arguments about the genesis of sexual aggression in adolescents. White and Smith (2004) is the first study to look longitudinally at the accumulation of risk factors, and further work of this kind should be hailed.

Three general impressions emerge from the material reviewed in this chapter. First, the causation of sexual aggression is multifactorial, and there will never be a simple answer to the question, "Why do men rape?" Second, there is a notable lack of data on adolescent sexual aggression in community- and school-based samples, in spite of convincing evidence that sexual aggression is occurring with great frequency at young ages. Third, there is an almost total absence of theory-driven research into the development of adolescent sexual aggression. White and Kowalski's (1998) ICD and the confluence model developed by Malamuth and colleagues (1991; Malamuth, Linz, Heavey, Barnes, & Acker, 1995) are two of the few theory-based inquiries into the development of sexual aggression.

It is heartening to see the growth in research on sexual aggression among acquaintances. Now that so many descriptive data have been proliferated, it is a good point in the development of the field for researchers to turn more of their attention toward adolescents and younger children. These potential research participants are in the active period of sexual socialization and closer to the traumatic childhood experiences that have been linked to sexually aggressive adult outcomes. There is a need to improve the database on adolescents, including prevalence data on sexual aggression, descriptive characteristics of the incidents that occur during junior high and high school, and measurement of those variables with predictive power for adult sexually aggressive behavior.

In this review, we have described the integrative contextual developmental model and specific variables that appear promising. Research on adolescents will not be an easy task given the institutional barriers that block research access to adolescents and our society's discomfort with children's sexuality. We can only hope that some will be encouraged to try.

References

Abbey, A., McAuslan, P., Zawacki, T., Clinton, A. M., & Buck, P. O. (2001). Attitudinal, experiential, and situational predictors of sexual assault perpetration. *Journal of Interpersonal Violence, 16,* 784–807.

Abbey, A., Zawacki, T., Buck, P. O., Clinton, A. M., & McAuslan, P. (2001). Alcohol and sexual assault. *Alcohol Research and Health, 25,* 43–51.

Aberle, C. C., & Littlefield, R. P. (2001). Family functioning and sexual aggression in a sample of college men. *Journal of Interpersonal Violence, 16,* 565–579.

Ageton, S. S. (1983). *Sexual assault among adolescents.* Lexington, MA: Heath.

Barbaree, H. E., Hudson, S. M., & Seto, M. C. (1993). Sexual assault in society: The role of the juvenile offender. In H. E. Barbaree, W. L. Marshall, & S. M. Hudson (Eds.), *The juvenile sex offender* (pp. 1–24). New York: Guilford Press.

Baron, L., & Straus, M. A. (1989). *Four theories of rape in American society: A state-level analysis.* New Haven, CT: Yale University Press.

Belknap, J. (1989). The sexual victimization of unmarried women by nonrelative acquaintances. In M. A. Pirog-Good & J. E. Stets (Eds.), *Violence in dating relationships: Emerging social issues* (pp. 205–218). New York: Praeger.

Beneke, T. (1982). *Men who rape.* New York: St. Martin's Press.

Billingham, R. E. (1987). Courtship violence: The patterns of conflict resolution strategies across seven levels of emotional commitment. *Family Relations, 36,* 283–289.

Bondurant, B., & Donat, P. L. N. (1999). Perceptions of women's sexual interest and acquaintance rape: The role of sexual overperception and affective attitudes. *Psychology of Women Quarterly, 23,* 691–705.

Burkhart, B., & Bohmer, C. (1990). Hidden rape and the legal crucible: Analysis and implications of epidemiological, social, and legal factors. *The Expert Witness, the Trial Lawyer, the Trial Judge, 5*, 3–6.

Calhoun, K. S., Bernat, J. A., Clum, G. A., & Frame, C. L. (1997). Sexual coercion and attraction to sexual aggression in a community sample of young men. *Journal of Interpersonal Violence, 12*, 392–406.

Check, J. V. P., & Malamuth, N. M. (1983). Sex role stereotyping and reaction to depictions of stranger versus acquaintance rape. *Journal of Personality and Social Psychology, 45*, 344–356.

Clark, L., & Lewis, D. (1977). *The price of coercive sexuality.* Toronto, Ontario, Canada: Women's Press.

Cleveland, H. H., Koss, M. P., & Lyons, J. (1999). Rape tactics form the survivors' perspective: Contextual dependence and within-event independence. *Journal of Interpersonal Violence, 14*, 532–547.

Cohen, L. E., & Felson, M. (1979). Social change and crime rate trends: A routine activity approach. *American Sociological Review, 44*, 588–608.

Dean, K. E., & Malamuth, N. M. (1997). Characteristics of men who aggress sexually and of men who imagine aggressing: Risk and moderating variables. *Journal of Personality and Social Psychology, 73*, 449–455.

Duthie, B., & McIvor, D. L. (1990). A new system for cluster-coding child molester MMPI profile types. *Criminal Justice and Behavior, 17*, 199–214.

Dutton, D. G. (1988). Research advances in the study of wife assault: Etiology and prevention. In D. N. Weisstub (Ed.), *Law and mental health: International perspectives* (Vol. 4, pp. 161–220). Elmsford, NY: Pergamon.

Ellickson, P. L., & McGuigan, K. A. (2000). Early predictors of adolescent violence. *American Journal of Public Health, 90*, 566–572.

Ellis, L. (1989). A synthesized (biosocial) theory of rape. *Journal of Consulting and Clinical Psychology, 59*, 631–642.

Federal Bureau of Investigation. (1999). *Crime in the United States: Uniform crime reports.* Washington, DC: U.S. Department of Justice.

Federal Bureau of Investigation. (2000). *Crime in the United States: Uniform crime reports.* Washington, DC: U.S. Department of Justice.

Federal Bureau of Investigation. (2001). *Crime in the United States: Uniform crime reports.* Washington, DC: U.S. Department of Justice.

Feild, H. S., & Bienen, L. B. (1980). *Jurors and rape: A study in psychology and law.* Lexington, MA: Heath.

Forbes, G. (2001). Experiences with sexual coercion in college males and females: Role of family conflict, sexist attitudes, acceptance of rape myths, self-esteem, and the Big-Five personality factors. *Journal of Interpersonal Violence, 16*, 865–889.

Frintner, M. P., & Rubinson, L. (1993). Acquaintance rape: The influence of alcohol, fraternity membership, and sports team membership. *Journal of Sex Education and Therapy, 19*, 272–284.

Goldstein, M. J., & Kant, S. H. (1973). *Pornography and sexual deviance: A report of the Legal and Behavioral Institute, Beverly Hills, California.* Berkeley: University of California Press.

Goodchilds, J. D., Zellman, G. L., Johnson, P. B., & Giarrusso, R. (1988). Adolescents and their perceptions of sexual interactions. In A. W. Burgess (Ed.), *Rape and sexual assault* (Vol. 2, pp. 245–270). New York: Garland.

Hammock, G. S., & Richardson, D. R. (1997). Perceptions of rape: The influence of closeness of relationship, intoxication and sex of participant. *Violence and Victims, 12,* 237–246.

Hill, M. S., & Fischer, A. R. (2001). Does entitlement mediate the link between masculinity and rape-related variables? *Journal of Counseling Psychology, 48,* 39–50.

Humphrey, S. E., & Kahn, A. S. (2000). Fraternities, athletic teams, and rape: Importance of identification with a risky group. *Journal of Interpersonal Violence, 15,* 1313–1322.

Johnson, D. (1997). Exposure, affective responses and sexual arousal to sexually explicit materials. *Dissertation Abstracts International, 57*(10-B), 6605. (UMI No. AAM 9707386)

Johnson, G. M., & Knight, R. A. (2000). Developmental antecedents of sexual coercion in juvenile sex offenders. *Sexual Abuse: A Journal of Research and Treatment, 12,* 165–178.

Kalmuss, D. S. (1984). The intergenerational transmission of marital aggression. *Journal of Marriage and Family, 46,* 11–19.

Kanin, E. J. (1985). Date rapists: Differential sexual socialization and relative deprivation. *Archives of Sexual Behavior, 14,* 218–232.

Koss, M. P. (1988). Hidden rape: Sexual aggression and victimization in a national sample of students in higher education. In A. W. Burgess (Ed.), *Rape and sexual assault* (Vol. 2, pp. 3–25). New York: Garland.

Koss, M. P. (1990). The woman's mental health research agenda: Violence against women. *American Psychologist, 45,* 374–380.

Koss, M. P., & Dinero, T. E. (1989). Discriminant analysis of risk factors for sexual victimization among a national sample of college women. *Journal of Consulting and Clinical Psychology, 57,* 242–250.

Koss, M. P., & Gaines, J. A. (1993). The prediction of sexual aggression by alcohol use, athletic participation, and fraternity affiliation. *Journal of Interpersonal Violence, 8,* 94–108.

Koss, M. P., Gidycz, C. A., & Wisniewski, N. (1987). The scope of rape: Incidence and prevalence of sexual aggression and victimization in a national sample of higher education students. *Journal of Consulting and Clinical Psychology, 55,* 162–170.

Kosson, D. S., Kelly, J. C., & White, J. W. (1997). Psychopathy-related traits predict self-reported sexual aggression among college men. *Journal of Interpersonal Violence, 12,* 241–254.

Kowalski, R. M. (1993). Inferring sexual interest from behavioral cues: Effects of gender and sexually-relevant attitudes. *Sex Roles, 29,* 13–31.

Lang, R. A., Flor-Henry, P., & Frenzel, R. R. (1990). Sex hormone profiles in pedophilic and incestuous men. *Annals of Sex Research, 3,* 59–74.

Lanier, C. A. (2001). Rape-accepting attitudes: Precursors to or consequences of forced sex. *Violence Against Women, 7,* 876–885.

Lerner, R. M. (1991). Changing organism context relations as the basic process of development: A developmental contextual perspective. *Developmental Psychology, 27*, 27–32.

Lisak, D., & Roth, S. (1988). Motivational factors in nonincarcerated sexually aggressive men. *Journal of Personality and Social Psychology, 55*, 795–802.

Lloyd, S. A. (1991). The dark side of courtship. *Family Relations, 40*, 14–20.

Lodico, M. A., Gruber, E., & DiClemente, R. J. (1996). Childhood sexual abuse and coercive sex among school-based adolescents in a midwestern state. *Journal of Adolescent Health, 18*, 211–217.

Lorh, B. A., Adams, H. E., & Davis, J. M. (1997). Sexual arousal to erotic and aggressive stimuli in sexually coercive and noncoercive men. *Journal of Abnormal Psychology, 106*, 230–242.

Lundberg-Love, P., & Geffner, R. (1989). Date rape: Prevalence, risk factors, and a proposed model. In M. Pirog-Good & J. E. Stets (Eds.), *Violence in dating relationships* (pp. 169–184). New York: Praeger.

Mahoney, E. R., Shively, M. D., & Traw, M. (1986). Sexual coercion and assault: Male socialization and female risk. *Sexual Coercion and Assault, 1*, 2–8.

Malamuth, N. M. (1986). Predictors of naturalistic sexual aggression. *Journal of Personality and Social Psychology, 50*, 953–962.

Malamuth, N. M. (1998). The confluence model as an organizing framework for research on sexually aggressive men: Risk, moderators, imagined aggression, and pornography consumption. In R. G. Geen & E. Donnerstein (Eds.), *Human aggression: Theories, research, and implications for social policy* (pp. 229–245). San Diego, CA: Academic.

Malamuth, N. M., Addison, T., & Koss, M. (2000). Pornography and sexual aggression: Are there reliable effects and can we understand them? *Annual Review of Sex Research, 11*, 26–91.

Malamuth, N. M., Linz, D., Heavey, C. L., Barnes, G., & Acker, M. (1995). Using the confluence model of sexual aggression to predict men's conflict with women: A 10-year follow-up study. *Journal of Personality and Social Psychology, 69*, 353–369.

Malamuth, N. M., Sockloskie, R. J., Koss, M. P., & Tanaka, J. S. (1991). Characteristics of aggressors against women: Testing a model using a national sample of college students. *Journal of Consulting and Clinical Psychology, 59*, 670–681.

Malamuth, N. M., & Thornhill, N. W. (1994). Hostile masculinity, sexual aggression, and gender-biased domineeringness in conversations. *Aggressive Behavior, 20*, 185–194.

Muehlenhard, C., & Schrag, J. (1991). Nonviolent sexual coercion. In A. Parrot & L. Bechhofer (Eds.), *Acquaintance rape: The hidden crime* (pp. 115–128). New York: Wiley.

Muehlenhard, C. L., & Linton, M. A. (1987). Date rape and sexual aggression in dating situations: Incidence and risk factors. *Journal of Consulting Psychology, 34*, 186–196.

Office of Juvenile Justice and Delinquency Prevention. (1999). *Juvenile offenders and victims: 1999 National Report* (NCJ 178257). Retrieved May 19, 2003, from www.ncjrs.org/html/ojjdp/nationalreport99/toc.html.

Olday, D., & Wesley, B. (1983). *Premarital courtship violence: A summary report*. Unpublished manuscript, Moorehead State University, Moorehead, KY.

Palmer, C. T. (1988). Twelve reasons why rape is not sexually motivated: A skeptical examination. *Journal of Sex Research, 25*, 512–530.

Rapaport, K. R., & Posey, D. D. (1991). Sexually coercive college males. In A. Parrot & L. Bechhofer (Eds.), *Acquaintance rape: The hidden crime* (pp. 83–95). New York: Wiley.

Richardson, D., & Hammock, G. (1991). The role of alcohol in acquaintance rape. In A. Parrot & L. Bechhofer (Eds.), *Acquaintance rape: The hidden crime* (pp. 217–228). New York: Wiley.

Riggs, D. S. (1993). Relationship problems and dating aggression: A potential treatment target. *Journal of Interpersonal Violence, 8*, 18–35.

Roscoe, B., & Kelsey, T. (1986). Dating violence among high school students. *Psychology, 23*, 53–59.

Rose, S., & Frieze, I. H. (1993). Young singles' contemporary dating scripts. *Sex Roles, 28*, 499–509.

Ross, V. M. (1977). Rape as a social problem: A byproduct of the feminist movement. *Social Problems, 25*, 75–89.

Rozee, P. D. (1993). Forbidden or forgiven? Rape in cross-cultural perspective. *Psychology of Women Quarterly, 17*, 499–509.

Scully, D., & Marolla, J. (2001). "Riding the bull at Gilley's": Convicted rapists describe the rewards of rape. In J. M. Henslin (Ed.), *Down to earth sociology: Introductory readings* (11th ed., pp. 45–60). New York: Free Press.

Sechrist, S. M., & White, J. W. (2003, March). *The confluence model in the prediction of sexual aggression: Adolescence through college*. Paper presented at the meeting of the Southeastern Psychological Association, New Orleans, LA.

Seto, M. C., Maric, A., & Barbaree, H. E. (2001). The role of pornography in the etiology of sexual aggression. *Aggression and Violent Behavior, 6*, 35–53.

Shotland, R. L. (1992). A theory of the causes of courtship rape: Part 2. *Journal of Social Issues, 48*, 127–143.

Stith, S. M., Rosen, K. H., Middleton, K. A., Busch, A. L., Lundberg, K., & Carlton, R. P. (2000). The intergenerational transmission of spouse abuse: A meta-analysis. *Journal of Marriage and the Family, 62*, 640–654.

Testa, M. (2002). The impact of men's alcohol consumption on perpetration of sexual aggression. *Clinical Psychology Review, 22*, 1239–1263.

U.S. Department of Justice. (2001). *Table 59: Personal and property crimes 2001: Percent distribution of incidents, by type of crime and time of occurrence*. Retrieved October 17, 2003, from Office of Justice Programs, Department of Justice web site, www.ojp.usdoj.gov/bjs/abstract/cvus/time_of_occurrence.htm.

Warshaw, R. (1988). *I never called it rape*. New York: Harper & Row.

Wheeler, J. G., George, W. H., & Dahl, B. J. (2002). Sexually aggressive college males: Empathy as a moderator in the "Confluence Model" of sexual aggression. *Personality and Individual Differences, 33*, 759–775.

White, J. W., & Humphrey, J. A. (1990, April). A theoretical model of search assault: An empirical test. In J. W. White (Chair), *Sexual assault: Research, treatment, and education.* Symposium conducted at the meeting of the Southeastern Psychological Association, Atlanta, GA.

White, J. W., & Koss, M. P. (1993). Adolescent sexual aggression within heterosexual relationships: Prevalence, characteristics, and causes. In H. E. Barbaree, W. L. Marshall, & S. M. Hudson (Eds.), *The juvenile sex offender* (pp. 182–202). New York: Guilford Press.

White, J. W., & Kowalski, R. M. (1998). Male violence toward women: An integrated perspective. In R. G. Green & E. Donnerstein (Eds.), *Human aggression: Theories, research, and implications for social policy* (pp. 203–228). San Diego, CA: Academic.

White, J. W., & Smith, P. H. (2004). Sexual assault perpetration and re-perpetration: From adolescence to young adulthood. *Criminal Justice and Behavior, 31,* 182–202.

White, S., & Shuntich, R. J. (1991, March). *Some home environment correlates of male sexual coerciveness/aggressiveness.* Paper presented at the annual meeting of the Southeastern Psychological Association, New Orleans, LA.

Wilson, A. E., Calhoun, K. S., & McNair, L. D. (2002) Alcohol consumption and expectancies among sexually coercive college men. *Journal of Interpersonal Violence, 17,* 1145–1159.

CHAPTER 7

The Female Juvenile Sex Offender

John A. Hunter
Judith V. Becker
Lenard J. Lexier

The sexual abuse and assault of children and females in our society continues to be a growing public health concern. The preponderance of the literature on this topic focuses on males as the perpetrators of these assaults. Over the past two decades, clinicians and researchers have also turned their attention to females who commit sexual offenses. More recently, the literature has focused on the topic of juvenile female sexual offenders.

The prevalence of sexual abuse perpetrated by females is difficult to assess due to the low incidence and/or underreporting of the phenomenon (Becker, Hall, & Stinson, 2001). Data available from official statistics (Federal Bureau of Investigation [FBI], 2001) indicate that 98% of individuals arrested for forcible rape in 2001 were male and 1.2% female. During this reporting period, 92% of individuals arrested for other sex offenses (excluding forcible rape and prostitution) were male and 8% were female. When these offenses are broken down by age, 40 females under the age of 18 were arrested for forcible rape and 959 for another sexual offense (excluding forcible rape and prostitution) in the cited year. These percentages may be underestimates of actual incidence, given the likelihood that the majority of cases of child sexual abuse and assault do not come to the attention of law enforcement or other public agencies.

Developmental Perspectives and Risk Factors

In understanding juvenile female sexual offending, one must consider developmental issues. For females ages 12–18, tremendous maturation in physical growth and cognitive development is occurring. A hallmark of this time period is the development of sexual maturity, with a concomitant interest in sexual relationships. The sexual maturation of adolescent females encompasses a wide variety of psychophysiological changes, including the beginning of menstruation and the subsequent development of secondary sexual characteristics and reproductive capacity. These changes in bodily appearance and function can be psychologically challenging for young females, particularly when they occur in advance of the youth's peer group.

A number of longitudinal studies suggest that the early developmental occurrence of puberty in females is associated with an elevated risk of emotional, social, and behavioral maladjustment (Caspi, Lynam, Moffitt, & Silva, 1993). In contrast to later developing females, those with early menarche have been found to have more body image disturbances, less academic success, an earlier onset to sexual behavior, and a greater risk for delinquency (Caspi et al., 1993; Simmons & Blyth, 1987; Stattin & Magnusson, 1990).

Related research suggests that family conflict, maternal depression, and biological father absence are associated with early menarche in females (Moffitt, Caspi, Belsky, & Silva, 1992; Ellis & Garber, 2000). At issue is the exact mechanism or mechanisms of this effect. Some theorists argue that the preceding factors are mediated by psychosocial stress (Belsky, Steinberg, & Draper, 1991), whereas others point to genetic (Comings, Muhleman, Johnson, & MacMurray, 2002) or alternative sociobiological influences (Ellis & Garber, 2000).

During the adolescent period, reasoning ability becomes fully developed. Many adolescents are capable of advanced cognitive thinking and abstract problem solving. Concomitant with cognitive development is moral development and the capacity for empathy. Research suggests that youths with lower IQs are at higher risk for delinquent behavior and that delinquent youths have lower levels of moral maturation than controls (Bartek, Krebs, & Taylor, 1993; White, Moffitt, & Silva, 1989).

Advances in cognitive development are typically accompanied by intense introspection and a heightened sensitivity to how one is perceived by peers. This period has been defined by Erikson (1968) as a time of identity crisis in which adolescents question who they are and their role in life. As noted by Erikson (1968), during this time span adolescents face the task of developing a functional and stable self-concept.

If an adolescent is unable to develop a sense of identity, she may have difficulty forming and maintaining stable interpersonal relationships and developing life goals. Due to a search for identity and the tremendous hormonal changes that occur, this is a period in which adolescent females are at increased risk for developing depression and/or anxiety disorders and suicidal behavior.

Identity confusion and the risk of emotional maladjustment and acting-out behaviors may be intensified in those youths with histories of sexual and physical maltreatment. As reviewed in the following section, the incidence of child maltreatment in adolescent females who perpetrate sexual offenses is markedly elevated, and many of these young people suffer from abuse-related psychological sequelae. Thus child maltreatment experiences may loom large in the lives of these youths and may have altered how they view themselves and others. They may also have had a negative impact on sexual attitudes and feelings and on basic mood and impulse regulatory processes.

Closely associated with identity formation is the achievement of a greater sense of autonomy and the progressive movement away from a primary emotional dependence on parents. Research suggests that social skill acquisition in adolescents and a successful transition to greater autonomy are linked to a secure attachment to parents (Allen et al., 2002). Adolescents with insecure and preoccupied attachments show not only fewer gains in social skills than their more securely attached peers, but also a greater tendency to engage in delinquent behavior (Allen et al., 2002).

As youths attempt to gain greater independence from parents, the peer group becomes especially critical. Adolescent females want to feel accepted by their peer groups, and it is very painful when they are isolated. This is a period during which adolescents experiment with alcohol and drugs and negative peer group influences can be especially strong. It is not uncommon for adolescents to use substances in order to become a part of their peer group. Also, some adolescent girls who have been the victims of maltreatment may turn to alcohol or other drugs to medicate themselves.

Pair bonding and sexual experimentation also occur during this period of development. Those adolescent females who have a history of being sexually abused may engage in the sexual abuse of younger peers as a way of mastering their own abuse history. Other female adolescents who are lacking peer partners may, out of social isolation and loneliness, befriend and then sexualize relationships with younger children.

It is thus important to examine the sexual behavior of the adolescent female in the larger developmental and ecological context in which it occurs. Only through consideration of the youth's developmental history, her level of cognitive, emotional, and social maturation, and relevant familial and peer group influences can an evaluator glean an accurate understanding of her motivation for engaging in nonconsenting sexual activity and her intervention needs.

Clinical Presentation

As with their male counterparts, juvenile females who are referred for treatment of sexual behavior problems present with an array of offending behaviors and associated psychosocial, psychiatric, and familial problems. As such, they should be viewed as a heterogeneous clinical population consisting of both mildly and severely disturbed youths. A review of prominent characteristics of studied samples of juvenile female sexual offenders follows.

Developmental Characteristics

Available data suggest that child maltreatment, exposure to violence, and familial instability are prominent in the lives of adolescent females referred for sexual offending behavior. Fehrenbach and Monastersky (1988) found that approximately one fifth of the studied adolescent female sexual perpetrators had childhood histories of physical abuse and that one half had histories of sexual abuse. Mathews, Hunter, and Vuz (1997) found histories of physical abuse in 60% of a sample of 67 adolescent female sexual perpetrators and sexual abuse in over three fourths of these youths.

Exclusively residential samples of adolescent female sexual perpetrators tend to produce even higher estimates of child maltreatment. All of the 10 residentially placed youth surveyed by Hunter, Lexier, Goodwin, Browne, & Dennis (1993) had been sexually abused, and 86.6% of Hunter and Lexier's (2003) new residential sample of 15 female sexual offenders had chart-documented histories of sexual victimization. Sexual victimization rates also tend to be very high (> 90%) in samples of prepubescent female sexual perpetrators (Johnson, 1989).

Rates of child maltreatment in samples of adolescent female sexual perpetrators typically exceed those found in comparison samples of adolescent male sex offenders (Mathews et al., 1997). Furthermore, inspection of maltreatment data suggests that juvenile female sexual offenders often experienced more extensive and severe abuse than their male counterparts. For example, Mathews et al. (1997) found that 75% of adolescent female offenders, compared with 10% of the adolescent male offenders, reported having been victimized by more than one person; the females averaged 4.5 offenders each. These data also revealed that the adolescent female sex offenders were younger on average at the time of first sexual victimization and were more frequently subjected to sexual coercion or force than the studied males.

These maltreatment experiences often appear to have occurred in the context of severe family dysfunction with little environmental or caretaker support for the afflicted youths. These experiences include the witnessing of domestic violence and marital strife, as well as adult-modeled antisocial behavior. Theory and available empirical data suggest that it is both the magnitude of the experienced childhood trauma and its occurrence in the absence of significant social supports and protective factors that explain ensuing psychological and behavioral problems in abused youths (Kendall-Tackett, Williams, & Finkelhor, 1993; Hunter & Figueredo, 2000).

Sexual Offense Behavior

The majority of the "hands-on" sexual offenses committed by juvenile females are against younger children. Relatively few of these youths sexually aggress against peers or adults (Hunter & Mathews, 1997). At present, there is some controversy in the literature as to whether female sex offenders are more likely to molest male or female children (Grayston & De Luca, 1999). Fehrenbach and Monastersky (1988) reported that 35.7% of the adolescent females they studied assaulted males; 57.7%, females; and 7.1%, children of both sexes. In Hunter and Lexier's (2003) sample, 35.7% assaulted males; 42.8%, females; and 21.4%, children of both sexes. Conversely, Mathews et al. (1997) reported that 44.8% of their sample abused males only; 23.9%, females only; and 31.3%, both males and females.

In each of the cited studies, the majority of the victims of these youths were children under the age of 6. In keeping with the young age of their victims, a significant percentage of the child molestations perpetrated by adolescent females occurs in the context of child care or babysitting. The majority of their victims are therefore children to whom they are related or are acquainted with (Becker et al., 2001; Grayston & DeLuca, 1999). Sexual abuse of unknown children is relatively uncommon in this population, occurring in less than 10% of the cases (Mathews et al., 1997).

Juvenile females appear to engage in a broad spectrum of "hands-on" sexual offenses. Both Fehrenbach and Monastersky (1988), and Mathews et al. (1997), found that over one fourth of their studied samples engaged in vaginal or anal penetration of the victim; oral sexual activity was reported by nearly one half of the Mathews et al. (1997)

sample. Somewhat surprisingly, the latter researchers found that nearly the same number of juvenile female and male offenders reported that they used force in the commission of one or more of their sexual offenses (20–25%). This is in keeping with data suggesting that juvenile and adult female sexual offenders often both physically and sexually abuse their victims (Mathews et al., 1997; Grayston & DeLuca, 1999; Finkelhor & Williams, 1988).

Whereas the sexual offending of some of these youths may be limited to one or two offenses against a single victim, a sizable number appear to engage in repetitive offending against one or more victims. Over half of the Mathews et al. (1997) sample and 60% of the Hunter and Lexier (2003) cohort had sexually offended against more than one child. Thus, in at least a subset of these youths, the sexual offending appears to involve the active seeking out of children for sexual exploitation. As with males, sexual behavior disturbances in females may progress in frequency and severity over time.

Unlike with adult female sex offenders, it does not appear that there are a large number of juvenile females who sexually perpetrate in the context of a relationship with a male co-offender. Most of the youths in the Fehrenbach and Monastersky (1988), Mathews et al. (1997), Hunter et al. (1993), and Hunter and Lexier (2003) samples acted independently and on their own initiative. It does appear that a number of juvenile female sex offenders engage in multiple paraphiliac behavior, including "hands-off" sexual offenses. Both the Mathews et al. (1997) and Hunter et al. (1993) samples contained youths who engaged in exhibitionistic behavior, bestiality, and voyeurism in addition to the sexual molestation of children.

Psychiatric Characteristics

Psychiatric comorbidity in juvenile female sexual offenders referred for treatment appears to be high, especially in residential samples. Over one fourth of the females in the Mathews et al. (1997) mixed sample of community-based and residentially treated youths had substance abuse problems, nearly one fourth were learning disabled, and a third had a history of running away. Nearly 40% of these youths had experienced suicidal ideation or made a suicide attempt, and over 70% had previously received mental health treatment.

Especially prevalent in residential samples of juvenile female sexual offenders are mood disturbances and posttraumatic stress disorder (PTSD). All of the youths in the Hunter et al. (1993) residential sample had been diagnosed with an affective disorder, and 90% with PTSD. Over 93% of the Hunter and Lexier (2003) sample had an affective disorder diagnosis, and over 53% had the diagnosis of PTSD. In the latter sample, 60% of these youths had a diagnosis of dysthymic disorder, 26.7% major depression, and 20% bipolar disorder (note: some youths were diagnosed with concurrent disorders). Over 53% of these youths had a history of suicidal gesturing or attempts.

The preceding psychiatric diagnoses are consistent with the extensive maltreatment and exposure to violence that many of these young people experienced during childhood and early adolescence. These experiences often appear to be the focus of recurrent nightmares and intrusive thoughts. They also appear to be associated with avoidance of certain situations and relationships that engender memories of past trauma and ego identity confusion. As discussed in the section on treatment, chronic dysphoria and unresolved trauma experiences may serve as stimuli for both self-injurious behavior and aggressive and sexual acting out in this population.

Many juvenile female sexual offenders, especially those treated residentially, meet criteria for diagnosis of conduct disorder. In addition to a history of sexual perpetration, a sizable number of these young women have engaged in other forms of delinquent and antisocial behavior, such as lying, stealing, and physical assault. The presence of attention-deficit/hyperactivity disorder (ADHD; 53.3% in the Hunter & Lexier, 2003; sample) may also help account for the impulsive and acting-out behavior seen in many of these youths. Subsets of residentially treated female sex offenders manifest other major psychiatric disturbances, including schizoaffective and borderline personality disorders.

Typological Impressions

The relatively low numbers of juvenile female sex offenders found in clinical and legal settings limit the conduct of large-scale and more formal research on this population. What follows is a description of major subtypes of adolescent female sex offenders based on clinical impression and what can be gleaned from existent studies.

Mathews et al. (1997) describe three groups of juvenile female sexual offenders commonly seen in clinical settings. The first group could be termed "naïve/experimenters." These youths typically have engaged in limited sexual offending, usually in the context of babysitting. They generally have not used physical force or threat in the commission of the sexual offense(s), and absent is evidence of major psychopathology or sexual maladjustment. Instead, these young women can be characterized as somewhat fearful or anxious about sexuality and primarily motivated by curiosity. They do not appear to be at high risk for continued sexual acting out or antisocial behavior, and their treatment prognosis is typically considered to be good.

The second group consists of adolescents who have engaged in more extensive sexual acting out with one or more children, often for a period of several months. Notable in the histories of these young people is their own sexual victimization. This victimization may either precede or be concurrent with their victimization of younger children. In many cases, the perpetrating behavior parallels the victimization experience. These youths typically manifest a mild to moderate level of individual psychopathology and have had few prior age-appropriate sexual experiences. Approximately one half of these adolescents suffer from depression or an identity disturbance, and a number come from troubled and dysfunctional families. Although the treatment of these young people is generally more complicated and longer term than it is for the preceding group, their prognosis is generally good.

Case Example

T. was found alone in a car at 12 days of age—apparently abandoned by her biological mother. She was shortly thereafter adopted. At the age of 16, she was referred for treatment following a history of sexually molesting her 6-year-old adoptive brother. The molestations occurred on several occasions over a period of about 1 year and consisted of playing a "baby" game wherein she and her brother would take off their clothes and lie on each other, simulating intercourse. T. denied that there was ever vaginal penetration or that she had engaged in oral sexual activities with her brother.

T. stated that she learned this game from two male "cousins"— actually the sons of a friend of her adoptive mother who were, respectively, 5 and 12 years older than she. T. stated that these males first began playing this game with her when she was a toddler and continued until she was 16 years of age. Approximately 3 months after her last reported victimization by these older males, the sexual molestation of her brother was discovered.

T. does not have a history of sexually offending against other children. She does have a history of lying and stealing from her mother and friends and of chronic depression. She reportedly experienced intermittent nightmares from ages 10 through 14. However, there is no history of suicide attempts or gestures, psychotic activity, or significant substance abuse. She was mildly anxious but cooperative during her intake clinical interview and commented that she knew what she did with her brother was wrong.

The third group of adolescents represents those with more serious and pervasive sexual disturbance and related psychopathology. Their sexual acting out is generally longer standing and may involve multiple victims. Furthermore, these females may have engaged in more invasive sexual behaviors and/or utilized force or threats in committing their sexual offenses. In addition to their sexual behavior problems, they typically manifest severe emotional disturbances.

Not surprisingly, the developmental histories of this latter group of youths often reflect high levels of sexual and physical trauma, exposure to violence, and familial upheaval. Many of these young people meet diagnostic criteria for conduct disorder, PTSD, and major affective disorders. Within this group are those who experience recurrent sexual and aggressive impulses. These impulses may be either ego-syntonic or ego-dystonic; however, the majority of these young women have difficulty with mood regulation and impulse control, making their risk of sexual and/or aggressive acting out high. In addition, a number of these youths have disturbances in their thinking and thought processes and histories of intermittent psychotic symptomatology or episodes. Self-injurious and suicidal behavior within this subtype is relatively common. Treatment is obviously more complicated with this group of adolescents, with a number requiring intensive and extended community-based care or residential placement.

Case Example

B. was referred for residential placement at age 12 after putting a knife and pins in the vaginas of her 5-year-old paternal half-sister and 9-year-old stepsister. She had previously tried to suffocate one of the girls and kill her pet. She acknowledged homicidal thoughts toward both her sisters and her stepmother. She stated that she was intensely angry toward the latter for taking her away from one of the only friends she ever had—a girl who had introduced her to drug use and sexual activity in the preceding year.

When B. was 5 months of age, her mother gave her to her father to raise. This occurred after the mother reportedly began "dating" a 16-year-old male. The father married B.'s stepmother when B. was 8 years old. B. has a history of impulsive behavior and distractibility and has been diagnosed with ADHD. She stated in the intake interview that she has been depressed "forever." Her admission note documents frequent crying spells, anhedonia, insomnia, and hyperirritability. She began smoking "pot" at age 11 and has also been caught "huffing" cans of hair spray and air freshener. She has intermittently experienced suicidal ideation, but there have been no attempts to date. Her residential placement diagnoses included bipolar II disorder and borderline personality traits.

Assessment and Treatment Planning

Given the apparent high level of psychiatric comorbidity in juvenile female sexual offenders, it is imperative that conducted clinical assessments be comprehensive and directed at identifying and diagnosing all of the relevant emotional and behavioral problems of these young women. An emphasis should be placed on achieving an understanding of the manifest sexual behavior problem in the context of the adolescent's overall personality functioning and developmental and familial background.

Especially important is examining in considerable depth the young person's early development, including attachment to parents and the achievement of critical developmental milestones. The clinician must glean an understanding of the youth's premorbid functioning and the precipitants of her sexual acting out. Disruptive developmental influences require thorough examination. Simply identifying maltreatment and other potentially traumatic experiences is of limited utility. Instead, attention must be given to systematically exploring the specific manner in which these experiences may have altered perceptions of self and others, as well as mood and impulse regulatory processes and sexual cognitions.

Beyond gaining an integrated and holistic understanding of the young woman and her development, the clinician must specifically assess the nature and severity of her sexual behavior problems. This requires obtaining, through interview and perusal of available clinical and legal documents, a thorough sexual history and report of her perpetrating behaviors. Detailed information should be generated regarding the age and sex of victims, the displayed sexual behaviors and interactions with the victims, and the relationship and environmental context in which the offense(s) occurred. In addition, it is prudent to explore the cognitions and affect (including sexual feelings) of the perpetrating youth before, during, and following the offense. Gathered information should be sufficient to delineate the "modus operandi" of the offender, including explanation of how the victim was selected, how control over the victim was gained and maintained, and whether and how there was an attempt to maintain victim silence.

It is also important to attempt to ascertain the extent to which the perpetrating youth has empathy for the victim and/or remorse for the offending behavior. Research suggests that empathy may have both trait-like and state-like qualities and can be victim specific (Hunter, Figueredo, Malamuth, & Becker, in press). As it relates to the former, individuals who are characterologically impaired (i.e. antisocial and narcissistic) may have relatively little or no general empathy for others. Thus exploitation of others is ego-syntonic and does not engender anxiety or regret. For others, the capacity for empathy and respect for others' rights and welfare may be rudimentarily intact; however, specific moods, cognitions, and circumstances may negatively alter their capacity to empathize with a given victim. Discernment of the extent to which empathy deficits are proportionally the former or the latter is important to both diagnosis and treatment planning.

The previously described information has been largely gathered through clinical interviews and record reviews. Clinical interviews should include a review of mental health history and a mental status examination, as well as academic, vocational, and family functioning. When available and clinically or legally appropriate, parents and caretakers should also be interviewed. Such interviews can be the source of valuable information about both the youth and the adequacy and safety of the home environment.

Unlike the assessment of juvenile and adult male sexual offenders, there is a dearth of special sexual offender instrumentation available for the assessment of juvenile and adult female perpetrators. Clinicians are warned that the use of sexual cognition, interest, and risk assessment measures that were developed and validated on males in the assessment of female clients may produce misleading and erroneous results. Thus clinicians should either avoid the use of these instruments or be cautious and conservative in their application and interpretation.

Traditional psychological evaluation (including intellectual and personality assessment) may be of value in assessing referred youths. Although such testing usually does not generate information directly related to the nature and severity of the young woman's sexual behavior problems or her risk of sexual reoffending, it can provide information that is relevant to comprehensive diagnosis and treatment planning. The latter includes fostering an understanding of the adolescent's overall intellectual capacity and specific learning strengths and weaknesses, as well as specific cognitive and emotional processes and impairments that may have indirectly contributed to her sexual offending behavior. Such evaluation can also be helpful in identifying comorbid conditions that require therapeutic attention.

Assessment information should be used in support of clinical and legal decision making. Where legal action is pending, clinicians are advised to conduct their evaluations postadjudication and presentencing. Preadjudication evaluations are fraught with legal and ethical complexity and generally should be avoided when possible (Hunter & Lexier, 1998; Hunter & Mathews, 1997).

Assessment reports should address the following: (1) evaluation of the nature of the sexual behavior problem and risk of further sexual and nonsexual offenses; (2) an understanding of operative factors and dynamics contributing to the sexual offense(s) and specific risk factors; (3) comorbid conditions and familial/environmental issues that need to be addressed in a comprehensive plan of intervention; (4) the youths' accountability for their behavior and amenability to treatment; and (5) the most appropriate level and type of care. The latter should include the delineation of specific treatment goals and objectives, summarization of a plan of action for their achievement, and a projected timetable for their accomplishment.

Treatment

As discussed by Hunter and Mathews (1997), the treatment of female sexual offenders has been advanced in recent years. Prior to the mid-1980s, many juvenile and adult females were placed in treatment programs along with males, with little sensitivity to gender differences or the potential negative impact of such mixing on both sexes. Today, it is generally recognized that females require specialized treatment programming that reflects an understanding of female psychosexual development and of the unique etiology and psychopathology that is associated with the emergence of sexual offending in this population. Thus we argue for both age- and gender-specific treatment of females who have engaged in sexual offending behaviors. This includes separate treatment groups and, in the case of residential placement, separate milieu placement and management.

The majority of young women in the first two of the discussed prototypic subtypes can be successfully treated and managed in community settings, given the development of appropriate community-based resources. As with males, the clinical care of juvenile females involved with the legal system should be carefully coordinated with their legal management. This includes close consultation with probation and parole officers so as to ensure that the legal management plan reflects an understanding of the youth's risk factors and supervision and monitoring needs. Mutual exchange of information between clinicians and legal authorities and coordination of intervention planning can also help ensure that youths and families are afforded all of the social and mental health services that they require.

Treatment of young people within the first subtype is generally short term (e.g., 3–6 months) and consists of some combination of individual, group, and family therapy. The focus within these modalities includes the provision of sex education, the enhancement of self-esteem and social skills, and the improvement of family communication and support. Females in the second subtype typically require a longer term of clinical care. Especially important is exploring and working through unresolved conflicts and problems stemming from their own sexual victimizations. This includes helping these young women understand how these maltreatment experiences may have contributed to their current problems.

Adolescents within the second subtype may benefit from focused intervention directed at correcting distorted or confused sexual cognitions, teaching healthy female sexuality and relationship development, and improving impulse control and empathy. As many of these young women have more extensive familial and/or comorbid problems, it is important to ensure that these issues are adequately addressed, as well. Depending on the circumstances of their sexual perpetrations and family environment, some of these youths may require out-of-home placement (e.g., placement with a relative or in a foster or group home). In making placement decisions, professional workers should obviously be attentive to the risk that these individuals pose to younger children and avoid placing them in settings where younger children reside.

The treatment of youths within the third subtype is generally more intensive and lengthy than that of the first two subtypes. As such, they often require intensive community-based care or residential placement. The viability of the former often depends on whether the particular community in question has the necessary resources to meet the extensive clinical intervention, support, and monitoring and supervision services these young people require.

Because of their potential danger to themselves and others, the majority of adolescents within the third subtype require 24-hour supervision. Supervision, even within the confines of a residential treatment program, can be a daunting task given the emotional volatility and impulsiveness that many of these youths display. Both aggression toward others and suicidal gestures and attempts can occur with little warning—particularly in young people suffering from PTSD, borderline personality disorder, and major affective disorders. Such afflicted adolescents may be very vulnerable to decompensation under conditions of stress, with emotional reactions often appearing to be disproportionate to the external stimulus or trigger.

The effective residential or community management of these youths requires a thorough understanding of their underlying psychopathology and risk factors for sexual and aggressive acting out and self-injurious behavior. This knowledge must be imparted to caretakers and reflected in a comprehensive case management plan. In the case of young people suffering from PTSD, it is important that both the youths and caretakers understand how particular stimuli may trigger strong emotional reactions and that they have a firm grasp of helpful coping and behavior management strategies.

Treatment of Comorbid PTSD

Hunter and Mathews (1997) discuss the potential complexity of treating adolescent females with comorbid PTSD and comment that their sexual acting out may be compulsive in nature and reflect an attempt to discharge painful affects and pent-up sexual tensions. These youths and those with borderline personality traits may form negative therapeutic transferences and have difficulty trusting others. As such, therapists and caretakers may be severely tested. The successful treatment of these young females requires both an understanding of relational dynamics and effective interventions for allaying negative affects and increasing self-control.

Of relevance to the latter, the treatment of PTSD (including that secondary to rape and sexual trauma) has been advanced in recent years by research on cognitive-behavioral approaches to symptom management and resolution. Studies suggest that cognitive-behavioral approaches are superior to supportive counseling in attenuating PTSD symptomatology, including intrusive thoughts, avoidance, and feelings of depression (Bryant, Harvey, Dang, Sackville, & Basten, 1998; Foa, Rothbaum, Riggs, & Murdock, 1991).

One such cognitive-behavioral approach, "prolonged exposure," entails a psychoeducational component (i.e., common reactions to rape), relaxation training, imaginal reliving of the rape memory, exposure to trauma cues, and cognitive restructuring (Jaycox, Zoellner, & Foa, 2002). Within this approach, both the exposure (imaginal and in vivo cues) and cognitive restructuring elements appear to be critical to long-term recovery. The former is thought to result in a dampening of excitatory processes through stimulus habituation (Foa, Hearst-Ikeda, & Perry, 1995). The latter addresses distorted thinking pertinent to self-blame and expectations of event recurrence, both of which are highly relevant to understanding prolonged psychological distress (Boeschen, Koss, Figueredo, & Coan, 2001; Koss, Figueredo, & Prince, 2002).

Of special note, recent research suggests that the use of some cognitive-behavioral approaches with patients with PTSD may result in symptom exacerbation during the early phases of treatment (Nishith, Resick, & Griffin, 2002). This is believed to be the product of disruption of avoidance as a defense mechanism and the intentional introduction of painful memories and trauma cues. Although these symptoms eventually remit and long-lasting therapeutic gains are achieved, they may trigger a withdrawal from treatment in some individuals (Nishith et al., 2002). Cloitre, Koenen, Cohen, and Han (2002) demonstrated that a two-phase therapeutic approach, wherein females with histories of child abuse first received skills training in affect and interpersonal regulation and then subsequently prolonged exposure, was particularly effective. These researchers showed that "phase one" therapeutic alliance and attained skills in regulating negative moods predicted success in "phase two."

Medical Management

A number of juvenile female sexual offenders, especially those within the third subtype, require careful medical management. This includes the judicious utilization of psychotropic medications. Medication management can be difficult with this population of adolescents, especially those with character pathology and PTSD. The latter often act out with prescribed medication, intentionally missing doses or attempting excessive self-medication. They may also attempt to sell medications because of their "street value." Not infrequently, these problems are compounded by a basic distrust of the physician and his or her interventions.

The forging of an effective working relationship with these young people is paramount to their successful medical management. The physician must understand the manner in which trauma experiences have contributed to their suspiciousness and wariness of caretakers and severely damaged their self-esteem and sense of self-worth. It is also important for physicians to recognize that many of these young women have had prior negative experiences with psychotropic medication.

Many of the frequently utilized medications have side effects, including weight gain. The latter is particularly true with some of the selective serotonin reuptake inhibitors (SSRIs), and the atypical antipsychotic medications. Such troublesome side effects can further damage self-esteem and exacerbate body image disturbances. It is strongly recommended that attending physicians have frank discussions with the young women on the risks and benefits of the various medications they are prescribed and attempt to select medications that do not include weight gain as a side effect.

The medical management of youths suffering from posttraumatic stress disorder can be especially challenging because of the extent of their underlying psychiatric impairment. Many of these young people are prone to dissociation, and their suspiciousness and hypervigilance can border on frank paranoia. At times, it is clinically difficult to discern between brief reactive psychotic periods and severe, triggered PTSD events. SSRIs are approved by the FDA for this indication and have been found to be particularly helpful in treating hyperarousal and obsessive sexual thinking. However, we have found that the more severely impaired adolescents (what has been termed PTSD-p in the literature) may also require the use of low-dose atypical neuroleptics. This has led us to use the newer atypical neuroleptic medications, as well as escitalopram (Lexapro) and citalopram (Celexa). Naltrexone (ReVia) may also be helpful in treating "flashbacks" and dissociative episodes in more severely afflicted youths.

In the Hunter and Lexier (2003) cohort described in this chapter, a large number of adolescents have established diagnoses of ADHD. Yet, at the time of admission, very few of these girls were treated with stimulant medication. This may be attributable to the referenced difficulties with medication compliance and the potential for abuse of these medications. Many these young women complain, even with the long-acting amphetamines, of an up-and-down or "yo-yo" effect with regard to their moods. We have found the extended-release methylphenidate (Concerta) preparation to be helpful when the girls complain of the biphasic onset of the long-acting amphetamine preparations. We have also been encouraged with the use of atomoxetine (Strattera), though it typically takes 3 to 4 weeks before youngsters will show a therapeutic response. It is clear that a lot of young people, particularly those admitted with many medications, including mood stabilizers, antidepressants, and atypical antipsychotics, clearly benefit from the judicious use of medicine that affects their ADHD problems.

References

Allen, J. P., Marsh, P., McFarland, C., McElhaney, K. B., Boykin, K., Land, D. J., et al. (2002). Attachment and autonomy as predictors of the development of social skills and delinquency during midadolescence. *Journal of Consulting and Clinical Psychology, 70*(1), 56–66.

Bartek, S. E., Krebs, D. L., & Taylor, M. C. (1993). Coping, defending, and the relations between moral judgment and moral behavior in prostitutes and other female juvenile delinquents. *Journal of Abnormal Psychology, 102*(1), 66–73.

Becker, J. V., Hall, S. R., & Stinson, J. D. (2001). Female sexual offenders: Clinical, legal, and policy issues. *Journal of Forensic Psychology Practice, 1*(3), 29–50.

Belsky, J., Steinberg, L., & Draper, P. (1991). Childhood experience, interpersonal development, and reproductive strategy: An evolutionary theory of socialization. *Child Development, 62*(4), 647–670.

Boeschen, L. E., Koss, M. P., Figueredo, A. J., & Coan, J. A. (2001). Experiential avoidance and post-traumatic stress disorder: A cognitive mediational model of rape recovery. *Journal of Aggression, Maltreatment, and Trauma,* 4(2), 211–245.

Bryant, R. A., Harvey, A. G., Dang, S. T., Sackville, T., & Basten, C. (1998). Treatment of acute stress disorder: A comparison of cognitive-behavioral therapy and supportive counseling. *Journal of Consulting & Clinical Psychology,* 66(5), 862–866.

Caspi, A., Lynam, D., Moffitt, T. E., & Silva, P. A. (1993). Unraveling girls' delinquency: Biological, dispositional, and contextual contributions to adolescent misbehavior. *Developmental Psychology,* 29(1), 19–30.

Cloitre, M., Koenen, K. C., Cohen, L. R., & Han, H. (2002). Skills training in affective and interpersonal regulation followed by exposure: A phase-based treatment for PTSD related to childhood abuse. *Journal of Consulting and Clinical Psychology,* 70(5), 1067–1074.

Comings, D. E., Muhleman, D., Johnson, J. P., & MacMurray, J. P. (2002). Parent–daughter transmission of the androgen receptor gene as an explanation of the effect of father absence on age of menarche. *Child Development,* 73(4), 1046–1051.

Ellis, B. J., & Garber, J. (2000). Psychosocial antecedents of variation in girls' pubertal timing: Maternal depression, stepfather presence, and marital and family stress. *Child Development,* 71(2), 485–501.

Erikson, E. H. (1968). *Identity: Youth and crisis.* Oxford, UK: Norton.

Federal Bureau of Investigation. (2001). *Crime in the United States (Uniform Crime Reports).* Retrieved February 2, 2003, from www.fbi.gov/ucr/Olcius.htm

Fehrenbach, P. A., & Monastersky, C. (1988). Characteristics of female adolescent sexual offenders. *American Journal of Orthopsychiatry,* 58(1), 148–151.

Finkelhor, D., & Williams, L. M. (1988). Perpetrators. In D. Finkelhor, L. M. Williams, N. Burns, & M. Kalinowski (Eds.), *Nursery crimes: Sexual abuse in day care* (pp. 27–69). Newbury Park, CA: Sage.

Foa, E. B., Hearst-Ikeda, D., & Perry, K. J. (1995). Evaluation of a brief cognitive-behavioral program for the prevention of chronic PTSD in recent assault victims. *Journal of Consulting and Clinical Psychology,* 63(6), 948–955.

Foa, E. B., Rothbaum, B. O., Riggs, D. S., & Murdock, T. B. (1991). Treatment of posttraumatic stress disorder in rape victims: A comparison between cognitive-behavioral procedures and counseling. *Journal of Consulting and Clinical Psychology,* 59(5), 715–723.

Grayston, A. D., & De Luca, R. V. (1999). Female perpetrators of child sexual abuse: A review of the clinical and empirical literature. *Aggression and Violent Behavior,* 4(1), 93–106.

Hunter, J. A., & Figueredo, A. J. (2000). The influence of personality and history of sexual victimization in the prediction of offense characteristics of juvenile sex offenders. *Behavior Modification,* 24(2), 241–263.

Hunter, J. A., Figueredo, A. J., Malamuth, N. M., & Becker, J. V. (2003). Juvenile sex offenders: Toward the development of a typology. *Sexual Abuse: A Journal of Research and Treatment, 15*(1), 27–48.

Hunter, J. A., Figueredo, A. J., Malamuth, N. M., & Becker, J. V. (in press). Non-sexual delinquency in juvenile sex offenders: The mediating and moderating influences of emotional empathy. *Journal of Family Violence.*

Hunter, J. A., & Lexier, L. J. (2003). *A survey of residentially treated juvenile female sexual offenders.* Unpublished manuscript.

Hunter, J. A., Lexier, L. J., Goodwin, D. W., Browne, P. A., & Dennis, C. (1993). Psychosexual, attitudinal, and developmental characteristics of juvenile female sexual perpetrators in a residential treatment setting. *Journal of Child and Family Studies, 2*(4), 317–326.

Hunter, J. A., Jr., & Lexier, L. J. (1998). Ethical and legal issues in the assessment and treatment of juvenile sex offenders. *Child Maltreatment: Journal of the American Professional Society on the Abuse of Children, 3*(4), 339–348.

Hunter, J. A., Jr., & Mathews, R. (1997). Sexual deviance in females. In D. R. Laws & W. T. O'Donohue (Eds.), Sexual deviance: Theory, assessment, and treatment (pp. 465–480). New York: Guilford Press.

Jaycox, L. H., Zoellner, L., & Foa, E. B. (2002). Cognitive-behavior therapy for PTSD in rape survivors. *Journal of Clinical Psychology, 58*(8), 891–906.

Johnson, T. C. (1989). Female child perpetrators: Children who molest other children. *Child Abuse and Neglect, 13,* 571–585.

Kendall-Tackett, K. A., Williams, L. M., & Finkelhor, D. (1993). Impact of sexual abuse on children: A review and synthesis of recent empirical studies. *Psychological Bulletin, 113*(1), 164–180.

Koss, M. P., Figueredo, A. J., & Prince, R. J. (2002). Cognitive mediation of rape's mental, physical, and social health impact tests of four models in cross-sectional data. *Journal of Consulting and Clinical Psychology, 70*(4), 926–941.

Mathews, R., Hunter, J. A., Jr., & Vuz, J. (1997). Juvenile female sexual offenders: Clinical characteristics and treatment issues. *Sexual Abuse: A Journal of Research and Treatment, 9*(3), 187–199.

Moffitt, T. E., Caspi, A., Belsky, J., & Silva, P. A. (1992). Childhood experience and the onset of menarche: A test of a sociobiological model. *Child Development, 63*(1), 47–58.

Nishith, P., Resick, P. A., & Griffin, M. G. (2002). Pattern of change in prolonged exposure and cognitive-processing therapy for female rape victims with posttraumatic stress disorder. *Journal of Consulting and Clinical Psychology, 70*(4), 880–886.

Simmons, R. G., & Blyth, D. A. (1987). *Moving into adolescence: The impact of pubertal change and school context.* Hawthorne, NY: Aldine de Gruyter.

Stattin, H., & Magnusson, D. (1990). *Pubertal maturation in female development.* Hillsdale, NJ: Erlbaum.

White, J. L., Moffitt, T. E., & Silva, P. A. (1989). A prospective replication of the protective effects of IQ in subjects at high risk for juvenile delinquency. *Journal of Consulting and Clinical Psychology, 57*(6), 719–724.

CHAPTER 8

Conduct Problems and Juvenile Sexual Offending

Michael C. Seto
Martin L. Lalumière

One of the central theoretical questions regarding the causes of juvenile sexual offending is the contribution of antisocial tendencies. This question is central because it is clear that antisocial tendencies contribute to other forms of juvenile delinquency: Juveniles who commit crimes tend to score higher than juveniles who do not commit crimes on measures of early conduct problems, aggression, antisocial attitudes and beliefs, association with delinquent peers, antisocial personality, and other indicators of antisocial tendencies (reviewed in Quinsey, Skilling, Lalumière, & Craig, 2004). It is a logical step to wonder about the extent to which juvenile sexual offending is also explained by general antisocial tendencies.

Becker (1988) suggested that some juvenile sex offenders are motivated by paraphilic sexual interests such as pedophilia, whereas others offend as a result of general antisocial tendencies. In the first edition of this book, France and Hudson (1993) suggested that approximately half of juvenile sex offenders have nonsexual offense histories and that a majority would meet the diagnostic criteria for conduct disorder (American Psychiatric Association, 2000). They also added that "it is possible that theoretical and treatment formulations for nonsexual disturbances in conduct may have useful explanatory power for at least some types of juvenile sex offending" (p. 225). In fact, several recent explanatory models of juvenile sexual offending have emphasized the role of such conduct problems as aggression toward peers, disruptive school behavior, and involvement in nonsexual crimes (e.g., Johnson & Knight, 2000; Hunter, Figueredo, Malamuth, & Becker, 2003; Knight & Sims-Knight, 2003).

In this chapter we examine the relevance of conduct problems—as one manifestation of antisocial tendencies—in juvenile sexual offending by quantitatively reviewing publicly available studies that have compared male juvenile sex offenders[1] with male juveniles who have committed offenses of a nonsexual nature. We begin with an account of several lines of research that suggest that juvenile sexual offending may be a manifestation of general antisocial tendencies. We follow with the results of a meta-analysis of 24 studies that compared juvenile sex offenders and nonsexual offenders on measures of criminal history (reflecting past conduct problems of an illegal nature) and measures of general and specific conduct problems. We conclude with a discussion of the results and suggestions for future research.

The Link between Sexual and Nonsexual Offending

Different lines of research suggest that juvenile sexual offending may be underlain by general antisocial tendencies. First, few juvenile sex offenders specialize in sexual crimes; many have also committed nonsexual offenses (see France & Hudson, 1993). Second, juvenile sex offenders are generally more likely to reoffend nonsexually than sexually (reviewed in Caldwell, 2002). Third, analyses of the criminal careers of young repeat offenders suggest that sexual assaults tend to be committed after an escalating history of nonsexual offenses (Elliott, 1994). Fourth, the variables that predict future offending among juvenile sex offenders—for example, offender age, criminal history, and antisocial personality—also predict reoffending quite well among juvenile non-sex-offenders (Caldwell, 2002; Lipsey & Derzon, 1998). Many of these variables reflect general antisocial tendencies.

From this research, we expect that juvenile sex offenders and non-sex-offenders should not differ on measures of their criminal histories and conduct problems. This expectation does not rule out unique factors such as paraphilic interests to explain some sexual offending, but it does suggest that general antisocial tendencies are important. Another possibility, however, is that a subgroup of juvenile sex offenders are particularly antisocial, reflected in the fact that they have committed particularly serious crimes (compared with, for example, stealing or possessing illegal drugs as common nonsexual crimes). If this possibility is correct, then we would expect that an undifferentiated group of juvenile sex offenders would score higher on measures of criminal history and conduct problems than a group of non-sex-offenders. A third possibility is that a subgroup of juvenile sex offenders are not generally antisocial and restrict their antisocial conduct to the sexual domain, so that an undifferentiated group of juvenile sex offenders would score lower on measures of criminal history and conduct problems than a group of non-sex-offenders. We tested these different possibilities in the meta-analysis reported in this chapter. In particular, we distinguished juveniles who sexually offend against peers or adults from those who sexually offend against children.

Adult sex offenders who target other adults (usually female) are quite similar to non-sex-offenders on measures of antisocial tendencies but are more antisocial than adult sex offenders who target children (reviewed in Lalumière, Harris, Quinsey, & Rice, 2005). Adult sex offenders who target children show more offense specialization than other groups (Hanson, Morton, & Harris, 2003; Quinsey, Rice, & Harris, 1995; Walker, 1998) and are more likely to display pedophilic interests in phallometric assessments than other sex offenders, non-sex-offenders, or nonoffenders (reviewed in Quinsey & Lalumière, 2001). One might expect a similar pattern among juvenile sex offenders distinguished according to victim age: Sex offenders against peers or adults may be similar to other juvenile offenders with regard to antisocial tendencies, whereas offenders against children may show fewer of those tendencies. Thus the magnitude of any difference in antisocial tendencies found between an undifferentiated group of juvenile sex offenders and a group of non-sex-offenders would depend on the proportion of the juvenile-sex-offender sample who had victimized children.

In sum, we expect that juvenile sex offenders will show substantial conduct problems, but it is unclear how they will compare with juveniles who have engaged in nonsexual offenses only. We expect that the magnitude of any group difference will be affected by the composition of the juvenile-sex-offender sample with regard to victim age. Because the source of information about conduct problems varies across studies, we also examined the impact of this potential moderator on the magnitude of group differences.

We now report a quantitative review of studies comparing juvenile sex offenders and non-sex-offenders on conduct problems, in terms of criminal history, school behavior problems, aggression, and other behaviors consistent with a diagnosis of conduct disorder. Many of the indicators of conduct problems are well-established risk factors for recidivism in the juvenile delinquency literature (for a recent meta-analytic review, see Cottle, Lee, & Heilbrun, 2001).

Meta-Analysis

Selection of Studies

We conducted a search of the electronic database PsycInfo and reviewed the reference lists of relevant studies, as well as the reference lists of review articles and book chapters. We selected studies that included at least one group of adjudicated (i.e., those who had appeared in court[2]) juvenile sex offenders and at least one group of adjudicated juveniles who had committed nonsexual offenses. Both groups had to be assessed in the same or equivalent setting (correctional, mental health, or community). We selected studies that had adolescent samples, which we defined as ages 12–18, so studies of children engaging in sexually aggressive behavior were not included. Some studies included younger juveniles (e.g., ages 10 and 11; Krauth, 1998) and others included older ones (e.g., age 19, Zakireh, 2000), but most participants were between the ages of 12 and 18. Studies that selected participants on the basis of characteristics other than having committed a sexual or nonsexual offense were excluded. For example, Napolitano (1996) required non-sex-offenders to have a diagnosis of conduct disorder.

Sex offenders could have a nonsexual offense in their history, but non-sex-offenders could not have any known sexual offenses. Subgroups of sex offenders or non-sex-offenders were merged for the main meta-analysis (e.g., violent and nonviolent non-sex-offenders were combined when they were reported separately). We excluded studies published before 1970, in part because older studies might include sex offenders who would no longer be considered as such under contemporary laws (e.g., Atcheson & Williams, 1954, which included youths designated as "sexual delinquents" because of promiscuity).

We restricted our search to published articles, book chapters, theses, or dissertations. Unpublished manuscripts were not included because they would not be readily available to readers, because their methods have not been scrutinized through peer or academic review, and because there was no clear a priori reason to expect a publication bias favoring a particular pattern of results. Studies had to provide sufficient information to calculate an effect size, operationalized as Cohen's d (see subsequent section). Our search led to the inclusion of 24 independent studies published between 1979 and 2003, representing a total of 1,652 juvenile sex offenders and 8,148 juvenile non-sex-offenders.

Selection of Variables

All study variables having to do with criminal history and general or specific conduct problems were included, except for variables reflecting conduct problems specifically in the sexual domain. This exclusion is not perfect because sexual items are embedded in some composite measures (e.g., "total conduct problems" has an item about forcing sex on someone). We organized all of these variables into eight categories, with three major domains: (1) Age at First Contact with the criminal justice system; (2) Extent of Criminal History, defined as the number (or presence) of charges, arrests, or convictions; and (3) Conduct Problems. The first two domains reflect the onset and extent, respectively, of conduct problems that are illegal, whereas the third domain reflects conduct problems that may or may not be illegal, with six subdomains.

The first Conduct Problems subdomain comprised general measures of delinquency, antisocial behavior, or conduct problems (e.g., Delinquent Behavior score on the Child Behavior Checklist; Achenbach, 1991). The second subdomain had to do with school behavioral problems, excluding academic achievement problems. We created this subdomain because of the many studies that reported specifically on school behavioral problems. The other four subdomains corresponded to the criteria for the DSM-IV-TR diagnosis of conduct disorder: aggression, destruction of property, deceitfulness and theft, and serious rule violations (American Psychiatric Association, 2000). Truancy is given as a specific example of serious rule violations in the DSM-IV-TR, so we placed it in this subdomain rather than in the School Behavioral Problem subdomain.

Effect Size

We used Cohen's d in this meta-analysis, which represents the standardized mean difference between groups: $(M_{JSO} - M_{NSO}) / SD_{pooled}$, where M_{JSO} represents the mean score for the juvenile-sex-offender group, M_{NSO} represents the mean score for the juvenile-non-sex-offender group, and SD_{pooled} represents the pooled standard deviation across the two groups. All d's were coded in the same direction, so that a positive score reflected greater conduct problems among juvenile sex offenders (or a younger age at first contact). A d value of $+0.50$, for example, means that juvenile sex offenders scored one half standard deviation higher than non-sex-offenders on that variable. Because d was rarely reported, we calculated it from group means and standard deviations when these were available; otherwise, we calculated d from t-test values. Chi-square statistics (corrected for continuity) were calculated for comparisons reported as percentages (e.g., proportion of offenders with prior offense histories) and then transformed into a d value. We did not include variables with insufficient information to calculate a precise d (e.g., statements about the presence or absence of a statistically significant difference without any accompanying statistics).

Each study could contribute only one effect size to each of the eight categories. When one study reported more than one variable for a given category, an average effect size for these variables was calculated and used in our meta-analysis. For example, Butler and Seto (2002) reported two variables—Total Conduct Problems and Externalizing scale score on the Youth Self-Report form—that were assigned to the category of General Conduct Problems; a weighted average effect size was calculated for these two variables (sample size sometimes varied from variable to variable within a study). All effect sizes were independent within a category, whereas individual studies could contribute effect sizes to multiple categories. Study effect sizes were weighted by sample size for all analyses so that a larger study contributed more to the mean effect size value. We used a commercially available statistical program, Comprehensive Meta-Analysis v1.0.25 (Biostat Inc., Englewood, NJ) for the calculation of average d values, 95% confidence intervals, and heterogeneity of d values (fixed effects model).

Results

The main results are reported in Tables 8.1 and 8.2. These tables show the effect size for each variable (or group of variables) by study, along with the sample size and the mean or percentage values for each variable. The lines in **bold** indicate the meta-analytic calculations for the variable category, including overall sample size, mean d, the 95% confidence intervals (CIs) for d, and the Q statistic of heterogeneity among the d values. Confidence intervals for d that include zero indicate that the two groups—juvenile sex offenders and juvenile non-sex-offenders—do not significantly differ from each other. Significant heterogeneity indicates that one or more study characteristics moderate effect sizes.

Age at First Contact

Seven studies reported age at first contact with police or the criminal justice system (see Table 8.1). One study accounted for the very large sample of non-sex-offenders (Jonson-Reid & Way, 2001). Age at first contact was early for both groups. Juvenile sex offenders were slightly older than non-sex-offenders at age of first contact, but this very small difference was not statistically significant. We obtained the same finding when we looked at the four studies that reported age at first contact based on information from official records (police, court, or correctional files).

TABLE 8.1. Age at First Contact (7 Studies) and Extent of Criminal History (16 Studies)

Study	Domain/variable	Mean or %		n		d	95% CI	Heterogeneity (Q)
		JSO	NSO	JSO	NSO			
K = 7	**Age at First Contact**			**819**	**6,318**	-0.07	-0.16 to +0.02	22.7, p < .001
K = 4	**Official Records Only**			**471**	**6,087**	-0.03	-0.13 to +0.07	13.0, p < .005
Barham (2001)	Age first offense	13.2	13.3	42	32	0.03		
Flores (2003)	Age first charge[a]	13.6	12.2	30	34	-0.72		
Hilliker (1997)	Age first arrest	12.7	11.9	289	138	-0.33		
Jacobs et al. (1997)	Age first state referral[a,b]	12.7	12.0	78	78	-0.33		
Jonson-Reid & Way (2001)	Incarcerated before 15[a]	9%	6%	304	5,778	0.05		
Lewis et al. (1979, 1981)	Age first juvenile court	11.6	12.3	17	61	0.37		
Milloy (1994)	Age first conviction[a]	13.4	13.4	59	197	0.00		
K = 16	**Criminal History**			**1,393**	**7,742**	-0.43	-0.50 to -0.36	72.8, p < .0001
K = 10	**Prior History Only**			**739**	**7,171**	-0.32	-0.40 to -0.23	38.3, p < .0001
K = 5	**Prior, Official Records Only**			**508**	**6,160**	-0.33	-0.43 to -0.23	26.9, p < .0001
Abbott (1991)	Any prior history	32%	75%	40	40	-0.88		
Barham (2001)	Number of priors	1.5	2.6	42	32	-0.51		
Butler & Seto (2002)	Number of prior charges[a]	2.8	6.8	32	81	-1.02		
Flores (2003)	Number of charges[a]	4.8	12.5	30	34	-1.35		
Ford & Linney (1995)	Any priors[a]	54%	96%	35	26	-0.93		
Hill (2000)	Number of court referrals[a]	4.4	8.6	26	110	-0.91		
Hilliker (1997)	Number of charges	7.0	11.5	289	138	-0.49		
Jacobs et al. (1997)	Number of priors[a]	12.1	17.0	78	78	-0.45		
Jonson-Reid & Way (2001)	2+ prior petitions[a]	37%	58%	304	5,778	-0.18		

Krauth (1998)	Number of juvenile referrals[a]	1.6	2.9	218	200	-0.71
Maring (1998)	Number of arrests	1.9	2.9	60	55	-0.46
Milloy (1994)	Number of prior convictions[c]	3.9	7.0	59	197	-0.61
Ness (2001)				47	90	-0.20
	% with previous . . .[c]					
	Breaking and entering	8%	23%			
	Stolen property	0%	9%			
	Unlawful driving auto	0%	12%			
	Assault and battery	8%	22%			
	Retail fraud	13%	21%			
	Larceny	8%	16%			
	Destruction of property	6%	13%			
	Home invasion	4%	13%			
	Curfew violation	4%	10%			
	Parole/probation breach	4%	9%			
	Felonious assault	6%	7%			
	Incorrigibility	8%	4%			
	Weapons	0%	6%			
	Other criminal behavior	26%	49%			
	Other status offenses	2%	8%			
Shields & Jordan (1995)	2+ prior convictions	50%	59%	52	800	-0.06
Sivley (1998)	Convicted any	26%	59%	31	34	-0.63
Zakireh (2000)	Number of prior arrests	1.7	1.9	50	49	-0.15

Note. For age at first contact *d* is reversed (positive *d* means younger age at first contact for juvenile sex offenders than for non-sex-offenders). K refers to the number of studies in each category.
[a]Information from official records.
[b]First referral to state juvenile correctional authorities.
[c]Includes only crimes with a base rate of 5% or more for one of the two groups, in order to avoid diluting any real group difference by including many crimes with very low base rates.

TABLE 8.2. Conduct Problems (15 Studies)

Study	Domain/variable	Mean or %		n		d	95% CI	Heterogeneity (Q)
		JSO	NSO	JSO	NSO			
K = 8	**General Conduct Problems**			287	289		−0.52 to −0.17	26.9, p < .0005
Awad & Saunders (1991)	Antisocial behavior	53%	88%	94	24	−0.35		
Blaske, Borduin, Henggeler, & Mann (1989)	RBPC conduct disorder	9.6	11.0	15	30	−0.54		
Butler & Seto (2002)	Total conduct problems	9.4	15.8	30	47	−0.22		
	YSR externalizing[a]	55.5	59.2	30	75	−0.66		
Etherington (1993)	K-SADS conduct disorder[a]	63.1	59.2	20	20	0.83		
Ford & Linney (1995)	Other delinquency[a]	28%	15%	35	26	0.24		
Nagel (1996)	YSR externalizing[a]	57.1	61.8	27	23	−0.36		
Ness (2001)	Delinquency	64%	93%	47	90	−0.76		
Symboluk et al. (2001)	CBCL delinquent behavior	63.0	65.1	19	15	−0.24		
K = 6	**School Behavioral Problems**			476	1,207	−0.41	−0.53 to −0.28	22.4, p < .0005
Awad & Saunders (1991)	School behavioral problems	67%	78%	94	24	−0.01		
	Kindergarten difficult	22%	25%					
Butler & Seto (2002)	YOLSI education/employment[b]	3.2	4.8	32	82	−0.90		
Ford & Linney (1995)	Ever suspended from school	71%	88%	35	26	−0.22		
	Emotional problems in class	26%	35%					
Krauth (1998)	Suspended last year	54%	83%	216	185	−0.63		
Ness (2001)	Disciplinary school problems	32%	46%	47	90	−0.24		

174

Study	Measure			n₁	n₂	d	95% CI	Q
Shields & Jordan (1995)	Poor classroom behavior[a]	39%	42%	52	800	-0.02		
	Suspended or expelled[a]	81%	84%					
K = 8	**Aggression**			429	735	-0.04	-0.17 to +0.08	42.0, p < .0001
Blaske et al. (1989)	Mom MPRI aggression	0.15	0.58	15	30	-0.32		
	Teacher MPRI aggression	-0.16	0.03					
	RBPC aggression	4.0	6.7					
Davis-Rosanbalm (2003)	Nonsexual violence[a]	5.9	4.1	43	46	0.53		
Ford & Linney (1995)	Fighting[a]	14%	19%	35	26	0.14		
	Cruelty to animals[a]	11%	0%					
Krauth (1998)	Physically aggressive	43%	73%	185	188	-0.43		
	Cruel to animals	4%	4%					
	Weapon use	16%	48%					
Milloy (1994)	Verbal threats	41%	38%	59	197	0.02		
	Assaults	25%	28%					
	Assaults (special security)	9%	6%					
	Used weapon in offense	17%	19%					
	Excessively aggressive	25%	21%					
Spaccarelli, Bowden, Coatsworth, & Kim (1997)	Serious violence[a]	38%	50%	24	186	-0.14		
Symboluk et al. (2001)	CBCL aggressive scale	61.4	60.3	19	15	0.11		
Zakireh (2000)	MASA expressive aggression	0.72	0.37	49	47	0.85		
K = 3	**Destruction of Property**			246	308	0.33	+0.16 to +0.50	1.6, p = .44
Ford & Linney (1995)	Fire setting[a]	17%	4%	35	26			

cont.

TABLE 8.2. cont.

Study	Domain/variable	Mean or %		n		d	95% CI	Heterogeneity (Q)
		JSO	NSO	JSO	NSO			
Krauth (1998)	Arson	13%	5%	164	192	0.27		
Ness (2001)	Fire setting	13%	0%	47	90	0.54		
K = 2	**Deceitfulness and Theft**			216	222	−0.78	−0.97 to −0.59	17.6, p < .0001
Ford & Linney (1995)	Stealing[a]	14%	4%	35	26	0.23		
Krauth (1998)	Theft	25%	68%	181	196	−0.94		
K = 5	**Serious Rule Violations**			386	540	−0.34	−0.48 to −0.21	16.7, p < .005
Etherington (1993)	MAPI attendance[a]	57.4	48.2	20	20	0.49		
Krauth (1998)	Truancy	25%	63%	200	178	−0.60		
	Running away	12%	32%					
Maring (1998)	MAPI attendance[a]	52.6	54.6	60	55	−0.10		
Milloy (1994)	Previous escape from custody	14%	21%	59	197	−0.14		
Ness (2001)	Truancy	26%	46%	47	90	−0.35		
	Running away	11%	27%					

Note. CBCL, Child Behavior Checklist; K-SADS, Kiddie Schedule of Affective Disorders and Schizophrenia; MASA, Multidimensional Assessment of Sex and Aggression; MAPI, Millon Adolescent Personality Inventory; MPRI, Missouri Peer Relations Inventory; RBPC, Revised Behavior Problem Checklist; YOLSI, Young Offender Level of Supervision Inventory; YSR, Youth Self-Report Form. K refers to the number of studies in each category.
[a]Based on self-report.
[b]Six of 10 items pertain to school behavioral problems.

Effect sizes were heterogeneous for both the overall and official record comparisons, suggesting the presence of one or more additional moderator variables.

Extent of Criminal History

Sixteen studies reported information regarding the number or presence of charges, arrests, or convictions (see Table 8.1). Both groups had extensive criminal histories, but every single study found that juvenile sex offenders had less extensive criminal histories than non-sex-offenders. It is worth noting that this consistent finding was obtained despite the fact that non-sex-offenders were constrained in their offense history because they could not have committed sexual offenses (which would have resulted in their assignment to the juvenile-sex-offender group), whereas sex offenders could also have committed nonsexual offenses. Four studies specifically examined nonsexual offense histories, with similar results (Flores, 2003; Hilliker, 1997; Ness, 2001; Zakireh, 2000).

The mean effect size for criminal history was statistically significant and moderate in size (see Cohen, 1992). A similar result was observed when we examined the 10 studies that provided information on prior offenses only or the 5 studies that provided information on prior offenses only and relied on official records. The effect sizes were heterogeneous in all of these comparisons.

Conduct Problems

Fifteen studies reported at least one variable for one of the six Conduct Problems subdomains (see Table 8.2). Eight studies were included in the subdomain General Conduct Problems. Both groups scored fairly high on these variables, but six of the eight studies found that juvenile non-sex-offenders had higher scores. The overall effect size was negative, statistically significant, and small to moderate, again with significant heterogeneity.

All six studies reporting on School Behavioral Problems found that juvenile non-sex-offenders had more problems, with an average effect size that was negative, statistically significant, heterogeneous, and moderate in size. However, both groups showed extensive school behavioral problems (e.g., the proportions who were suspended or expelled from school).

In the following section we examine the four subdomains that correspond to the components of the DSM-IV-TR diagnosis of conduct disorder. The overall effect size in the Aggression subdomain (eight studies) was very small (near zero), negative, heterogeneous, and not statistically significant.

All three studies that contributed to the subdomain Destruction of Property reported on fire setting. The result of this comparison differed from the results of all of the other comparisons: About a sixth of the juvenile sex offenders who were studied had engaged in fire setting or arson, a proportion that was significantly higher than for juvenile non-sex-offenders; the average effect size was small and homogeneous.

There were only two studies in the subdomain Deceitfulness and Theft; both of them reported on stealing. The overall effect size was negative, statistically significant, heterogeneous, and large. Finally, there were five studies in the subdomain Serious Rule Violations. More problems were noted among juvenile non-sex-offenders, with a small to moderate negative effect size that was statistically significant and heterogeneous.

Source of Conduct Problems Data

All but one category of effect sizes were heterogeneous in the domain of Conduct Problems, but there were too few studies within each category to look for factors to explain this variability. Therefore, we combined all the variables in this domain and examined the impact of the source of information on the magnitude of the group difference. Some variables were based on the offenders' self-reports only, whereas others were based on reports from collaterals (e.g., parents, teachers, clinicians). We calculated, for each study, an average (weighted) effect size for all variables based on self-report only and an average (weighted) effect size for all variables based on other sources of information. Only two studies (Butler & Seto, 2002; Ford & Linney, 1995) produced an average effect for both self-report and other sources of information.

Nine studies had variables based solely on self-report, for an average weighted effect size of 0.11 (95% CI = −0.02 to 0.25, Q = 30.3, p < .0005), suggesting that juvenile sex offenders tended to have *more* conduct problems than non-sex-offenders, with significant heterogeneity. Eight studies had variables that were based on sources other than self-report. The weighted average of these nine effect sizes was −0.35 (95% CI = −0.48 to −0.22, Q = 17.6, p < .05), suggesting that juvenile sex offenders had significantly fewer conduct problems than juvenile non-sex-offenders, with some heterogeneity in effect sizes. The difference between these two effect sizes was significant, suggesting that source of information is an important moderator of effect sizes. The only two studies that used both self-report and other sources of information (albeit on different variables) obtained the same pattern of results: The group difference was larger and negative when data were obtained from sources other than self-report (Butler & Seto, 2002; Ford & Linney, 1995).

Victim Age

We next examined whether the magnitude of the group difference was related to the proportion of juveniles who victimized at least one child (these sex offenders against children could have peer or adult victims as well) in the sex-offender samples.[3] For this analysis we calculated an average study effect size for all variables (in all three domains) reported in each study.[4] Nine studies reported sufficient information for us to calculate the exact proportion of juvenile sex offenders who had any child victims: Awad and Saunders (1991), Butler and Seto (2002), Davis-Rosanbalm (2003), Flores (2003), Ford and Linney (1995), Krauth (1998), Lewis, Shanok, and Pincus (1979, 1981), Nagel (1996), and Zakireh (2000).

The correlation between the proportion of the juvenile-sex-offender sample that targeted a child victim and the average d, statistically controlling for total sample size, was r (6) = −.61 (p = .11),[5] indicating that samples with a greater proportion of juvenile sex offenders against children had fewer conduct problems, relative to the comparison samples of juvenile non-sex-offenders, than samples with a lower proportion.

We also classified studies into those in which *less* than 50% of the sex-offender sample had a child victim (n = 3) and those in which *50% or more* of the sex-offender sample had a child victim (n = 7). A tenth study could be included in this analysis (Symboluk, Cummings, & Leschied, 2001[6]). Consistent with the results of the correlational analysis, studies in which less than 50% of the sex-offender sample had a child victim produced significantly higher effect sizes (weighted mean d = +0.17, 95% CI = −0.10 to +0.43) than studies in which 50% or more had a child victim (weighted mean d = −0.41, 95% CI = −0.55 to −0.27). This result suggests that juvenile-sex-offender samples with a majority of offenders against peers or adults were similar to non-sex-offenders in the extent of their conduct problems, whereas juvenile-sex-offender samples with a majority of offenders against children had fewer conduct problems.

To pursue this question further, we examined seven studies that explicitly compared juvenile sex offenders against peers or adults and those against younger children on the same conduct problem variables. Three of these studies were part of our meta-analysis (Awad & Saunders, 1991; Ford & Linney, 1995; Krauth, 1998); the other four studies were not included in the main meta-analysis because they did not include a group of juvenile non-sex-offenders (Hsu & Starzynski, 1990; Jacobs, 1999; Kavoussi, Kaplan, & Becker, 1988; Way, 2000).[7] We calculated an effect size for each study, averaging over all conduct problem variables (across all three domains). Consistent with the results reported earlier, juvenile sex offenders against peers or adults tended to have more conduct problems than those who offended against children, although this difference was not statistically significant, $d = 0.12$ (95% CI = −0.04 to +0.29, $Q = 3.4$, ns). The same pattern was found when we focused only on the variables that were not based on self-report (K = 5): $d = 0.17$ (95% CI = −0.01 to +0.36, $Q = 4.3$, ns).

Publication Bias

Finally, to examine the possibility of a publication bias, we prepared a funnel graph showing the average effect size for each of the 24 studies comparing juvenile sex offenders and juvenile non-sex-offenders (one average effect size per study, based on all variables) as a function of the log transformed total sample size. If there is no publication bias toward statistically significant results, then the funnel graph should show greater variation in effect sizes around the overall mean effect size at small sample sizes than at large sample sizes and should be symmetrical around the overall mean across all sample sizes. Figure 8.1 shows a fairly symmetrical funnel narrowing at higher sample size values, suggesting there was no publication bias in the studies we examined.

To further examine the possibility of publication bias, we compared studies published in peer-reviewed journals with those that were reported in government publications, theses, or dissertations. Again, each study produced a single average effect size for this analysis, collapsed across the eight categories of conduct problem variables. The nine peer-reviewed studies produced an average effect size ($d = -0.13$, 95% CI = −0.23 to −0.04) that was smaller than the average effect size produced by the 15 studies that were not peer reviewed ($d = -0.31$, 95% CI = −0.39 to −0.22). Both types of studies, however, produced statistically significant negative effect sizes.

Summary and Conclusions

We found in this quantitative review that juvenile sex offenders had substantial histories of criminal and other conduct problems but, nonetheless, generally scored lower in these conduct problems than their nonsexually offending counterparts. Juvenile-sex-offenders had their first official contact with the criminal justice system at around the ages of 12 or 13 and did not significantly differ in this domain from non-sex-offenders; this might reflect a floor effect, because of the age at which criminal responsibility begins in most legal jurisdictions. Many of the juvenile sex offenders had prior offense histories, with a quarter to half

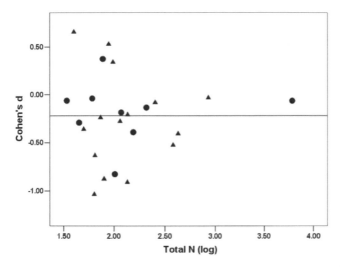

FIGURE 8.1. Funnel graph on the relation between the size of the group difference (*d*) and sample size. Each circle represents a peer-reviewed study, whereas each triangle represents a non-peer-reviewed study. The horizontal line represents the overall average.

having any prior offenses, but as a group they had a less extensive criminal history than juvenile non-sex-offenders. Finally, many juvenile sex offenders showed evidence of conduct problems, but juvenile non-sex-offenders had even more conduct problems (with one exception). Interestingly, the only published comparison of female juvenile sex offenders and non-sex-offenders we could locate (not included in this meta-analysis) found the same pattern of results with regard to criminal history, school behavioral problems, and fighting (Kubik, Hecker, & Righthand, 2002).

Interestingly, the general pattern observed in this meta-analysis obscured a difference between juvenile sex offenders who target peers or adults and those who target children. We found that samples that contained more sex offenders who target children had fewer conduct problems relative to non-sex-offenders. Unfortunately, only a small number of studies directly compared these sex-offender subgroups on measures of conduct problems; these studies found that those who offended against children showed a nonsignificant tendency to have fewer conduct problems than those who offended against peers or adults. At the beginning of the chapter we mentioned the possibility that there might be subgroups of juvenile sex offenders who show few conduct problems and restrict their antisocial conduct to the sexual domain; the preliminary results presented here are consistent with this possibility and suggest that juvenile sex offenders who target children may be such a group. Perhaps, as Becker (1988) suggested, these offenders have a pedophilic interest that motivates their behavior (for phallometric evidence that some adolescent sex offenders against children show pedophilic interest, see Seto, Lalumière, & Blanchard, 2000). We hope these results will encourage investigators to record and examine the gender and age of victims when studying juvenile sex offenders, as is typically done with adult sex offenders.

There was one intriguing exception to the general pattern of results we observed: Juvenile sex offenders were significantly more, rather than less, likely to have histories of setting fires than non-sex-offenders. Moreover, the two studies that directly compared juvenile sex offenders according to victim age found that those who targeted children were more likely to engage in fire setting than those who targeted peers or adults (Ford & Linney, 1995; Krauth, 1998). This exception to the general pattern of fewer or less severe conduct problems among juvenile sex offenders, and fewer still among sex offenders against children, is puzzling, especially in light of evidence that fire setting is positively correlated with other conduct problems among juveniles (e.g., Forehand, Wierson, Frame, Kempton, & Armistead, 1991; Kolko, Kazdin, & Meyer, 1985; Martin, Bergen, Richardson, Roeger, & Allison, 2004).

One possible explanation, albeit a very speculative one, is that fire setting is an expression of an atypical sexual interest. A reanalysis of data originally reported by Quinsey, Chaplin, and Upfold (1989) found that adult fire setters significantly differed from adult non-fire-setters in sexual arousal elicited by stories describing the setting and watching of fires (Harris, Rice, Quinsey, Chaplin, & Earls, 1992). Case reports of individuals with sexual arousal to fires have also been published (e.g., Bourget & Bradford, 1987). If there is a link between fire setting and atypical sexual interests, and given the co-occurrence of paraphilic interests found in clinical samples of adult sex offenders (e.g., Freund, Seto, & Kuban, 1997), we might expect paraphilic individuals (e.g., pedophiles) to be more likely than nonparaphilic individuals to engage in fire setting. We are not aware of any studies addressing this question. Other possible explanations for the relationship between juvenile sexual offending and fire setting involve potential common factors such as lower intelligence, neurodevelopmental problems, or assertiveness deficits (Chen, Arria, & Anthony, 2003; Jacobs, Kennedy, & Meyer, 1997; Katz, 1990; Rice & Harris, 1991).

The source of data in the Conduct Problems domain was related to the magnitude of group differences in a curious way: Juvenile sex offenders scored significantly lower than non-sex-offenders when the data were obtained from parents, teachers, or clinicians, but they scored (nonsignificantly) higher when the data were obtained from the offenders themselves. There are three possible explanations for this finding: (1) juvenile sex offenders do in fact have as many conduct problems as non-sex-offenders, but they are better able to avoid detection; (2) juvenile sex offenders overreport conduct problems, perhaps as a result of the emphasis on disclosure in many juvenile-sex-offender treatment programs; or (3) juvenile non-sex-offenders underreport conduct problems, reflecting their greater antisocial tendencies (which could include lying and impression management). We believe the third explanation is the most plausible, but we are not aware of studies that allow us to examine this issue more closely.

There are several limitations or caveats to keep in mind when interpreting the results of this meta-analysis. First, it is possible that there is ascertainment bias such that juvenile sex offenders are more likely to be referred for treatment or placed in custody than juvenile non-sex-offenders, simply because their misconduct was sexual in nature, whereas only the most conduct-disordered non-sex-offenders are admitted to a clinical or correctional setting. This would result in a significant difference in conduct problems, even when examining data collected at the same setting for both groups. Second, it is possible that unpublished studies tend not to find a significant difference between juvenile sex offenders and non-sex-offenders, so that our results are biased because we included only published studies. The funnel graph suggested no publication bias in the studies we did include, but studies published in peer-reviewed journals produced smaller effect sizes than studies reported in government publications, theses, or dissertations. The significant group difference was obtained, however, in both types of studies. Finally, because of space limitations, we did not quantitatively review other variables indicative of antisociality, such as antisocial personality traits, antisocial attitudes and beliefs, and associations with delinquent peers. We would predict, based on the results presented here, that juvenile sex offenders would score lower than non-sex-offenders on these variables and that sex offenders against children would score lower than sex offenders against peers or adults.

Despite these limitations and caveats, we believe the results of this quantitative review are informative. The high prevalence of conduct problems among juvenile sex offenders suggests that current developmental models of juvenile delinquency (e.g., Quinsey et al., 2004) must have relevance in explaining juvenile sexual offending. After all, sexual offending is an antisocial behavior. At the same time, juvenile sex offenders scored lower in conduct problems than non-sex-offenders, suggesting that juvenile sex offenders are in fact different in some respects and that juvenile sexual offending may have unique causes. Comparing juvenile sex offenders and non-sex-offenders on variables pertaining to putative specific causes of sexual offending (especially variables assessing atypical sexual interests) would greatly inform theory development, assessment, and treatment.

Notes

1. Our focus is on male sex offenders who have committed offenses involving physical contact with a victim, although some of the studies we examine in our meta-analysis included juveniles who committed offenses such as indecent exposure. We did not examine studies of juveniles who committed offenses that did not directly involve a victim, such as possession of illegal pornography or prostitution. Males commit the large majority of sexual offenses, and there are few studies of female offenders, whether juvenile or adult.
2. The one exception was Ness (2001), in which both juvenile sex offenders and non-sex-offenders were referred to a residential treatment center by the courts or by social service agencies; the proportion referred by the courts was not reported.
3. In the studies we examined for this analysis, child victims were defined as 3 to 6 years younger than the offender. Victims who were closer in age or older than the offender were categorized as "peers or adults." Ideally, one would want to categorize child versus peer/adult victims based on their pubertal status (see Seto, 2002).
4. There was no association between the number of variables in each study and the size of the group difference.
5. The proportion of offenders against children and the total sample size were log transformed because the distributions were not normal. The corresponding correlation for untransformed data was −.59.
6. We could infer that the proportion in Symboluk et al. (2001) was either 95% or 100%.
7. The maximum age of the child victims was 11 years old with no minimum age difference in Hsu and Starzynski (1990); at least 4 years younger than the offender in Jacobs (1999); 10 years old in Kavoussi et al. (1988); and 12 years old with a minimum age difference of 3 years in Way (2000).

References

Asterisks indicate references that provided data for the main meta-analysis.

Abbott, B. R. (1991). Family dynamics, intergenerational patterns of negative events and trauma, and patterns of offending behavior: A comparison of adolescent sexual offenders and delinquent adolescents and their parents. *Dissertation Abstracts International, 51*(8-B), 4037. (UMI No. 9029096)*

Achenbach, T. M. (1991). *Integrative guide for the 1991 CBCL/4-18, YSR, and TRF profiles.* Burlington: University of Vermont, Department of Psychiatry.

American Psychiatric Association. (2000). *Diagnostic and statistical manual of mental disorders* (4th ed., text rev.). Washington, DC: Author.

Atcheson, J. D., & Williams, D. C. (1954). A study of juvenile sex offenders. *American Journal of Psychiatry, 111,* 366–370.

Awad, G. A., & Saunders, E. B. (1991). Male adolescent sexual assaulters: Clinical observations. *Journal of Interpersonal Violence, 6,* 446–460.*

Barham, M. D. (2001). A comparison of juvenile sexual offenders, dual offenders, and nonsexual offenders on heterosocial skills, social self-efficacy, psychopathy, impulsivity, and attitudes toward sexual abuse. *Dissertation Abstracts International, 61*(7-B), 3829. (UMI No. 9979892)*

Becker J. V. (1988). Adolescent sex offenders. *Behavior Therapist, 11,* 185–187.

Blaske, D. M., Borduin, C. M., Henggeler, S. W., & Mann, B. J. (1989). Individual, family, and peer characteristics of adolescent sex offenders and assaultive offenders. *Developmental Psychology, 25,* 846–855.*

Bourget, D., & Bradford, J. (1987). Fire fetishism, diagnostic and clinical implications: A review of two cases. *Canadian Journal of Psychiatry, 32,* 459–462.

Butler, S. M., & Seto, M. C. (2002). Distinguishing two types of juvenile sex offenders. *Journal of the American Academy of Child and Adolescent Psychiatry, 41,* 83–90.*

Caldwell, M. F. (2002). What we do not know about juvenile sexual reoffense risk. *Child Maltreatment, 7,* 291–302.

Chen, Y.-H., Arria, A. M., & Anthony, J. C. (2003). Firesetting in adolescence and being aggressive, shy, and rejected by peers: New epidemiologic evidence from a national sample survey. *Journal of the American Academy of Psychiatry and the Law, 31,* 44–52.

Cohen, J. (1992). A power primer. *Psychological Bulletin, 112,* 155–159.

Cottle, C. C., Lee, R. J., & Heilbrun, K. (2001). The prediction of criminal recidivism in juveniles: A meta-analysis. *Criminal Justice and Behavior, 28,* 367–394.

Davis-Rosanbalm, M. K. (2003). A comparison of social information processing in juvenile sexual offenders and violent nonsexual offenders. *Dissertation Abstracts International, 64*(4-B), 1897. (UMI No. 3086328)*

Elliott, D. S. (1994). Serious violent offenders: Onset, developmental course and termination. *Criminology, 32,* 1–22.

Etherington, R. (1993). Diagnostic and personality differences of juvenile sex offenders, non-sex-offenders, and non-offenders. *Dissertation Abstracts International, 54*(4-B), 2195. (UMI No. 9324334)*

Flores, G. T. (2003). Empathy, cognitive distortions, and delinquent behaviors in adolescent male violent sex offenders and non-sex-offenders. *Dissertation Abstracts International, 63*(8-B), 3912. (UMI No. 3062287)*

Ford, M. E., & Linney, J. A. (1995). Comparative analysis of juvenile sexual offenders, violent nonsexual offenders, and status offenders. *Journal of Interpersonal Violence, 10,* 56–70.[*]

Forehand, R., Wierson, M., Frame, C. L., Kempton, T., & Armistead, L. (1991). Juvenile firesetting: A unique syndrome or an advanced level of antisocial behavior? *Behaviour Research and Therapy, 29,* 125–128.

France, K. G., & Hudson, S. M. (1993). The conduct disorders and the juvenile sex offender. In H. E. Barbaree, W. L. Marshall, & S. M. Hudson (Eds.), *The juvenile sex offender* (pp. 225–234). New York: Guilford Press.

Freund, K., Seto, M. C., & Kuban, M. (1997). Frotteurism and the theory of courtship disorder. In D. R. Laws & W. T. O'Donohue (Eds.), *Sexual deviance: Theory, assessment and treatment* (pp. 111–130). New York: Guilford Press.

Hanson, R. K., Morton, K. E., & Harris, A. J. R. (2003). Sexual offender recidivism risk: What we know and what we need to know. *Annals of the New York Academy of Sciences, 989,* 154–166.

Harris, G. T., Rice, M. E., Quinsey, V. L., Chaplin, T. C., & Earls, C. (1992). Maximizing the discriminant validity of phallometric assessment data. *Psychological Assessment, 4,* 502–511.

Hill, R. A. (2000). A discriminant analysis between adolescent sexual offenders and nonsexual offenders. *Dissertation Abstracts International, 60*(12-A), 4332. (UMI No. 9953865)[*]

Hilliker, D. R. (1997). The relationship between childhood sexual abuse and juvenile sexual offending: Victim to victimizer. *Dissertation Abstracts International, 58*(5-B), 2678. (UMI No. 9731636)[*]

Hsu, L. K. G., & Starzynski, J. (1990). Adolescent rapists and adolescent child sexual assaulters. *International Journal of Offender Therapy and Comparative Criminology, 34,* 23–30.

Hunter, J. A., Figueredo, A. J., Malamuth, N. M., & Becker, J. V. (2003). Juvenile sex offenders: Toward the development of a typology. *Sexual Abuse: Journal of Research and Treatment, 15,* 27–48.

Jacobs, W. L., Kennedy, W. A., & Meyer, J. B. (1997). Juvenile delinquents: A between-group comparison study of sexual and nonsexual offenders. *Sexual Abuse: Journal of Research and Treatment, 9,* 201–217.[*]

Johnson, G. M., & Knight, R. A. (2000). Developmental antecedents of sexual coercion in juvenile sexual offenders. *Sexual Abuse: Journal of Research and Treatment, 12,* 165–178.

Jonson-Reid, M., & Way, I. (2001). Adolescent sexual offenders: Incidence of childhood maltreatment, serious emotional disturbance, and prior offenses. *American Journal of Orthopsychiatry, 71,* 120–130.[*]

Katz, R. C. (1990). Psychosocial adjustment in adolescent child molesters. *Child Abuse and Neglect, 14,* 567–575.

Kavoussi, R. J., Kaplan, M., & Becker, J. V. (1988). Psychiatric diagnoses in adolescent sex offenders. *Journal of the American Academy of Child and Adolescent Psychiatry, 27,* 241–243.

Knight, R. A., & Sims-Knight, J. E. (2003). The developmental antecedents of sexual coercion against women: Testing alternative hypotheses with structural equation modeling. *Annals of the New York Academy of Sciences, 989*, 72–85.

Kolko, D. J., Kazdin, A. E., & Meyer, E. C. (1985). Aggression and psychopathology in childhood firesetters: Parent and child reports. *Journal of Consulting and Clinical Psychology, 53*, 377–385.

Krauth, A. A. (1998). A comparative study of male juvenile sex offenders. *Dissertation Abstracts International, 58*(8-B), 4455. (UMI No. 0598312)[*]

Kubik, E. K., Hecker, J. E., & Righthand, S. (2002). Adolescent females who have sexually offended: Comparisons with delinquent adolescent female offenders and adolescent males who sexually offend. *Journal of Child Sexual Abuse, 11*, 63–83.

Lalumière, M. L., Harris, G. H., Quinsey, V. L., & Rice, M. E. (2005). *The causes of rape: Understanding individual differences in male propensity for sexual aggression.* Washington, DC: American Psychological Association.

Lewis, D. O., Shanok, S. S., & Pincus, J. H. (1979). Juvenile male sexual assaulters. *American Journal of Psychiatry, 136*, 1194–1196.[*]

Lewis, D. O., Shanok, S. S., & Pincus, J. H. (1981). Juvenile male sexual assaulters: Psychiatric, neurological, psychoeducational, and abuse factors. In D. O. Lewis (Ed.), *Vulnerabilities to delinquency* (pp. 89–105). New York: SP Medical and Scientific.[*]

Lipsey, M. W., & Derzon, J. H. (1998). Predictors of violent or serious delinquency in adolescence and early adulthood: A synthesis of longitudinal research. In R. Loeber & D. P. Farrington (Eds.), *Serious and violent juvenile offenders: Risk factors and successful interventions* (pp. 86–105). Thousand Oaks, CA: Sage.

Maring, J. E. (1998). Using the Millon Adolescent Personality Inventory to differentiate sexually offending from nonsexually offending conduct-disordered adolescents. *Dissertation Abstracts International, 59*(2-B), 0879. (UMI No. 9824364)[*]

Martin, G., Bergen, H. A., Richardson, A. S., Roeger, L., & Allison, S. (2004). Correlates of firesetting in a community sample of young adolescents. *Australian and New Zealand Journal of Psychiatry, 38*, 148–154.

Milloy, C. D. (1994, June). *A comparative study of juvenile sex and non-sex-offenders.* Olympia: Washington State Institute for Public Policy.[*]

Nagel, H. E. (1996). A comparison of adolescent sexual offenders and nonsexually offending juvenile delinquents on familial, sexual and social variables. *Masters Abstract International, 35*(01), 348. (UMI No. 1381034)[*]

Napolitano, S. A. (1996). *Depression, cognitive characteristics, and social functioning in adolescent sex offenders and conduct disordered adolescents in residential treatment.* Unpublished doctoral dissertation, University of Texas–Austin.

Ness, C. M. (2001). Emotional expressiveness and problematic behaviors among male juvenile sexual offenders, general offenders, and nonoffenders. *Dissertation Abstracts International, 61*(9-B), 4966. (UMI No. 9988432)[*]

Quinsey, V. L., Chaplin, T. C., & Upfold, D. (1989). Arsonists and sexual arousal to fire setting: Correlation unsupported. *Journal of Behavior Therapy and Experimental Psychiatry, 20,* 203–209.

Quinsey, V. L., & Lalumière, M. L. (2001). *Assessment of sex offenders against children* (2nd ed.). Thousand Oaks, CA: Sage.

Quinsey, V. L., Rice, M. E., & Harris, G. T. (1995). Actuarial prediction of sexual recidivism. *Journal of Interpersonal Violence, 10,* 85–105.

Quinsey, V. L., Skilling, T. S., Lalumière, M. L., & Craig, W. M. (2004). *Juvenile delinquency: Understanding the origins of individual differences.* Washington, DC: American Psychological Association.

Rice, M. E., & Harris, G. T. (1991). Firesetters admitted to a maximum security psychiatric institution: Characteristics of offenders and offenses. *Journal of Interpersonal Violence, 6,* 461–475.

Seto, M. C. (2002). Precisely defining pedophilia. *Archives of Sexual Behavior, 31,* 498–499.

Seto, M. C., Lalumière, M. L., & Blanchard, R. (2000). The discriminative validity of a phallometric test for pedophilic interests among adolescent offenders against children. *Psychological Assessment, 12,* 319–327.

Shields, I. W., & Jordan, S. A. (1995). Young sex offenders: A comparison with a control group of non-sex offenders. *Forum on Corrections Research, 7,* 56–58.[*]

Sivley, J. O. (1998). A comparison of personality characteristics between juvenile sex offenders and delinquent non-sex offending adolescents. *Dissertation Abstracts International, 58*(11-B), 6247. (UMI No. 9813993)[*]

Spaccarelli, S., Bowden, B., Coatsworth, J. D., & Kim, S. (1997). Psychosocial correlates of male sexual aggression in a chronic delinquent sample. *Criminal Justice and Behavior, 24,* 71–95.[*]

Symboluk, A., Cummings, A. L., & Leschied, A. W. (2001). Family, social and personal variables in adolescent sex offenders. *Irish Journal of Psychology, 22,* 198–212.[*]

Walker, W. D. (1998). Patterns in sexual offending. *Dissertation Abstracts International, 58*(9-B), 5147. (UMI No. NQ20594)

Way, I. F. (2000). Adolescent sexual offenders: The role of cognitive and emotional victim empathy in the victim-to-victimizer process. *Dissertation Abstracts International, 61*(1-A), 367. (UMI No. 9959970)

Zakireh, B. (2000). Residential and outpatient adolescent sexual and nonsexual offenders: History, sexual adjustment, clinical, cognitive, and demographic characteristics. *Dissertation Abstracts International, 61*(2-B), 1102. (UMI No. 9962106)[*]

CHAPTER 9

Assessment and Treatment of Criminogenic Needs

Gary O'Reilly
Alan Carr

In this chapter we consider the assessment and treatment of criminogenic factors in young people who engage in sexually abusive behavior. Evidence from the theoretical and research literature will be used to highlight the extent of this problem and the significant role played by a coercive style of family interaction in its etiology. We put forward our view that a useful approach to tackling nonsexual criminal and antisocial behavior among juvenile sexual offenders involves referring to the "what works" literature concerning young people who present with conduct disorder. Consistent with ideas presenting an etiological role for dysfunctional family interaction in sexual and nonsexual criminal and antisocial behavior, the what-works literature provides an evidence base that points to a continuum of therapeutic response ranging from parental behavioral training to functional family therapy, multisystemic therapy, and special foster-care placement. We conclude the chapter by illustrating a functional family therapy approach to assessing, formulating, and intervening with a young person whose sexually abusive behavior is part of more general criminal and antisocial activities, with reference to a case example.

Insights from the Theoretical Literature

In recent years a number of theoretical models have appeared in the literature that aim to describe the development of sexually abusive behavior (O'Reilly & Carr, 2004a). Although much of this literature is concerned with adults, it has relevance for juveniles who sexually abuse. A common feature of many theoretical models is that they either incorporate as a central component the development of aspects of individual psychological functioning that promote criminal behavior or, alternatively, they divide sexual offenders into typologies, one of which usually represents a group whose sexual offending is part of a broader pattern of more general antisocial and criminal behavior. In this section we briefly outline relevant aspects of some of these theoretical models as they inform the clinical assessment and treatment of criminogenic needs in juvenile sexual offenders.

The Marshall and Barbaree Model

A highly influential model that fundamentally incorporates the development of criminal and antisocial behavior with the emergence of sexual offending is that of Marshall and Barbaree (Barbaree, Marshall, & McCormick, 1998; Marshall & Barbaree, 1990). In their model they trace the individual origins of sexual offending to key experiences in early childhood. Marshall and Barbaree propose that a developmental pathway that has the potential to culminate in sexual offending begins with relationships with attachment figures (usually parents) that are of a significantly poorer quality than those experienced by most people, usually reflecting abusive, neglectful, or nonnurturing home environments. In these circumstances although parents may be physically present, they are frequently emotionally unavailable, often due to substance abuse or other personal difficulties. A young child in this type of home environment may seek parental attention through disruptive and demanding behavior. When parents respond to the child's disruptive behavior with an aggressive, coercive, and manipulative parenting style, the child experiences a model of parental behavior that promotes aggression, coercion, and manipulation while severely limiting the child's experience with positive interpersonal skills. The next significant step in the Marshall and Barbaree model occurs when a child whose developmental experiences were predominantly as characterized previously begins to attend school. Such a child is unlikely to successfully manage the many opportunities for prosocial development offered by the school environment. Instead of developing good relationships with peers and teachers, a child whose interpersonal style is predominantly aggressive, coercive, and manipulative is unlikely to form stable and satisfying relationships. Consequently, the developmental benefits offered by the successful formation of relationships outside of school do not accrue to the child. Instead, he or she develops a negative self-image and a lack of self-confidence and is further blocked in his or her potential for interpersonal development. Marshall and Barbaree regard the intermediate childhood outcome of this developmental trajectory as culminating in a "syndrome of social disability" that has five defining features. These are (1) an inability to establish and maintain intimate relationships, (2) low self-esteem, (3) diverse antisocial, criminal attitudes and behaviors, (4) a lack of empathic skill, and (5) cognitive distortions that support and justify criminal behavior. From this point Marshall and Barbaree's model continues by describing the emergence and consolidation of sexually abusive behavior in adolescence and adulthood. However, from the point of view of this chapter, it is significant to note that according to the Marshall and Barbaree model, the developmental pathway that leads to sexually abusive behavior is described as one that fundamentally promotes antisocial criminal attitudes and behaviors. This clearly provides a theoretical rationale that suggests that key aspects of assessment and intervention with young people who sexually offend ought to be concerned with understanding and suitably intervening to tackle any aspects of individual or family functioning that promote more general criminal and antisocial behavior.

The Ward and Siegart Model

Further theoretical support for the need to assess and intervene with more general problems of antisocial and criminal behavior in young people who sexually offend comes from Ward and Siegart (2002). They offer a model of sexual offending that attempts to integrate what they regard as the best elements of other key models that have appeared in the literature. In doing so, they draw on the work of Marshall and Barbaree (1990), Finkelhor (1984), and Hall and Hirschman (Hall, 1996; Hall & Hirschman, 1991, 1992). In essence, Ward and Siegart's integrative model outlines five distinct developmental pathways that may lead to sexual offending. These are (1) an intimacy-and-social-skills-deficit pathway; (2) a deviant-sexual-script pathway (in which sexual behavior is erroneously equated with the expression of interpersonal closeness); (3) an emotional-dysregulation pathway; (4) an antisocial-cognitions pathway; and (5) a multiple-dysfunctional-mechanisms (pedophilic) pathway. Of these five developmental routes to sexual offending, the antisocial-cognitions pathway has the greatest relevance to our discussion.

Unfortunately, Ward and Siegart (2000) are vague on the developmental experiences of those whose development is characterized by the antisocial-cognitions pathway, but they do describe them in the following terms. Their sexually abusive behavior is part of a wider pattern of more general criminal behavior that includes substance abuse, theft, and violent assault. They commonly have impulse-control difficulties and frequently engage in behaviors that are consistent with a diagnosis of conduct disorder from early childhood. As their sexually abusive behavior is part of more general criminal behavior that often has a childhood onset, sexual offending for those on pathway 4 may begin at a relatively early age. Consequently, this group of offenders may be overrepresented among adolescents who sexually abuse. This theoretical model implies the clinical connotation that, unless those aspects of current psychological functioning that are supportive of more general criminality are tackled for juveniles on pathway 4, we can expect that interventions that are exclusively sexual offense specific will be less successful.

The Becker and Kaplan Model

A final theoretical speculation that provides a useful insight into the importance of more general criminality among adolescents who sexually offend is that offered by Becker and Kaplan (1988). They suggest that there are three post-offense pathways that a young person may follow. The first is termed a "dead-end pathway," in which the young person's sexual offending comes to a dead end and consequently discontinues. Its cessation may be reflective of the experience of negative consequences that have followed from the offense or perhaps the positive impact of intervention. The second pathway identified by Becker and Kaplan is a "deviant sexual interest pathway," in which the young person perpetrates additional sexual offences, consolidating a paraphilic pattern of sexual arousal. They suggest that the following factors may be instrumental in promoting young people's development in this direction: (1) they may have found their sexual offending to be very pleasurable; (2) they may have experienced minimal consequences in response to their offending; (3) they may reinforce their sexually abusive behavior through fantasy and masturbation; (4) they continue to have deficits in their ability to relate to age-appropriate peers. The third post-offense pathway described by Becker and Kaplan (1988) is a "delinquency pathway." Here the young person continues to engage in sexually abusive behavior as part of a continued and broader pattern of engagement in other nonsexual crimes and antisocial behavior.

Implications of Theoretical Models

Apart from illustrating the fondness of theorists for using analogies about pathways, these three models highlight four important features of criminogenic and antisocial behavior among young people who sexually abuse. These are: (1) sexual and nonsexual offending behavior share at least some common developmental features; (2) young people who sexually abuse may be thought of as a heterogeneous population, some but not all of whom have substantial difficulties with more general criminal and antisocial behavior; (3) the child and adolescent psychiatric diagnostic category of conduct disorder may provide a valuable construct that allows us to organize ideas that are useful and effective in tackling criminogenic and antisocial behavior problems in young people who also engage in sexually abusive behavior; (4) post-sexual-offense development should be considered in terms of potential for both sexual and nonsexual recidivism. In the next section we review some recent research literature that highlights pertinent information that adds to our understanding of criminogenic and antisocial behavior among young people who sexually abuse.

Insights from the Empirical Literature

The empirical research literature on juveniles who sexually offend provides many insights into the extent of criminal and antisocial behavior among this population. In a recent review, Epps and Fisher (2004) make the following points:

1. A significant number of studies subsequent to that of Becker, Cunningham-Rathner, and Kaplan (1986) have consistently confirmed its findings concerning the extent of nonsexual antisocial and criminal behavior problems among samples of young people who sexually abuse. Becker et al. reported that 55% of their sample of young abusers had a previous arrest for a nonsexual offense, and 63% met the criteria for a diagnosis of conduct disorder.

2. The variety of disordered conduct among young abusers is evident from a study by Bladon (2000). She reports the following levels of antisocial behavior in a sample of 166 young people who had engaged in sexual offending: aggressive behavior (70%), bullying (44%), vandalism (38%), fire setting (26%), cruelty to animals (20%), shoplifting (20%), drug abuse (15%), and alcohol abuse (10%).

3. Considerable differences are found in the rates of antisocial behavior among young people who sexually abuse, depending on a number of variables—in particular, whether the sample in question is drawn from a residential or a community treatment program and whether certain behaviors are a feature of their sexual offending behavior, such as use of violence or selecting victims who are peers or adults rather than children. Consistently, samples drawn from residential facilities or that

include sexual offenders who use violence or who offend against peers or adults are found to have higher rates of other antisocial and criminal behaviors. It is important that these variables are carefully identified and controlled in research investigating the psychological characteristics of young people who sexually abuse.

4. Evidence shows that young people who abuse and whose base rates of antisocial behavior are high have considerable risk of recidivating nonsexually at alarmingly high levels. For example, Hagan, King, and Patros (1994) reviewed 50 young people who sexually offended 2 years after release from a state correctional facility. They reported that, whereas 8% had reoffended sexually, 46% had reoffended nonsexually.

Two studies that illustrate the importance of some of the distinctions highlighted by Epps and Fisher (2004) are those of Rubinstein, Yeager, Goodstein, and Lewis (1993) and Sipe, Jensen, and Everett (1998). A particularly important feature of these two studies is that they provide information on sexual and nonsexual reoffense rates for adolescent abusers as they mature into adulthood. Rubinstein et al. report data on 17 adolescents who had sexually offended with violence and whose lives were characterized by multiple problems in comparison with 41 youths who had perpetrated violent but nonsexual crimes. Recidivism rates using official police, FBI, and adult correctional facility records for both groups were established 8 years after the adolescents had been released from a juvenile correctional facility. The average age at the time of follow-up was 24 years. The adolescent sexual offender group had a subsequent rate of first- or second-degree sexual offense of 37% and a subsequent violent but nonsexual offense rate of 89% in adulthood (see Table 9.1). In contrast, nonsexually violent youths had a subsequent rate of first- or second-degree sexual offending of 10% and a violent nonsexual offense rate of 69%. These findings suggest that the 17 young people who sexually offended in Rubinstein et al.'s study had considerable potential for sexual and nonsexual offending. It also illustrates that some of those young people who come to the attention of authorities (10% in this study) for violent nonsexual offending are at risk of subsequently engaging in sexual crimes.

Sipe et al. (1998) reported data on a slightly different sample of young people who sexually offended, comparing them with a mixed group of nonsexual offenders. In their study they established the reoffense rates for 124 adolescents who, before they reached 16 years of age, had perpetrated nonviolent sexual crimes against younger children. All young people whose sexual crimes included violent elements were removed from the study. The comparison group in Sipe et al.'s study were 132 juveniles who had committed a mixture of nonsexual crimes,

TABLE 9.1. Reoffense Rates for Adolescents Who Perpetrate Sexual and Nonsexual Offenses Followed Up in Adulthood

Offense	Juvenile sexual offender group	Juvenile nonsexual offender group
Rubenstein, Yeager, Goodstein, & Lewis (1993)		
First-/second-degree sexual offense	37%	10%
Violent nonsexual offense	89%	69%
Sipe, Jensen, & Everett (1998)		
Sexual offense	9.7%	3.0%
Violent offense	5.6%	12.1%
Property offense	16.1%	32.6%
Other offense	15.3%	22.7%
Any arrest	32.3%	43.9%

such as burglary, theft, assault, and robbery. All the young people in the study had attended the Idaho Juvenile Diagnostic Unit during the time period 1978–1993. Follow-up began when a young person reached 18 years of age. The average follow-up period was 6 years (ranging from 1 to 14 years). Sipe et al. report the following rates of reoffending for the two groups: juvenile sexual offender group, sexual offense 9.7%, violent nonsexual offense 5.6%, property offenses 16.1%, other nonsexual offenses 15.3%, any subsequent arrest 32.3%; juvenile nonsexual offender group, sexual offense 3%, violent nonsexual offense 12.1%, property offense 32.6%, other nonsexual offenses 22.7%, any subsequent arrest 43.9%. Of these differing rates of reoffending between sexually and nonsexually offending juveniles, only two reached statistical significance. The sexual offender group were more likely to reoffend sexually, whereas the nonsexual offender group were more likely to perpetrate property offenses.

Three studies that have attempted to identify individual factors associated with increased risk of reoffending provide additional insights. Most recently, Langstrom and Grann (2000) report data on 44 males and 2 females between 15 and 20 years of age ($M = 18.13$ years) who were referred by courts for forensic psychiatric evaluation following the perpetration of sexual offenses. Of the 46 participants in Långström and Grann's study, 28 were responsible for rape or attempted rape, 12 had committed nonrape contact sexual offenses, and 6 were convicted of noncontact sexual offenses, typically exhibitionism. The average postinstitutional release time for subsequent reoffending was 60.95

months. In their study, Långström and Grann (2000) reviewed the research literature and identified 22 factors they deemed likely to predict subsequent sexual or general reoffending among young sexual abusers. They explored the retrospective value of each in light of the reconviction data for the 46 young people who had completed a full forensic psychiatric evaluation. At the end of the follow-up period, 30 (65%) of the young people had been reconvicted of a subsequent crime. Of these, 9 (20%) had been reconvicted of a sexual offense. Four risk factors were retrospectively found to be sensitive to sexual reconviction. Young people were 3.5 times more likely to reoffend sexually if their assessment profile included any one of the following features: sexual offending prior to the study's index offense, having poor social skills, victimizing males, and offending against two or more victims. Five different factors that did not predict sexual recidivism were predictive of nonsexual criminal recidivism. These were: (1) signs of conduct-disordered behavior before age 15 (excluding sexual misconduct), according to DSM-IV (American Psychiatric Association, 1994) criteria; (2) any prior violent conviction; (3) three or more previous convictions for any type of crime; (4) a score on the Psychopathy Check-List (Revised) of 26 or more; and (5) use of death threats or weapons as part of the index sexual crime.

Långström and Grann's (2000) study adds to the knowledge gained from two previous investigations in this area. Smith and Monastersky (1986) reported data on criminal recidivism over a minimum time period of 17 months in a group of 112 juvenile sexual offenders who had completed a community-based intervention program. They reported that engaging in noncontact sexual offenses, assaulting peer or adult victims (rather than younger children), having a male victim, and victimizing a stranger were factors associated with sexual-offense-recidivism. Kahn and Chambers (1991) reported data from 221 young people who had perpetrated sexual offenses followed up over an average time period of 20 months. Subsequent sexual offending was associated with denial, blaming the victim for the sexual assault, using verbal threats during sexual offending, and relatively younger age. Nonsexual criminal recidivism was associated with school-based behavioral problems, poor social skills, and relatively younger juveniles.

Implications from the Empirical Literature

These studies, which have reasonably good methodologies, clearly confirm a range of nonsexual criminal and antisocial behaviors as a significant feature in the lives of young people who sexually offend. Their severity reflects a number of factors, particularly the level of the antisocial behavior at the time of the index offence, and the gender and age of the victim. It appears that to a certain extent different risk factors may be associated with sexual and nonsexual offending. The literature also suggests the need for good judgment in avoiding the development of one-size-fits-all intervention programs that are sexual offense specific but that fail to tackle other types of nonsexual offending behavior. Finally, it reminds us that, just as juveniles who sexually offend have a potential for nonsexual recidivism, some young people who come to the attention of authorities for nonsexual crimes also have a potential for future sexual offending.

Conduct Disorder as a Useful Conceptual Framework for Planning Effective Assessment and Intervention

As we have seen in reviewing both the empirical and theoretical literature, many authors have included reference to the diagnostic category of conduct disorder when considering the problem of general criminality in young people who engage in sexually abusive behavior. The criteria for conduct disorder are outlined in Table 9.2 and reflect a variety of criminal and antisocial activities that are of concern for a subpopulation of young sexual abusers (American Psychiatric Association, 1994; World Health Organization, 1992, 1996). The true extent of conduct-disordered-type problems among this population is a matter to be determined more definitively in further empirical research but is linked to factors such as severity of offending behavior and gender of victim. Diagrammatically, it is useful to think of a relationship between sexual offending, conduct disorder, and general criminality of a sub-conduct-disorder threshold in such a way as is illustrated in Figure 9.1. That is, some young people who abuse do not have difficulties with other types of criminal or antisocial behavior. Others do to the extent that they also meet the criteria for a DSM-IV or ICD-10 diagnosis of conduct disorder. Others engage in sexual offending behavior and, to some degree, other types of antisocial or criminal behavior, but not to such an extent that they would meet the criteria for a conduct disorder diagnosis. It is clear from Table 9.2 that the behaviors listed accurately reflect the main categories of criminal activities evident from studies (such as that of Blandon, 2000, described earlier) of juvenile sexual abusers who commit broader acts of criminal behavior. Consequently, in order to outline material in this chapter that may assist in assessment of and intervention with criminogenic needs, we make reference to the category of conduct disorder for the remainder of our discussion, as it allows us to present approaches to clinical practice that have been evaluated and found to be effective in research studies of a high quality. In this way we hope to sug-

TABLE 9.2. Diagnostic Criteria for Conduct Disorder as Outlined in DSM–IV and ICD 10

DSM-IV	ICD-10
A. A repetitive and persistent pattern of behavior in which the basic rights of others or major age-appropriate societal norms or rules are violated, as manifested by the presence of three or more of the following criteria in the past 12 months with at least one criterion present in the past 6 months:	Conduct disorders are characterized by a repetitive and persistent pattern of dissocial, aggressive, or deviant conduct. Such behavior, when at its most extreme for the individual should amount to major violations of age-appropriate social expectations, and is therefore more severe than ordinary childish mischief or adolescent rebelliousness.

Aggression to people or animals

1. often bullies, threatens, or intimidates others
2. often initiates physical fights
3. has used a weapon that can cause serious physical harm to others
4. has been physically cruel to people
5. has been physically cruel to animals
6. has stolen while confronting a victim
7. has forced someone into sexual activity

Destruction of property

8. has deliberately engaged in fire setting . . .
9. has deliberately destroyed others' property . . .

Deceitfulness or theft

10. has broken into someone else's house, building, or car
11. often lies to obtain goods or favors or to avoid obligations
12. has stolen items without confronting the victim

Serious violation of rules

13. often stays out late at night despite parental prohibitions (before 13 years of age)
14. has run away from home overnight at least twice while living in parental home or once without returning for a lengthy period
15. is often truant from school before the age of 13

B. The disturbance in behavior causes clinically significant impairment in social, academic, or occupational functioning.

C. In those over 18 years, the criteria for antisocial personality disorder are not met.

Specify childhood onset (prior to 10 years) or adolescent onset.

Specify severity (mild, moderate, or severe).

Examples of the behaviors on which the diagnosis is based include the following: excessive levels of fighting or bullying; cruelty to animals or other people; severe destructiveness to property; fire-setting; stealing; repeated lying; truancy from school and running away from home; unusually frequent and severe temper tantrums; deviant provocative behavior and persistent and severe disobedience. Any one of these categories, if marked, is sufficient for the diagnosis, but isolated dissocial acts are not.

Exclusion criteria include serious underlying conditions such as schizophrenia, hyperkinetic disorder, or depression.

The diagnosis is not made unless the duration of the behavior is 6 months or longer.

Specify:

Conduct disorder confined to a family context where the symptoms are confined to the home

Unsocialized conduct disorder where there is a pervasive abnormality in peer relationships

Socialized conduct disorder where the individual is well integrated into a peer group

Note. Adapted from American Psychiatric Association (1994) and World Health Organization (1996). Copyright 1994 by the American Psychiatric Association and 1996 by the World Health Organization. Adapted by permission.

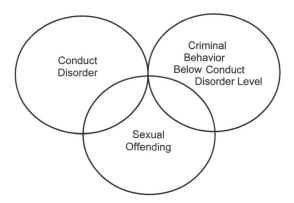

FIGURE 9.1. A way to conceptualize the relationship between adolescent sexual offending, conduct disorder, and criminal behavior of a sub-conduct-disordered level; exact proportions of overlap unknown.

gest an integration of important aspects of the conduct disorder literature in the assessment and treatment of young people who sexually offend and engage in broader forms of criminal and antisocial behavior. The approaches outlined in the remainder of this chapter should be regarded as supplemental to a full clinical assessment that is informed by more offense-specific concerns such as that outlined by O'Reilly and Carr (2004b).

What Works in Assessment and Intervention

In recent years a number of authors have given serious consideration to reviewing the literature on what works in psychological intervention with a broad range of difficulties experienced by children, adolescents, and adults. Among many valuable sources of information on what is effective and not effective in the clinical management of antisocial and criminal behavior in those who meet the criteria for a DSM-IV or ICD 10 diagnosis of conduct disorder are reviews by Brosnan and Carr (2000) and Wolpert et al. (2002). Brosnan and Carr (2000) reviewed empirical studies on the effectiveness of interventions in alleviating conduct-disordered behaviors in adolescents. This is part of a more complete review of effective interventions with children, adolescents, and their families for a wide range of psychological and psychiatric disorders. One of the features of these reviews is that they are based on a meta-analysis of studies that meet the criteria of methodologically sound research as conceptualized by Carr (2000a). Studies that do not meet criteria that allow them to be considered methodologically strong were excluded from the review. The outcome of this approach is that clinical guidelines are established on a solid basis of evidence. Wolpert et al. (2002) also addressed the question of what the evidence tells us works in clinical practice for young people and their families who present with a variety of psychological and psychiatric disorders, including disorders of conduct. However, their report differs from that of Brosnan and Carr (2000) in that it considered evidence that was deemed to be methodologically strong, in addition to useful tentative evidence based on studies that could be considered to be methodologically weaker.

In summary, Brosnan and Carr (2000) reported the following based on their meta-analysis of the literature. A continuum of therapeutic intervention is an appropriate and effective response for adolescents who present with conduct disorder reflecting its severity. This continuum should range from training parents in the behavioral management of their children (more than 45 hours of intervention in a 1-year period) to family therapy (up to 36 hours of intervention) to multisystemic therapy (up to 20 hours for between 2 to 47 months) to special foster care. Describing this continuum more specifically, intensive behavioral parent training supported by telephone contact may sufficiently improve parenting skill to effectively reduce adolescent recidivism during and after the intervention. The goal of functional family therapy should be to help parents to cooperate and develop problem-solving skills concerning the management of the teenagers' problematic behavior and to improve family communication. This approach has been effective with adolescents with severe delinquent behavior who hail from a range of socioeconomic backgrounds. It can also help reduce arrest rates among the siblings of the referred client. In multisystemic therapy, the intervention is designed to target maintaining factors related to the young person's conduct disorder that are features of the many social systems of which he or she is a part (such as family, peer group, school, and community). This approach has been found to be effective with repeat adolescent offenders from low socioeconomic backgrounds by improving family functioning, reducing behavioral problems at home, and halving recidivism. In special foster care, the foster parents are provided with specialist training based on the principles of social learning theory that they implement to help a young person resocialize his or her behavior from more antisocial patterns. This approach can be effective with repeat offenders and those hospitalized because of severe conduct problems.

Wolpert et al. (2002) also make very clear statements on the clinical implications of the what-works literature in relation to disturbances of conduct. When children younger than 8 years of age present with conduct disorder, parent training is the most appropriate intervention, especially in circumstances in which there is less comorbidity, moderate severity, and less social disadvantage. With children ages 8–12 years, or with younger children with more severe disturbances of conduct, parent training should be supplemented with individual interventions for the child that offer problem-solving and social-skills training. For adolescents and younger children with moderate conduct problems, functional family therapy should be considered and combined with individual interventions that focus on reducing opportunities for antisocial behavior and promoting problem-solving, coping, and social skills. For severe and long-term conduct problems in adolescents, multisystemic therapy is the most effective intervention. However, this is an approach that requires high levels of professional resources and that consequently requires careful planning and targeting. Specialist foster care placements can be a useful aspect of intervention for chronic and severe conduct problems. There is insufficient evidence in the literature to allow us to make statements regarding the effectiveness of psychodynamic approaches to treatment. Although there is some limited evidence to suggest that selected forms of psychotropic medication can lower aggressiveness, medication should not be used as the initial form of intervention for conduct problems.

Therapeutic Assessment and Intervention

Carr (1995, 2000b) outlines a conceptual model of functional family-based assessment and treatment that lends itself to assessment of and intervention with criminal and antisocial behavior in young people who engage in sexually abusive behavior. Carr's model is based on the idea that within families an individual's psychological dysfunction, such as conduct-disordered behavior in a teenager, can be understood according to a three-column formulation that reflects predisposing and precipitating factors, maintaining cognitive factors, and a pattern of interaction in which the dysfunctional behavior is expressed in interpersonal exchanges between family members. Through careful family interviews, it is possible to develop for an individual family a formulation that reflects their particular difficulties and that can be used collaboratively by the family and their therapist to develop solutions to the problems they face. In the next section we outline how this model of assessment, formulation, and intervention can be implemented for a young person referred for sexually abusive behavior who also presents with criminal and antisocial behavior using a fictional but realistic case example. In doing so, we attempt to outline how this type of approach, indicated by the what-works literature and reflective of the etiological and maintaining role attributed to coercive patterns of family interaction, may be used to supplement interventions aimed more specifically at changing sexually abusive behavior.

Case Example

Timmy is 14 years old. He has been accused of sexually abusing James, his 6-year-old cousin, while babysitting. Timmy denied his offense at first. However, he later admitted to the behavior after he was threatened with a beating by his father, George, if he did not tell the truth regarding the allegation.

Timmy's parents report that they have always had problems with his behavior. Timmy has had a history of disruptive behavior since he began to attend primary school. He was referred to the local child guidance service at 6 years of age because he repeatedly stole the belongings of other pupils and fought with them on the playground. He has struggled to make progress in class and has a specific reading difficulty. He is currently in his second year in secondary school and is frequently absent without permission.

Timmy is the eldest of five children, who range in age from 5 to 14 years. His father, George, has an alcohol abuse problem. He has served a prison sentence for burglary and aggravated assault. Timmy's family is known to the local community services due to past episodes of family violence related to George's drinking. Timmy's mother, Dorothy, has a history of depression. She is currently taking antidepressant medication prescribed by her local general practitioner. Her extended family refuses to have any contact with her, as they disapprove of her relationship with George.

Timmy has three friends with whom he spends most of his time in the evenings and on weekends. He frequently stays out with them until after midnight, ignoring parental rules on curfew times. Most of their time is spent hanging around the local shopping center. Timmy and his friends have been in trouble with the local police for shoplifting, underage drinking, and marijuana use. He has been suspended from school for fighting, is suspected of serious bullying at school, and has a reputation as a troublemaker within his local community. It is suspected that he has been involved in joyriding [car theft]. Timmy's father is not living in the house at present and has declined the invitation to take part in this assessment. However, his mother is prepared to attend.

The following is an extract from part of the assessment interview with Timmy and his mother, Dorothy. The therapist was trying to get a working description of a pattern of interaction within the family concerning the presenting problem of Timmy's disruptive and antisocial behavior. In doing so he asked them to describe a recent example of a time they fought. The therapist was interested in understanding what happened in the interaction and the thoughts and feelings of Timmy and Dorothy. This segment was subsequently used by the therapist to complete a three-column problem formulation that was the starting point for Timmy, Dorothy, and the therapist to problem solve alternative strategies they all could implement as they attempted to avoid this pattern of interaction repeating itself in the future. In adopting his model for practice with conduct-disordered adolescents, Carr (2000b) made a number of points regarding behavioral and cognitive features of family interaction that should be kept in mind when conducting an assessment. First, the coercive style of interaction, common in the families of adolescents with conduct-disordered, criminal, and sexually abusive behavior, promotes the cognitive bias in individuals that social interactions are likely to lead to conflict. This increases the likelihood that ambiguous or neutral situations will be interpreted in a hostile manner. Second, the coercive style of interaction promotes the belief that there is something intrinsically wrong with the adolescent who presents with antisocial or criminal behavior, making attempts to bring about change seem futile. Third, there is usually an absence of positive interaction within such families. Among other things, this limits the development of positive self-regard in the adolescent and limits his or her experience of healthy relationships and associated interpersonal and problem-solving skills. Fourth, the parents frequently, inconsistently and ineffectively "punish" the adolescent. Finally, the parents unintentionally promote antisocial behavior in the adolescent by brief confrontation and punishment, followed by withdrawal from the situation when the young person intensifies his or her antisocial behavior. In developing a three-column formulation based on this assessment session conversation with Dorothy and Timmy, the therapist looked for these features in their interaction.

THERAPIST: You have told us that you and Timmy often fight at home. I wonder if you would both describe to me the last time this happened. As you do, it's important to remember that we simply want to get a description of what happened that includes everyone's perspective. For now it doesn't matter who was right or wrong. Can you remember when you last had a fight?

DOROTHY: (*Laughs.*) That should be easy! Probably yesterday when he refused to go back to school after lunch.

THERAPIST: Okay. Do you both agree that we can talk about this example of a time when you fought?

DOROTHY: Yeah, that's fine.

THERAPIST: What about you, Timmy? Is that okay?

TIMMY: Suppose.

THERAPIST: Good. How did the fight start?

DOROTHY: The same as always. It started with Timmy. He came in from school about 12 and I could see by his face that he was in a fouler [bad mood]. He barely grunted hello and went to his room. Isn't that right?

TIMMY: So what. . . .

THERAPIST: (*to Timmy*) Okay, so what happened next?

TIMMY: Nothin'. I just went to me room that's all. I just went there and stayed there.

THERAPIST: What did you do while you were there?

TIMMY: Watched TV.

THERAPIST: Okay, so what happened next?

DOROTHY: I asked him if he wanted anything to eat and he didn't bother to answer.

THERAPIST: Why do you think he didn't answer?

DOROTHY: 'Cause when he's in one of his moods he is impossible to talk to.

THERAPIST: Did you hear your Ma ask you if you wanted something to eat?

TIMMY: No.

DOROTHY: Yes, you did.

TIMMY: Yeah, well, only when you started shouting and banging on the door.

THERAPIST: So you both weren't in the same room when you were having this conversation?

DOROTHY: No (*slightly annoyed at therapist*). He was in his room and he locks the door and no one can get in and he turns on the TV full blast so you have to shout or he doesn't hear you. Not that he answers when he does.

THERAPIST: Errr, what happened next?

DOROTHY: Nothing. He didn't answer so I gave up.

THERAPIST: What were you thinking as you gave up?

DOROTHY: Mm, something like ungrateful little . . . brat. . . .

THERAPIST: What were you thinking at this point, Timmy?

TIMMY: Nothin'. Just glad she was gone.

THERAPIST: All right. So what happened after that?

DOROTHY: The usual, he refused to go back to school.

THERAPIST: Oh, how did that happen?

DOROTHY: Well, he has to leave by half-twelve if he's going to be back in school on time at a quarter to one. He knows this but he's always late. Since he didn't bother to answer me earlier, I thought, I'm not going to run after him to get him back to school. By a quarter to one he was still in his room, so I banged on the door to remind him to get out. He told me to "fuck off" and to mind my own business. I'll put up with a lot but, my God, I won't have him talk to me in that kind of language in my own home. So, I made him open the door.

THERAPIST: How did you do that?

DOROTHY: I told him I'd get his Da to sort him out later if he didn't open the door.

THERAPIST: What happened after you opened the door?

TIMMY: (voice slightly raised) She was there, screaming like a bleedin' madwoman. Screamin' at me to get out so I got out.

THERAPIST: Did you go back to school?

TIMMY: What?

THERAPIST: Where did you go to after you left the house?

TIMMY: I just went out. . . . I met Steo and Razor [friends] and we went to the field and hung around and played some football [U.S. soccer].

DOROTHY: A likely story.

THERAPIST: What were you thinking as you left the house?

TIMMY: Dunno, eh, that it's always the same. It's always bleedin' me that she picks on. It's never the others, it's always me, it's not fair.

THERAPIST: How were you feeling, Dorothy, when Timmy left the house?

DOROTHY: Me nerves were in shreds. He really upsets me. I know it's terrible to say but I was just glad that he was out of my sight.

THERAPIST: When did you see him again?

DOROTHY: I didn't. At least not yesterday. He sneaked in after midnight after I'd gone to bed. I was fed up waiting for him to come back.

THERAPIST: Okay. Thanks, both of you.

Within this model of practice the therapist applies the specific information gathered from the assessment conversation with Dorothy and Timmy to generate an individualized preliminary three-column formulation. In the right-hand column, the therapist simply restates the pattern of interaction within the family as described by Dorothy and Timmy. In the left-hand column, the therapist lists predisposing factors that are relevant to the presenting problem and pertinent to the pattern of interaction within the family. In the middle column, the therapist lists the maintaining cognitions and beliefs that link the predisposing factors to the pattern of interaction. An example of this type of formulation based on assessment information offered by Dorothy and Timmy is illustrated in Figure 9.2. This preliminary formulation is presented to Timmy and Dorothy on completion of the assessment when a contract for treatment is being negotiated. At this time, their views are sought on its accuracy in describing the pattern of interaction they described and the links hypothesized by the therapist between that interaction and predisposing factors combined with linking beliefs and cognitions. It is also an opportunity to present family members with a broader perspective on the important influences on family life and relationships, based on the intricacies of how they behave as they interact with each other. This formulation should be discussed fully when presented in session and refined in response to feedback from family members. Once this formulation is agreed on, it becomes the basis for inviting family members to brainstorm alternatives to the choices made in interactions as described in the formulation, alternatives that they can work toward implementing in their family life.

An essential complement to the three-column problem formulation that can help families to generate alternatives is to complete the same process of assessment and formulation for an exception to the problem. An exception to the problem is a time when the problem could potentially have happened but did not. In our case example, this might reflect a time when Dorothy and Timmy did not fight but interacted in a manner that both of them found to be more positive. The following session extract illustrates how the therapist continued the earlier conversation to glean information from Dorothy and Timmy in order to develop a three-column formulation that accurately reflects an exception to their problematic

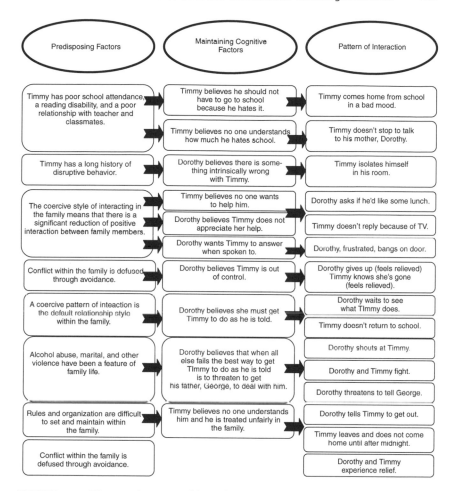

FIGURE 9.2. Three-column problem formulation for Timmy and Dorothy.

interactions that support Timmy's antisocial and criminal behavior (see Figure 9.3). In subsequently reviewing the exception to the problem formulation when a contract for treatment is being negotiated, Dorothy and Timmy are invited to identify what was different in the way they thought, felt, and behaved and to consider whether setting themselves the goal of engaging in a similar way of thinking, feeling, and behaving in the future might help prevent a repeat of the problem behavior.

THERAPIST: Okay, so that's an example of a recent time when you fought. I wonder if you would tell me about a time when the oppo-

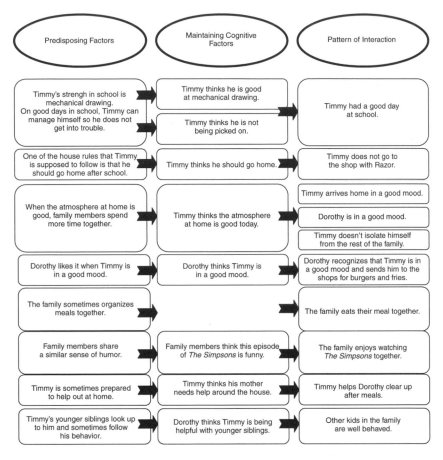

FIGURE 9.3. Three-column formulation for an exception to the problem for Timmy and Dorothy.

site happened. By this I mean a time when you didn't fight, didn't avoid each other, but got on okay.

DOROTHY: Do you mean a recent time?

THERAPIST: Yes, a recent time.

DOROTHY: Hmm . . . can you think of a time?

TIMMY: Dunno . . . last week maybe . . . that time when we had burgers for tea and watched *The Simpsons*.

DOROTHY: Oh, yeah.

THERAPIST: Good. Would you mind telling me about what happened?

DOROTHY: We had burgers from the chipper [fast-food shop] and watched TV. There was me, Timmy, and the other kids.

THERAPIST: What day was this?

DOROTHY: Let me think . . . was it Thursday? Yeah, Thursday, I think, 'cause I got paid on Thursday.

THERAPIST: Oh, was that a school day for you, Timmy?

TIMMY: Yeah.

THERAPIST: What kind of day was it in school?

TIMMY: All right. Nothin' really happened.

THERAPIST: Does that mean you didn't have any problems or worries in school last Thursday?

TIMMY: Yeah.

THERAPIST: Can you think of why that was? Is Thursday different from other school days?

TIMMY: Not really. I have double mechanical drawing, which is deadly [very good].

DOROTHY: He has Mr. McKiernan for mechanical drawing. He always does well in that class. He's the only teacher in that school who's any use.

THERAPIST: Did you get into any fights in school on Thursday?

TIMMY: No.

THERAPIST: How did you manage that?

TIMMY: Dunno. Just no one picked on me, that's all.

THERAPIST: So what kind of mood were you in when you got home?

TIMMY: Good, I suppose.

THERAPIST: Did you go straight home from school, or did you do anything along the way?

TIMMY: I met Razor. He was going to the shop for his Ma but I didn't bother going with him.

THERAPIST: So what happened when you got home?

TIMMY: Me Ma was there. She's usually in a good mood on a Thursday 'cause it's her night for going out. She told me to go to the chipper and get burgers and chips. So, I went and got them. When I came home we ate them in the kitchen. *The Simpsons* was on so we watched that. Me Ma thinks Mr. Cleary across the road looks like Ned Flanders.

DOROTHY: No, I don't. (*Laughs.*)

TIMMY: She says "How-didily-doodily neighbor" whenever she sees him. (*Laughs.*)

THERAPIST: What did you think when Timmy came home from school on Thursday?

DOROTHY: Nothing, really. I could see he was in a good mood. He's good when he's like that. He even helped me clear up afterwards. That's what I don't understand. He's good when he wants to be. Like when he helps with the younger ones. And when he's good, sometimes they're good, too.

THERAPIST: Why do you think that is?

DOROTHY: They look up to him, I suppose.

THERAPIST: Okay. That sounds like a nice evening. Thank you.

As mentioned previously, on completion of the assessment phase of intervention, the next step in Carr's (2000b) model is to develop a contract for intervention. The three primary aims of intervention are to use the three-column formulations to help the family move away from repeating the coercive style of interacting with one another, to increase the number of positive exchanges within the family, and to help the adolescent learn how to manage his or her behavior so that he or she engages in a more socially acceptable manner. During the development of a contract for intervention, practical arrangements concerning the number of sessions and their location and time should be clearly outlined. Suitable arrangements that will help prevent nonattendance should be put in place. These arrangements may include support from involved systems such as social services, the provision of transportation to appointments, or arranging to conduct sessions in the client's home. As we have seen from the what-works literature, the more chronic the adolescent's antisocial and criminal behavior, the more intensive and long-term the functional family therapy that is likely to be required. These details may be put into a written contract that is signed by family members, the therapists, and other involved members of the family's support network.

Intervention Techniques

In the intervention phase a number of techniques can be implemented that will help to decrease coercive interactions, increase positive interactions, and facilitate parents in helping the young person to learn how to manage his or her behavior. These include helping parents to monitor and understand the pattern of family interaction and its reflection of broader influences on behavior in a manner similar to that illustrated by the three-column formulation process. Helping family members to positively reframe problem interactions can be achieved either by helping them to externalize the problem behavior of the young person, rather than interpreting it as something intrinsically wrong with him or her, or by reemphasizing some positive element of the behavior. Other techniques include planned special time, using reward systems to promote behavioral control, enhancing parenting skills, improving communication skills in family members, and improving problem-solving skills. These and other approaches are described in detail in Carr (2000b) and in other, similar sources on clinical practice. In the remainder of this section we describe three of these techniques in greater detail in order to give a picture of what the intervention process may be like.

Planned Special Time

In planned special time an attempt is made to break the coercive pattern of interaction between parent(s) and adolescent by scheduling positive time to be spent together. In doing so, the parents and the adolescent plan and agree on a specific activity in which all parties can enjoy participating. The activities themselves do not have to be elaborate or incur any significant expense. With teenagers, the special time might be as simple as going for a walk together once a week or choosing a video to watch together and then having a conversation about it afterward (however, generally speaking, overly passive activities are less useful). The choice of activity for the planned special time should reflect the interests and resources of the family. There are a number of important aspects for therapists to emphasize in establishing this intervention. These include helping parents to develop positive attributions concerning the adolescent by asking parents to notice how much they enjoy spending time with their son or daughter. To improve the expression of boundaries and clear positive emotional statements within the family, therapists may ask parents to conclude the activity by verbalizing a review of what they have done together, along with their positive feelings regarding the time spent together. Asking parents to foresee and preempt rule breaking that could potentially occur related to the activity, rather than allowing it to unfold, can help the development of parenting skills.

Enhancing Parenting Skills

A key element of successful intervention is to enhance effective parenting skills. A number of parent training manuals, videos, and programs are available that facilitate this goal. In this section we describe a CD-ROM-based intervention known as Parenting Adolescents Wisely that is well suited to this task. It combines instructional video clips on problems and possible solutions to the difficulty of parenting adolescents with disruptive and problematic behavior with educational instruction and content review quizzes. It was developed by Donald Gordon in the United States but has been implemented in a number of other countries, including Ireland, the United Kingdom, and Australia. It was designed to specifically promote parenting practices the absence of which has been consistently linked to juvenile delinquency. In developing a CD-ROM—based intervention, Gordon was building on research evidence that demonstrates that video training is an effective way to improve parenting practices and knowledge and is as successful in improving child behavior problems as are educational groups for parents or direct instruction from a therapist. It also has the advantage of offering a format that is low cost and flexible for service providers, as it does not require staff training and can be implemented in a family's home through a laptop computer.

The format of Parenting Adolescents Wisely presents video clips illustrating nine parent–adolescent problem situations (including completing homework, sibling conflict, defiance, avoiding chores, disrespectful talk, associating with undesirable peers). At the conclusion of each video clip illustrating the problem, parents are given three strategies to choose from in response to the young person's behavior. The parents are invited to choose the response that best reflects the way they would handle the situation. The parents' choice of parenting strategy is then illustrated in another video clip that portrays the outcome of this approach. After the video clip is played, a series of questions and answers appear on the screen that allow the parent to consider the positive and negative aspects of their choice of parenting strategy. If the response chosen by the parent is not the solution most reflective of good parenting principles, the computer program invites the respondent to select another option, which is also illustrated in a video clip. When the optimal solution has been illustrated on video, the parent completes an on-screen quiz that facilitates a content review of the good parenting practices exemplified. Within the Parenting Adolescents Wisely program a number of effective parenting behavioral management techniques are illustrated and reviewed. These include active listening, using "I" statements to express emotions, supervision, contracting with teenagers for positive behavior, using appropriate discipline, and contingency management.

Gordon (2002) states that the goals of the Parenting Adolescents Wisely CD-ROM are fivefold. Firstly, to increase parents' knowledge of the principles of good and successful approaches to parenting teenagers.

Secondly, to improve their actual parenting behavior in addition to knowledge gains. Thirdly, to facilitate the improvement of problematic behavior among teenagers. Fourthly, to improve family functioning, and finally to enhance parents' satisfaction with their ability to be effective in managing their children when they present with difficult behavior. Gordon (2002) reviews evidence from six studies that indicate that the Parenting Adolescents Wisely program effectively achieves these aims. In summary, these empirical studies attest to the effectiveness of the program with teenagers and their families who were referred from outpatient clinics and a residential center for juvenile delinquents or who were identified with problem behaviors in a public school; with teenagers who are themselves parents of young children; with court-referred juvenile delinquents from low-income homes; with at-risk socially disadvantaged families; and with families in which there is spousal conflict and family violence.

Reward Systems and Behavioral Control Programs

Another key element of successful family intervention for adolescents with antisocial and criminal behavior is to assist parents in directly promoting prosocial behavior and in directly discouraging antisocial behavior through the use of reward systems and behavioral-control programs without recourse to a coercive style of interaction. Reward systems provide an intervention well designed to promote prosocial behavior. They are an equivalent to approaches such as star charts that are used with younger children but that are obviously unsuitable for adolescents. A format that is more acceptable to teenagers is one in which parents and the young person agree to work on one or two positive behaviors that they would like to see the young person do more of (such as getting up at a certain time, speaking to family members in a regular voice, helping with a chore such as clearing up after a meal, doing homework at a set time). A preagreed number of points is offered for the successful completion of the specified task. A menu of rewards is also preagreed. It outlines benefits that can be claimed for an agreed number of reward points that have been accumulated by the adolescent. Rewards are usually extra privileges (such as watching TV for an extra hour, staying up an extra half-hour, having a friend over to visit for 2 hours). Some key elements are helpful in successfully establishing this type of system. These include setting up the program as one in which the aim is not to control the adolescent's behavior but to help him or her to consolidate habits that are more prosocial. Another useful approach is to begin the program on a successful footing by including behaviors that are already within the teenager's repertoire at the outset. It is also important that the program work on a small number of manageable goals rather than a large number of unmanageable ones, that parents are encouraged to engage in behaviors that positively model those encouraged in the adolescent, that the program is implemented consistently, that parents are encouraged to quickly offer praise and positive feedback in addition to point rewards to the young person when positive behaviors are displayed, and that all parties adopt an open-minded approach to revising the system until one is found that works for the individual family.

An inescapable but infinitely more difficult aspect of the intervention concerns the use of behavioral-control programs. These are similar to reward programs in that they aim to encourage positive prosocial behavior, but they differ in that they entail sanctions for engaging in negative behavior and rule breaking. In establishing a behavioral-control program, the primary caregivers pick a small number of rules that they would like to promote (such as getting up at a certain time in the morning; speaking to family members in a calm, nonaggressive manner; or returning home by a certain time in the evening). As before, a system of reward points that can be accumulated and exchanged for preagreed privileges is established. However, an additional feature of the system is that points are deducted if the young person engages in rule breaking. The number of penalty points deducted within the system is also agreed in advance of the implementation of the program. Engaging in this type of intervention is usually very stressful for families, particularly at the outset. A typical feature of their implementation is that the young person responds by escalating the intensity of his or her inappropriate behavior. In the three-column problem formulation outlined for Timmy, there are two instances in which this happens: (1) Timmy deliberately ignores Dorothy when she starts banging on his bedroom door, and she becomes further frustrated and leaves; (2) later Dorothy shouts at Timmy, and Timmy responds by shouting back at her. Having these types of illustrations in the problem formulation helps prepare the family for what they should expect as they begin to implement a behavioral-control program, as they are based on the real-life interactions of the family. They serve to highlight the coercive style of intrafamily interaction, demonstrating how both Timmy and Dorothy use this approach as the default interaction technique within the family. They illustrate the outcome that when a parent tries to exert control, the adolescent continues to defy or to escalate his or her defiance in response, the frustrated parent gives up, and both parties experience relief. During the intervention phase, the aim is to help the parents introduce appropriate parental control and not repeat the unintentional rewarding of inappropriate behavior. This would undoubtedly be a very difficult challenge for any parent. As part of preparing the family for this element of a functional family therapy intervention, it is important to emphasize that all adults within the system must implement the program consistently, to ensure that adults are mutually supportive of the program and have access to other forms of social support as appropriate, and that the adults agree that, in implementing the program, they will not engage in parenting toward the adolescent that is physically, emotionally or verbally punitive. In addition, this element of intervention is unlikely to meet with any success if it is not equally accompanied by the development of positive relationship interactions, positive reframing, and problem-solving skills. Given the initial resistance that will be elicited by this type of intervention, it is very tempting for family members and therapists to repeat the usual outcome of intensified behavioral response by backing down. Consequently, appropriately maintaining the program when initial resistance is encountered is very important.

Summary and Conclusions

In this chapter we have shown that many theorists have acknowledged that more general criminal behavior is a significant feature in a subset of those young people who engage in sexually abusive behavior. A key aspect in the development of sexual and nonsexual criminal behavior is theorized to be living in a family in which interpersonal interaction is characterized by a coercive and manipulative style. The empirical literature confirms that nonsexual criminal behavior is evident among many young people who sexually offend and is particularly associated with those whose lifestyles and offenses are characterized by certain features such as sexual offending against peers or adults or against male victims. However, the exact extent of the problem of nonsexual criminal and antisocial behavior among juveniles who sexually offend needs to be established through empirical investigation. Studies that have monitored development of young people who sexually abuse into adulthood clearly indicate that both sexual and nonsexual recidivism are issues that need to be assessed and addressed when offering therapeutic services. In this chapter we referred to the clear findings from the what-works literature for children and adolescents regarding effective interventions for those who present with conduct disorder, as this diagnostic category incorporates many aspects of criminal and antisocial behavior that the empirical literature indicates are features of the behavior of some adolescents who sexually abuse others. Consistent with the hypothesized importance of coercive family interactions in the etiology of sexual and nonsexual offending, the what-works literature suggests comprehensive family-based interventions as the most appropriate and most effective therapeutic response. Using a case example, we concluded this chapter by outlining a model of functional family assessment, formulation, and intervention conceptualized by Carr (1995, 2000b). It is our hope that this chapter has highlighted the importance of addressing other types of criminal and antisocial behaviors among a subset of adolescents who engage in sexually abusive behavior. We also hope that it has presented an evidenced and practical introduction for practitioners who may wish to further consider addressing these needs within existing or developing services.

References

American Psychiatric Association. (1994). *Diagnostic and statistical manual of the mental disorders* (4th ed.). Washington, DC: Author.

Barbaree, H. E., Marshall, W. L., & McCormick, J. (1998). The development of sexually deviant behaviour among adolescents and its implications for prevention and treatment. *Irish Journal of Psychology, 19*(1), 1–31.

Becker, J., Cunningham-Rathner, J., & Kaplan, M. S. (1986). Adolescent sexual offenders: Demographics, criminal and sexual histories, and recommendations for reducing future sexual offenses. *Journal of Interpersonal Violence, 1,* 431–445.

Becker, J., & Kaplan, M. S. (1988). The assessment of adolescent sexual offenders. *Advances in Behavioral Assessment of Children and Families, 4,* 97–114.

Bladon, E. M. M. (2000). *Child and adolescent sexual offending: Nature of offending, diagnoses and treatment outcome.* Unpublished doctoral dissertation, Institute of Psychiatry, London.

Brosnan, R., & Carr, A. (2000). Adolescent conduct problems. In A. Carr (Ed.), *What works with children and adolescents? A critical review of psychological interventions with children, adolescents and their families.* London: Routledge.

Carr, A. (1995). *Positive practice: A step-by-step approach to family therapy.* Reading, UK: Harwood.

Carr, A. (Ed.). (2000a). *What works with children and adolescents? A critical review of psychological interventions with children, adolescents and their families.* London: Routledge.

Carr, A. (2000b). *Family therapy: Concepts, process and practice.* Chichester, UK: Wiley.

Epps, K., & Fisher, D. (2004). A review of the research literature on young people who sexually abuse. In G. O'Reilly, W. L. Marshall, A. Carr, & R.

Beckett (Eds.), *Handbook of clinical intervention for young people who sexually abuse*. London: Routledge.

Finkelhor, D. (1984). *Child sexual abuse: New theory and research*. New York: Free Press.

Gordon, D. (2002). Intervening with families of troubled youth: Functional family therapy and parenting wisely. In J. Maguire (Ed.), *Offender rehabilitation and treatment: Programs and policies to reduce re-offending*. New York: Wiley.

Hagan, M. P., King, R. P., & Patros, R. L. (1994). Recidivism among adolescent perpetrators of sexual assault against children. *Journal of Offender Rehabilitation, 21*, 127–137.

Hall, G. C. N. (1996). *Theory-based assessment, treatment and prevention of sexual aggression*. New York: Oxford University Press.

Hall, G. C. N., & Hirschman, R. (1991). Towards a theory of sexual aggression: A quadripartite model. *Journal of Consulting and Clinical Psychology, 59*(5), 662–669.

Hall, G. C. N., & Hirschman, R. (1992). Sexual aggression against children: A conceptual perspective on etiology. *Criminal Justice and Behavior, 19*, 8–23.

Kahn, T. J., & Chambers, H. J. (1991). Assessing reoffense risk with juvenile sexual offenders. *Child Welfare, 70*, 333–344.

Långström, N., & Grann, M. (2000). Risk for criminal recidivism among young sex offenders. *Journal of Interpersonal Violence, 15*, 855–871.

Marshall, W. L., & Barbaree, H. E. (1990). An integrated theory of the etiology of sexual offending. In W. L. Marshall, D. R. Laws, & H. E. Barbaree (Eds.), *Handbook of sexual assault: Issues, theories, and treatment of the offender*. New York: Plenum Press.

O'Reilly, G., & Carr, A. (2004a). A review of theoretical models of sexual offending. In G. O'Reilly, W. L. Marshall, A. Carr, & R. Beckett (Eds.), *Handbook of clinical intervention for young people who sexually abuse*. London: Routledge.

O'Reilly, G., & Carr, A. (2004b). The clinical assessment of young people with sexually abusive behaviour. In G. O'Reilly, W. L. Marshall, A. Carr, & R. Beckett (Eds.), *Handbook of clinical intervention for young people who sexually abuse*. London: Routledge.

Rubenstein, M., Yeager, C. A., Goodstein, C., & Lewis, D. O. (1993). Sexually assaultive male juveniles: A follow-up. *American Journal of Psychiatry, 150*, 262–265.

Sipe, R., Jensen, E. L., & Everett, R. S. (1998). Adolescent sexual offenders grown up: Recidivism in young adulthood. *Criminal Justice and Behaviour, 25*, 109–124.

Smith, W. R., & Monastersky, C. (1986). Assessing juvenile sexual offenders' risk for reoffending. *Criminal Justice and Behaviour, 25*, 109–124.

Ward, T., & Siegart, R. J. (2002). Towards a comprehensive theory of child sexual abuse: A theory knitting perspective. *Psychology, Crime and Law, 8*, 319–351.

Wolpert, M., Fuggle, P., Cottrell, D., Fonaghy, P., Philips, J., Pilling, S., Stein, S., et al. (2002). *Drawing on the evidence: Advice for mental health professionals working with children and adolescents*. Leicester, UK: British Psychological Society.

World Health Organization. (1992). *The ICD-10 classification of mental and behavioural disorders*. Geneva: Author.

World Health Organization. (1996). *Multi-axial classification of child and adolescent psychiatric disorders: ICD-10 classification of mental disorders in children and adolescents*. Cambridge, UK: Cambridge University Press.

CHAPTER 10

Risk of Sexual Recidivism in Adolescents Who Offend Sexually
Correlates and Assessment

James R. Worling
Niklas Långström

Adolescents who commit sexual offenses are unique human beings. Not surprisingly, therefore, they are heterogeneous with respect to virtually every variable that one chooses to study. For example, adolescents who offend sexually have diverse experiences of childhood victimization ranging from none to extensive sexual victimization by numerous perpetrators. They exhibit varying emotional and behavioral control ranging from extreme impulsivity to extreme overcontrol, and they demonstrate varying sexual interest in prepubescent children ranging from none to preferential sexual interest in younger children. The onset and persistence of severe or violent antisocial behavior in adolescents is the result of complex interactions between a multitude of risk and protective factors (cf. Loeber & Farrington, 1998). These factors include temperament or personality characteristics, parental or family factors, peer traits, and neighborhood/social environment attributes. These factors are likely to interact not only within each domain but also across several of them. Because of the variability of these characteristics between different adolescents, it should be no surprise that the risk of sexual reoffending is also a heterogeneous characteristic.

Even when the risk of reoffending sexually is viewed as a dichotomous variable, there are at least five possible outcomes. First, there is likely a group of adolescents who have committed sexual assaults, who are never detected by authorities or treatment providers, and who stop offending on their own. Researchers have rarely studied these individuals, and it would be informative to investigate these individuals to understand both the prevalence of adolescent sexual offending in the general population and to identify the mechanisms by which these individuals were able to terminate their offending behaviors without professional intervention. Second, there are adolescents who commit sexual assaults but are never detected and who continue to offend sexually as adults. Although many adults who offend sexually are never detected, published data indicate that many adults who are caught for sexual offenses acknowledge that they began offending sexually as teens (e.g., Elliott, Browne, & Kilcoyne, 1995; Prentky & Knight, 1993). The third group consists of adolescents who have offended sexually and who stop offending forever once they have been detected by authorities. For these adolescents, it may be the shame and embarrassment connected with the detection of the behavior that results in termination of sexual offending. Fourth, there are adolescents who have committed a sexual offense and will stop only after being both detected and treated. Finally, there is a group of adolescents who have offended sexually and continue to do so despite being detected and treated.

Despite the obvious variability in outcome, there is a tendency for some people to view *all* adolescents who sexually offend as "high risk." When this bias influences judgment, many adolescents who are truly lower risk are erroneously labeled as "high risk," resulting in unnecessary and potentially deleterious and irreversible consequences, such as severe restrictions on their personal freedom, family separation, intensive offense-specific treatment, and long-term legal restrictions. Furthermore, when low-risk adolescents are inaccurately labeled high risk, precious specialized treatment resources will not be provided to those who are most in need. At the other end of the spectrum, some authors have pointed to selected recidivism data and have stated that the risk for sexual reoffending among adolescents is low. Therefore, they question the need for specialized assessment and treatment. When this bias is operating, many adolescents who are truly at high risk of reoffending sexually are not provided with appropriate restrictions or treatment, and the result may be further sexual offenses. The high stakes involved in making decisions regarding risk calls for empirically derived data on risk and protective factors for recidivism and improved procedures for risk assessment.

Published Recidivism Data

Although recidivism data are often equated with actual sexual reoffending, recidivism figures based on "official" statistics are typically conservative estimates. The accuracy of registered data is contingent on many factors, such as the victimized person's willingness to report the offense; the ability of an adult in the victimized person's environment to correctly perceive and act on this information; the ability of child protection agencies or the police to investigate a complaint; the decision of police and prosecutors to press charges that reflect the sexual nature of the crime; the accurate and timely entry of the charge into the database; and, finally, the ability of the researcher to access the official data. Naturally, when a court conviction is used as a recidivism estimate, the measurement of recidivism is additionally dependent on charges not being dropped or altered to a nonsexual charge through plea bargaining and on the outcome of any adjudication process.

We located 22 published follow-up investigations of unique (or slightly overlapping) samples of juveniles who had committed a sexual offense (see Table 10.1). Published sexual assault recidivism rates range quite dramatically from 0% to almost 40% across studies. Mean follow-up periods vary from 6 months to 9 years. On average, authors using criminal charges as an estimate of reoffending cited a sexual assault recidivism rate of 15% (127 of 846), and investigators using more conservative estimates such as convictions, court records, self-report, or adult-only charges reported a recidivism rate for sexual offenses of 14% (226 of 1,593). This dissimilarity is not significant, χ^2 (1, n = 2,439) = 0.30, $p < .05$. However, when the examined outcome was any criminal (including sexual) recidivism, investigators using charges found that 54% (455 of 846) of adolescents were charged with any reoffense, whereas those using more conservative measures reported an overall criminal recidivism rate of 42% (422 of 998) and this difference is significant, $\chi^2(1, n = 1,844) = 24.27, p < .001$.

The generalizability of empirically derived recidivism base rates is also dependent on the length of the follow-up period. In the case of adults who have offended sexually, longer follow-up times typically yield higher recidivism rates (Quinsey, Harris, Rice, & Cormier, 1998). For the investigations in Table 10.1, the average follow-up period was matched against sexual-reoffense data. For studies in which the mean follow-up time was not specified, we used the median time. For example, Kahn and Lafond (1988) reported a follow-up of "several weeks" to 5 years; therefore, we used 30 months as the average follow-up period for that study. As in the case of research with adults who offend sexually, there was a significant linear relationship between length of follow-up and sexual assault recidivism, $r = 0.61; F_{(1,19)} = 11.37, p < .01$. This relationship was also observed for any criminal recidivism, $r = 0.66; F_{(1,15)} = 11.63, p < .01$. Therefore, it is important for those examining recidivism rates to be mindful of both the source of the data (i.e., charges vs. convictions) and the length of the follow-up interval when conclusions are drawn.

TABLE 10.1. Published Recidivism Rates for Adolescents Who Have Offended Sexually

Study	Age	Treatment group n	Comparison group n	Specialized treatment (community-based vs. residential)	Follow-up period	Recidivism measure	Any recidivism (%)	Sexual recidivism (%)
Borduin et al. (1990)	M = 14	8	8	Community	M = 3 years	Charges, local and state records	25—treatment (2/8) 88—comparison (7/8)	13—treatment (1/8) 75—comparison (6/8)
Borduin & Schaeffer (2001)	"youths" (Not specified)	24	24	Community	M = 8 years	Charges, local and state records	29—treatment (7/24) 63—comparison (15/24)	13—treatment (3/24) 42—comparison (10/24)
Brannon & Troyer (1991)	13–18 (M = 16.5)	53	0	Residential	Not specified	Survey of parole workers	34 (18/54)	2 (1/54)
Brannon & Troyer (1995)	14–19	36	0	Residential	4 years	Adult incarceration, statewide	17 (6/36)	3 (1/36)
Bremer (1992)	12–18	193	0	Residential	Several months to 6 years (Estimated median = 3 years)	Self-report	Not specified	11 (18/193)
Gretton et al. (2001)	12–18	220	0	Community	7–106 months (M = 55 months)	Charges, national database	51 (112/220)	15 (33/220)

cont.

Study	Age	N	N	Treatment	Follow-up	Outcome measure	Recidivism	Recidivism
Hagan, Gust-Brey, Cho, & Dow (2001)	12–19	100	0	Residential	8 years	Convictions, state records	Not specified	18 (18/100)
Kahn & Chambers (1991)	8–18 (M = 14.7)	221	0	Both	M = 20 months	Convictions, state records	45 (99/221)	7.5 (16/221)
Kahn & Lafond (1988)		350	0	Residential	Several weeks to 5 years (Estimated median = 2.5 years)	Not specified	17 (no numbers reported: assumed to be 60/350)	9 (no numbers reported; assumed to be 32/350)
Lab et al. (1993)	M = 14	46	109	Community	1–3 years (Estimated mean = 2 years)	Convictions, juvenile court records	24—treatment (11/46) 17—comparison (18/109)	2—treatment (1/46) 4—comparison (4/109)
Långström (2002)	15–20	117	0	No treatment	M = 115 months	Convictions, national database	79 (92/117)	30 (35/117)
Långström & Grann (2000)	15–20 (M = 18.13)	46	0	No treatment	M = 61 months	Convictions, national database	65 (30/46)	20 (9/46)
Nisbet et al. (2004)	10–18 (M = 16)	292	0	Not specified	M = 7.3 years	Convictions, state records	Not specified	29 (84/292)
Prentky et al. (2000)	9–20	75	0	Community	1 year	Court records, city	11 (8/75)	4 (3/75)
Mazur & Michael (1992)	13–17	10	0	Community	6 months	Self- and parent-report	Not specified	0 (0/10)
Miner (2002)	14–19 (M = 17.2)	86	0	Residential	M = 4.29 years (a few months to 6.5 yrs.)	Arrest, conviction, or parole violation, state records	55 (47/86)	8 (8/86)

TABLE 10.1. *cont.*

Study	Age	Treatment group *n*	Comparison group *n*	Specialized treatment (community-based vs. residential)	Follow-up period	Recidivism measure	Any recidivism (%)	Sexual recidivism (%)
Rasmussen (1999)	7–18 (M = 14)	170	0	Both	5 years	Juvenile convictions, state records	58 (100/170)	14 (24/170)
Rubinstein, Yeager, Goodstein, & Lewis (1993)	Not specified	19	0	Not specified	8 years	Adult arrests, state and FBI records	89 (17/19)	37 (7/19)
Schram et al. (1992)	M = 14.5	197	0	Both	5 years	Charges	63 (124/197)	12 (24/197)
Sipe, Jensen, & Everett (1998)	11–18	124	0	Not specified	M = 6 years	Adult charges, state records	32 (40/124)	10 (12/124)
Smith & Monastersky (1986)	10–16 (M = 14.1)	112	0	Community	M = 28 months	Juvenile charges, state records	49 (55/112)	14 (16/112)
Worling & Curwen (2000)	12–19 (M = 15.5)	58	90	Community	2–10 years (M = 6.23 years)	Charges, national database	35—treatment (20/58) 54—comparison (49/90)	5—treatment (3/58) 18—comparison (16/90)

In an effort to identify relevant risk factors for criminal recidivism for adolescents who had offended sexually, we (Worling & Långström, 2003) completed a narrative review of the published literature. In that review, we categorized risk factors for sexual recidivism into the following four categories: *empirically supported, promising, possible*, and *unlikely*. The support for each factor was concluded from empirical studies of risk factors for sexual reoffending in adolescents who had committed sexual offenses and contrasted against clinical guidelines and checklists developed by expert practitioners in the field. The latter documents represent attempts to structure clinical observations and theoretically derived assumptions concerning factors related to reoffending risk among adolescents. Further, when available, findings were also compared with data from meta-analyses on risk factors for recidivism in adults who offended sexually (Hanson & Bussière, 1998), serious or violent offending among adolescents in the general population (Lipsey & Derzon, 1998), and recidivism in adolescents known for having committed crimes (Cottle, Lee, & Heilbrun, 2001).

Empirically Supported Risk Factors

For each of the risk factors described in this section, there have been at least two independent empirical investigations statistically linking the risk factor to sexual reoffending. Furthermore, no contradictory findings have been published so far. As these risk factors have the most defensible empirical support relative to other factors described later, they should be relied upon most in the assessment of sexual-reoffending risk. Support for these risk factors also comes from several clinical guidelines and checklists.

Deviant Sexual Interest

Adolescents who offend sexually and who are sexually interested in prepubescent children and/or in sexual violence are at increased risk of committing subsequent sexual offenses. Worling and Curwen (2000) found that self-reported sexual interest in children was a risk factor for sexual reoffending. Kenny, Keogh, and Seidler (2001) found that adolescents with a previous charge for sexual offending ("recidivists") were more likely to report deviant sexual fantasies that reflected sexual interest in the use of force or in young children. Finally, Schram, Malloy, and Rowe (1992) found that adolescents rated by clinicians as most likely to have deviant sexual interests more often reoffended sexually. Several authors of risk assessment guidelines for adolescents who offended sexually have suggested that deviant sexual interests increase risk for sexual reoffending (Calder, Hanks, & Epps, 1997; Epps, 1997; Lane, 1997; Rich, 2001; Ross & Loss, 1991).

Although deviant sexual interest as measured by penile plethysmography (PPG) is a robust predictor of sexual-assault recidivism for *adults* (Hanson & Bussière, 1998), Gretton, McBride, Hare, O'Shaughnessy, and Kumka (2001) were not able to show that deviant arousal assessed by PPG was related to sexual reoffending for adolescents. Therefore, empirical support for the contribution of deviant sexual interest to sexual-reoffending risk is presently limited to adolescent self-report or therapist ratings.

Prior Criminal Sanctions for Sexual Offending

Adolescents who continue to commit sexual offenses despite prior legal sanctions are at higher risk of sexual assault recidivism. Schram et al. (1992) found that adolescents with at least one conviction for a sexual assault before the index sexual offense were more likely to recidivate sexually. In investigations by Långström and Grann (2000) and Långström (2002; including the sample from Långström & Grann, 2000), a history of previous sexual offenses, including prior convictions, was related to sexual assault recidivism. A prior criminal charge for a sexual offense is also considered a risk factor in the risk assessment checklist outlined by Ross and Loss (1991). In studies with adults who have offended sexually, a history of prior legal sanctions for sexual assaults (i.e., charges or convictions) is clearly associated with later sexual offending (Hanson & Bussière, 1998).

Sexual Offending Against More than One Victim

Adolescents who have committed sexual offenses against two or more victims are at higher risk of reoffending sexually. Rasmussen (1999) found that the number of assaulted female victims was related to subsequent sexual offenses. Långström (2002) and Worling (2002) independently reported that adolescents who offended against two or more victims were more likely to be reconvicted of a sexual crime than were adolescents with one known victim. In addition, several authors of risk assessment guidelines also suggest that adolescents with a history of sexual offenses against multiple victims are more likely to reoffend sexually (Epps, 1997; Lane, 1997; Perry & Orchard, 1992; Ross & Loss, 1991; Steen & Monnette, 1989). It is difficult to comment on the empirical support for this risk factor based on research with adults, as researchers have typically focused on the number of prior charges or convictions rather than on the number of victims, per se.

Sexual Offending against a Stranger Victim

Adolescents who have ever targeted a stranger as victim in a sexual offense are at greater risk of continued sexual offending. Smith and Monastersky (1986) and Långström (2002) found that the selection of strangers as victims was moderately associated with sexual reoffending for adolescents. In their list of potential risk factors, Ross and Loss (1991) suggested that adolescents who consistently target strangers are at a higher risk of a sexual reoffense. Results of research with primarily adult males indicate that the selection of victims who are strangers is related to sexual reoffending (Hanson & Bussière, 1998).

Social Isolation

Adolescents who offend sexually and who are unable to form or uninterested in forming emotionally intimate peer relationships or who are socially isolated are at higher risk to commit further sexual offenses. Långström and Grann (2000) found that adolescents with limited social contacts were more than three times as likely to be reconvicted for a sexual crime. Similarly, Kenny et al. (2001) reported that adolescents who displayed poor social skills and who had weak relationships with peers were more likely to be sexual assault recidivists than adolescents who had better social relationships. In their meta-analysis, Lipsey and Derzon (1998) noted that social isolation was a robust risk factor for violent (including sexual) offending in adolescents. Cottle et al. (2001) found a similar relationship between social isolation and criminal reoffending among antisocial youths ages 12 to 21 years.

Social isolation or social difficulties are listed as indicators of sexual-reoffending risk in guidelines for adolescents who have offended sexually (Epps, 1997; Lane, 1997; Perry & Orchard, 1992; Rich, 2001; Ross & Loss, 1991). With reference to adults who offend sexually, Grubin (1999) suggested that a long-standing history of social isolation is a risk indicator. Hanson (2000) stated that an inability to form and maintain intimate relationships is a promising dynamic risk factor for sexual recidivism in adults.

Uncompleted Offense-Specific Treatment

Adolescents who have not participated in specialized treatment for their sexual offending behavior are at higher risk to reoffend sexually than are adolescents who have completed such treatment. There are very few published studies with both treatment and comparison groups. Nevertheless, available data suggest that adolescents who complete comprehensive treatment combining a strong family-relationship component with offense-specific interventions are less likely to commit further sexual and nonsexual offenses (Borduin, Henggeler, Blaske, & Stein, 1990; Worling & Curwen, 2000). Authors of most clinically based risk guidelines list unwillingness to engage in treatment as a risk factor for sexual reoffending (Epps, 1997; Lane, 1997; Perry & Orchard, 1992; Rich, 2001; Ross and Loss, 1991; Steen & Monnette, 1989). The results of a meta-analytic review of the effectiveness of psychological treatment for primarily adult males who have offended sexually are supportive of a treatment effect (Hanson et al., 2002).

Promising Risk Factors

The following factors have been listed in published risk-factor checklists for adolescents and are supported by a single published study focused specifically on adolescent sexual-assault recidivism. Although assessors will likely want to examine these factors when formulating a risk estimate, they presently have limited empirical support.

Problematic Parent–Adolescent Relationships

Adolescents with a history of sexual offending who also have problematic relationships with parents are likely at higher risk of further sexual assaults. Worling and Curwen (2000) reported a moderate correlation between perceived parental rejection and sexual recidivism in adolescents. Poor parent–child relationships were related to later violent (including sexual) offending in a meta-analysis of risk factors for criminal behavior in adolescents and young adults in general (Lipsey & Derzon, 1998) and to any criminal recidivism in another meta-analysis based on studies of young individuals already known for committing crimes (Cottle et al., 2001).

Ross and Loss (1991) and Lane (1997) suggested that the quality of the parent–child relationship is related to risk of sexual reoffending in their risk-assessment guidelines. There has not been much published research regarding family-of-origin relationships and adult sexual assault recidivism. However, Hanson and Bussière (1998) noted that adult males who described negative relationships with their mothers were more likely to reoffend sexually.

Attitudes Supportive of Sexual Offending

Adolescents who believe that sexual assaults are invited by victims, are educational, or are harmless are probably at higher risk of committing sexual assaults again. Kahn and Chambers (1991) found that adolescents who blamed their victims were more likely to have a subsequent conviction for a sexual offense. Authors of risk assessment guidelines note that offending-supportive attitudes such as victim blame and the belief that sexual assaults are not wrong or harmful are risk indicators (Calder et al., 1997; Epps, 1997; Perry & Orchard, 1992). In research with adults, attitudes supportive of sexual offending are related to increased risk for subsequent sexual assaults (e.g., Hanson & Harris, 1998; Hudson, Wales, Bakker, & Ward, 2002; Thornton, 2002).

Possible Risk Factors

Some authors presently view these risk factors as related to sexual assault recidivism. However, one should use considerable caution when basing risk assessments on these factors given the current lack of empirical support.

High-Stress Family Environment

In their meta-analysis of research regarding risk factors for violence (including sexual violence) among adolescents, Lipsey and Derzon (1998) found that family distress was correlated with violent (including sexual) or other serious offending. Current risk assessment guidelines include extreme family dysfunction or distress as a risk indicator for adolescent sexual reoffending (Lane, 1997; Perry & Orchard, 1992; Rich, 2001; Ross & Loss, 1991; Steen & Monnette, 1989; Wenet & Clark, 1986). As noted earlier, family relationships have not been examined often in recidivism research with adults who sexually offend.

Impulsivity

Epps (1997), Lane (1997), and Rich (2001) suggested that impulsive adolescents are at greater risk to reoffend sexually. There is no empirical support for this factor specifically in adolescents who offend sexually, and it has yet to be researched. There is, however, ample evidence that impulsivity is related to general juvenile delinquency and nonsexual reoffending (e.g., Cottle et al., 2001; Lipsey & Derzon, 1998). Hanson (2000) suggested that general self-regulation is one of the more promising dynamic risk factors for adult sexual-assault recidivism.

Antisocial Interpersonal Orientation

Although a history of antisocial behaviors or a delinquent orientation has been suggested as a risk factor for continued sexual assaults in most risk guidelines for adolescents (Epps, 1997; Lane, 1997; Perry & Orchard, 1992; Rich, 2001; Ross & Loss, 1991), the empirical support for such an association is lacking. For example, in two investigations in which psychopathy was measured using a structured scale, no relationship was shown between psychopathy and adolescent sexual-assault recidivism (Gretton et al., 2001; Långström & Grann, 2000). Similarly, Worling and Curwen (2000) found that antisocial personality features were not associated with sexual assault recidivism. In contrast, but consistent with meta-analyses of risk factors for serious antisocial behavior and criminal recidivism in juveniles (Cottle et al., 2001; Lipsey & Derzon, 1998), antisocial personality traits were associated with *nonsexual* criminal recidivism in all three investigations (see Risk Factors for Nonsexual Reoffending). Hanson and Bussière (1998) found that an antisocial personality was related to sexual assault recidivism in adults who had offended sexually.

Interpersonal Aggression

Available risk assessment checklists for adolescents who have offended sexually suggest that a history of interpersonal aggression is related to a heightened risk for continued sexual offending (Epps, 1997; Perry & Orchard, 1992; Rich, 2001; Ross & Loss, 1991; Wenet & Clark, 1986). Långström (2002) found no relationship between prior violent nonsexual criminal convictions and sexual recidivism risk among adolescents who had offended sexually. However, Hanson and Bussière (1998) reported a small correlation between anger problems and sexual assault recidivism in their meta-analysis of recidivism studies with primarily adult males.

Negative Peer Associations

Some authors of risk assessment guidelines for adolescents who have offended sexually include association with an antisocial peer group as an indicator of higher risk for sexual assault recidivism (Rich, 2001; Ross & Loss, 1991), although the association of this variable with sexual reoffending has not yet been researched. Undoubtedly, association with delinquent peers is a well-established risk factor for both the onset and persistence of antisocial behavior (e.g., Cottle et al., 2001; Lipsey & Derzon, 1998).

Although only very little research is available regarding the impact of peer associations on adult sexual assault recidivism, Hanson (2000) noted that adults who associate with peers who support deviant lifestyles or inadequate coping strategies are at greater risk of reoffending sexually.

Sexual Preoccupation

Authors of risk assessment guidelines for adolescents note the need to assess sexual preoccupation (Epps, 1997; Lane, 1997; Steen & Monnette, 1989), compulsive ideation regarding past offenses (Perry & Orchard, 1992), and compulsive, deviant masturbatory fantasies (Ross & Loss, 1991; Wenet & Clark, 1986). Sexual preoccupation has yet to be examined in research with adolescents, although it has been described as a promising dynamic variable for adults and it is included in the SONAR (Hanson & Harris, 2000), an actuarial tool to examine dynamic risk factors for adult sexual offense recidivism.

Sexual Offending against a Male Victim

In research with adults who have offended sexually, an increase in risk of sexual reoffending is found for males who victimize male children (Hanson & Bussière, 1998). At this point, the findings for adolescents are contradictory. Male adolescents who abuse male victims are more likely to commit a subsequent sexual offense, according to two studies (Långström & Grann, 2000; Smith & Monastersky, 1986). On the other hand, others (Rasmussen, 1999; Worling & Curwen, 2000) found that the number of male victims and victim gender, respectively, were unrelated to sexual reoffending. Further, in an extension of the Långström and Grann (2000) study, based on the original sample and completing it by adding more participants and conducting a longer follow-up, Långström (2002) no longer found an association between any male victim and sexual recidivism. This may indicate that the previous positive association was spurious.

Sexual Offending against a Child

In their lists of risk factors, Rich (2001) and Ross and Loss (1991) suggested that adolescents who sexually abuse young children are at higher risk to reoffend sexually. The empirical data from retrospective studies with adolescents who have offended sexually are mixed. Some authors have not found evidence that having a child victim is related to increased risk for sexual recidivism (Hagan & Cho, 1996; Långström, 2002; Rasmussen, 1999; Smith & Monastersky, 1986; Worling & Curwen, 2000). However, Kahn and Chambers (1991) and Sipe, Jensen, and Everett (1998) found that a past sexual assault against a child victim was related to the risk of further sexual assaults. In their meta-analysis of recidivism studies with primarily adults, Hanson and Bussière (1998) found that child-victim choice was unrelated to reoffending. Perhaps victim age, like victim gender, is a weaker marker of risk for sexual recidivism in adolescents given that sexual preferences are usually not as "fixed" for teens as for adults.

Threats, Violence, or Weapons in Sexual Offense

Many authors of risk assessment guidelines have commented that adolescents who have used violence or weapons during their sexual assaults are at higher risk to reoffend sexually (Epps, 1997; Lane, 1997; Perry & Orchard, 1992; Rich, 2001; Ross & Loss, 1991; Steen & Monnette, 1989; Wenet & Clark, 1986). Although Kahn and Chambers (1991) found that adolescents who made verbal threats during their sexual assaults were more likely to reoffend sexually, Långström (2002) found that the use of weapons or death threats was related to nonsexual violent reoffending but not to subsequent sexual assaults. Perhaps these contradictory findings are a result of the focus on death threats but not other threats of violence in the latter study, or perhaps these characteristics have a stronger association with sexual recidivism in less generally violent adolescents who offend sexually. Hanson and Bussière (1998) found that the use of force and physical victim injury were not related to sexual assault recidivism in their meta-analysis of studies of primarily adults who had offended sexually.

Environment Supporting Reoffending

When estimating risk of a future behavior, the individual's current and future environment should be considered. For example, poor adult supervision and access to pornography and potential victims could increase risk for some adolescents. Epps (1997) and Ross and Loss (1991) suggested that adolescents who have unsupervised access to potential victims are at higher risk to reoffend sexually. Despite the intuitive logic, few data related to this factor are available with either adolescents or adults who have offended sexually. In an investigation with adults, however, Hanson and Harris (1998) found that sexual assault recidivists were more likely than nonrecidivists to place themselves in situations providing greater access to victims.

Unlikely Risk Factors

Given the present contrary empirical evidence, the factors listed here should not be used when formulating risk estimates for adolescents. The collection of additional data, or the use of better measurement techniques, may lead to evidence that supports some of these risk factors. Of course, it is also possible that researchers will confirm that these factors are clearly not related to adolescent sexual reoffending.

Adolescent's Own History of Sexual Victimization

Some authors of guidelines for professional assessment suggest that adolescents who offend sexually and who are victims of child sexual abuse are at greater risk for reoffending sexually (Perry & Orchard, 1992; Rich, 2001; Steen & Monnette, 1989; Wenet & Clark, 1986). However, available data indicate that a childhood sexual abuse history (measured dichotomously) is not predictive of sexual reoffending (Hagan & Cho, 1996; Rasmussen, 1999; Worling & Curwen, 2000). Although childhood sexual abuse may be linked, under some conditions, to the onset of adolescent sexual aggression for some adolescents (Borowsky, Hogan, & Ireland, 1997; Morris, Anderson, & Knox, 2002), there is no support for this variable as a risk marker for continued sexual offending once an adolescent has been detected. With respect to research with adults, Hanson and Bussière (1998) reported no relationship between an offending adult's childhood sexual victimization history and sexual offense recidivism.

History of Nonsexual Offending

A history of nonsexual crimes is listed as a risk factor for adolescent sexual assault recidivism in most expert clinical guidelines (Epps, 1997; Perry & Orchard, 1992; Rich, 2001; Ross & Loss, 1991; Wenet & Clark, 1986). Although a history of nonsexual criminal charges is related to sexual assault recidivism for adult males (Hanson & Bussière, 1998), researchers have consistently demonstrated that this variable is not related to subsequent sexual offenses among adolescents (Kahn & Chambers, 1991; Lab, Shields, & Schondel, 1993; Långström, 2002; Sipe et al., 1998; Rasmussen, 1999; Worling & Curwen, 2000). As expected, however, most researchers have found that a history of nonsexual crimes is related to nonsexual reoffending.

Sexual Offending Involving Penetration

Authors of available checklists and guidelines suggest that adolescents who engage in penetrative (anal, vaginal, or oral) sexual assaults are at higher risk of reoffending sexually (Epps, 1997; Ross & Loss, 1991; Steen & Monnette, 1989). However, Långström (2002) reported that victim penetration was negatively related to subsequent convictions for sexual offenses. In their meta-analysis of factors related to recidivism primarily in adults, Hanson and Bussière (1998) found a weak relationship between being involved in exhibitionistic acts and sexual recidivism risk. However, no relationship was identified between the degree of sexual contact and sexual recidivism. Perhaps researchers and clinicians should examine separately the occurrence of noncontact offenses, such as exhibitionistic acts, and the extent of penetration within contact sexual offenses. These may be independent risk factors, and combining them may conceal important information.

Denial of Sexual Offending

Authors of all available guidelines for the assessment of adolescent sexual recidivism risk claim that denial of the sexual offense is a risk marker (Epps, 1997; Perry & Orchard, 1992; Rich, 2001; Ross & Loss, 1991; Steen & Monnette, 1989; Wenet & Clark, 1986). On the contrary, however, available research indicates that adolescents who deny their sexual crimes are less likely to reoffend sexually (Kahn & Chambers, 1991; Långström & Grann, 2000; Worling, 2002). This finding is counterintuitive to most clinicians working with adolescents who commit sexual offenses. However, the negative correlation between denial and reoffending may be the result of the relationship between these variables in a subgroup of generally antisocial adolescents who also offend sexually. These adolescents may be more motivated or skilled to deny offending and, at the same time, at a lower risk to reoffend sexually— perhaps less motivated by deviant sexual interests when committing sexual assaults. Alternatively, perhaps some mechanisms that result in denial of the sexual offense (e.g., shame and embarrassment) also act somehow to reduce the odds of a future sexual offense. In their meta-analysis of studies of primarily adult males, Hanson and Bussière (1998) found no relation between denial of the sexual offense and sexual assault recidivism.

Low Victim Empathy

Most published guidelines include lack of remorse or empathy as evidence of heightened risk for sexual recidivism for adolescents with a history of sexual offenses (Epps, 1997; Perry & Orchard, 1992; Rich, 2001; Ross & Loss, 1991; Steen & Monnette, 1989; Wenet & Clark, 1986). However, there are currently no data supporting this suggestion. Smith and Monastersky (1986) found no relation between the adolescent's inability to understand the exploitative character of the sexual offense and sexual recidivism. Similarly, Långström and Grann (2000) found that adolescents with low general empathy were no more at risk of being reconvicted for a sexual crime than those with more empathy.

In their meta-analysis concerning adults who offended sexually, Hanson and Bussière (1998) found no relation between low empathy for victims and sexual assault recidivism. Many measures of victim empathy assess the ability to cognitively recognize emotional distress in others. Although this is certainly an important component of empathy, very few existing measures tap compassion for others or affective empathy, abilities that may prevent future sexual offending. If researchers devised different measures of victim empathy, compassion, or remorse, they might find support for the use of this variable.

Risk Factors for Adolescents versus Adults

Some authors have stressed that factors related to adolescent sexual offending are unique when contrasted with what is known about adults and that there is little useful overlap when it comes to risk assessment. Conversely, other clinicians have denied any distinctions between the two groups and have used actuarial risk instruments designed for adults in their assessment of adolescents. We believe, from the current review, that a defensible position is somewhere in between these two extremes. On one hand, many of the empirically supported risk factors for adolescent sexual assault recidivism (e.g., stranger victim, prior legal sanction for a sexual assault, social isolation, incomplete offense-specific treatment, and deviant sexual interests) are also well-supported risk factors for adults who sexually offend. General impulsivity, sexual preoccupation, and access to potential victims are also promising risk factors for both age groups. Furthermore, a number of factors are evidently not related to risk of sexual reoffending for either adolescents or adults (e.g., denial of the offense and history of childhood sexual abuse). These results are suggestive of considerable overlap with respect to risk factors.

On the other hand, there are unique risk factors for both groups, indicating that checklists and actuarial tools designed to estimate risk for one group should not be used for the other. For example, although a history of nonsexual crimes, deviant arousal measured by PPG, and marital status are predictive of sexual reoffending risk for adults, these variables should not be used to estimate risk for adolescents. Similarly, other variables, such as problematic parent–child relationships, are likely to have much more bearing on future risk for adolescents than for adults.

Risk Factors for Minority–Ethnicity Adolescents and Adolescent Females

So far, ethnically mixed samples from Canada, the United States, the United Kingdom, Sweden, and Australia have been used for the study of recidivism risk factors among adolescents who commit sexual offenses. Particularly in these countries, the careful use of the risk factors presented previously also with non-majority-ethnicity male adolescents who have offended sexually seems warranted. However, researchers have yet to report on whether the relative importance of risk factors for sexual recidivism in adolescents varies with race or ethnicity.

Systematic reviews have not revealed distinct differences in risk factors across gender in adolescents, either for aggressive behavior (Leschied, Cummings, Van Brunschot, Cunningham, & Saunders, 2000) or for general (including sexual) offending (Simourd & Andrews, 1994). However, we could not identify any study focused specifically on risk factors for recidivism among adolescent females who have offended sexually. We suggest that risk factors identified in studies with male adolescents who offend sexually should be employed with substantial caution for the assessment of adolescent females who commit sexual offenses.

Risk Factors for Nonsexual Reoffending

As noted in Table 10.1, adolescents who commit sexual offenses are, on average, more likely to be detected for nonsexual reoffenses than for sexual reoffenses. In agreement with the literature with adults who offend sexually (cf. Hanson & Bussière, 1998), Långström and Grann (2000) found that factors related to any criminal recidivism among adolescents who offended sexually were clearly different from factors associated with sexual recidivism. Conduct disorder symptoms before age 15 (DSM-IV; American Psychiatric Association, 1994), number of previous convictions (for any offense), Psychopathy Checklist—Revised (PCL-R) psychopathy (Hare, 1991), and sexual-offense-related use of weapons or death threats were all related to *any recidivism*, but not to sexual assault recidivism. Similarly, Gretton et al. (2001) found psychopathy to relate to any recidivism, but not to sexual assault recidivism. When extending his previous study, Långström (2002) established that early-onset conduct disorder, a prior violent conviction, and sexual-offense-related variables such as use of threats or weapons and causing physical victim injury were all risk factors for *violent* nonsexual recidivism. Again, none of these factors was associated with sexual assault recidivism. Finally, Worling and Curwen (2000) reported that factors including lower socioeconomic status, hostility, aggression, antisocial personality, and previous criminal charges predicted violent and nonviolent *nonsexual*, but not sexual, recidivism.

Approaches to Risk Assessment

In addition to the identification of the adolescent's unique strengths, concerns, and treatment needs, current best-practice guidelines suggest that the risk of a reoffense should be addressed in assessments (Association for the Treatment of Sexual Abusers [ATSA], 2001). Estimates of the risk for future sexual offending assist with decisions regarding critical issues such as the level of community access, the timing of family reunification, and the delivery of specific treatment interventions.

When providing assessments of risk of reoffending sexually, it is generally held that—at least for adults—actuarial assessments are superior to unstructured clinical judgment (e.g., Barbaree, Seto, Langton, & Peacock, 2001; Hanson, 2000). Unlike unstructured clinical judgments, actuarial assessments are based on an objective scoring system for a fixed number of risk factors. Additionally, the risk factors included in most actuarial systems were identified through an examination of follow-up research with large samples of individuals. Furthermore, for a scale to be actuarial, the total score must correspond to a probabilistic estimate of risk over a fixed period (e.g., 30% likelihood of a sexual reoffense over a 5-year period).

Clinicians working with adults have access to a number of actuarial risk estimation tools that have been studied empirically, such as the Static-99 (Hanson & Thornton, 1999), the Rapid Risk Assessment of Sexual Offense Recidivism (RRASOR; Hanson, 1997), and the Sex Offender Risk Appraisal Guide (SORAG; Quinsey et al., 1998). Although juveniles represent at least 20% of all those charged with sexual offenses in North America (Federal Bureau of Investigation, 1993; Statistics Canada, 1997), there has not yet been enough published research to develop, refine, and test actuarial tools for sexual reoffense risk in adolescents.

Some clinicians working with adolescents who have offended sexually continue to base risk estimates on unstructured clinical judgment. However, there are serious concerns regarding the accuracy of clinical judgment with respect to predicting sexual assault recidivism (Hanson, 2002). To provide more structured judgments, many assessors use one or more of the popular checklists or guidelines developed based on expert clinical opinion (Calder et al., 1997; Epps, 1997; Lane, 1997; Perry & Orchard, 1992; Rich, 2001; Ross & Loss, 1991; Steen & Monnette,

1989; Wenet & Clark, 1986). At present, however, no empirical data support these guidelines in their current forms, and certain factors contained within some of the checklists are no longer supported by published research. Furthermore, most checklists and guidelines do not have objective scoring rules, and it would be difficult to assess or enhance interrater agreement.

Empirically Guided Structured Checklists

Although there is not yet enough follow-up research to establish and validate an actuarial tool for adolescents, simply identifying relevant risk factors may be important. Identified risk factors could then be used to inform clinical decisions, in what Hanson (2000) has called *empirically guided clinical judgment*. Unlike actuarial scales, there is no definitive link between a total score and a specific probability of a reoffense using this approach. As such, the overall determination of risk using any empirically guided decision tool remains a clinical judgment. The advantage of empirically guided clinical judgment, in comparison with both unstructured clinical prediction and the available checklists or guidelines, is the promise of higher accuracy given the scientific evidence in favor of the risk factors. Furthermore, the empirically guided approach is more systematic and should lead to better agreement among professionals (cf. Boer, Hart, Kropp, & Webster, 1997).

Two such instruments in use in North America have been described as promising (Doren, 2002; Leversee & Pearson, 2001): the Juvenile Sexual Offender Assessment Protocol (J-SOAP; Prentky & Righthand, 2001, 2003) and the Estimate of Risk of Adolescent Sexual Offense Recidivism (ERASOR; Worling & Curwen, 2001). Both tools offer explicit scoring instructions for a fixed number of risk factors, and both are designed to assist clinicians to estimate the risk of a sexual reoffense for individuals ages 12–18.

Juvenile Sex Offender Assessment Protocol

The original version of the J-SOAP had scoring criteria for 23 factors in four risk domains: (1) Sexual Drive/Sexual Preoccupation, (2) Impulsive, Antisocial Behavior, (3) Clinical/Treatment, and (4) Community Adjustment. The 18 factors included in the first two risk domains were static, or historical, factors, whereas the remaining 5 factors in the last two domains were dynamic, or potentially alterable, risk factors. Risk factors are scored 0, 1, or 2, and evaluators are provided with a score sheet to compute total scores. The authors caution, however, that the scores are not yet meaningful for interpretation, as follow-up data need to be collected. Based on file-review data for juveniles ages 9–20, the authors reported interrater agreement (using Pearson *r*) ranging from .59 to .91, with most values above .80 (Prentky, Harris, Frizzell, & Righthand, 2000). The authors also collected recidivism data over a 12-month period. However, the low official recidivism statistics over this period prevented evaluation of the scale's predictive validity. With respect to concurrent validity, on the other hand, the J-SOAP appears to be highly related to general juvenile delinquency. The authors reported a substantial correlation of .91 between the J-SOAP total score and the total score from the Youth Level of Service/Case Management Inventory (YLS/CMI; Hoge & Andrews, 2003), a measure of risk for general juvenile delinquency.

Based on preliminary psychometric analyses, the J-SOAP was revised in 2001, and Prentky and Righthand (2001) presented very encouraging results regarding the revised 26-item (16 static and 10 dynamic factors) measure with respect to interrater agreement, internal consistency, and item–total correlations. Promising results regarding the *postdictive* validity of modified and partial J-SOAP scores based on archival data have also been presented (Hecker, Scoular, Righthand, & Nangle, 2002; Waite, Pinkerton, Wieckowski, McGarvey, & Brown, 2002). The J-SOAP was designed to be an actuarial risk assessment tool. Given the lack of prospective follow-up data, however, the authors stress that it should presently be used only as a checklist for the systematic review of risk factors.

The J-SOAP was revised once more in 2003 based on both a reanalysis of the available risk research and on the psychometric properties of the previous version. (The revised, 28-item J-SOAP-II is available free of charge at www.csom.org, and its authors are actively involved in further research with the scale.)

The Estimate of Risk of Adolescent Sexual Offense Recidivism

The J-SOAP was designed and tested as an instrument that could be coded from archival file data, and the majority of the items on that scale are static, or historical, in nature. In contrast, the ERASOR was constructed to be used by evaluators following a clinical assessment, and most risk factors are dynamic so that treatment targets can be identified and reevaluated. The ERASOR was modeled after the Sexual Violence Risk—20 (SVR-20; Boer et al., 1997), an empirically guided clinical checklist for adults who have offended sexually. Unlike the J-SOAP, a total score is not computed with the ERASOR.

The ERASOR was developed following initial field testing with a pilot version at the Sexual Abuse: Family Education and Treatment

(SAFE-T) Program in Toronto, Canada. The 25 risk factors included in the ERASOR (Version 2.0; Worling & Curwen, 2001) fall into five categories: (1) Sexual Interests, Attitudes, and Behaviors, (2) Historical Sexual Assaults, (3) Psychosocial Functioning, (4) Family/Environmental Functioning, and (5) Treatment. The 16 dynamic items (all but the 9 Historical Sexual Assault items) are coded using a 6-month time frame. The ERASOR coding manual contains information regarding the rationale for the inclusion of each risk factor. Specific coding instructions guide the coding of risk factors as *not present*, *possibly or partially present*, *present*, or *unknown*.

Studies of the reliability and validity of the ERASOR are underway in North America and Europe, and preliminary data are supportive. In one such investigation (Worling, 2004), ratings were collected from 28 masters' and doctoral level clinicians immediately following comprehensive assessments of 136 adolescents. With respect to interrater agreement, average-rating intraclass correlation coefficients (ICC) were at or above .70 for 22 of the 25 ERASOR factors, and the average-rating ICC for the overall risk rating for risk of sexual reoffending (*low, moderate,* or *high*) was .91. For evidence of validity, it was found that ERASOR ratings were moderately efficient in differentiating adolescents known to have offended sexually again after being sanctioned by an adult versus those who had never been sanctioned (area under the receiver operating characteristic [ROC] curve = .74; 90% CI = .64–.94). ERASOR risk ratings also differentiated adolescents assessed at community-based clinics from those seen at a specialized residential facility for high-risk/high-needs youths. As in the case of the J-SOAP, however, prospective data regarding the predictive validity of the ERASOR are not yet available. Instructions for both the J-SOAP and the ERASOR specify that it is best for multiple assessors to formulate risk estimates for each adolescent and to combine the independently formed judgments for the final estimate. (The ERASOR manual is also available free of charge by contacting the author at jworling@ican.net.)

Conducting Risk Assessments with Adolescents

Regardless of the specific approach that is taken to formulate a risk estimate, a number of important issues should be considered (cf. Boer et al., 1997; Borum, 2000). First, evaluators should have sufficient training and experience regarding the assessment of adolescents and their families and, particularly, regarding adolescents who offend sexually. Specifically, they should have a good working knowledge of current research regarding etiology, assessment, treatment, and recidivism related to adolescent sexual offending. Second, assessors should cover multiple domains of the adolescent's functioning. These include sexual (e.g., sexual arousal and attitudes), intrapersonal (e.g., affective expression, impulsivity), interpersonal (e.g., social involvement, aggression), familial (e.g., parent–child relationships, family distress), and biological (e.g., neuropsychiatric or physical health) domains. Third, although empirically supported risk factors are most justifiable, there are other compelling risk factors—such as the adolescent's stated intention to reoffend—that will be important to consider (Hanson, 2002). It is important to be aware that many risk factors have yet to be examined in research. Fourth, information should be collected from multiple sources and informants, such as the adolescent him- or herself, police (including victim statements), child protection or social services, family members, residential staff, and other mental health professionals who are familiar with the adolescent and his or her family. Of course, risk assessments based on information collected solely from the adolescent should be interpreted with considerable caution. For example, the shame and embarrassment typically connected with sexual offending will likely affect the validity of his or her account. Fifth, professionals should use multiple methods of data collection, including interviews (with the adolescent and other informants), psychological tests, reviews of prior assessments and case notes, and direct behavioral observation. Finally, evaluators should collect information regarding both static (historic and unchangeable) and dynamic (variable and potentially changeable) factors.

Communicating Risk Estimates

Risk estimates can result in substantial consequences for the adolescent, for his or her family, and for the community. Therefore, any estimate of risk for future reoffending should be limited and qualified. All too often, risk estimates are made without reference to the quality of the information gathered, the empirical support for the judgments, or the need to reevaluate risk (Hoge, 2002). The following suggestions regarding the communication of risk estimates were inspired by previous work by Boer et al. (1997).

First, evaluators should inform recipients of risk judgments about the current scientific limitations of estimating the risk of offense recidivism. For instance, although risk assessments can be based on the best available research and consensus in expert opinion, it is essential to communicate that *precise* evaluations of risk for individual adolescents are impossible. Although most assessors are well aware of this fact, many consumers of risk assessments are not. Second, it is critical to describe any limitations specific to the assessment at hand, such as lack of detailed information from the victim(s), use of experimental psychophysiological measures, lack of access to parents, and so forth. The anticipated impact of these specific limitations on the risk estimate should be noted. Third, evaluators should stress that their estimates of recidivism risk are strictly time limited. Extensive (and sometimes rapid) social, physical, sexual, emotional, and cognitive developmental changes take place during adolescence. In addition, most risk-factor research is based on average follow-up periods of 4 years or less. Taken together, it is important to note that risk assessments are time limited and should be repeated within certain time intervals or following major change in one or more of the risk factors. Guidelines published by the Association for the Treatment of Sexual Abusers (2001) suggest that treatment providers should consider reevaluation of risk and treatment needs if an assessment had not been completed in the previous year.

Naturally, this time limitation should have significant implications for assessors involved with the perplexing task of addressing long-term risk of criminal reoffending, such as assessments under "sexually violent predator" designations. No published data support making such long-term estimates for adolescents. Fourth, evaluators of risk should make sexual assault recidivism estimates as specific as possible. For example, the evaluator should try to specify qualitative aspects of potential reoffending, such as imminence, frequency, and severity. More specifically, Långström (2002) found that risk factors that were *on average* associated with sexual recidivism among adolescents who had sexually assaulted were not necessarily related to risk for *immediate* or *violent* sexual recidivism. Fifth, evaluators should justify their risk estimates by referring to the presence (or absence) of specific risk or protective factors. It would be helpful for both the adolescent and the recipient of the risk estimate to comment specifically on the reasons why an adolescent is at a particular level of risk. Sixth, in an attempt to individualize assessments founded in group-based empirical data, evaluators should list circumstances that might exacerbate the short-term risk of reoffending in a particular youth. It is usually helpful to try to describe situations that could be warning signs for those working with the adolescent. For example, proximity to prepubescent males or availability of a certain form of sexual media could be noted if they were anticipated to increase risk for a particular adolescent. Finally, evaluators should list strategies that they believe would be helpful in managing and reducing the adolescent's risk to reoffend. In addition to possible therapeutic interventions, this may include recommendations regarding placement, community supervision, and the timing and intensity of family reunification.

In conclusion, although the focus of this chapter is on the risk of sexual reoffending, there are certainly a number of additional important risks to consider in the assessment of an adolescent who has committed a sexual offense. Given the importance of providing a holistic and comprehensive assessment, assessors should also address other risks, such as the risk of self-harm, the risk of substance abuse, the risk of nonsexual (re)offending, and the risk of the adolescent being victimized by others.

References

American Psychiatric Association. (1994). *Diagnostic and statistical manual of mental disorders* (4th ed.). Washington, DC: Author.

Association for the Treatment of Sexual Abusers. (2001). *Practice standards and guidelines for members of the Association for the Treatment of Sexual Abusers.* Beaverton, OR: Author.

Barbaree, H. E., Seto, M. C., Langton, C. M., & Peacock, E. J. (2001). Evaluating the predictive accuracy of six risk assessment instruments for adult sex offenders. *Criminal Justice and Behavior, 28,* 490–521.

Boer, D. P., Hart, S. D., Kropp, P. R., & Webster, C. D. (1997). *Manual for the Sexual Violence Risk—20.* Burnaby, British Columbia, Canada: Simon Fraser University, Mental Health, Law, and Policy Institute.

Borduin, C. M., Henggeler, S. W., Blaske, D. M., & Stein, R. J. (1990). Multisystemic treatment of adolescent sexual offenders. *International Journal of Offender Therapy and Comparative Criminology, 34,* 105–113.

Borduin, C. M., & Schaeffer, C. M. (2001). Mulitsystemic treatment of juvenile sexual offenders: A progress report. *Journal of Psychology and Human Sexuality, 13,* 25–42.

Borowsky, I. M., Hogan, M., & Ireland, M. (1997). Adolescent sexual aggression: Risk and protective factors. *Pediatrics, 100(6),* e6.

Borum, R. (2000). Assessing violence risk among youth. *Journal of Clinical Psychology, 56,* 1263–1288.

Brannon, J. M., & Troyer, R. (1991). Peer group counseling: A normalized residential alternative to the specialized treatment of adolescent sex offenders. *International Journal of Offender Therapy and Comparative Criminology, 35,* 225–234.

Brannon, J. M., & Troyer, R. (1995). Adolescent sex offenders: Investigating adult commitment-rates four years later. *International Journal of Offender Therapy and Comparative Criminology, 39,* 317–326.

Bremer, J. (1992). Serious juvenile sex offenders: Treatment and long-term follow-up. *Psychiatric Annals, 22,* 326–332.

Bremer, J. F. (1998). Challenges in the assessment and treatment of sexually abusive adolescents. *Irish Journal of Psychology, 19,* 82–92.

Calder, M. C., Hanks, H., & Epps, K. J. (1997). *Juveniles and children who sex-*

ually abuse: A guide to risk assessment. Lyme Regis, Dorset, UK: Russell House.

Cottle, C. C., Lee, R. J., & Heilbrun, K. (2001). The prediction of criminal recidivism in juveniles. *Criminal Justice and Behavior, 28,* 367–394.

Doren, D. M. (2002). The state of recidivism risk assessment. *Forum, 14*(2), 4–5.

Elliott, M., Browne, K., & Kilcoyne, J. (1995). Child sexual abuse prevention: What offenders tell us. *Child Abuse and Neglect, 19,* 579–594.

Epps, K. J. (1997). Managing risk. In M. S. Hoghughi, S. R. Bhate, & F. Graham (Eds.), *Working with sexually abusive adolescents* (pp. 35–51). London: Sage.

Federal Bureau of Investigation. (1993). *Crime in the United States: Uniform crime reports.* Washington, DC: U.S. Department of Justice.

Gretton, H. M., McBride, M., Hare, R. D., O'Shaughnessy, R., & Kumka, G. (2001). Psychopathy and recidivism in adolescent sex offenders. *Criminal Justice and Behavior, 28,* 427–449.

Grubin, D. (1999). Actuarial and clinical assessment of risk in sex offenders. *Journal of Interpersonal Violence, 14,* 331–343.

Hagan, M. P., & Cho, M. E. (1996). A comparison of treatment outcomes between adolescent rapists and child sexual offenders. *International Journal of Offender Therapy and Comparative Criminology, 40,* 113–122.

Hagan, M. P., Gust-Brey, K. L., Cho, M. E., & Dow, E. (2001). Eight-year comparative analyses of adolescent rapists, adolescent child molesters, other adolescent delinquents, and the general population. *International Journal of Offender Therapy and Comparative Criminology, 45,* 314–324.

Hanson, R. K. (1997). *The development of a brief actuarial risk scale for sexual offense recidivism* (User Report 97–04). Ottawa, Ontario, Canada: Department of the Solicitor General of Canada.

Hanson, R. K. (2000). *Risk assessment.* Beaverton, OR: Association for the Treatment of Sexual Abusers.

Hanson, R. K., & Bussière, M. T. (1998). Predicting relapse: A meta-analysis of sexual offender recidivism studies. *Journal of Consulting and Clinical Psychology, 66,* 348–362.

Hanson, R. K., Gordon, A., Harris, A. J., Marques, J. K., Murphy, W., Quinsey, V. L., & Seto, M. C. (2002). First report of the collaborative outcome data project on the effectiveness of psychological treatment for sex offenders. *Sexual Abuse: A Journal of Research and Treatment, 14,* 169–194.

Hanson, R. K., & Harris, A. J. R. (1998). *Dynamic predictors of sexual recidivism* (User Report 1998–01). Ottawa, Ontario, Canada: Department of the Solicitor General of Canada.

Hanson, R. K., & Harris, A. J. R. (2000). *The Sex Offender Need Assessment Rating (SONAR): A method for measuring change in risk levels* (User Report 2000–1). Ottawa, Ontario, Canada: Department of the Solicitor General of Canada.

Hanson, R. K., & Thornton, D. (1999). *Improving actuarial risk assessments for sex offenders* (User report 1999–02). Ottawa, Ontario, Canada: Department of the Solicitor General of Canada.

Hare, R. D. (1991). *Manual for the Hare Psychopathy Checklist—Revised.* Toronto, Ontario, Canada: Multi-Health Systems.

Hecker, J., Scoular, J., Righthand, S., & Nangle, D. (2002, October). *Predictive validity of the J-SOAP over 10-plus years: Implications for risk assessment.* Paper presented at the annual meeting of the Association for the Treatment of Sexual Abusers, Montreal, Quebec, Canada.

Hoge, R. D. (2002). Standardized instruments for assessing risk and need in youthful offenders. *Criminal Justice and Behavior, 29,* 380–396.

Hoge, R. D., & Andrews, D. A. (2003). *The Youth Level of Service/Case Management Inventory: Manual.* Toronto, Ontario, Canada: Multi-Health Systems.

Hudson, S. M., Wales, D. S., Bakker, L., & Ward, T. (2002). Dynamic risk factors: The Kia Marama Evaluation. *Sexual Abuse: A Journal of Research and Treatment, 14,* 103–119.

Kahn, T. J., & Chambers, H. J. (1991). Assessing reoffense risk with juvenile sexual offenders. *Child Welfare, 70,* 333–345.

Kahn, T. J., & Lafond, M. A. (1988). Treatment of the adolescent sexual offender. *Child and Adolescent Social Work, 5,* 135–148.

Kenny, D. T., Keogh, T., & Seidler, K. (2001). Predictors of recidivism in Australian juvenile sex offenders: Implications for treatment. *Sexual Abuse: A Journal of Research and Treatment, 13,* 131–148.

Lab, S. P., Shields, G., & Schondel, C. (1993). Research note: An evaluation of juvenile sexual offender treatment. *Crime and Delinquency, 39,* 543–553.

Lane, S. (1997). Assessment of sexually abusive youth. In G. Ryan & S. Lane (Eds.), *Juvenile sexual offending: Causes, consequences, and correction* (rev. ed., pp. 219–263). San Francisco: Jossey-Bass.

Långström, N. (2002). Long-term follow-up of criminal recidivism in young sex offenders: Temporal patterns and risk factors. *Psychology, Crime and Law, 8,* 41–58.

Långström, N., & Grann, M. (2000). Risk for criminal recidivism among young sex offenders. *Journal of Interpersonal Violence, 15,* 855–871.

Leschied, A. W., Cummings, A., Van Brunschot, M., Cunningham, A., & Saunders, A. (2000). *Female adolescent aggression: A review of the literature and the correlates of aggression* (User Report 2000-4). Ottawa, Ontario, Canada: Solicitor General of Canada.

Leversee, T., & Pearson, C. (2001). Eliminating the pendulum effect: A balanced approach to the assessment, treatment, and management of sexually abusive youth. *Journal of the Center for Families, Children and the Courts, 3,* 45–57.

Lipsey, M. W., & Derzon, J. H. (1998). Predictors of violent or serious delinquency in adolescence and early adulthood: A synthesis of longitudinal research. In R. Loeber & D. P. Farrington (Eds.), *Serious and violent juvenile offenders: Risk factors and successful interventions* (pp. 86–105). London: Sage.

Loeber, R., & Farrington, D. P. (1998). *Serious and violent juvenile offenders: Risk factors and successful interventions.* Thousand Oaks, CA: Sage.

Mazur, T., & Michael, P. M. (1992). Outpatient treatment for adolescents with sexually inappropriate behaviour: Program description and six-month follow-up. *Journal of Offender Rehabilitation, 18,* 191–203.

Miner, M. H. (2002). Factors associated with recidivism in juveniles: An analysis of serious juvenile sex offenders. *Journal of Research in Crime and Delinquency, 39,* 421–436.

Morris, R. E., Anderson, M. M., & Knox, G. W. (2002). Incarcerated adolescents' experiences as perpetrators of sexual assault. *Archives of Pediatrics and Adolescent Medicine, 156,* 831–835.

Nisbet, I. A., Wilson, P. H., & Smallbone, S. W. (2003). A prospective longitudinal study of sexual recidivism among adolescent sex offenders. *Sexual Abuse: A Journal of Research and Treatment, 16,* 223–234.

Perry, G. P., & Orchard, J. (1992). *Assessment and treatment of adolescent sex offenders.* Sarasota, FL: Professional Resource Exchange.

Prentky, R., Harris, B., Frizzell, K., & Righthand, S. (2000). An actuarial procedure for assessing risk with juvenile sex offenders. *Sexual Abuse: A Journal of Research and Treatment, 12,* 71–93.

Prentky, R., & Knight, R. A. (1993). Age of onset of sexual assault: Criminal and life history correlates. In G. C. Nagayama Hall, R. Hirschman, J. R. Graham, & M. S. Zaragoza (Eds.), *Sexual aggression: Issues in etiology, assessment, and treatment* (pp. 43–62). Washington, DC: Taylor & Francis.

Prentky, R. A., & Righthand, S. C. (2001). *Juvenile sex offender assessment protocol: Manual.* Available online at www.csom.org

Prentky, R. A., & Righthand, S. C. (2003). *Juvenile sex offender assessment protocol–II: Manual.* Available online at www.csom.org

Quinsey, V. L., Harris, G. T., Rice, M. E., & Cormier, C. A. (1998). *Violent offenders: Appraising and managing risk.* Washington, DC: American Psychological Association.

Rasmussen, L. A. (1999). Factors related to recidivism among juvenile sexual offenders. *Sexual Abuse: A Journal of Research and Treatment, 11,* 69–85.

Rich, P. (2001). *J-RAT: Juvenile (Clinical) Risk Assessment Tool—Assessment of risk for sexual re-offending.* Unpublished manuscript.

Ross, J., & Loss, P. (1991). Assessment of the juvenile sex offender. In G. D. Ryan & S. L. Lane (Eds.), *Juvenile sexual offending: Causes, consequences, and correction* (pp. 199–251). Lexington, MA: Lexington Books.

Rubinstein, M., Yeager, C. A., Goodstein, C., & Lewis, D. O. (1993). Sexually assaultive male juveniles: A follow-up. *American Journal of Psychiatry, 150,* 262–265.

Schram, D. D., Malloy, C. D., & Rowe, W. E. (1992, July). Juvenile sex offenders: A follow-up study of reoffense behavior. *Interchange,,* 1–3.

Simourd, L., & Andrews, D. A. (1994). Correlates of delinquency: A look at gender differences. *Forum on Corrections Research, 6,* 26–31.

Sipe, R., Jensen, E. L., & Everett, R. S. (1998). Adolescent sexual offenders grown up: Recidivism in young adulthood. *Criminal Justice and Behavior, 25,* 109–124.

Smith, W. R., & Monastersky, C. (1986). Assessing juvenile sexual offenders' risk for reoffending. *Criminal Justice and Behavior, 13,* 115–140.

Statistics Canada. (1997). *Canadian crime statistics, 1996.* Ottawa, Ontario, Canada: Statistics Canada, Canadian Centre for Justice Statistics.

Steen, C., & Monnette, B. (1989). *Treating adolescent sex offenders in the community.* Springfield, IL: Thomas.

Thornton, D. (2002). Constructing and testing a framework for dynamic risk assessment. *Sexual Abuse: A Journal of Research and Treatment, 14,* 139–153.

Waite, D., Pinkerton, R., Wieckowski, E., McGarvey, E., & Brown, G. L. (2002, October). *Tracking treatment outcome among juvenile sexual offenders: A nine-year follow-up study.* Paper presented at the annual meeting of the Association for the Treatment of Sexual Abusers, Montreal, Quebec, Canada.

Wenet, G. A., & Clark, T. F. (1986). *The Oregon report on juvenile sexual offenders.* Salem, OR: Department of Human Resources, Children Services Division.

Worling, J. R. (2002). Assessing risk of sexual assault recidivism with adolescent sexual offenders. In M. C. Calder (Ed.), *Young people who sexually abuse: Building the evidence base for your practice* (pp. 365–375). Lyme Regis, Dorset, UK: Russell House.

Worling, J. R. (2004). The Estimate of Risk of Adolescent Sexual Offense Recidivism (ERASOR): Preliminary psychometric data. *Sexual Abuse: A Journal of Research and Treatment, 16,* 235–254.

Worling, J. R., & Curwen, T. (2000). Adolescent sexual offender recidivism: Success of specialized treatment and implications for risk prediction. *Child Abuse and Neglect, 24,* 965–982.

Worling, J. R., & Curwen, T. (2001). Estimate of risk of adolescent sexual offense recidivism (The ERASOR: Version 2.0). In M. C. Calder (Ed.), *Juveniles and children who sexually abuse: Frameworks for assessment* (pp. 372–397). Lyme Regis, Dorset, UK: Russell House. (Available from the author, jworling@ican.net)

Worling, J. R., & Långström, N. (2003). Assessment of criminal recidivism risk with adolescents who have offended sexually. *Trauma, Violence, and Abuse: A Review Journal, 4,* 341–362.

CHAPTER 11

Conceptual Issues in Treatment Evaluation Research with Juvenile Sexual Offenders

Calvin M. Langton
Howard E. Barbaree

There has been much discussion about the treatment outcome literature with sexual offenders since Furby, Weinrott, and Blackshaw's (1989) oft-cited review (see, e.g., Brown & Kolko, 1998; Day & Marques, 1998; Hanson, 1997a; Hanson et al., 2002; Marshall & Fernandez, 2004; Marshall, Jones, Ward, Johnston, & Barbaree, 1991; Marshall & Pithers, 1994; McConaghy, 1998, 1999; Miner, 1997; Quinsey, Harris, Rice, & Lalumière, 1993; Rice & Harris, 2003; Worling & Curwen, 2000). Our intention in this chapter is not to recapitulate this debate by further critiquing the treatment outcome literature on sexual offenders (adults or juveniles), nor will we revisit here those methodological issues in treatment evaluation research that we (Langton & Barbaree, 2004) and others have discussed elsewhere (see Henggeler, Smith, & Schoenwald, 1994, and Kazdin, 1991, for excellent reviews of the broader psychotherapy treatment outcome literature). Rather, we want to identify a number of conceptual foci that we feel offer promising directions for future treatment evaluation research efforts with young sexual abusers.

At the outset, it should be noted that we will use the terms "juvenile sexual offender" and "young sexual abuser," as well as "child" and "adolescent," interchangeably (Barbaree, Hudson, & Seto, 1993). This is not an implicit endorsement of imprecision in sample description, theoretical specificity, or data analysis. Rather, it permits us to retain an emphasis on common concepts pertinent to our discussion. Similarly, we will use the terms "treatment" and "intervention" to refer to the provision of any program that represents an independent variable introduced to change sexually abusive behavior. "Sexually abusive behavior," as defined by the National Task Force on Juvenile Sexual Offending (1993), refers to "any sexual behavior which occurs 1) without consent; 2) without equality; or 3) as a result of coercion" (p. 11). As such, references to sexually abusive behavior and sexual offending reflect our use of these terms as general descriptors.

To inform our discussion, we first briefly introduce a number of the concepts concerning experimental validity (Cook & Campbell, 1979), noting in passing some of the general methodological problems frequently mentioned by researchers. We then introduce two "themes" that run through the chapter, namely, the place of theory in treatment evaluation research and the measurement of homogeneity and heterogeneity in samples or groups under study, with a view to underscoring the importance of each in carrying out and interpreting evaluation research. Our discussion then examines the relevance of three main principles empirically demonstrated to be related to positive treatment effects in the wider criminological literature when planning and implementing treatment outcome research.

Internal validity refers to the extent to which an observed effect can be taken to have been caused by the independent variable (for example, the treatment program). There are many threats to internal validity to which researchers should attend. These include a number of statistical concerns, such as: low power to detect differences or changes between groups assigned to the experimental treatment(s) and no treatment–treatment-as-usual conditions (e.g., different tests vary in their sensitivity to detect differences; comparative designs may have insufficient numbers of participants to detect differences between groups, resulting in a Type II error; see Kazdin, 1991, and Barbaree, 1997, for more complete discussion of this problem); capitalizing on chance (multiple testing of a data set produces an increased likelihood of a statistically significant result by chance, a Type I error, and therefore requires correction procedures); violations of statistical assumptions (certain statistical analyses are suitable only for use with certain types of data); and statistical regression of test scores to the mean, all of which can result in erroneous inference of treatment effects when changes are observed over the course of the intervention or experimental manipulation.

Other threats to internal validity include history, which here refers to events (such as changes in policing or supervision policies and practices) that occur (either to participants or to the larger context in which the study is conducted) that affect the outcome of interest (e.g., reoffense rates) but are not related to the independent variable (i.e., treatment). Similarly, maturation is a notable threat to internal validity in studies with children and adolescents. Poor reliability of assessment measures and therapists' adherence to treatment principles and procedures both also represent important threats to internal validity (Wagner, Frank, & Steiner, 1992). Testing can threaten internal validity if the assessment process itself influences outcome (whether the problem involves the test's susceptibility to response bias or practice effects or test administrator effects). Importantly, the selection process employed in a design can threatened internal validity if there are systematic differences between groups under comparison, which might account for differences on outcome measures (Larzelere, Kuhn, & Johnson, 2004). Mortality (i.e., participants who are removed or drop out from a treatment program or are lost to follow-up in an treatment evaluation study prior to completion), particularly, can affect outcomes and so threaten internal validity if the data are treated inappropriately.

External validity refers to the extent to which the results of a study can be generalized beyond the testing conditions to other samples or circumstances. Construct validity is important here and is concerned with what the treatment actually involves, what mechanisms of change are implicated, and for whom the treatment works. Treatment strength (i.e., likelihood of an effect) will be expected to vary according to duration, frequency, and intensity of the intervention, all of which are important considerations for the researcher. Also important is the integrity with which the treatment is implemented (Henggeler et al., 1994). As Miner (1997) notes, construct validity is undermined when interventions are poorly operationalized, and when aspects of the intervention are not measured. The importance of theory is central here and we will expand on this shortly.

The selection process can also undermine external validity if the participants under study represent an experimental group (e.g., a carefully screened research sample) unrepresentative of those found in applied settings (e.g., a heterogeneous institutional or community facility sample), such that the findings likely cannot be generalized to other samples or populations. Kazdin (2003) discusses the many differences that exist between clinical and research practices. Such differences should be afforded close attention with young sexual abusers because research findings must have validity for populations typically found in applied contexts to be of any practical importance (Weisz, Weiss, & Donenberg, 1992).

The Place of Theory in Treatment Evaluation Research

One of the safeguards against threats to experimental validity is to ensure that the theoretical rationale for the experimental manipulation is clearly stated. In terms of the clinical interventions with which we are concerned here, this requires that the treatment be based on a theory in which elements of the treatment, the mechanisms by which they are expected to work, and their relationship to both etiological theory and outcomes (from symptomology to recidivism) are all specified (Kazdin, 2002). Unfortunately, there is often a marked lack of theoretical specificity in treatment evaluation studies in our field. If detailed procedural aspects of an experimental manipulation or treatment program alone are provided, it may be possible to replicate the intervention in clinical work in applied settings (when it appears efficacious), but little is gained in terms of understanding the mechanisms of change or, indeed, why the treatment was comprised as it was. However, when the intervention is based on explicit theory, construct validity can be enhanced if components are directly examined using appropriate measures. Here we are talking about demonstrating that the treatment is effective.

As a simplified example, if a treatment program for juvenile sexual offenders is expected to reduce reoffending behavior through the reduction of cognitive distortions, the enhancement of empathy, the development of a relapse prevention plan, and disengagement from delinquent peer associates, as well as improvements in social skills and sexual knowledge, changes in these *proximal* measures of outcome (which can be referred to as "within-treatment targets" or "clinical change") must be shown to occur over the course of treatment and then be shown to be related to the *ultimate* outcome measure (i.e., recidivism, although relating treatment change to recidivism outcomes can require considerable patience given the need to utilize a sufficiently long follow-up time to provide a meaningful picture and avoid interpretative problems associated with low bases; see, for example, Barbaree, 1997). Furthermore, the fidelity with which the intervention is carried out is itself an important component warranting monitoring and assessment (Henggeler, Schoenwald, Liao, Letourneau, & Edwards, 2002). Just as with any experimental manipulation, then, in treatment evaluation research with young sexual abusers, it is important to formally test hypotheses generated from the theoretical rationale for the treatment. In this manner an indication of response to treatment is obtained that either supports or contradicts the theoretical rationale. Importantly, it provides an opportunity to reject the null hypothesis that no change occurs (Finkelhor & Berliner, 1995).

Selection of outcome measures should be determined by the design of the treatment (i.e., its intended targets or goals) as informed by the theory, and the measures need to be selected with attention to their psychometric properties (that is, their demonstrated reliability and validity). Although reviews of proximal outcome measures suggest that further work is needed to develop treatment-specific measures with acceptable psychometric properties for sexual offenders (Hanson, Cox, & Woszczyna, 1991), there has been increased attention to theoretical specificity and operationalization of constructs in a number of areas (see Calder, 2001), affording researchers potentially useful tools to incorporate in evaluation study designs. By obtaining normative data (for children and adolescents who sexually abuse, as well as for nonclinical samples in these age groups), a number of pre–post comparisons (both within- and between-groups) could be made, which, importantly, would allow specific tests of theory. As well as allowing for various types of statistical comparisons, posttreatment scores that are a number of standard deviations above the pretreatment mean for the clinical group and posttreatment scores that enter the normative range of a nonclinical group mean represent ways to gauge meaningful clinical change in constructs targeted in treatment beyond reliance on tests of statistical significance between groups (Jacobson & Revenstorf, 1988; Jacobson & Truax, 1991).

In terms of measures of ultimate outcomes, official records of rearrest or reconviction will likely continue to be used despite wide recognition that they underestimate reoffending behavior. As a result, in addition to the possible overestimation of a treatment effect (through undetected recidivism, which would represent a bias expected to affect both treated and comparison group data), researchers face the problem of working with what might be spurious relationships; from their data on detected and undetected but self-reported sexual offenses, Knight and Prentky (1993) observed, "being apprehended for sexual coercion entailed a number of characteristics that were different from the correlates of only engaging in sexual coercion. Clearly, such data indicate that when data only from criminal record sources are available, extreme caution must be exerted in interpreting the correlates of specific crimes or in predicting criminal outcome" (p. 76). The use of self-report and collateral interviews represent additional sources of information that could be used as measures of ultimate outcome and considerably improve the confidence one can have in the findings (Furby et al., 1989; Heilbrun, Nezu, Keeney, Chung, & Wasserman, 1998; Quinsey, Rice, & Harris, 1995).

In summary here, a focus on the theory underlying a treatment would be expected to foster greater attention to implementation and assessment of proximal and ultimate outcomes. It would also enable the discernment of differences in emphasis and approach in clinical interventions. Following two decades of intervention work that has lacked theoretical precision, combined with equivocal (certainly contested on methodological grounds) results from outcome studies and the finding that general delinquency is common among young sexual abusers, a number of clinicians and researchers have even begun to question whether *specialized* treatment for sexually abusive youths is actually required, or at least whether it is indicated in all cases (see Berliner, 1998; Milloy, 1998; Ryan, 1998). Clearly, this is an empirical question that has significant implications for current theories of treatment (and the etiological theories informing these), and it invites evaluation work in which specialized treatment is compared with nonspecialized interventions.

Two studies, both employing random assignment designs, with children demonstrating sexual behavior problems have looked at contrasting treatment models. Pithers, Gray, Busconi, and Houchens (1998) compared a relapse-prevention (RP)-based intervention (adapted for children) with expressive play therapy and found an interaction effect for treatment type and child type (to which we return further on). Similarly, Bonner, Walker, and Berliner (1999) compared cognitive-behavioral treatment and dynamic play therapy, but no significant differences were found between treatments. Unfortunately, in both these studies, specific testing of theoretical rationales for the treatment models was not reported.

With adolescents, a growing body of evidence supports the use of multisystemic therapy (MST; Henggeler, Schoenwald, Borduin, Rowland, & Cunningham, 1998; Henggeler & Lee, 2003) with serious juvenile offenders (Borduin et al., 1995). Importantly, MST researchers have investigated mechanisms of change relating to treatment effects; for example, Huey, Henggeler, Brondino, and Pickrel (2000) reported that the relationship between reductions in delinquent behavior and caregiver-rated adherence (the extent to which adolescent offenders' caregivers engaged in behaviors consistent with the principles of MST) was mediated by changes in family relations and delinquent peer affiliation.

Data from MST treatment evaluation research using random assignment procedures reported for adolescent sexual offenders are very encouraging (Borduin, Henggeler, Blaske, & Stein, 1990; Borduin & Schaeffer, 2001). An adaptation of MST for juvenile sexual offenders (Swenson, Henggeler, Schoenwald, Kaufman, & Randall, 1998) could usefully be compared with the RP model (Gray & Pithers, 1993; Murphy & Page, 2000), with theoretical distinctions and differing treatment emphases being tested using a combined set of proximal (both clinical and service-related) outcome measures, which eventually can be examined in terms of their associations with ultimate outcomes. Indeed, such an investigation is under way and should prove, in time, highly informative (Letourneau, 2003).

Of particular interest for our discussion, Letourneau, Schoenwald, and Sheidow (2004) recently reported a study using MST in which clinically relevant and statistically significant reductions in problem behaviors in a variety of spheres (sexual, school, aggression, and substance use assessed using measures with established psychometric properties) were found from pre- to posttreatment for youths, regardless of whether they had had no, low, or high levels of sexual behavior problems at pretreatment. Although no significant differences were found in follow-up arrest, conviction, incarceration, or placement outcomes between these three groups, these outcome data were collected only up to discharge from treatment (approximately 4 months' duration). Distinct patterns and associations between clinically relevant within-treatment changes and these outcomes might be discernable once data for the sample can be collected using a longer follow-up time. Although discussions of MST with juvenile sex offenders are optimistic with respect to outcomes, it is unclear how practical or realistic the implementation of MST would be in many community settings given concerns about cost and resources.

The Subject of Study and the Issue of Heterogeneity

In evaluating the efficacy of any intervention, the question of "who" we wish to see evincing change seems a primary one, and it should be answered in terms of where the focus (or foci) of treatment lies. Certainly the child or adolescent who has committed a sexually abusive act represents the most obvious focus, but other candidates for study include the parents and families of the offender, as well as their social networks and associated ethnic and cultural variables (National Task Force on Juvenile Sexual Offending, 1993). Current theory implicates the home environment and caregivers as important components in the etiology and also the treatment of sexually assaultive behavior in youths (Bentovim, 1998; National Task Force on Juvenile Sexual Offending, 1993; Swenson et al., 1998). As we have noted, treatment evaluation studies should include assessments of theoretically important constructs; clearly, parental, peer, and other environmental variables should therefore be assessed in interventions intended to influence them.

An important question is whether the families themselves should participate in the treatment, for example with family therapy, in order to prevent further acts of sexually inappropriate behavior by the youth (Henggeler et al., 1998) or whether these families need "only" be part of the treatment, for example by supporting the youth's efforts and fulfilling a monitoring function (Gray & Pithers, 1993; Murphy & Page, 2000). Clearly, these other candidates for inclusion as subjects of study are important. However, here we limit ourselves to consideration of the degree of homogeneity characterizing study samples of the offending youths themselves.

In any research with young offenders, the description of samples under study should be as detailed as possible so that the applicability of the findings to other samples is evident to the reader but also so that the degree of heterogeneity in the sample (and the potential impact this can have on results) can be considered or, indeed, statistically controlled for. Recent studies examining recidivism rates have attempted to focus more specifically on particular groups of interest. For example, Hagan and Cho (1996) compared the reoffense rates for those adolescents who had committed sexual assaults against younger children with the rates of those who had committed sexual assaults against victims their own age or older. No differences were found in a 2-year follow-up period. This is in contrast to the findings reported for adult sexual offenders who victimize particular age groups (e.g., Prentky, Lee, Knight, & Cerce, 1997). Although the relatively short time at risk might account for this lack of difference, it is also possible that the groups studied by Hagan and Cho lacked homogeneity despite the authors' efforts to focus on subtypes of the juvenile sexual offender.

Sipe, Jensen, and Everett (1998) compared the reoffense rates of juveniles who had committed nonviolent sexual offences with those of nonsexual juvenile offenders. Following the juveniles into adulthood (follow-up ranged from 1 to 14 years), these researchers reported a higher rate of later sexual recidivism but lower rates of later nonsexual criminal offenses for the sexual-offender group than for the nonsexual juvenile offenders. Interestingly, no differences were found in reoffense rate between juveniles known to have committed multiple sexual offenses and those understood to have committed only one sexual offense before follow-up (although the number of these juveniles with multiple sexual offenses who went on to reoffend sexually as adults was very small, $n = 4$).

Data reported by Nisbet, Wilson, and Smallbone (2004) for a relatively large sample of 303 adolescent male sexual offenders, followed up for an average 7.3 years, revealed substantial diversity and persistence in criminal behavior. Of particular interest here is the fact that almost 25% were convicted of later sexual offenses while still adolescents but only a very small group of individuals ($n = 5$) recidivated sexually both as adolescents and again later as adults, suggesting that important differences in risk of sexual recidivism characterized the sample. Also, those adolescents whose initial victims were peers or adults were significantly more likely to be charged with sexual offenses as adults. Both findings underscore potentially important differences between types of adolescent sexual offenders and later recidivism, which would have implications for treatment and, importantly here, for interpretation of treatment evaluation research data.

It should be obvious from our earlier comments on experimental validity that a significant threat to the validity of research with children and adolescents who sexually abuse is the lack of homogeneity in samples studied. Given the possibility of selection bias, it would be counterintuitive to assume that children or adolescents who have committed sexually coercive acts represent a unitary class when constructing theories or analyzing data (Mulvey & Phelps, 1988). Additionally, both clinical experience and empirical evidence clearly indicate that heterogeneity is a defining hallmark of sexual offenders across the age range (Knight & Prentky, 1990, 1993) and gender (Matthews, Hunter, & Vuz, 1997). Recognition of this has prompted a number of researchers and clinicians to propose various typologies of children and adolescents who exhibit sexually abusive behaviors. Some have been deductively derived and based largely on clinical impressions (e.g., O'Brien & Bera, 1986), whereas others have used inductive procedures to empirically deduce subtypes within more generic groupings (Bonner et al., 1999; Långström, Grann, & Lindblad, 2000; Pithers et al., 1998; Worling, 2001). Others have examined the applicability that empirically validated typologies of adult sexual offenders have for young sexual abusers (Knight & Prentky, 1993). We are not concerned here with the details of these important efforts; rather, we wish to point out how the incorporation of typological considerations into treatment evaluation research could be useful.

Detecting important differences between types of juvenile sexual offenders is clearly important both for theoretical understanding, contributing as it can to the discernment of contrasting developmental pathways (Johnson & Knight, 2000), and for providing direction for clinical interventions (Butler & Seto, 2002; Hunter, Figueredo, Malamuth, & Becker, 2003). Specifically, the different etiological pathways and factors that maintain the abusive behavior identified for subtypes will be associated with a range of needs, both of the adolescents themselves and of their families, which can be optimally addressed in specifically designed programs of intervention. Differential experience of, and response to, treatment among adolescent sexual offenders would suggest that certain treatment modalities, models, or components might be appropriate for use with one subtype but contraindicated with others (Allam, Middleton, & Browne, 1997). As Becker (1998) notes, "further research is needed to develop typologies and to tailor treatment and intervention to the specific needs of the youth. We can no longer afford to take the one-size fits all approach with these adolescents. It has not been empirically supported, is potentially costly, and, in some cases, may be detrimental to youth and their families" (p. 318). More directly related to treatment evaluation research, subtype may function as a moderator variable, affecting the association between independent (e.g., study group) and dependent (proximal and ultimate outcomes) variables. Failure to take differential characteristics among a study sample into account will permit potential confounds to obscure results.

As a final comment on the issue of heterogeneity, it is worth noting here the ethical concern that arises in proposing classification systems for children and adolescents who are sexually aggressive or who demonstrate other sexual behavior problems. Quite appropriately, a number of clinicians and researchers have expressed reservations about the use of labels and the language used to refer to these individuals. Due attention must be paid to the stigmatizing effects of diagnoses and proper consideration given to the influence that assessments will have on the dispositions that follow. The ethical issue here is that without a theoretical rationale and empirical evidence attesting to the clinical utility of the classification, simply labeling a young person as a type of sexual offender (or psychopathic; see later discussion) might deprive them of the very sources of support and services that they require in order to desist from their harmful behaviors. There are ethical grounds, then, for encouraging research that develops empirically validated and clinically meaningful typologies so that classification is functional and that serves to inform case management practices, data analytic strategies, and interpretation of results.

Having introduced the themes of theory and heterogeneity, we turn now to three principles that will clearly illustrate the importance of both themes in designing treatment evaluation studies.

The Principles of Risk, Need, and Responsivity

The notion of matching intervention to client is the essence of a set of principles described by Andrews, Bonta, and their colleagues (e.g., Andrews & Bonta, 2003; Andrews, Bonta, & Hoge, 1990; Andrews, Zinger, et al., 1990). From their meta-analytic reviews, these authors identify three principles that characterize treatment interventions shown to be effective in reducing recidivism in general criminal populations. The first is the *risk principle*, which holds that the intensity of treatment should match the risk level (risk for reoffense) of the offender so that high-risk offenders receive high-intensity interventions, whereas offenders assessed to be at relatively lower risk participate in less intensive interventions. The second principle, the *needs principle*, focuses on deficits of the offender and indicates that for interventions to be effective in reducing reoffending behavior they must specifically target the problem areas or needs shown to be empirically associated with criminal behavior. The third principle is the *responsivity principle*, which emphasizes the importance of matching treatment modality with offender characteristics (such as learning style and personality). Given the strong empirical basis for these principles in the wider criminological literature, as well as growing recognition of their importance with adult sexual offenders (Gordon & Nicholaichuk, 1996; Langton, 2003), exploration of their utility for evaluation research and clinical work with young sexual abusers seems appropriate. Our interest in them here is primarily in terms of their relevance to treatment evaluation research. As Andrews, Robinson, and Balla (1986) observe,

> one of the best predictors of postintervention status is preintervention level of functioning. The existence of such a predictive correlation means that pre-treatment assessments of risk may serve two control functions in program evaluations (Cook & Campbell, 1979): Some control may be introduced over selection as a threat to internal validity, and statistical conclusion validity may be improved through any accompanying reduction in the magnitude of the error terms. A third control function involves the extension of external validity through the inclusion of tests of Risk × Treatment interactions. It is this moderator function of risk assessments that has direct clinical significance in differential treatment planning. (p. 203)

When a main effect (what researchers are looking for when they ask, Does this intervention make a difference?) for a program is not found (perhaps because of a lack of homogeneity in the groups), inclusion of risk as a variable permits the researcher to check for an interaction effect (what researchers look for when they ask, Does this treatment make a difference that varies according to some third variable?). As an illustration of this, consider the program evaluation study described by Andrews et al. (1986) that examined the effects of an intensive, nonresidential support program for children referred to a child protection agency. As the program was intended to prevent residential placement, the outcome of interest was incidence of placement in residential care. The authors reported no main effect for the program. However, exploration of the significant interaction effect between condition (program participants, selected on a "first come, first served" basis, vs. nonparticipants, who made up the wait-list control group for the program) and risk level (a summed score using the Delinquency, Education, Parents, and Personality/Skills subtotals of an early version of the Youth Level of Service/Case Management Inventory [YLS/CMI]; Hoge & Andrews, 2002) showed that higher risk participants did in fact benefit from the specialized program (i.e., showed lower admission rates into residential care and lower mean number of days in care) compared with equivalent-risk nonparticipants. No such treatment effect was evident for lower risk cases, accounting for the lack of a main effect.

Another reason to find means to incorporate some empirically based index of risk in treatment evaluation designs is illustrated by Bonta, Wallace-Capretta, and Rooney (2000). These researchers reported that low-risk nonsexual offenders who received high-intensity treatment recidivated at a higher rate than untreated low-risk nonsexual offenders, a pattern that the authors postulated may be attributable to the fact that the low-risk individuals and the high-risk individuals received treatment together, with the latter thought to have negatively influenced the former. Research with children and adolescents at risk for problem behaviors indicates that interventions that involve association with deviant peers may similarly exacerbate problems (Dishion & Andrews, 1995; Dishion, McCord, & Poulin, 1999). This raises the issue of iatrogenic effects of interventions, to which researchers and clinicians must be alert. The risk principle affords us one means by which to examine this more closely.

As well as its value in treatment evaluation research, this moderating function of risk level has direct clinical significance because it can be used to inform the intensity of service provision and treatment. Although determining optimal levels of intensity (in terms of, for example, duration and frequency) remains to established with sexual abusers of any age, the importance of incorporating risk level in clinical case management and treatment decisions with young sexual abusers is underscored by their differential reoffense rates according to subtype (Långström et al., 2000; Nisbet et al., 2004). We would hypothesize from the literature on general criminal (including juvenile) populations that differing levels of case management and intensity of treatment and supervision will have a differential effect on recidivism rates in young sexual abusers according to risk level.

As Andrews et al. (1986) observe, incorporation of risk as a variable also introduces a measure of control over threats to the internal validity of an evaluation design. For example, in a nonrandomized study that compares reoffense rates for treatment completers, treatment dropouts, and treatment refusers, one concern that precludes attribution of a treatment effect would be the presence of a selection bias, such as internal motivation on the part of treatment completers, which would be unrelated to the intervention. However, when all participants share the same relative probability of reoffending according to a risk assessment tool with established predictive validity (such as can be achieved statistically, by controlling for risk level, or experimentally, by matching across groups on risk at pretreatment), we might be permitted qualified confidence in inferring a treatment effect (e.g., Barbaree, Langton, & Peacock, 2003; McGrath, Cumming, Livingston, & Hoke, 2003).

Whereas the risk principle is concerned with level of risk and probability of reoffense and its interaction with intervention, the needs principle is more directly relevant to what is generally understood as risk assessment, because it concerns the identification and prioritization of those factors that are associated with reoffending behavior. Importantly, however, according to the needs principle, the risk factors identified should be amenable to intervention (i.e., changeable, dynamic risk factors rather than historical, static risk factors; see Hanson, 1998). Andrews and Bonta (2003) refer to these as *criminogenic needs*. Given the research indicating that many of the factors predictive of general criminal recidivism among juvenile sexual offenders do not appear also to predict sexual recidivism (Långström, 2002; Rasmussen, 1999; Worling & Curwen, 2000), a further distinction should be drawn between criminogenic needs related to general recidivism and criminogenic needs related to sexual recidivism with this group.

In contrast to the work of Andrews, Bonta, and their colleagues, research on assessment of risk for violent and sexual recidivism with adult sexual offenders has produced instruments composed primarily of static (that is, historical and therefore usually unchangeable) factors (e.g., Sex Offender Risk Appraisal Guide [SORAG]; Quinsey, Harris, Rice, & Cormier, 1998; Static 99; Hanson & Thornton, 1999). As such, this progress has been separate from and has preceded work on the assessment of needs (representing temporally proximal, changeable factors empirically associated with reoffense behavior) in sexual offenders. Promising work reported by Hanson and Harris (2000, 2001) represents a notable advance toward a criminogenic needs-based assessment for adult sexual offenders. Similarly, Gilgun's Clinical Assessment Package for Assessing Client Risks and Strengths (CASPARS; Gilgun, 1999), which comprises scales focusing on family relationships, emotional expressiveness, family embeddedness in community, peer relationships, and sexuality) is designed to inform intervention efforts and may serve as a useful criminogenic needs-based assessment package for juvenile sexual offenders. So, too, Bremer's (1998) Protective Factors Scale represents an important effort to assess variables in the domains of general behavior, offense characteristics, offense denial, social adjustments, emotional adjustment, cooperation, and family style that serve to focus treatment efforts. Although reliability and validity data reported for these initiatives are encouraging (J. F. Bremer, personal communication, September 27, 2004; Gilgun, Keskinen, Marti, & Rice, 1999), the predictive validity of the instruments has not yet been clearly established and replicated. However, preliminary support for the predictive validity of revisions of the Level of Service Inventory—Revised (LSI-R; Andrews & Bonta, 1995) with adult sexual offenders (Girard & Wormith, 2004) suggests that examination of the youth version (YLS/CMI; Hoge & Andrews, 2002) should be investigated with young sexual abusers.

The clinical significance of the needs principle lies in the contribution that a needs-based assessment of risk can make to the planning of target-specific interventions. It remains to be demonstrated empirically, but the hypothesis would be that different subtypes of young sexual abuser actually require different interventions, some needing social skills training or treatment to develop anger management and impulse control, whereas others may require more direct interventions to specifically address, for example, sexual deviance (Ryan, 1998). To underscore the significance of the needs principle for treatment evaluation research, we must return to our earlier discussion of the importance of theoretical rationale in intervention work and the emphasis we placed on the incorporation of proximal outcome measures in research designs. It will be recalled that we suggested that proximal outcome measures be approached as tests of explicit hypotheses about the nature of the intervention and what it is intended to do. If the theory underlying an intervention is informed by the empirical literature, it will implicate factors associated with reoffending behavior. If the intervention is grounded in this theory, it will target these factors, and researchers can measure within-in-treatment change and, eventually, relate this to ultimate outcomes (i.e., rearrest, reoffense). Thus, the needs principle should drive treatment evaluation research just as it should inform treatment planning.

Despite the evident importance of risk–needs assessment for clinical case management with young sexual abusers and the potential utility of incorporating risk and need as variables in treatment evaluation research, there has been relatively little research undertaken in this area (National Task Force on Juvenile Sexual Offending, 1993). In contrast to the literature on risk assessment with adult sexual offenders—which has witnessed the development and validation of a number of assessment instruments with demonstrated predictive validity for sexual, violent, and general criminal recidivism (Hanson, 1998; Barbaree, Seto, Langton, & Peacock, 2001)—a similar degree of progress with risk assessment procedures for younger offenders remains to be attained (see Worling & Långström, 2003, for a review). Promising work by Prentky and his colleagues (Prentky, Harris, Frizzell, & Righthand, 2000; Righthand, Carpenter, & Prentky, 2001) and Worling and his colleagues (Worling, 2004; Worling & Curwen, 2001) have drawn on research identifying factors associated with reoffending behaviors in young sexual offenders to produce structured clinical guidelines for assessing risk for reoffense. Unfortunately, there is a paucity of data on the validity of these efforts in predicting sexual or general criminal recidivism.

In an attempt to address this situation, Morton (2003) employed a retrospective design to investigate the psychometric properties of four risk assessment instruments with adolescent sexual offenders. She used archived file materials to code the Rapid Risk Assessment of Sex Offense Recidivism (RRASOR; Hanson, 1997b) and the Static-99 (Hanson & Thornton, 1999, 2000), and also to score the Estimate of Risk of Adolescent Sexual Offense Recidivism (ERASOR; Worling & Curwen, 2001), and the YLS/CMI (Hoge & Andrews, 2002). The first two are well-validated risk assessment instruments widely used with adult sexual offenders, whereas the latter two are risk assessment instruments developed for use with adolescents. Importantly, Morton's study represented the first examination of the predictive validity of the ERASOR and YLS/CMI with adolescent sexual offenders (although the YLS-CMI has been shown to have predictive validity among a sample of nonsexual adolescent offenders; see Catchpole & Gretton, 2003, and Jung & Rawana, 1999).

Among her sample of 77 adolescent male sexual offenders followed up for an average of 68 months, Morton (2003) found that none of the four instruments predicted sexual recidivism at levels significantly above chance, although the Static-99 did predict general recidivism among the sample, and various subscales on the ERASOR and YLS/CMI predicted serious (any violent, including sexual) recidivism. Morton acknowledges a number of limitations to her study, including the small sample size, lack of range of some of the instrument scores, and reliance on file information for coding the instruments (a potential problem for the valid assessment of dynamic items that would be expected to change over time, particularly if targeted in treatment). However, using post hoc analyses, Morton was able to identify items in the ERASOR and YLS/CMI that distinguished between juveniles who reoffended sexually and those who did not. Taken together with the demonstrated association that scores on these two instruments had with later interpersonal aggression and the good internal and concurrent validities also reported, Morton's results are encouraging. Although there is considerable work still to be done in terms of the development and validation of objective risk–need assessment procedures for use with young sexual abusers, the potential of such efforts should be clear for treatment evaluation research purposes and, of course, clinical practice.

Another important consideration in risk–need-driven treatment evaluation research is the identification of factors that serve to ameliorate the effects of risk factors and that are actually associated with successful outcomes. Such factors, referred to as protective or compensatory factors according to the mechanism by which they operate (Luthar, 1993), have been considered in the wider literature on resilience with children and adolescents (e.g., Cicchetti, Rogosch, Lynch, & Holt, 1993) and also with adult correctional populations (Gilgun, Klein, & Pranis, 2000), but they are only just beginning to receive attention in research endeavors with young sexual abusers (Bremer, 1998; Gilgun, 1999). Studies with both nonoffending samples (e.g., Grossman et al., 1992; Stouthamer-Loeber et al., 1993) and high-risk adjudicated youths (Hoge, Andrews, & Leschied, 1996) indicate that protective factors (such as positive peer relations, good school achievement, positive response to authority, and effective use of leisure time) do operate in the presence of risk factors to reduce negative outcomes (such as poor adjustment, incidence of delinquency, noncompliance with orders, and reoffending behavior). In addition to the implications of these findings for assessment and interventions, and of direct relevance to our discussion, protective and compensatory factors would be very important to consider in treatment evaluation research because they will likely add to the variability within groups and therefore also to the error term in analyses if they are not incorporated in the research design.

Before we move on to the responsivity principle and its relevance to treatment evaluation research, we should acknowledge the ethical concerns that are associated with risk assessment and prediction. Perhaps most obviously, there is the practical problem of false positives and negatives. Application of the risk principle in practice will mean that a given number of individuals (which will vary according to the sensitivity and specificity of the risk assessment instrument) will be incorrectly classified as high or low risk. The injustices associated with misclassification and consequent exclusion from services (such as intensive treatment and supervision) and incentives and privileges (such as bail, probation, or parole), as well as those associated with mandatory participation in unnecessary (and even potentially harmful) treatments, are clearly undesirable. In research, erroneous classification will undermine the experimental validity of the study. As Le Blanc (1998) notes, there is no clear ethical solution to this quandary, only an incentive to reduce prediction errors. However, the use of a risk–needs assessment that is focused on deficits or problem areas to be addressed (i.e., criminogenic needs) goes some way toward addressing ethical concerns with risk assessment and classification based on predictions because it places the emphasis on remedial intervention rather than proscriptive classification.

Turning finally to the responsivity principle, recall that an important factor associated with effective interventions with correctional populations is treatment modality, with behavioral, cognitive-behavioral, and multimodal models shown to effect greatest improvements with juvenile offenders (e.g., Lipsey, 1992; Redondo, Sanchez-Meca, & Garrido, 1999). Application of this principle would include attending to the learning styles of clients and adapting interventions accordingly (Felton, 1994). Schoenwald, Halliday-Boykins, and Henggeler (2003) reported that therapists' adherence to MST treatment principles varied according to certain youth and family characteristics such as criminality, substance abuse, and educational disadvantage, as well as caregiver–therapist ethnic match. Indeed, based on research with adult sexual offenders, therapeutic-group climate and therapist characteristics could be hypothesized to affect juvenile sexual offenders' response to treatment (Beech & Fordham, 1997; Marshall & Serran, 2004), although little research attention has been paid to these variables in treatment evaluation research with juvenile sexual offenders (see Henggeler et al., 1998, for discussion of these variables in treatment evaluation research with juvenile offenders more generally).

Just as treatment modality is associated with treatment outcome, it is likely that treatment model is important. Rich (1998) emphasizes an approach to the treatment of adolescent sexual offenders that is developmentally sensitive, rather than merely involving a revision of adult sexual offender treatment. For example, she questions the usefulness of offense-cycle work as undertaken in adult programs because it appears incompatible with adolescents' abilities and suggests instead alternative conceptualizations using metaphors that are more intuitively comprehensible to adolescents.

If we consider the responsivity principle in light of the heterogeneity characteristic of young sexual abusers noted earlier, we might hypothesize that different subtypes will respond differently to a given intervention. Indeed, a good illustration of the responsivity principle is evident in a comparative treatment study that considered subtypes. Pithers et al. (1998) examined changes in scores on a proximal outcome measure (the Child Sexual Behavior Inventory—Third Edition; Friedrich et al., 1992), for five subtypes (empirically derived from historical variables, offense dynamics, and psychometric data) after 16 weeks of a planned 32-week treatment regimen of either modified relapse prevention or expressive therapy. The authors reported that the "highly traumatized" child subtype who participated in the expressive therapy showed a slight increase in sexualized behavior midway through treatment, whereas those "highly traumatized" children participating in the modified relapse prevention treatment showed a large reduction in sexualized behavior after 16 weeks (no p values reported beyond those for the ANCOVA and chi-square analyses, which were significant). Additionally, Pithers et al. (1998) reported that a greater percentage of the "sexually aggressive" subtype who participated in the expressive therapy showed significant clinical change (13% improved, 13% deteriorated) in their sexual behaviors than did this child type participating in the modified relapse prevention treatment, for whom, as Pithers et al. (1998) note, treatment appeared inert. Although Pithers et al. (1998) are appropriately cautious about the importance of these preliminary findings, the results do allow us to point to the potential importance of the responsivity principle in designing interventions, assigning individuals to interventions, and evaluating the efficacy of interventions. Thus, in light of the applicability of the responsivity principle, a third focus in future treatment evaluation research with sexually abusive youths must be to investigate possible interactions between subtypes and treatment models and modalities.

Psychopathy, too, is relevant here. Consistent with findings widely reported for adult offender populations, psychopathy, as measured by the Psychopathy Checklist: Youth Version (PCL:YV; Forth, Kosson, & Hare, 2003), has been shown to function as a risk factor, predicting general recidivism (Catchpole & Gretton, 2003) and violent recidivism (Gretton, Hare, & Catchpole, 2004) among young offenders, as well as among young offenders with sexual offenses specifically (Gretton, McBride, Hare, O'Shaughnessy, & Kumka, 2001). Importantly, however, psychopathy can also be understood to function as a responsivity factor, and its assessment therefore has relevance for both risk and responsivity issues in treatment evaluation research and clinical applications. Among adjudicated youths with substance abuse problems participating in a hospital-based treatment program, O'Neill, Lidz, and Heilbrun (2003) found that psychopathic characteristics were negatively associated with program attendance; with ratings of quality of participation in treatment activities, as well as clinical improvement; and with percentage of clean urine screens during program participation (while conversely showing a positive association with rearrests over the 1-year follow-up period after treatment participation). Testing for a moderating function of psychopathy between treatment response and recidivism outcomes would clearly be an important design consideration in treatment evaluation research with juvenile sexual abusers also (see Langton, 2003, for preliminary work along these lines with adult male sexual offenders).

Summary and Conclusions

In this chapter we have suggested that researchers design treatment evaluation studies (and indeed interventions) that are theoretically driven and that incorporate (1) proximal measures of outcome (such as pre–post measures) that serve both to enhance internal validity and test hypotheses about the mechanisms of change in the treatment and (2) ultimate outcome measures (i.e., rearrest or reconviction rates). Attention to the needs principle should be central to this work, because it focuses researchers' attention on those factors that are associated with negative outcomes, as well as the amenability of these factors to treatment specifically targeted to them. In addition, we have drawn attention to the importance of reducing heterogeneity in samples in order to enhance both internal validity (through increased experimental sensitivity to treatment effects) and external validity (through tests of client–treatment interactions that will indicate for which population a particular treatment model, program, or component is efficacious). Application of the risk principle and subtyping of young offenders represent two important practical avenues for researchers to explore in efforts to analyze more homogeneous subgroups in treatment evaluation studies. We also highlighted the importance of the responsivity principle as a concern for researchers (i.e., determining who responds best to what) that, in turn, will reduce the gap between treatment evaluation research and clinical practice and better inform case management and treatment plans.

References

Allam, J., Middleton, D., & Browne, K. (1997). Different clients, different needs? Practical issues in community-based treatment for sex offenders. *Criminal Behaviour and Mental Health, 7,* 69–84.

Andrews, D. A., & Bonta, J. (1995). *The Level of Service Inventory—Revised.* Toronto, Ontario, Canada: Multi-Health Systems.

Andrews, D. A., & Bonta, J. (2003). *The psychology of criminal conduct* (3rd ed.). Cincinnati, OH: Anderson.

Andrews, D. A., Bonta, J., & Hoge, R. D. (1990). Classification for effective rehabilitation: Rediscovering psychology. *Criminal Justice and Behavior, 17,* 19–52.

Andrews, D. A., Robinson, D., & Balla, M. (1986). Risk principle of case classification and the prevention of residential placements: An outcome evaluation of the Share the Parenting program. *Journal of Consulting and Clinical Psychology, 54,* 203–207.

Andrews, D. A., Zinger, I., Hoge, R. D., Bonta, J., Gendreau, P., & Cullen, F. T. (1990). Does correctional treatment work? A clinically relevant and psychologically informed meta-analysis. *Criminology, 28,* 369–404.

Barbaree, H. E. (1997). Evaluating treatment efficacy with sexual offenders: The insensitivity of recidivism studies to treatment effects. *Sexual Abuse: A Journal of Research and Treatment, 9,* 111–128.

Barbaree, H. E., Hudson, S. M., & Seto, M. C. (1993). Sexual assault in society: The role of the juvenile offender. In H. E. Barbaree, W. L. Marshall, & S. M. Hudson (Eds.), *The juvenile sex offender* (pp. 1–24). New York: Guilford Press.

Barbaree, H. E., Langton, C. M., & Peacock, E. J. (2003, October). *The evaluation of sex offender treatment efficacy using samples stratified by actuarial risk.* Paper presented at the annual Research and Treatment Conference, Association for the Treatment of Sexual Abusers, St. Louis, MO.

Barbaree, H. E., Seto, M. C., Langton, C. M., & Peacock, E. J. (2001). Evaluating the predictive accuracy of six risk assessment instruments for adult sex offenders. *Criminal Justice and Behavior, 28,* 490–521.

Becker, J. V. (1998). What we know about the characteristics and treatment of adolescents who have committed sexual offenses. *Child Maltreatment, 3,* 317–329.

Beech, A., & Fordham, A. S. (1997). Therapeutic climate of sexual offender treatment programs. *Sexual Abuse: A Journal of Research and Treatment, 9,* 219–237.

Bentovim, A. (1998). Family systemic approach to work with young sex offenders. *Irish Journal of Psychology, 19,* 119–135.

Berliner, L. (1998). Juvenile sex offenders: Should they be treated differently? *Journal of Interpersonal Violence, 13,* 645–646.

Bonner, B. L., Walker, C. E., & Berliner, L. (1999). *Children with sexual behavior problems: Assessment and treatment.* Washington, DC: U.S. Department of Health and Human Services

Bonta, J., Wallace-Capretta, S., & Rooney, J. (2000). A quasi-experimental evaluation of an intensive rehabilitation supervision program. *Criminal Justice and Behavior, 27,* 312–329.

Borduin, C. M., Henggeler, S. W., Blaske, D. M., & Stein, R. (1990). Multisystemic treatment of adolescent sexual offenders. *International Journal of Offender Therapy and Comparative Criminology, 34,* 105–113.

Borduin, C. M., Mann, B. J., Cone, L. T., Henggeler, S.W., Fucci, B. R., Blaske, D. M., & Williams, R. A. (1995). Multisystemic treatment of serious juvenile offenders: Long-term prevention of criminality and violence. *Journal of Consulting and Clinical Psychology, 63,* 569–578.

Borduin, C. M., & Schaeffer, C. M. (2001). Multisystemic treatment of juvenile sexual offenders: A progress report. *Journal of Psychology and Human Sexuality, 13,* 25–42.

Bremer, J. F. (1998). Challenges in the assessment and treatment of sexually abusive adolescents. *Irish Journal of Psychology, 19,* 82–92.

Brown, E. J., & Kolko, D. J. (1998). Treatment efficacy and program evaluation with juvenile sexual abusers: A critique with directions for service delivery and research. *Child Maltreatment, 3,* 362–373.

Butler, S. M., & Seto, M. C. (2002). Distinguishing two types of adolescent sex offenders. *Journal of the American Academy of Child and Adolescent Psychiatry, 41,* 83–90.

Calder, M. C. (2001). *Juveniles and children who sexually abuse: Frameworks for assessment* (2nd ed.). Dorset, UK: Russell House Publishing.

Catchpole, R. E. H., & Gretton, H. M. (2003). The predictive validity of risk assessment with violent young offenders: A 1-year examination of criminal outcome. *Criminal Justice and Behavior, 30,* 688–708.

Cicchetti, D., Rogosch, F. A., Lynch, M., & Holt, K. D. (1993). Resilience in maltreated children: Processes leading to adaptive outcome. *Development and Psychopathology, 5,* 629–647.

Cook, T. D., & Campbell, D. T. (1979). *Quasi-experimentation, design and analysis for field issues.* Boston: Houghton Milflin.

Day, D. M., & Marques, J. K. (1998). A clarification of SOTEP'S method and preliminary findings: Reply to Nathaniel McConaghy. *Sexual Abuse: A Journal of Research and Treatment, 10,* 162–166.

Dishion, T. J., & Andrews, D. W. (1995). Preventing escalation in problem behaviors with high-risk young adolescents: Immediate and 1-year outcomes. *Journal of Consulting and Clinical Psychology, 63,* 538–548.

Dishion, T. J., McCord, J., & Poulin, F. (1999). When interventions harm: Peer groups and problem behavior. *American Psychologist, 54,* 755–764.

Felton, T. L. (1994). The learning modes of an incarcerated population. *Journal of Correctional Education, 45,* 118–121.

Finkelhor, D., & Berliner, L. (1995). Research on the treatment of sexually abused children: A review and recommendations. *Journal of the American Academy of Child and Adolescent Psychiatry, 34,* 1408–1423.

Forth, A. E., Kosson, D. S., & Hare, R. D. (2003). *The Hare Psychopathy Checklist: Youth Version.* Toronto, Ontario, Canada: Multi-Health Systems.

Friedrich, W. N., Grambsch, P., Damon, L., Hewitt, S. K., Koverola, C., Lang, R., et al. (1992). Child Sexual Behavior Inventory: Normative and clinical comparisons. *Psychological Assessment, 4,* 303–311.

Furby, L., Weinrott, M. R., & Blackshaw, L. (1989). Sex offender recidivism: A review. *Psychological Bulletin, 105,* 3–30.

Gilgun, J. F. (1999). CASPARS: New tools for assessing client risks and strengths. *Families in Society, 80,* 450–459.

Gilgun, J. F., Keskinen, S., Marti, D. J., & Rice, K. (1999). Clinical applications of the CASPARS instruments: Boys who act out sexually. *Families in Society, 80,* 629–641.

Gilgun, J. F., Klein, C., & Pranis, K. (2000). The significance of resources in models of risk. *Journal of Interpersonal Violence, 15,* 631–650.

Girard, L., & Wormith, J. S. (2004). The predictive validity of the Level of Service Inventory—Ontario Revision on general and violent recidivism among various offender groups. *Criminal Justice and Behavior, 31,* 150–181.

Gordon, A., & Nicholaichuk, T. (1996). Applying the risk principle to sex offender treatment. *Forum on Corrections Research, 8*(2). Retrieved May 5, 2004, from www.csc-scc.gc.ca/text/pblct/forum/e082/e0821_e.shtml

Gray, A. S., & Pithers, W. D. (1993). Relapse prevention with sexually aggressive adolescents and children: Expanding treatment and supervision. In H. E. Barbaree, W. L. Marshall, & S. M. Hudson (Eds.), *The juvenile sex offender* (pp. 289–319). New York: Guilford Press.

Gretton, H. M., Hare, R. D., & Catchpole, R. H. (2004). Psychopathy and offending from adolescence to adulthood: A 10-year follow-up. *Journal of Consulting and Clinical Psychology, 72,* 636–645.

Gretton, H. M., McBride, M., Hare, R. D., O'Shaughnessy, R., & Kumka, G. (2001). Psychopathy and recidivism in adolescent sex offenders. *Criminal Justice and Behavior, 28,* 427–449.

Grossman, F. K., Beinashowitz, J., Anderson, L., Sakurai, M., Finnin, L., & Flaherty, M. (1992). Risk and resilience in young adolescents. *Journal of Youth and Adolescence, 21,* 529–550.

Hagan, M. P., & Cho, M. E. (1996). A comparison of treatment outcomes between adolescent rapists and child sexual offenders. *International Journal of Offender Therapy and Comparative Criminology, 40,* 113–122.

Hanson, R. K. (1997a). How to know what works with the sexual offenders. *Sexual Abuse: A Journal of Research and Treatment, 9,* 129–145.

Hanson, R. K. (1997b). *The development of a brief actuarial risk scale for sexual offense recidivism* (User Report 1997-04). Ottawa, Ontario, Canada: Department of the Solicitor General of Canada.

Hanson, R. K. (1998). What do we know about sex offender risk assessment? *Psychology, Public Policy, and Law, 4,* 50–72.

Hanson, R. K., Cox, B. J., & Woszczyna, C. (1991). Assessing treatment outcome for sexual offenders. *Annals of Sex Research, 4,* 177–208.

Hanson, R. K., Gordon, A. J. R., Marques, J. K., Murphy, W., Quinsey, V. L., & Seot, M. C. (2002). First report of the Collaborative Outcome Data Project on the Effectiveness of Psychological Treatment for Sex Offenders. *Sexual Abuse: A Journal of Research and Treatment, 14,* 169–194.

Hanson, R. K., & Harris, A. J. R. (2000). Where should we intervene? Dynamic predictors of sexual offense recidivism. *Criminal Justice and Behavior, 27,* 6–35.

Hanson, R. K., & Harris, A. J. R. (2001). A structured approach to evaluating change among sexual offenders. *Sexual Abuse: A Journal of Research and Treatment, 13,* 105–122.

Hanson, R. K., & Thornton, D. (1999). *Static-99: Improving actuarial risk assessments for sex offenders* (User Report 1999-02). Ottawa, Ontario, Canada: Department of the Solicitor General of Canada.

Hanson, R. K., & Thornton, D. (2000). Improving risk assessments for sex offenders: A comparison of three actuarial scales. *Law and Human Behavior, 24,* 119–136.

Heilbrun, K., Nezu, C. M., Keeney, M., Chung, S., & Wasserman, A. L. (1998). Sexual offending: Linking assessment, intervention, and decision making. *Psychology, Public Policy, and Law, 4,* 138–174.

Henggeler, S. W., & Lee, T. (2003). Multisystemic treatment of serious clinical problems. In A. E. Kazdin & J. R. Weisz (Eds.), *Evidenced-based psycho-*

therapies for children and adolescents (pp. 301–322). New York: Guilford Press.

Henggeler, S. W., Schoenwald, S. K., Borduin, C. M., Rowland, M. D., & Cunningham, P. B. (1998). *Multisystemic treatment of antisocial behavior in children and adolescents.* New York: Guilford Press.

Henggeler, S. W., Schoenwald, S. K., Liao, J. G., Letourneau, E. J., & Edwards, D. L. (2002). Transporting efficacious treatments to field settings: The link between supervisory practices and therapist fidelity in MST programs. *Journal of Clinical Child and Adolescent Psychology, 31,* 155–167.

Henggeler, S. W., Smith, B. H., & Schoenwald, S. K. (1994). Key theoretical and methodological issues in conducting treatment research in the juvenile justice system. *Journal of Clinical Child Psychology, 23,* 143–150.

Hoge, R. D., & Andrews, D. A. (2002). *Youth Level of Service/Case Management Inventory: User's manual.* Toronto, Ontario, Canada: Multi-Health Systems.

Hoge, R. D., Andrews, D. A., & Leschied, A. W. (1996). An investigation of risk and protective factors in a sample of youthful offenders. *Journal of Child Psychology and Psychiatry and Allied Disciplines, 37,* 419–424.

Huey, S. J., Jr., Henggeler, S. W., Brondino, M. J., & Pickrel, S. G. (2000). Mechanisms of change in multisystemic therapy: Reducing delinquent behavior through therapist adherence and improved family and peer functioning. *Journal of Consulting and Clinical Psychology, 68,* 451–467.

Hunter, J. A., Figueredo, A. J., Malamuth, N. M., & Becker, J. V. (2003). Juvenile sex offenders: Toward the development of a typology. *Sexual Abuse: A Journal of Research and Treatment, 15,* 27–48.

Jacobson, N. S., & Revenstorf, D. (1988). Statistics for assessing the clinical significance of psychotherapy techniques: Issues, problems, and new developments. *Behavioral Assessment, 10,* 133–145.

Jacobson, N. S., & Truax, P. (1991). Clinical significance: A statistical approach to defining meaningful change in psychotherapy research. *Journal of Consulting and Clinical Psychology, 59,* 12–19.

Johnson, G. M., & Knight, R. A. (2000). Developmental antecedents of sexual coercion in juvenile sex offenders. *Sexual Abuse: A Journal of Research and Treatment, 12,* 165–178.

Jung, S., & Rawana, E. P. (1999). Risk and need assessment of juvenile offenders. *Criminal Justice and Behavior, 26,* 69–89.

Kazdin, A. E. (1991). Effectiveness of psychotherapy with children and adolescents. *Journal of Consulting and Clinical Psychology, 59,* 785–798.

Kazdin, A. E. (2002). The state of child and adolescent psychotherapy research. *Child and Adolescent Mental Health, 7,* 53–59.

Kazdin, A. E. (2003). *Research design in clinical psychology* (4th ed.). Needham Heights, MA: Allyn & Bacon.

Knight, R. A., & Prentky, R. A. (1990). Classifying sexual offenders: The development and corroboration of taxonomic models. In W. L. Marshall, D. R. Laws, & H. E. Barbaree (Eds.), *Handbook of sexual assault: Issues, theories, and treatment of the offender* (pp. 23–52). New York: Plenum Press.

Knight, R. A., & Prentky, R. A. (1993). Exploring characteristics for classifying juvenile sex offenders. In H. E. Barbaree, W. L. Marshall, & S. M. Hudson (Eds.), *The juvenile sex offender* (pp. 45–83). New York: Guilford Press.

Långström, N. (2002). Long-term follow-up of criminal recidivism in young sex offenders: Temporal patterns and risk factors. *Psychology, Crime and Law, 8*, 41–58.

Långström, N., Grann, M., & Lindblad, F. (2000). A preliminary typology of young sex offenders. *Journal of Adolescence, 23*, 319–329.

Langton, C. M. (2003). *Contrasting approaches to risk assessment with adult male sexual offenders: An evaluation of recidivism prediction schemes and the utility of supplementary clinical information for enhancing predictive accuracy.* Unpublished doctoral dissertation, University of Toronto.

Langton, C. M., & Barbaree, H. E. (2004). Ethical and methodological issues in evaluation research with juvenile sexual abusers. In G. O'Reilly, W. L. Marshall, A. Carr, & R. C. Beckett (Eds.), *The handbook of clinical intervention with young people who sexually abuse* (pp. 419–441). Hove, UK: Brunner-Routledge.

Larzelere, R. E., Kuhn, B. R., & Johnson, B. (2004). The intervention selection bias: An underrecognized confound in intervention research. *Psychological Bulletin, 130*, 289–303.

Le Blanc, M. (1998). Screening of serious and violent juvenile offenders: Identification, classification, and prediction. In R. Loeber & D. P. Farrington (Eds.), *Serious and violent juvenile offenders: Risk factors and successful interventions* (pp. 167–193). Thousand Oaks, CA: Sage.

Letourneau, E. J. (2003, October). *Effectiveness trial: MST with juvenile sex offenders.* Paper presented at the annual Research and Treatment Conference, Association for the Treatment of Sexual Abusers, St. Louis, MO.

Letourneau, E. J., Schoenwald, S. K., & Sheidow, A. J. (2004). Children and adolescents with sexual behavior problems. *Child Maltreatment, 9*, 49–61.

Lipsey, M. W. (1992). The effect of treatment on juvenile delinquents: Results from meta-analysis. In F. Lösel, D. Bender, & T. Bliesener (Eds.), *Psychology and law: International perspectives* (pp. 131–143). Oxford, UK: de Gruyter.

Luthar, S. S. (1993). Annotation: Methodological and conceptual issues in research on childhood resilience. *Journal of Child Psychology and Psychiatry, 34*, 441–453.

Marshall, W. L., & Fernandez, Y. M. (2004). Treatment outcome with juvenile sexual offenders. In G. O'Reilly, W. L. Marshall, A. Carr, & R. C. Beckett (Eds.), *The handbook of clinical intervention with young people who sexually abuse* (pp. 442–452. Hove, UK: Brunner-Routledge.

Marshall, W. L., Jones, R. L., Ward, T., Johnston, P., & Barbaree, H. E. (1991). Treatment outcome with sex offenders. *Clinical Psychology Review, 11*, 465–485.

Marshall, W. L., & Pithers, W. D. (1994). A reconsideration of treatment outcome with sex offenders. *Criminal Justice and Behavior, 21*, 10–27.

Marshall, W. L., & Serran, G. A. (2004). The role of the therapist in offender treatment. *Psychology, Crime, and Law, 10,* 309–320.

Matthews, R., Hunter, J. A., & Vuz, J. (1997). Juvenile female sexual offenders: Clinical characteristics and treatment issues. *Sexual Abuse: A Journal of Research and Treatment, 9,* 187–199.

McConaghy, N. (1998). Neglect of evidence that relapse prevention is ineffective in treatment of incarcerated sexual offenders. *Sexual Abuse: A Journal of Research and Treatment, 10,* 159–162.

McConaghy, N. (1999). Methodological issues concerning evaluation of treatment for sexual offenders: Randomization, treatment dropouts, untreated controls, and within-treatment studies. *Sexual Abuse: A Journal of Research and Treatment, 11,* 183–193.

McGrath, R. J., Cumming, G., Livingston, J. A., & Hoke, S. E. (2003). Outcome of a treatment program for adult sex offenders: From prison to community. *Journal of Interpersonal Violence, 18,* 3–17.

Milloy, C. D. (1998). Specialized treatment for juvenile sex offenders: A closer look. *Journal of Interpersonal Violence, 13,* 653–656.

Miner, M. H. (1997). How can we conduct treatment outcome research? *Sexual Abuse: A Journal of Research and Treatment, 9,* 95–110.

Morton, K. E. (2003). *Psychometric properties of four risk assessment measures with male adolescent sexual offenders.* Unpublished master's dissertation, Carleton University, Ottawa, Ontario, Canada.

Mulvey, E. P., & Phelps, P. (1988). Ethical balances in juvenile justice research and practice. *American Psychologist, 43,* 65–69.

Murphy, W. D., & Page, I. J. (2000). Relapse prevention with adolescent sex offenders. In D. R. Laws, S. M. Hudson, & T. Ward (Eds.), *Remaking relapse prevention with sex offenders: A source book* (pp. 353–368). Thousand Oaks, CA: Sage.

National Task Force on Juvenile Sexual Offending. (1993). Revised report. *Juvenile and Family Court Journal, 44,* 1–61.

Nisbet, I. A., Wilson, P. H., & Smallbone, S. W. (2004). A prospective longitudinal study of sexual recidivism among adolescent sex offenders. *Sexual Abuse: A Journal of Research and Treatment, 16,* 223–234.

O'Brien, M., & Bera, W. H. (1986). Adolescent sexual offenders: A descriptive typology. *Preventing Sexual Abuse: A Newsletter of the National Family Life Education Network, 1,* 2–4.

O'Neill, M. L., Lidz, V., & Heilbrun, K. (2003). Adolescents with psychopathic characteristics in a substance abusing cohort: Treatment process and outcomes. *Law and Human Behavior, 27,* 299–313.

Pithers, W. D., Gray, A., Busconi, A., & Houchens, P. (1998). Children with sexual behavior problems: Identification of five distinct child types and related treatment considerations. *Child Maltreatment, 3,* 384–406.

Prentky, R. A., Harris, B., Frizzell, K., & Righthand, S. (2000). An actuarial procedure for assessing risk with juvenile sex offenders. *Sexual Abuse: A Journal of Research and Treatment, 12,* 71–93.

Prentky, R. A., Lee, A. F. S., Knight, R. A., & Cerce, D. (1997). Recidivism rates among child molesters and rapists: A methodological analysis. *Law and Human Behavior, 21,* 635–659.

Quinsey, V. L., Harris, G. T., Rice, M. E., & Cormier, C. A. (1998). *Violent offenders: Appraising and managing risk.* Washington, DC: American Psychological Association.

Quinsey, V. L., Harris, G. T., Rice, M. E., & Lalumière, M. L. (1993). Assessing treatment efficacy in outcome studies of sex offenders. *Journal of Interpersonal Violence, 8,* 512–523.

Quinsey, V. L., Rice, M. E., & Harris, G. T. (1995). Actuarial prediction of sexual recidivism. *Journal of Interpersonal Violence, 10,* 85–105.

Rasmussen, L. A. (1999). Factors related to recidivism among juvenile sexual offenders. *Sexual Abuse: A Journal of Research and Treatment, 11,* 69–86.

Redondo, S., Sanchez-Meca, J., & Garrido, V. (1999). The influence of treatment programmes on the recidivism of juvenile and adult offenders: An European meta-analytic review. *Psychology, Crime and Law, 5,* 251–278.

Rice, M. E., & Harris, G. T. (2003). The size and sign of treatment effects in sex offender therapy. *Annals of the New York Academy of Sciences, 989,* 428–440.

Rich, S. A. (1998). A developmental approach to the treatment of adolescent sexual offenders. *Irish Journal of Psychology, 19,* 102–118.

Righthand, S., Carpenter, E. M., & Prentky, R. A. (2001). *Risk assessment in a sample of juveniles who have sexually offended: A comparative analysis.* Poster presented at the annual Research and Treatment Conference, Association for the Treatment of Sexual Abusers, San Antonio, TX.

Ryan, G. (1998). What is so special about specialized treatment? *Journal of Interpersonal Violence, 13,* 647–652.

Schoenwald, S. K., Halliday-Boykins, C. A., & Henggeler, S. W. (2003). Client-level predictors of adherence to MST in community settings. *Family Process, 42,* 345–359.

Sipe, R., Jensen, E. L., & Everett, R. S. (1998). Adolescent sexual offenders grown up: Recidivism in young adulthood. *Criminal Justice and Behavior, 25,* 109–124.

Stouthamer-Loeber, M., Loeber, R., Farrington, D. P., Zhang, Q., van Kammen, W., & Maguin, E. (1993). The double edge of protective and risk factors for delinquency: Interrelations and developmental patterns. *Development and Psychopathology, 5,* 683–701.

Swenson, C. C., Henggeler, S. W., Schoenwald, S. K., Kaufman, K. L., & Randall, J. (1998). Changing the social ecologies of adolescent sexual offenders: Implications of the success of multisystemic therapy in treating serious antisocial behavior in adolescents. *Child Maltreatment, 3,* 330–338.

Wagner, E. F., Frank, E., & Steiner, S. C. (1992). Discriminating maintenance treatments for recurrent depression: Development and implementation of a rating scale. *Journal of Psychotherapy Practice and Research, 1,* 280–290.

Weisz, J. R., Weiss, B., & Donenberg, G. R. (1992). The lab versus the clinic: Effects of child and adolescent psychotherapy. *American Psychologist, 47,* 1578–1585.

Worling, J. R. (2001). Personality-based typology of adolescent male sexual offenders: Differences in recidivism rates, victim-selection characteristics, and personal victimization histories. *Sexual Abuse: A Journal of Research and Treatment, 13,* 149–166.

Worling, J. R. (2004). The Estimate of Risk of Adolescent Sexual Offense Recidivism (ERASOR): Preliminary psychometric data. *Sexual Abuse: A Journal of Research and Treatment, 16,* 235–254.

Worling, J. R., & Curwen, T. (2000). Adolescent sexual offender recidivism: Success of specialized treatment and implications for risk prediction. *Child Abuse and Neglect, 24,* 965–982.

Worling, J. R., & Curwen, T. (2001). Estimate of Risk of Adolescent Sexual Reoffense Recidivism (The ERASOR—Version 2.0). In M. C. Calder (Ed.), *Juveniles and children who sexually abuse: Frameworks for assessment* (pp. 372–397). Dorset, UK: Russell House.

Worling, J. R., & Långström, N. (2003). Assessment of criminal recidivism risk with adolescents who have offended sexually: A review. *Trauma, Violence, and Abuse, 4,* 341–362.

CHAPTER 12

Legal Consequences of Juvenile Sex Offending in the United States

Elizabeth J. Letourneau

This chapter reviews the application of special legislation designed for high-risk adult sex offenders to juvenile sex offenders and whether such applications are likely to have intended effects (e.g., reducing sexual recidivism) and/or unintended effects (e.g., reducing detection of juvenile sex offenders). Recent changes in legal procedures have resulted in significantly altered consequences to juvenile sex offenders. Specifically, many juvenile sex offenders are now required to register personal information on publicly available sex-offender registries. These registries are maintained by local or state law enforcement agencies and list offenders who have committed specific sexual crimes. Likewise, many juvenile offenders are also subjected to community notification procedures, in which persons external to law enforcement are informed about the specific sexual crimes of some youths. Per federal guidelines, registration and notification policies exclude juvenile offenders except for those youths prosecuted as adults. However, several states have extended registration and notification requirements to juvenile sex offenders.

It is noteworthy that juvenile justice sanctions that were developed in the late 1980s and throughout the 1990s remain in place and have, in many cases, intensified during the period of time in which juvenile sex offending was declining. In addition to registration and notification, these sanctions include longer sentences, increased use of out-of-home placements, and extension of civil commitment procedures to include juveniles. As is discussed subsequently, the potential for reduced offending or improved community safety seems limited, whereas the potential for harm to youthful offenders from these practices seems likely (Caldwell, 2002; Trivits & Reppucci, 2002; Zimring, 2004). Thus, although wide consensus exists on the need for improved community safety from sex offenders, substantial debate continues regarding the effectiveness of registration and notification procedures and the potentially negative impact of such practices, particularly as applied to juveniles (Edwards & Hensley, 2001; Lieb, 1996; Prentky, 1996; Redlich, 2001; Zimring, 2004). Hampering the ability of policy makers to make informed decisions is the almost complete lack of empirical data on the effects of registration and notification on juvenile sex offenders. The degree to which sex-offender registration reduces recidivism or deters new sexual offenses is unknown. Moreover, data from two states (presented subsequently) suggest the possibility of unintended effects of particularly harsh registration practices. In the subsequent sections, each issue pertaining to the legal treatment of juvenile sex offenders is reviewed. For a more detailed review of the legal consequences to juvenile sex offenders, including a cogent discussion of problems with laws against sex with minors (as those laws are applied to minors), the reader is referred to Zimring (2004). The reader is also advised that civil commitment procedures are not covered in this chapter but are increasingly applied to juveniles. I am unaware of a ready source for information on the application of civil commitment to juveniles.

Recent Legal Policies

Following several highly publicized sexual assaults committed by repeat offenders, three federal statutes were enacted that resulted in the development of sex-offender-specific legislation (SEARCH, 1998). These statutes carry the names of the victims in whose memories they were created: the federal version of the Jacob Wetterling Crimes Against Children and Sexually Violent Offender Registration Act (enacted under the federal Violent Crime Control and Law Enforcement Act of 1994); the federal version of "Megan's Law" (enacted in 1996); and the Pam Lychner Sexual Offender Tracking and Identification Act (enacted in 1996). The Jacob Wetterling Act requires that states: (1) compel certain sexual offenders to register (based on their conviction offense); (2) maintain updated and accurate registries; (3) distribute registries to law enforcement personnel; and (4) provide the public with information when necessary for safety (SEARCH, 1998). Megan's Law amended the

Jacob Wetterling Act and set forth requirements for mandatory public notification regarding states' most serious sex offenders (SEARCH, 1998). The Pam Lychner Sexual Offender Tracking and Identification Act further modified the Jacob Wetterling Act to require more stringent registration procedures (SEARCH, 1998). Thus all offenders who register must do so for a minimum of 10 years, and offenders identified by a state as "high risk" must register for life.

As originally defined by federal statutes, registration and community notification were two distinct procedures. This distinction has blurred considerably in states that do not distinguish between low-, medium-, or high-risk sex offenders. Because states are required to publicly identify high-risk sex offenders, states that have no formal mechanism for distinguishing between risk levels are, by default, identifying all registered sex offenders as high risk. In such states, the notification procedures include all sex offenders listed on the registry. Often, this is accomplished by making the registry public via the Internet. This type of notification has been labeled "broad community notification" and represents the widest dissemination of offender information to the public (Matson & Lieb, 1997, p. 5). The majority of states currently operate Internet-based registries and many, including South Carolina, include offenders adjudicated delinquent as minors (National Center for the Prosecution of Child Abuse, 1999). That Internet-based registries truly serve as community notification is evidenced by the high volume of "hits" on these sites. For example, the Florida Internet-based registry logged more than 40,000 inquiries during the first 3 weeks of implementation (SEARCH, 1998).

The goals of registration and notification are to (1) deter would-be sex offenders, (2) reduce recidivism by known sex offenders, (3) track offenders in the community, (4) assist in investigations, and (5) provide community residents with information to help protect their children (Center for Sex Offender Management, 1999; SEARCH, 1998). These laudable goals resulted from horrific acts. However, most states were compelled to create and ratify legislation quickly under penalty of losing federal grant funding (Center for Sex Offender Management, 1999; SEARCH, 1998). Thus registration and notification laws were enacted under tight deadlines and in the absence of empirical data regarding the impact of such laws on actual deterrence, recidivism rates, community safety, and other goals. These policies were also apparently enacted without considering whether such laws might have unintended or even detrimental side effects. To date, there remains little empirical data regarding the impact of registration or community notification on any of the goals for which these laws were enacted. Those studies that do exist are reviewed subsequently. First, however, theories regarding specific mechanisms by which registration and notification might reduce sexual offending are reviewed briefly.

Deterrence

One mechanism by which criminal justice sanctions can reduce crime is via deterrence. That is, the threat of detection and punishment (and/or the severity of punishment) might be sufficient to deter people from committing initial (or, in the case of criminals, additional) crimes (Nagin, 1998). Thus deterrence might be considered primary or secondary prevention in that crimes are avoided. Research across different crimes and using different research methodologies shows deterrence effects in the commission of new crimes (Nagin, 1998). For example, interrupted time-series studies have indicated that targeted interventions have an initial effect of reducing the specific targeted crime (often minor crimes but also including drunk driving, drug marketing, disorderly behavior, tax fraud, gun control, and other more serious crimes). Perceptual deterrence studies, which generally focus on participants' understanding of the likelihood of detection and punishment, have consistently demonstrated that increased perception of risk detection and punishment is linked to lowered self-reported offending or intentions to offend (Nagin, 1998). Importantly, an early study on deterrence of sexual assault supported the hypothesis that risk of sanctions (operationalized as arrest or dismissal from college) is a significant deterrent for date rape as self-reported by male college students (Bachman, Paternoster, & Ward, 1992).

In the case of registration and notification, a deterrent effect might be evidenced in two ways: an overall reduction in first-time sex offending and a specific reduction in sexual recidivism rates of registered offenders. Although research generally supports the deterrence effects of the perceived threat of criminal justice sanctions, and although at least one study supports the deterrence effects of formal sanctions for date rape, there are several reasons to suspect that sex offender registration and community notification might not deter initial sex crimes (as opposed to recidivism, which is addressed later) by minors. First, the effect of deterrence varies by age (Sampson & Cohen, 1988), with juveniles showing less deterrence than adults, perhaps due to the greater impulsivity of youth or the generally greater consequences experienced by adults. Second, deterrence would depend on a relatively complex, multistep process of reasoning in which youths must (1) identify themselves as individuals who might one day commit sexual offenses; (2) expect to be caught and punished; and (3) expect that, following punishment, registration would be compelled. Third (and related to step 3), deterrence would depend on a youth having a working understanding of sex-offender registration and community notification policies. It is my experience that even criminal justice experts, other professionals who examine criminal justice data, and parents of juvenile sex offenders are largely unaware of state registration and notification laws as applied to minors, and it therefore seems defensible to posit that most youths neither know nor care about these laws. Fourth, deterrence appears to work best when policing agents are mobilized in a very specific manner to address very specific crimes (Nagin, 1998). Because sexual assault most commonly occurs in secrecy, because it can occur virtually anywhere and most often within the privacy of homes (e.g., see Pastore & Maguire, 2002, Table 3.33), and because it rarely leaves physical evidence (De Jong, 1992), it is difficult to imagine how a targeted policy intervention could have a substantial effect on sexual offending.

Although registration and notification policies probably do not exert a deterrent effect on initial sexual offending, it seems entirely possible that these polices have a significant deterrent effect on those youths subjected to these policies (that is, registered offenders). One likely mechanism for this effect is that youths who are registered may perceive an increased threat of detection for new crimes, given that their names, addresses, and even pictures are available specifically to law enforcement officers (via the registry) and more generally to the public (via Internet accessibility to the registry). The fact that some registries (e.g., South Carolina's) hold records for life certainly removes the threat of being "reregistered" and consequently might reduce the deterrent effect of registration. However, more salient to youths might be the perception of risk of detection and punishment, regardless of whether punishment carries with it the additional threat of renewed registration or notification. Thus deterrent effects for registration and notification seem possible for those youths subjected to these policies. However, as discussed subsequently, the low recidivism rates of most juvenile sex offenders may make it difficult to detect statistically significant reductions in sexual recidivism rates.

Incapacitation

A second mechanism by which criminal justice sanctions might reduce crime is via incapacitation (Nagin, 1998). Simply put, when criminals are behind bars they cannot commit additional crimes (at least not in the community). Over the past two decades, the prison population in the United States has grown by nearly 500% (Nagin, 1998, p. 356) and it has been hypothesized that this increase is responsible, at least in part, for the general reduction in violent offending that occurred during the

1990s (Blumstein, 2000). Increased incapacitation has also been posited as a specific mechanism by which sexual offending has declined in the past decade (Finkelhor & Jones, 2004). Although it seems obvious that incapacitation would result in fewer crimes (cf. DiIulio, 1995), several arguments have been made against such an effect (see, for example, Nagin, 1998; Tonry, 2004).

Registration and notification do not equate to incarceration—in fact, most states compel incarcerated offenders to register only after (or just prior to) their release. Registration might exert a type of incapacitation effect, however, by increasing the likelihood of apprehending recidivists. Registries might make it easier for law enforcement to develop hypotheses about *who* might have committed a newly reported sex crime (e.g., by having lists of known sex offenders' names and their types of crimes on hand). Moreover, registries might make it easier for law enforcement to develop hypotheses about *where* potential assailants might be (e.g., by having, in addition to the names of sex offenders, their current addresses listed on the registry). Indeed, limited evidence regarding high-risk adult sex offenders (reviewed in greater detail subsequently) indicates that those who registered and whose communities were warned of their presence were rearrested faster than men with similar index offenses who were released prior to enactment of these laws (Lieb, 1996; Schram & Milloy, 1995). Furthermore, anecdotal information suggests that registries help law enforcement officers winnow the field of potential sex offenders by providing information on known offenders in a given geographical area (SEARCH, 1998).

Given the effects by which deterrence and incapacitation work, it is hypothesized that registration and notification polices will not affect general rates of sexual offending but might affect sexual recidivism rates among juvenile sex offenders. However, there are problems in addition to a low base rate that might attenuate such effects. First, evidence suggests that penalties perceived as too harsh can lead judges and juries to refuse to convict offenders (Ross, 1982). In states with harsh registration and/or notification policies (e.g., lifetime registration on Internet-based registries), officials may be less willing to prosecute or adjudicate youths of registry offenses (this concern is discussed in detail subsequently).

Second, in states in which all sex offenders convicted of registry offenses are considered high risk (i.e., in states that do not discriminate between risk levels), there is an issue akin to the "net widening" effect frequently seen with intermediate sanctions (Tonry, 1998). With net widening, sanctions intended to divert offenders from (costly) incarceration are often applied by risk-averse judges to offenders who would have been placed on probation (and not incarcerated) in the first place. This practice results in reduced capacity to determine an effect of the intermediate sanctions (easier to detect if only the highest risk offenders had participated in the new program) and a loss of cost effectiveness. Registration and notification procedures were initially developed to address threats to community safety posed by high-risk, repeat sexual offenders. However, not all sex offenders, or even the subsample of sex offenders who commit serious sexual offenses, are at high risk to recidivate. For example, the base rate for sexual recidivism among juvenile offenders is low, averaging 10% for most studies (Alexander, 1999; Caldwell, 2002). In the absence of accurate risk assessment, the (predominantly) low-risk offenders will be included in intervention groups with the (rarer) high-risk offenders, a mix that is likely to attenuate intervention effects. To summarize, three problems will make it difficult to determine the effectiveness of registration and notification policies: (1) a low base rate in which most juvenile sex offenders are never again apprehended for new sex crimes; (2) the practice of prosecuting and adjudicating juvenile sex offenders for non-sex crimes; and (3) the overuse of registration or notification for low-risk youth. Nevertheless, well-designed research with large samples should be able to determine whether these policies have their intended effects of reducing sex crimes. Such research that exists is reviewed next.

Previous Research on Intended Effects of Registration and Notification

In the discussion of deterrence and incapacitation theories of punishment, brief references were made to research on adult sex offenders. The remainder of this section reviews in greater detail extant research on registered adult sex offenders, the single study that has been published on registered juvenile sex offenders, and research on related issues.

Recall that the intended effects of registration and notification include five primary goals: (1) to deter would-be sex offenders; (2) to reduce recidivism by known sex offenders; (3) to track offenders in the community; (4) to assist in investigations; and (5) to provide community residents with information to help protect their children. Surprisingly little empirical research has been published regarding the effects of these policies on any of these goals. Anecdotal information, however, suggests that registration is an effective tool for law enforcement personnel (goals 3 and 4). For example, following an attempted rape, law enforcement personnel were able to quickly identify known sex offenders residing in the area in which the alleged offense took place and located the alleged assailant (SEARCH, 1998). Anecdotal reports also suggest that community residents utilize registries to improve the safety of their children (goal 5). Specifically, citizens have called the police when they recognized registered sex offenders at Boy Scout meetings or volunteering as children's coaches (SEARCH, 1998). Thus there is some information supporting the usefulness of registries to law enforcement personnel and the usefulness of community notification policies in the protection of children. However, one study casts doubt on the likelihood that notification increases the safety of adult women (Petrosino & Petrosino, 1999). In this study, records of high-risk sex offenders released prior to implementation of registration and notification laws were reviewed, and incidents of sexual recidivism were examined. Based on Wisconsin's notification procedures, the authors estimated the likelihood that the actual victims of recidivists would have received notification about their assailants had the offenders been subjected to community notification. The authors determined that it was highly unlikely that most victims would have received any notification about their offenders. The authors further noted that, had these victims lived in the notification radius of the offender's address, for notification to have increased their safety the victims would have had to (1) been home at the time of the scheduled notification (or read a posted bulletin); (2) consider themselves potential targets; and (3) taken specific precautionary measures to avoid being victimized. The authors concluded that it was highly unlikely each condition would have been met and, therefore, unlikely that community notification offered a real improvement to community safety. Thus registries, coupled with notification, appear to provide a useful starting place for law enforcement investigating sexual crimes and for citizens to protect their children, but perhaps not themselves.

There are no studies examining the deterrence of would-be sex offenders (goal 1) and just one study of which I am aware pertaining to the reduction of sexual recidivism (goal 2). Schram and Milloy (1995) examined the recidivism rates of (mostly adult) sex offenders subjected to the highest level of community notification in Washington state during the first 4 years following enactment of community notification laws in that state. Ninety offenders designated as high risk were matched (on victim type—child or adult—and number of offenses) with a sample of 90 sex offenders released prior to enactment of community notification laws. Although not matched on other potentially important risk variables (such as age), the demographic characteristics of the two groups were nevertheless similar. Sexual recidivism rates (i.e., arrests for new sex offenses) and general recidivism rates (i.e., arrests for new offenses of any kind) were not statistically different between the two groups: 19% of the community notification group and 22% of the comparison group were arrested for new sexual offenses during a 4.5-year follow-up period. Thus notification did not appear to have an immediate deterrent effect. However, offenders subjected to community notification were arrested significantly more quickly than were offenders in the comparison group (median time to new arrest was 25.1 months vs. 61.7 months, respectively). Because the effects of incapacitation are gradual, this study might have uncovered a reduction in recidivism had the follow-up period been extended (see, for example, Ramirez & Crano, 2003).

Whereas data on the effect of notification is limited for adults, there are no data on the effects of registration or community notification on juvenile sex offenders. However, substantial research supports the view that juvenile sex offenders differ from their adult counterparts in meaningful ways and are not simply younger versions of adult offenders, as might be suggested by the wholesale application to juveniles of justice policies developed for adults (Chaffin, 1998; Seagrave & Grisso, 2002; Zimring, 2004). As recently emphasized (e.g., Caldwell, 2002; Chaffin, Letourneau, & Silovsky, 2002; Letourneau & Miner, in press; Seagrave & Grisso, 2002; Zimring, 2004), the independent study of the effects of sex-offender-specific legislation and sex offender treatment and assessment practices on juvenile offenders is necessary to determine the effectiveness of such interventions with young offenders. Limited descriptive information on youths subjected to community notification is available from the Washington State study described previously (Lieb, 1996; Schram & Milloy, 1995). Among the offenders identified as high risk in the broader study, 14 were juvenile offenders. Over the 4.5-year follow-up, 43% ($n = 6$ youths) were rearrested for new sex crimes (Lieb, 1996; Schram & Milloy, 1995). If this high rate of sexual recidivism is not an artifact of the small sample size (or some other extraneous factor), it suggests that those juvenile offenders were indeed at very high risk to reoffend, relative to most juvenile sex offenders, and perhaps warranted community notification. Clearly, additional research with larger samples and with control groups is warranted.

Previous Research on Unintended Effects of Registration and Notification

The provision of information about convicted sex offenders to people outside the criminal justice system has sparked substantial and ongoing debate regarding the legality, feasibility, effectiveness, and unintended consequences of these policies (Edwards & Hensley, 2001; Letourneau & Miner, in press; Lieb, 1996; Prentky, 1996; Redlich, 2001; Zimring, 2004). Specific concerns have been voiced regarding (1) increased burden on law enforcement personnel, (2) vigilantism, and (3) reduced reporting, prosecution, or adjudication of sex offenders due to the perceived harshness of sex-offender-specific laws (e.g., Edwards & Hensley, 2001; SEARCH, 1998; Zevitz & Farkas, 2000a). However, as with the intended effects of sex-offender-specific legislation, concerns about unintended effects remain largely speculative.

Regarding concerns about increased burden on staff, data suggest that sex-offender-specific legislation substantially increased the burdens on staff time and departmental budgets (SEARCH, 1998; Zevitz & Farkas, 2000a), an unintended but perhaps predictable effect. Regarding vigilantism, official reports indicate that between 3% and 10% of offenders subjected to community notification were also subjected to harassment (Matson & Lieb, 1997). Self-report data suggest even higher rates of harassment, with 29 of 30 adult male offenders indicating that community notification negatively affected their transition from prison to the community (Zevitz & Farkas, 2000b). Regarding juvenile offenders, anecdotal information indicates that some youths subjected to community notification have been subjected to physical and emotional harm, ostracism by peers and adults in their communities, and interrupted schooling (Trivits & Reppucci, 2002). These reports, coupled with the research on adult offenders, suggest that some incidents of vigilantism remain unreported and some types of negative reactions (e.g., being shunned by peers) are not officially recorded.

The third unintended effect, that sex-offender-specific legislation might reduce the likelihood of prosecuting sex offenders, has been raised previously for incest victims, whose identities might be inferred by the registration of the perpetrators. Indeed, one state changed the information included in its sex-offender registry to help protect the identity of incest victims (SEARCH, 1998). However, it is also possible that registration or notification laws have altered the ways in which members of the justice system behave toward sex offenders. As mentioned previously, particularly harsh policies can cause judges and juries to refuse to convict offenders (Ross, 1982). Importantly, research suggests that judges and law students have concerns regarding sex-offender-specific legislation. For example, Bumby and Maddox (1999) examined judges' beliefs and sentiments regarding sex-offender legislation and prosecution. Of 42 Midwestern trial judges, between 26 and 30% had concerns about community notification, and the majority of judges reported that it was more difficult to preside over sex-offender cases than other criminal cases (Bumby & Maddox, 1999). Another study found that, relative to law enforcement personnel and community residents, law students were significantly less likely to support community notification or to believe that all sex offenders should be required to register (Redlich, 2001). To the extent that judges and prosecutors have concerns about the application of registration or notification to adult sexual offenders

(Bumby & Maddox, 1999; Redlich, 2001), such concerns might be heightened when the offenders are minors.

Anecdotal conversations I had with several state officials support the view that some juvenile justice professionals are discouraged by harsh registration and notification policies when such policies are applied to youths and seek to avoid these consequences by "hiding" (as it was put by one former member of a state department of juvenile justice) juvenile sex offenders under other crimes, such as aggravated assault. The application of adult legal interventions to juvenile offenders (particularly those youths who are tried in juvenile court and not in adult court) can be viewed as running against traditional juvenile court philosophy that emphasizes rehabilitation over retribution (Trivits & Reppucci, 2002). This may be of particular concern if prosecutors or judges suspect that registration or notification leads to harassment or other unintended negative consequences; these professionals might be less willing to identify youths as sex offenders.

The possibility that youths who offend sexually are being prosecuted for other crimes or diverted out of juvenile justice altogether is also supported by data from two states, Illinois and South Carolina. A recent review of crime trends from an Illinois county revealed that the number of sexual assault charges brought against adolescents fell dramatically the same year that registration laws were modified to include minors (Keller, 2002). One apparent reason for the reduction was that many more juvenile sex offender cases were diverted out of juvenile justice altogether or adjusted downward (Keller, 2002). That is, fewer juvenile sex offenders were being formally adjudicated for their sex crimes. In South Carolina, statistics indicate a dramatic reduction in arrests for rape committed by minors. This reduction occurred in the year immediately following enactment of registration laws (which in South Carolina have always applied to both juvenile and adult offenders). A second reduction occurred in the year immediately following online availability of the South Carolina registry (McManus, 2002).

To the extent that registration and notification policies have had an impact on sexual crime rates or official responses to juvenile sex offenders, that impact might be greatest in states with the most comprehensive registration procedures. For this reason, South Carolina's policies are reviewed in more detail.

The South Carolina legislation that created the sex-offender registry is among the most aggressive examples of such legislation in the United States, particularly as applied to juvenile offenders. As noted previously, federal law provides guidelines for registration and notification, whereas states retain control of specific implementation details. States can make registries more (but not less) comprehensive. In every respect, the South

Carolina registry is more comprehensive than is required by federal law. Thus this registry applies to persons of any age (rather than being limited to adults or youths tried as adults); applies for life (rather than the federally mandated 10-year minimum); includes hands-off sex offenses (rather than only the mandated, hands-on offenses); does not distinguish between any risk levels; and subjects all registrants to notification (rather than only "high-risk" registrants) via the Internet, with some exceptions for very young offenders.

In addition to exceeding all federal guidelines, the South Carolina policy as applied to juveniles is also more aggressive than those of many other states. For example, several states limit the age of juveniles required to register (e.g., South Dakota); the length of time for which juveniles must register (e.g., Idaho); and access to information about juvenile sex offenders (e.g., New York; Center for Sex Offender Management, 1999; National Center for the Prosecution of Child Abuse, 1999). The South Carolina policies provide no such protections for teenagers convicted of sex crimes. Younger offenders are not placed on the Internet-based registry until they reach 12 years of age. On the other hand, the South Carolina registry is by no means unique. For example, the Illinois Supreme Court recently upheld that state's decision to require lifetime registration for a 12-year-old boy who met criteria as a "sexual predator" (*Illinois v. J.W.*, 2003).

The potential for harm from registration and notification policies as applied to minors seems self-evident. In addition to the potential for ostracism and vigilantism, research has found that being labeled as "deviant" may diminish a youth's social bonds, thus potentially freeing the youth to participate in criminal behavior, including sex offending (Paternoster & Iovanni, 1989; Triplett & Jarjoura, 1994). Longitudinal research has also indicated that such labeling puts youths at a risk of remaining involved with delinquent peers and thus maintaining delinquent behavior over time (Hayes, 1997). Accordingly, although punishment is not an intended effect of sex-offender-specific legislation, it appears to be a relatively likely outcome, especially with respect to increasing rejection from prosocial peers and groups and important organizations (Letourneau & Miner, in press). Finally, ongoing developmental research indicates that both the initiation of criminal behavior and its maintenance over time are related, in part, to feelings of powerlessness (Ross & Mirowsky, 1987) and an individual's level of bonding to conventional individuals and institutions (Huizinga, 1995; Menard, Elliott, & Wofford, 1993). It is possible, and perhaps even likely, that registration and notification policies negatively influence the development of a positive self-identity, with important ramifications for continued delinquent behavior.

Summary and Conclusions

The principal goals of registration and notification are to reduce initial sex offending and prevent recidivism. However, the impact of these policies on sexual criminal offending, as implemented with juvenile offenders, is completely unknown at the present time. Research must be developed and funded to examine whether registration has the intended effect of reducing sexual crimes in general, and sexual recidivism in particular, among juvenile offenders. Importantly, research must also examine whether certain registration and notification policies have unintended effects, such as reducing the probabilities of either prosecution or adjudication for registry offenses. If registration and notification are found to have independent effects of reducing general sexual offending, sexual recidivism, or both, such an impact would offset the costs and burdens of maintaining registries, to the extent that additional crime and victim-related costs are reduced and to the extent that communities are made safer. Alternately, if registration and notification fail to reduce sexual offending and sexual recidivism, the financial and physical burden of maintaining registries may be deemed wasteful of ever-shrinking state funds and resources. In either event, study results should place policy makers in a much better position to determine the relative cost–benefit ratio provided by comprehensive registration and notification policies. Furthermore, if aggressive registration practices, such as those employed in South Carolina and Illinois, actually have the effect of *reducing* the probability that juvenile sex offenders are prosecuted or adjudicated for registry offenses, such information would also be important in determining cost–benefit ratios and might indicate the need to alter such policies or provide specialized training to officials responsible for these youths.

Although all states have enacted registration and notification legislation, there is ongoing debate regarding the application of these laws to juvenile offenders. For example, the Illinois State Supreme Court recently heard a case of a 12-year-old child who was identified as a "sexual predator" and placed on the state's lifetime sex-offender registry. The Illinois Supreme Court upheld these decisions, and the defense requested a hearing from the United States Supreme Court. Although the United States Supreme Court refused to hear the case, it seems very likely that more requests for Supreme Court intervention will be made as states grapple with how to implement sex-offender-specific legislation.

It seems unlikely that the United States will retreat from registration and notification policies; thus research can and should be utilized to implement these policies in the most effective (and least destructive) manner. It is necessary and appropriate that effective policies be identified for reducing serious sex crimes and improving community safety.

However, care must also be taken that these same policies do not harm youths or otherwise undermine these important goals. Anecdotal information is insufficient for determining the effects of registration and notification on juvenile offenders. It is time now to examine these laws with an objective and empirical focus.

References

Alexander, M. A. (1999). Sexual offender treatment efficacy revisited. *Sexual Abuse: A Journal of Research and Treatment, 11*, 101–116.

Bachman, R., Paternoster, R., & Ward, S. (1992). The rationality of sexual offending: Testing a deterrence/rational choice conception of sexual assault. *Law and Society Review, 26*, 343–372.

Blumstein, A. (2000). Disaggregating the violence trends. In A. Blumstein & J. Wallman (Eds.), *The crime drop in America* (pp. 13–44). Cambridge, UK: Cambridge University Press.

Bumby, K. M., & Maddox, M. C. (1999). Judges' knowledge about sexual offenders, difficulties presiding over sexual offense cases, and opinions on sentencing, treatment, and legislation. *Sexual Abuse: A Journal of Research and Treatment, 11*, 305–315.

Caldwell, M. F. (2002). What we do not know about juvenile sexual reoffense risk. *Child Maltreatment, 7*, 291–302.

Center for Sex Offender Management. (1999). *Sex offender registries: Policy overview and comprehensive practices*. Silver Spring, MD. Retrieved February 23, 2003, from www.csom.org/pubs/sexreg.html

Chaffin, M. (1998). "Don't shoot, we're your children": Have we gone too far in our response to adolescent sexual abusers and children with sexual problems? *Child Maltreatment, 3*, 314–316.

Chaffin, M., Letourneau, E. J., & Silovsky, J. F. (2002). Adults, adolescents and children who sexually abuse children: A developmental perspective. In J. Myers (Ed.), *The APSAC handbook on child maltreatment* (pp. 205–232). Thousand Oaks, CA. Sage.

De Jong, A. R. (1992). Medical detection and effects of the sexual abuse of children. In W. O'Donohue & J. H. Geer (Eds.), *The sexual abuse of children: Clinical issues* (Vol. 2, pp. 71–99). Hillsdale, NJ: Erlbaum.

DiIulio, J. J. (1995). Arresting ideas: Tougher law enforcement is driving down urban crime. *Policy Review, 74*, 12–16.

Edwards, W., & Hensley, C. (2001). Contextualizing sex offender management legislation and policy: Evaluating the problem of latent consequences in community notification laws. *International Journal of Offender Therapy and Comparative Criminology, 45*, 83–101.

Finkelhor, D., & Jones, L. M. (2004, January). Explanations for the decline in child sexual abuse cases. *Juvenile Justice Bulletin*, NCJ 184741, pp. 1–12.

Hayes, H.D. (1997). Using integrated theory to explain the movement into juvenile delinquency. *Deviant Behavior: An Interdisciplinary Journal, 18,* 161–184.

Huizinga, D. (1995). Developmental sequences in delinquency: Dynamic typologies. In L. J. Crockett & A. C. Crouter (Eds.), *Pathways through adolescence. Individual development in relation to social contexts* (pp. 15–34). Mahwah, NJ: Erlbaum.

Illinois v. J. W. 204 Ill. 2d 50, *cert. denied,* 540 U.S. 983 (2003).

Keller, K. J. (2002). *Juvenile sex offender court history and outcomes.* Unpublished manuscript.

Letourneau, E. J., & Miner, M. H. (in press). Juvenile sex offenders: A case against the legal and clinical status quo. *Sexual Abuse: A Journal of Research and Treatment.*

Lieb, R. (1996). Community notification laws: A step toward more effective solutions. *Journal of Interpersonal Violence, 11,* 298–300.

Matson, S., & Lieb, R. (1997). *Megan's Law: A review of state and federal legislation* (Report No. 97-10-1101). Retrieved February 23, 2003, from the Washington State Institute for Public Policy website, www.wa.gov/wsipp

McManus, R. (2002). *South Carolina criminal and juvenile justice trends 2001.* Columbia, SC: South Carolina Department of Public Safety, Office of Justice Programs, Statistical Analysis Center.

Menard, S., Elliott, D. S., & Wofford, S. (1993). Social control theories in developmental perspective. *Studies on Crime and Crime Prevention, 2,* 69–87.

Nagin, D. S. (1998). Deterrence and incapacitation. In M. Tonry (Ed.), *The handbook of crime and punishment* (pp. 345–368). New York: Oxford University Press.

National Center for the Prosecution of Child Abuse (1999). *Child abuse and neglect state statutes elements: Investigations* (No. 17: Sex Offender Registration). Retrieved February 23, 2003, from www.ndaa-apri.org

Pastore, A. L., & Maguire, K. (2002). *Sourcebook of criminal justice statistics 2001.* Washington, DC: U.S. Department of Justice, Bureau of Justice Statistics.

Paternoster, R., & Iovanni, L. (1989). The labeling perspective and delinquency: An elaboration of the theory and assessment of the evidence. *Justice Quarterly, 6,* 359–394.

Petrosino, A. J., & Petrosino, C. (1999). The public safety potential of Megan's Law in Massachusetts: An assessment from a sample of criminal sexual psychopaths. *Crime and Delinquency, 45,* 140–158.

Prentky, R. A. (1996). Community notification and constructive risk reduction. *Journal of Interpersonal Violence, 11,* 295–298.

Ramirez, J. R., & Crano, W. D. (2003). Deterrence and incapacitation: An interrupted time-series analysis of California's three-strikes law. *Journal of Applied Social Psychology, 33,* 110–144.

Redlich, A. D. (2001). Community notification: Perceptions of its effectiveness in preventing child sexual abuse. *Journal of Child Sexual Abuse, 10,* 91–116.

Ross, C. E., & Mirowsky, J. (1987). Normlessness, powerlessness, and trouble with the law. *Criminology, 25,* 257–278.

Ross, H. L. (1982). *Deterring the drinking driver: Legal policy and social control.* Lexington, MA: Heath.

Sampson, R. J., & Cohen, J. (1988). Deterrent effects of police on crime: A replication and theoretical extension. *Law and Society Review, 22,* 163–189.

Schram, D. D., & Milloy, C. D. (1995). *Community notification: A study of offender characteristics and recidivism.* Washington State Institute for Public Policy. Olympia, WA. Retrieved February 23, 2003, from the Washington State Institute for Public Policy website, www.wa.gov/wsipp

Seagrave, D., & Grisso, T. (2002). Adolescent development and the measurement of juvenile psychopathy. *Law and Human Behavior, 26,* 219–239.

SEARCH. (1998). *National conference on sex offender registries: Proceedings of a BJS/SEARCH conference.* Retrieved February 1, 2003, from the U.S. Department of Justice website www.ojp.usdog.gov/bjs/pub/ascii/ncsor.txt

Tonry, M. (1998). Intermediate sanctions. In M. Tonry (Ed.), *The handbook of crime and punishment* (pp. 683–711). New York: Oxford University Press.

Triplett, R., & Jarjoura, G.R. (1994). Deterrence or labeling: The effects of informal sanctions. *Journal of Quantitative Criminology, 10,* 43–64.

Trivits, L. C., & Reppucci, N. D. (2002). Application of Megan's Law to juveniles. *American Psychologist, 57,* 690–704.

Zevitz, R. G., & Farkas, M. A. (2000a). The impact of sex-offender community notification on probation/parole in Wisconsin. *International Journal of Offender Therapy and Comparative Criminology, 44,* 8–21.

Zevitz, R. G., & Farkas, M. A. (2000b). Sex offender community notification: Managing high risk criminals or exacting further vengeance? *Behavioral Sciences and the Law, 18,* 375–391.

Zimring, F. E. (2004). An American travesty: Legal responses to adolescent sexual offending. Chicago: University of Chicago Press.

CHAPTER 13

Research on Adolescent Sexual Abuser Treatment Programs

David L. Burton
Joanne Smith-Darden
Sarah Jane Frankel

There is a paucity of research related to treatment processes and outcomes with juvenile sexual abusers. The extant research contains attempts to evaluate the efficacy of specific treatment programs by examining posttreatment recidivism of treated and untreated groups of adolescent male sexual abusers. Methodological difficulties abound in this research and involve issues such as ethical constraint (e.g., dealing with wait-list groups, nontreatment groups, etc.), poor research funding, short follow-up times, nonexperimental designs, and small sample sizes (Epps, 1994; Lab, Shields, & Schondel, 1993). The treatment evaluation studies are few in number (fewer than 15 studies have been published to date), so not surprisingly, few meta-analytic studies have been attempted. In general, these meta-analytic studies report effectiveness of current treatment with juvenile sexual abusers (Worling & Curwen, 2000; Alexander, 1999); however, it is important to note that questions about the methodological adequacy of this research have been raised (Weinrott, 1996).

Although program evaluations of this kind are crucially important to extend knowledge in the field, these studies have not offered guidance as to which specific treatment methods should be implemented or discontinued. As a result, no evidence-based treatment guidelines for juvenile sexual abusers are currently available. However, guidelines have been proposed based on expert opinion and currently accepted clinical practice. For instance, the National Task Force on Juvenile Sexual Abuser Treatment, affiliated with the National Adolescent Perpetrator Network, is currently revising recommendations that were originally developed in 1988 by providers in the field (National Adolescent Perpetrator Network, 1993). Another example of brief guidelines is a collection of experience-based standards for adolescents in residential facilities put together by a group of practitioners (Bengis et al., 1999). Finally, the Association for the Treatment of Sexual Abusers is currently developing guidelines for the treatment of adolescents. The lack of evidence-based guidelines may be due to the fact that treatment of juvenile sexual abusers is a relatively new field and that these youths make up less than 25% of the sexually abusive clients who are treated in the United States (McGrath, Cumming, & Burchard, 2003). However, despite the lack of evidence-based practice standards or guidelines, many treatment programs are already in place for juvenile sexual abusers, apparently in response to the perceived needs of this population of young offenders.

The Safer Society surveys, which started in 1986, provide us with a good description of these extant treatment programs. The survey's history has been discussed at length in previous publications (Burton & Smith-Darden, 2001; McGrath et al., 2003), but a brief summary is provided here: Honey Fay Knopp, Safer Society's founder and director, wanted to be able to offer treatment referrals on a national basis and also envisioned the creation of a network of treatment programs to support and inform one another. Hence, the original survey's questions were intended to elicit information about program characteristics that might be of interest to those who needed services, to program directors who might seek networking with other programs, or to those who might refer others to treatment programs (e.g., attorneys, social workers, and psychologists). Over the years of administering the survey, it grew in length from its original 2 pages to more than 15 pages, as the parties who were seeking treatment had more detailed questions about treatment providers. For example, in addition to the location of treatment programs, referral sources and individuals in need of treatment wanted to know the demographics of the populations served at various programs, the specific treatment methods implemented, and the various languages in which treatment services were provided. The survey moved into a new phase in the early 1990s with Robert Longo's involvement with Safer Society. Under his guidance, more research questions were added to allow for better program description, as well as the description of various services offered. We (Burton and colleagues) then assumed the survey analysis of the 1996 data (Burton & Smith-Darden, 2000) and the entire process of revision, collection, and analysis of the 2000 survey (Burton & Smith-

Darden, 2001). More recently, McGrath et al. (2003) undertook the entire process for the 2002 survey. This chapter first summarizes and compares critical treatment issues for adolescent sexual abusers, using data from the past two Safer Society surveys (Burton & Smith-Darden, 2001; McGrath et al., 2003) and then offers several previously unreported analyses from the 2000 survey data on programs that treat either male or female adolescent sexual abusers.

Method

A modified version of the empirically based total design method (Dillman, 1978) was employed to maximize the quantity of responses to the 2000 survey. To facilitate survey completion, the cover page provided survey instructions and contact information for the researchers so that respondent's questions could be easily answered via phone or e-mail. Surveys were sent to all programs and practitioners in the Safer Society referral database, covering programs located within the United States and Canada. One month after the initial mailing, a second, identical mailing was made, and then reminder postcards were sent at various intervals if the surveys were not returned. Telephone calls were made to those who did not respond to the mailed material. Additionally, surveys were passed out to all attendees of both the 1999 Association for the Treatment of Sexual Abusers conference and the 2000 National Adolescent Perpetration Network conference. For the 2002 survey, McGrath et al. (2003) utilized similar methods, but with a more extensive mailing list than was available for the 2000 survey. However, the 2002 survey process did not include Canadian programs (McGrath et al., 2003).

Whereas previous surveys had not defined the term "program," the 2000 and 2002 surveys defined a "program" as an entity treating *only* one age group and one gender. Programs were classified as either community based or residentially based. Although a program may have had multiple sites, it was counted as only one program if the sites used the same providers and the same model of treatment with the same age group and gender of offender (Burton & Smith-Darden, 2001; McGrath et al., 2003). If inpatient and outpatient services were available at the same site, providers were instructed to complete separate questionnaires for each.

The 2002 survey also included individual professional practices as programs—therefore, an individual professional working with one or several youths in a given area was counted as a program. In addition, in both the 2000 and 2002 surveys, participants were instructed to complete only one questionnaire per program and/or site to reduce double counting of programs.

Research Questions

The development of the survey questions, as described previously, has been quite flexible over the survey's eight iterations. In the 2000 survey, we endeavored to clarify some questions from previous versions of the survey and also to improve the method of distribution using Dillman's (1978) method. In 2002, McGrath et al. (2003) made additional improvements to both the mailing list and the clarity of the questions, in addition to adding more specific item-response choices. Historically, the survey had a particular set of questions that were retained for the sake of comparison over time. Additional questions were added with each version of the survey to meet changes in the field or improve the question set.

Summary and Comparison of Data from Previous Surveys

Descriptions of Programs

In the 2000 survey, Burton and Smith-Darden (2001) reported on 291 programs for adolescents. The majority of these were community-based (n = 190), and the remaining 101 were residential programs. This is approximately a 2:1 ratio of community to residential programs. In the 2002 survey, McGrath et al. (2003) reported on 937 programs for adolescents, with the majority again being community based (n = 726) and the remainder being residential (n = 131). This is about a 6:1 ratio of community to residential programs. This difference in community-to-residential-programs ratio between surveys is related to the intentional inclusion of individual practitioners in the 2002 survey (McGrath et al., 2003). As previously noted, McGrath et al. (2003) included individual treatment providers: 64% (310/484) of the survey respondents who treat adolescent males were private practitioners. Similarly, 62.4% (143/229) of the survey respondents who treat females were private practitioners. Once the individual practitioners are removed from the totals and programs are counted, the respondent totals are very similar to those found in the 2000 survey.

In 2000, male programs outnumbered female programs in community-based treatment by an almost 2:1 male-to-female-program ratio and in residential treatment by a 9:1 male-to-female-program ratio. In the 2002 survey, the gender ratios were very similar (2:1 and 6:1) (see Table 13.1).

By 2002, most programs had been in existence between 7 and 11 years. Residential programs for females were most recently established,

TABLE 13.1. Numbers of Programs/Respondents

	2000			2002		
	Community	Residential	Totals	Community	Residential	Totals
Males	118	91	209	486	188	674
Females	72	10	82	230	33	263
Totals	190	101	291	716	221	937

being in business an average of 7.23 years. The remaining program types (all male programs and community-based programs for females) reported average program ages between 10 and 11 years (McGrath et al., 2003). Presumably, many of the programs for females were established because of the recent increased recognition of the need for treatment of female abusers and as the number of females in the juvenile justice system has grown (Community Research Associates, 1998).

Program Theory

With respect to survey questions regarding program theory, there were again a few important differences in methodology between the 2000 and 2002 surveys (McGrath et al., 2003). The 2000 survey offered definitions of program theories to respondents, whereas in 2002, no definitions were provided to respondents. In 2000, respondents were asked to choose only one theory, whereas in 2002 respondents were asked to rank order three theories that best represented their program's theoretical basis. This was an attempt to capture the eclectic nature of treatment programs. In 2002, respondents also had slightly different theory choices than in previous surveys (e.g., social learning theory). In 2001 Burton and Smith-Darden reported that between 82 and 100% of the community and residential adolescent programs reported some form of cognitive-behavioral theory base (including response choices of "cognitive-behavioral/relapse prevention" and "classic cognitive behavioral/behavioral" based programs). This finding was echoed in 2002 with between 76 and 84% of male and female community programs and male residential programs choosing "cognitive-behavioral," "relapse prevention," or "social learning theory" as their primary practice theory (McGrath et al., 2003, p.28).

Interestingly, the responses regarding residential female programs varied between the two surveys. Whereas these programs fit in with the other program types on theory choice in the 2000 survey results (Burton

& Smith-Darden, 2001), in the 2002 survey results McGrath et al. (2003) reported that only 64% of the female residential programs chose "cognitive-behavioral," "relapse prevention," or "social learning theory" as their primary theory base (p. 28). The difference between years of the survey may be explained by the fact that, in 2002, 7.1% of the female residential programs reported "sexual trauma" as their theoretical base and an additional 7.1% chose "other" as the program's theoretical base (these options were not selected by any programs in 2000). This may reflect the more recent realization that program designers cannot assume that male and female offenders are similar and cannot simply clone male programming for females (Community Research Associates, 1998).

In the 2002 survey results, McGrath et al. (2003) present adolescent treatment dose (intensity of treatment) in sessions per week. Dose was found to be similar for males and females. However, dose of treatment differed by program type (i.e., community or residential). Based on a typical 4.3-week month, in community programs adolescent sexual abusers receive just over 4 group sessions per month, 2.7 individual sessions per month, and 1 family session per month. In residential settings, adolescent sexual abusers receive over 20 group sessions per month, over 5 individual sessions per month, and over 1.5 family sessions per month.

As can be seen in Tables 13.2 and 13.3, comparing these results with the survey findings in 2000, the number of both individual and family sessions per month has been reduced, whereas the number of group therapy sessions per month has increased (McGrath et al., 2003). These trends may reflect budgetary pressures and the differential costs of providing group versus individual and family treatment sessions. In a previous 10-year analysis of the survey, it was noted that family treatment in adolescent programs decreased between 1986 and 1996 (Burton et al., 2000). These latest findings may be a continuation of that trend.

Risk Assessment

In response to increasing demands for risk assessment in the field, McGrath et al. (2003) asked about specific recidivism risk assessment protocols for adolescent males (none are commonly in use for females yet). Although the tools in use for adolescent male sexual abusers are not actuarial, they are moving in that direction as more data are collected and the instruments are refined (see Worling & Långström, Chapter 10, this volume). Out of the community-based and residential programs that were surveyed, 21.0% reported using the ERASOR—the Estimated Risk of Adolescent Sexual Offender Recidivism (Worling & Curwen, 2000,

TABLE 13.2. Males: Average Sessions per Week

Sessions per week	2000		2002	
	Community (*n* = 118)	Residential (*n* = 91)	Community (*n* = 486)	Residential (*n* = 188)
Group	1.29	3.70	1.04	5.27
Individual	1.00	1.27	0.64	1.21
Family	0.74	0.81	0.27	0.34

2001)—and about 31% reported using J-SOAP—the Juvenile Sex Offender Assessment Protocol (Prentky, Harris, Frizzell, & Righthand, 2000; Prentky & Righthand, 2003). However, McGrath et al. (2003) did not ask about risk assessment for nonsexual offenses (e.g., violence, substance abuse, and other crimes) for juveniles. This may be an area for concern. For example, in summarizing the recidivism literature for adolescent male sexual abusers, Burton, Hedgepeth, Ryan, and Compton (2003) state that "sexual recidivism rates for treated adolescent sexual abusers are found to be between 0% and 20%, whereas their non-sexual crime recidivism rates are found to be between 8% and 65%" (p. 3). Given these statistics, it may be important for programs to assess the risk of other forms of recidivism prior to program completion.

Previously Unreported Results

An expert panel of 20 practitioners in this field were asked to score the importance of each item of unreported data from the 2000 survey (Burton & Smith-Darden, 2001) on a 3-point scale of the importance of the survey question to practitioners in the field. The 10 questions with the

TABLE 13.3. Females: Average Sessions per Week

Sessions per week	2000		2002	
	Community (*n* = 72)	Residential (*n* = 10)	Community (*n* = 230)	Residential (*n* = 33)
Group	1.07	4.11	0.92	5.10
Individual	0.96	1.50	0.66	1.17
Family	0.75	0.92	0.29	0.40

highest ratings are reported in this section in order of importance, determined by averaging the scores of the expert panel. Conclusions and recommendations follow these results.

Aftercare

Aftercare refers to the processes generally employed just before and after discharge of youths from a program. As indicated in Table 13.4, whereas the 2000 survey analyses revealed that about 80% or more of respondents indicated that program staff members assessed risk of recidivism in some fashion, according to the 2002 survey, as discussed previously, only about 30% of the staff members in the programs that work with males used the ERASOR or J-SOAP (McGrath et al., 2003). It is unknown what other tools or methods program staff are using to assess risk of recidivism; this emphasizes the need for further research on and development and validation of risk assessment measures for adolescent sexual abusers. This is especially a concern for programs that treat adolescent female abusers, as no commonly used or agreed-on recidivism risk assessment instruments currently exist.

   All of the residentially based programs assist in aftercare placement, but only 73% of the community-based programs do the same (see Table 13.4). Research indicates that residentially based youths typically have more severe victimization histories (Burton, 2000; Moody, Brissie, & Kim, 1994) and also commit more severe crimes (Burton, Miller, & Shill, 2002) when compared with community-based samples (Smith,

TABLE 13.4. Aftercare Process

	Residential programs		Community programs	
	Male (n = 91) %	Female (n = 10) %	Male (n = 118) %	Female (n = 72) %
Is a risk assessment done prior to discharge?	80.2	90.0	78.0	84.7
Does your agency assist in aftercare placement?	100.0	100.0	73.7	72.2
How is information shared with the next treatment provider(s)? Circle all that apply.				
In person	83.5	100.0	60.2	61.1
By telephone	94.5	100.0	88.1	91.7
Via packet/file	87.9	100.0	83.1	86.1

Monastersky, & Deisher, 1987; Worling, 2001). These differences may lead to a greater need for follow-up and additional placements for youths who have been in residential facilities than for those in community-based treatment, perhaps explaining the higher percentages of residential programs that are involved in aftercare processes as compared with the community-based programs in Table 13.4.

We have worked primarily in and with residential facilities. In our experience, many residential agencies send a packet of information to the next placement (e.g., a less secure facility, a halfway house). This packet usually contains criminal and legal information (e.g., court reports, victim statements, and court orders), psychological profiles and assessments, school and health records, psychosocial information, and some minimal information on treatment history. Sometimes additional treatment history or progress and other data are shared in person or on the phone as the placement is being planned and negotiated. The data in Table 13.4 support our experiences, and they also show that 100% of the residential programs that responded to the survey and that work with adolescent females use all three methods to communicate information to aftercare programs. Perhaps female sexual abusers are harder to place (i.e., fewer placements are available), and more information and communication may be needed in order to ensure the greatest chance of successful placement.

Psychoeducational Treatment

Many programs offer psychoeducational experiences to youths in order to enhance knowledge or reduce skill deficits. These experiences cover a broad range of areas, from sex education of various types to conflict resolution and communication skills. As can be seen from recent research (Knight & Sims-Knight, in press), adolescent sexual abusers are not homogenous in etiology or in areas of criminogenic need (e.g., social skills, dating skills, sexual knowledge). Although Table 13.5 illustrates that most programs offer many of these psychoeducational experiences to youths, it does not reveal how individual programs are applied to the individual youths. The research on heterogeneity of youths supports individualized programming for youths with different needs and backgrounds so that they receive what they need and do not participate in unnecessary or inapplicable classes.

Notably, the effectiveness of psychoeducational classes is rarely evaluated, but this type of intervention has shown promise for working with depression in adolescents (Ackerson, Scogin, McKendree-Smith, & Lyman, 1998) and aggressive behavior in children (Schechtman, 2000).

TABLE 13.5. Psychoeducational Classes/Experiences (Sorted alphabetically)

	Residential programs		Community programs	
	Male (n = 91) %	Female (n = 10) %	Male (n = 118) %	Female (n = 72) %
Assertiveness training	80.2	60.0	84.7	77.8
Communication skills	91.2	70.0	87.0	80.6
Conflict resolution	85.7	50.0	83.9	73.6
Dating skills	62.6	60.0	85.6	79.2
Frustration tolerance/ impulse control	76.9	40.0	78.0	70.8
Intimacy/relationship skills	78.0	60.0	85.6	77.8
Positive/prosocial sexuality	86.8	60.0	83.1	80.6
Sex role stereotyping, sexual lifestyles, etc.	71.4	50.0	72.0	65.3
Sexual attitude reassessment–SAR model	19.8	40.0	19.5	22.2
Sexually transmitted diseases	85.7	60.0	76.3	69.4
Values clarification	81.3	40.0	81.4	72.2

Adjunctive Techniques

The abuse of drugs and alcohol by adolescent sexual abusers has been briefly explored in the literature (Lightfoot & Barbaree, 1993; Zakireh, 2000). Many youths' sexual offenses are preceded by substance use and, indeed, substance abuse has been nationally recognized as a very serious issue among juvenile delinquent youths (McClelland, Teplin, & Abram, 2004), with 85.4% of youths having used drugs in the 6 months prior to their study. Finally, in our experience, substance abuse and sales of drugs are the primary crimes of recidivism for sexual abusers. Yet many programs do not offer some of the related adjunctive treatments (see Table 13.6).

Another surprising result was that not all of the programs had psychiatric consultation available to the youths (see Table 13.6). In a recent Office of Juvenile Justice and Delinquency Prevention (OJJDP) bulletin, Wasserman, Jensen, and Ko (2003) reviewed literature regarding mental health needs among youths in juvenile justice settings. These authors discussed how the mental health problems of these particular youths may be a contributing factor to their criminal behavior, as well as an impediment to their rehabilitation. Wasserman et al.'s (2003) study of nonsexually abusive delinquents revealed that 65% of their sample, after completing a relatively recently developed computerized self-administered version of the Diagnostic Interview for Children (DISC), had been found to have diagnoses of mental disorders. It is clear from such studies and clinical practice that many delinquent youths and many sexually abusive youths may have mental disorders that need assessment and treatment. Programs should therefore strongly consider having psychiatric consultation available to youths.

As mentioned previously, the number of programs that offer family therapy may be decreasing over time. Parent support groups seem to be lacking in the programs surveyed in 2000 as well (see Table 13.6). In residential programs, many youths' parents may be unavailable or uninterested or may live quite a distance from the program, which may help explain why the percentage of programs that offer parent support groups are lower for residential than for community programs. Research has not been conducted regarding the effectiveness of family therapy with adolescent sexual abusers except in the case of multisystemic therapy, which may, depending on the youth's needs, involve the youth's family. This treatment has been shown to be very effective with nonsexually abusing delinquents (Henggeler et al., 1991; Borduin, Schaeffer, & Ronis, 2003), as well as with sexually abusive youths (Borduin & Schaeffer, 2001).

TABLE 13.6. Adjunctive Techniques/Programs (Sorted alphabetically)

| | Residential programs | | Community programs | |
	Male (n = 91) %	Female (n = 10) %	Male (n = 118) %	Female (n = 72) %
Adult Children of Alcoholics (ACOA)	19.8	20.0	13.6	8.3
Alcoholics Anonymous (AA)	49.5	40.0	46.6	43.1
Employment/vocational training	67.0	10.0	37.3	27.8
Narcotics Anonymous (NA)	37.4	10.0	37.3	33.3
Parent support groups	39.6	30.0	49.2	54.2
Psychiatric consultations	82.4	50.0	70.3	63.9
Sexaholics Anonymous (SA)	7.7	0.0	5.1	4.2
Urinalysis monitoring	35.2	0.0	33.9	29.2

Medications

It is clear from the results reported in Table 13.7 that many programs use selective serotonin reuptake inhibitors (SSRIs) with some youths. According to a recent National Institute of Mental Health (2005) statement, although fluoxetine (i.e., Prozac) has been shown to help children with depression, other SSRIs have not been approved for use with children or adolescents. Nonetheless, many such drugs are prescribed and certainly may be useful with adolescents for anxiety disorders, bipolar disorder, depression, and so forth. However, caution and great care are obviously warranted, and easily accessible psychiatric consultation is strongly suggested.

The treatment of adolescent sexual abusers with antiandrogen drugs such as Lupron, Depo Provera, or Provera is controversial, but in many states, youths are retained in juvenile justice settings until the age of 21. Therefore, some of the youths who are treated with such drugs may be young adults, for whom these drugs are less dangerous, and protocols for giving antiandrogen drugs are better understood by providers. (See Bradford & Fedoroff, Chapter 16, this volume.)

Specific Techniques

It appears that many programs use bibliotherapy methods (e.g., journal keeping and autobiographies) with males but less so with females (see

TABLE 13.7. Medications (Sorted Alphabetically) (Reported in Less Detail in 2002)

	Residential programs		Community programs	
	Male (n = 91) %	Female (n = 10) %	Male (n = 118) %	Female (n = 72) %
Anafranil	19.8	40.0	8.5	6.9
Androcur (cyproterone acetate)	2.2	0.0	0.9	0.0
Buspar	31.9	40.0	13.6	9.7
Lithium carbonate	36.3	40.0	20.3	16.7
Lupron (leuprolide acetate)	7.7	0.0	6.8	0.0
Major tranquilizers	18.7	10.0	7.6	4.2
Minor tranquilizers	25.3	10.0	12.7	9.7
Provera or Depo-Provera	7.7	0.0	9.3	0.0
Selective serotonin reuptake inhibitors (SSRIs; e.g., Prozac, Paxil, Zoloft, Serzone	64.8	50.0	44.1	37.5

Table 13.8). These methods may be part of trauma resolution for youths, as well as part of helping youths recognize precursors to offenses and potential risk factors of reoffense. Many programs also work with youths on sexual fantasies. Presumably, this is to promote positive sexual fantasies and decrease negative and deviant ones. This may be relevant and important for some youths; for example, according to Johnson and Knight (2000), misogynistic sexual fantasies help predict the degree of sexual coercion used in the youths' offenses. Other researchers have also found that sexual fantasies of some sexually abusive young people may be of concern and thus an area for intervention (Daleiden, Kaufman, Hilliker, & O'Neil, 1998).

Bibliotherapy and fantasy work, two evidently popular methods of treatment, as well as the other techniques listed in Table 13.8, have not been shown either to have or not have a relationship with successful treatment outcomes. Our intent is not to disparage the use of such methods of treatment but rather to illustrate an important point: The lack of evidence of a relationship between these methods and treatment outcomes illustrates the great need for research regarding the various components of treatment for sexually abusive young people.

Program Evaluation

Fortunately, staff members from many programs report program evaluation activities (see Table 13.9). This may be related to the fact that many accrediting bodies (e.g., Council on Accreditation) require evidence of

TABLE 13.8. Specific Techniques/Interventions (Sorted Alphabetically)

	Residential programs		Community programs	
	Male ($n = 91$) %	Female ($n = 10$) %	Male ($n = 118$) %	Female ($n = 72$) %
Addictive cycle	42.9	40.0	39.0	34.7
Art therapies	38.5	30.0	23.7	22.0
Autobiography	79.1	50.0	64.0	61.1
Biofeedback	9.9	10.0	5.1	2.8
Bodywork/massage therapy	4.4	10.0	1.7	1.4
Dissociative state therapy	7.7	30.0	5.1	6.9
Experiential therapies	44.0	40.0	19.5	22.2
Fantasy work	79.1	60.0	78.0	63.9
Hypnosis	7.7	10.0	4.2	4.2
Journal keeping	84.6	60.0	72.0	70.8
Shaming	4.4	0.0	2.5	0.0

TABLE 13.9. Program Evaluation

	Residential programs		Community programs	
	Male (n = 91) %	Female (n = 10) %	Male (n = 118) %	Female (n = 72) %
Do you evaluate your program?	83.5	90.0	67.8	70.8
Do you collect and compare pre- and post- measures?	67.0	80.0	51.7	51.4
Posttreatment follow-up? (Circle all that apply.)				
6 months	48.4	60.0	35.6	43.1
12 months	33.0	20.0	35.6	40.3
2 years	26.4	30.0	12.7	13.9
Do you collect sexual abuser reoffense rates?	52.7	60.0	40.7	45.8
Do you collect sexual abuser rearrest rates on nonsexual charges?	45.1	60.0	22.0	25.0

program evaluation. However, it is unclear where the results of these evaluations are being stored and whether the results are being shared with other programs. Are the programs evaluating treatment as a whole, components of treatment, or both? It is strongly recommended that programs share data in a collaborative fashion in order to understand the effectiveness of various approaches to treatment.

Client Referrals to Respondent Programs

Table 13.10 presents the percentage of programs responding to the survey that indicated that they worked with young offenders referred by different referral types. As would be expected, the majority of juvenile sex offender programs worked with youths who had been adjudicated with sexually abusive behavior. The results of the question regarding young people who were mandated for treatment but who had not been adjudicated for sexual offending was a surprising result to us. A much larger percentage of programs were working with these youths than we had expected based on our experience in residential facilities for male offenders or community-based facilities for males. This large percentage of programs may be a result of concerns regarding registration policies (and evasion of registration) or of the recognized need for treatment of these youths who have otherwise evaded charges (e.g., a plea process or diversion program) related to sexual assault. Treatment of nonadjudicated young people can be very difficult. If a youth cannot discuss his crimes for fear of further prosecution or feels he can avoid admitting his crimes because he has not been adjudicated, then facilitating his sense of accountability and responsibility for past and future behavior may be challenging.

Access to Other Clients

Many young people who have been sexually abusive have also been sexually victimized (see Barbaree & Langton, Chapter 3 this volume). When clients are brought together for treatment, they therefore represent a group of youths all of whom perpetrated sexually abusive behaviors and many of whom are also working to resolve their own childhood victimizations. This combination results in a potentially risky situation wherein, if not extremely well supervised, youths may abuse one another. Most programs in the survey reported that young people had access to one another (see Table 13.11), but as can be seen in Tables 13.12 and 13.13, this access is limited to certain areas, and most of the programs responded that they are very careful in their supervision practices. Unfortunately, we did not ask how many programs had experienced sexual assaults between youths.

In our experience, bathrooms, work sites, residences in which more than one youth sleeps in a room, and schools are all areas of concern for potential reoffense. Therefore, line-of-sight supervision or practices in which only one youth is in a given area at any one time (i.e., the bathroom) are strongly recommended in order to prevent institutional offenses.

TABLE 13.10. Percent of Respondent Programs Receiving Referrals of Different Types (Sorted Alphabetically)

| | Residential programs | | Community programs | |
	Male ($n = 91$) %	Female ($n = 10$) %	Male ($n = 118$) %	Female ($n = 72$) %
Adjudicated for sexually abusive behavior	96.7	100.0	98.3	97.2
Mandated by law to seek treatment, but not adjudicated for sexual offending	48.4	80.0	68.6	70.8
Sent by children's protective services	52.7	70.0	68.6	76.4
Voluntary	27.5	70.0	67.8	72.2

TABLE 13.11. Access to Other Youths

	Residential programs		Community programs	
	Male (n = 91) %	Female (n = 10) %	Male (n = 118) %	Female (n = 72) %
Do sexual abusers have access to other clients at any time during treatment (e.g., housing, bathrooms, waiting rooms, hallways, adjunctive treatment activities, recreation, mealtimes)?	64.8	60.0	64.4	68.1

Diversity Training

Lewis (1999) has written of the need to incorporate an understanding of cultural differences into treatment for sexual abusers. Treatment programs in related areas (e.g., delinquency) that have integrated cultural differences into their treatment programs have shown success in decreasing negative behaviors and criminal charges (Botvin, Schinke, Epstein, Diaz, & Botvin, 1995). The 2000 survey results indicate that many programs provide some training for their staff on working with diverse cultural groups (see Table 13.14), yet this training is less than 6 hours per year on average. This seems like very little training for a growing and complicated area of important treatment knowledge.

Professional Affiliation

The research literature on professional and treatment provider burnout (Maslach, 2003) has indicated that burnout is primarily a result of organizational factors rather than individual treatment provider vulnerabilities. This research indicates that professional affiliation may be useful in preventing burnout, yet most agencies indicated that only one

TABLE 13.12. Access Available in Community Programs

	Bathroom	Hallway	Waiting room	Other
Male programs (n = 118)	13	25	45	15
Female programs (n = 72)	14	32	50	11

Note. Many of the responses indicated that youths were highly supervised in all areas.

TABLE 13.13. Access Available in Residential Programs

	Bathroom	Cafeteria	Hallway	In residence	School	Other
Male programs (n = 91)	3	12	10	18	21	30
Female programs (n = 10)	Not mentioned	20	Not mentioned	20	40	20

employee belonged to the primary professional organizations in the field (see Table 13.15). By belonging to the professional organization, that one employee may receive information, notice of conferences, related journals, and so forth, and pass these resources on to colleagues. But there is no indication that the other employees benefit from these resources. We suggest that the professional organizations working to reduce the levels of burnout of those that work in the field

TABLE 13.14. Diversity Training

	Residential programs		Community programs	
	Male (n = 91) %	Female (n = 10) %	Male (n = 118)%	Female (n = 72) %
Which ethnic/cultural group(s) of sexual abusers is/are your staff specifically trained to work with? (Circle all that apply.)				
African American	75.8	90.0	59.3	58.3
Anglo/Caucasian	80.2	100.0	72.9	75.0
Asian/Pacific Islander	26.4	30.0	26.3	31.9
Biracial/multicultural	49.5	70.0	44.9	50.0
Hispanic	56.0	80.0	53.4	51.4
Native American/First Nations	33.0	90.0	36.4	40.3
Other groups?	a		b	c
Are staff members who work with sexual abusers mandated to annually participate in diversity training/awareness?	51.6	50.0	31.4	31.9
If yes (to the previous question), how many hours annually [mean (SD)]?	5.2 (6.8)	6.2 (2.7)	5.1 (3.2)	5.5 (3.1)

[a]Hmong.
[b]Amish, Appalachian, fluent in Spanish, homosexual, non-Christian, Portuguese.
[c]Amish, homosexual, Portuguese.

TABLE 13.15. Staff Professional Affiliations

	Residential programs		Community programs	
Staff professional affiliations per program	Male (n = 91) % [Mean (SD)]	Female (n = 10) % [Mean (SD)]	Male (n = 118) % [Mean (SD)]	Female (n = 72) % [Mean (SD)]
Number of staff members who belong to the Association for the Treatment of Sexual Abusers (ATSA)	2.3 (1.8)	1.9 (1.8)	1.9 (1.5)	1.9 (1.5)
Number of staff members who belong to the American Professional Society on the Abuse of Children (APSAC)	1.7 (.9)	3 (0)[a]	1.5 (1.0)	1.4 (1.0)
Number of staff members who belong to the National Adolescent Perpetrator Network (NAPN)	1.8 (1.4)	2.1 (1.7)	1.6 (.96)	1.6 (.97)

[a]Only one program responded to this question.

might consider agency or group memberships in order to extend benefits to a larger number of professionals who work with sexually abusive youths.

Summary and Conclusions

In this chapter, we have summarized important characteristics of programs that treat adolescent sexual abusers, compared and contrasted data from the last two Safer Society surveys, and shared previously unreported data relevant to the treatment of adolescent sexual abusers. We were again struck by the need for research in many areas of this work. As a result of this realization and the preceding analyses, we offer the following recommendations for programs and practitioners:

• Greater collaboration and sharing of research among programs. Evidently, a great deal of evaluation is occurring, and many opportunities for research are being missed. Perhaps if more employees belonged to and were active in the field's professional organizations, greater opportunities for collaboration might be available to the field.

• More research on risk assessment. Many programs are assessing risk, and, more important, the instruments in use have not been validated. Given the low base rates of sexual reoffense for juvenile sexual abusers, a proposal such as the preceding—a collaborative effort—may be necessary to really understand reoffense risk factors and to test the validity of risk assessment instruments.

• A greater recognition of mental health needs and related psychiatric consultation in all programs. Individualized treatment—within fiscal reasonableness—is also suggested. The fact that young people are very different is clear, and programs may, as risk assessment and other forms of assessment increase, use these tools to decide how to personalize the treatment of sexually abusive youths.

• Further consideration of family and parent support groups as a means to decrease nonsexual recidivism. Experience with this kind of work reveals that youths often end up going home or to a relative after residential placement. Could further family treatment or parent support decrease the high rates of nonsexual recidivism? The research on multisystemic therapy raises this important question.

• Recognizing, assessing, and treating substance abuse as a factor that potentially contributes to sexual recidivism and is possibly a frequent nonsexual reoffense.

• A careful agency by agency analysis of the treatment of mandated but not adjudicated youths. This process and the treatment of these youths must be studied.

• A careful and cyclical analysis of potential access to other youths during the treatment process. This is essential for preventing our clients from reoffending and from being victimized while in professional care.

• Incorporating issues of diversity into treatment and practice. As the U.S. population continues to diversify and as related disciplines incorporate issues of diversity into their treatments and report success, the field of treatment of sexual abusers must incorporate those same issues into its treatments and practices.

References

Ackerson, J., Scogin, F., McKendree-Smith, N., & Lyman, R. D. (1998). Cognitive bibliotherapy for mild and moderate adolescent depressive symptomatology. *Journal of Consulting and Clinical Psychology, 66,* 685–690.

Alexander, M. (1999) Sexual offender treatment efficacy revisited. *Sexual Abuse: A Journal of Research and Treatment, 11,* 101–116.

Bengis, S., Brown, A., Longo, R., Matsuda, B., Ross, J., Singer, K., et al. (1999). *Standards of care for youth in sex offense specific residential treatment.* Holyoke, MA: Whitman.

Borduin, C. M., & Schaeffer, C. M. (2001). Multisystemic treatment of juvenile sexual offenders: A progress report. *Journal of Psychology and Human Sexuality, 13,* 25–42.

Borduin, C. M., Schaeffer, C. M., & Ronis, S. T. (2003). Multisystemic treatment of serious antisocial behavior in adolescents. In C.A. Essau (Ed.), *Conduct and oppositional defiant disorders: Epidemiology, risk factors, and treatment* (pp. 299–318). Mahwah, NJ: Erlbaum.

Botvin, G. J., Schinke, S. P., Epstein, J. A., Diaz, T., & Botvin, E. M. (1995). Effectiveness of culturally focused and generic skills training approaches to alcohol and drug abuse prevention among minority adolescents: Two-year follow-up results. *Psychology of Addictive Behaviors, 9,* 183–194.

Burton, D. (2000). Were adolescent sexual offenders children with sexual behavior problems? *Sexual Abuse: A Journal of Treatment and Research, 12,* 37–48.

Burton, D., Hedgepeth, M., Ryan, G., & Compton, D. (2003). *The relationship of trauma to non-sexual crimes committed by adolescent sexual abusers.* Manuscript submitted for publication.

Burton, D., Miller, D., & Shill, C. T. (2002). A social learning theory comparison of the sexual victimization of adolescent sexual offenders and nonsexual offending male delinquents. *Child Abuse and Neglect, 26,* 893–907.

Burton, D., & Smith-Darden, J. (2001). *North American survey of sexual abuser treatment and models summary data.* Brandon, VT: Safer Society Press.

Burton, D., & Smith-Darden, J. (with Levins, J., Fiske, J., & Freeman-Longo, R.). (2000). *The 1996 Safer Society Survey of sexual offender treatment programs.* Brandon, VT: Safer Society Press.

Community Research Associates. (1998). *Juvenile female offenders: A status of the states report.* Washington, DC: Office of Juvenile Justice and Delinquency Prevention.

Daleiden, E., Kaufman, K., Hilliker, D., & O'Neil, J. (1998). The sexual histories and fantasies of youthful males: A comparison of sexual offending, nonsexual offending, and nonoffending groups. *Sexual Abuse: A Journal of Research and Treatment, 10,* 195–209.

Dillman, D. (1978). *Mail and telephone surveys: The total design method.* New York: Wiley.

Epps, K. (1994). Treating adolescent sex offenders in secure conditions: The experience at Glenthorne Centre. *Journal of Adolescence, 17,* 105–122.

Henggeler, S. W., Borduin, C. M., Melton, G. B., Mann, B. J., Smith, L., et al. (1991). Effects of multisystemic therapy on drug use and abuse in serious juvenile offenders: A progress report from two outcome studies. *Family Dynamics of Addiction Quarterly, 1,* 40–51.

Johnson, G. M., & Knight, R. A. (2000). Developmental antecedents of sexual coercion in juvenile sexual offenders. *Sexual Abuse: A Journal of Research and Treatment, 12,* 165–178.

Knight, R. A., & Sims-Knight, J. E. (2001). *The developmental antecedents of sexual coercion against women in adolescents.* Manuscript submitted for publication.

Knight, R. A., & Sims-Knight, J. E. (in press). Testing an etiological model for juvenile sexual offending against women. In R. Geffner, K. C. Franey, T. G. Arnold, & R. Falconer (Eds.), *Identifying and treating youths who sexually offend: Current approaches, techniques, and research.* New York: Haworth Press.

Lab, S. P., Shields, G., & Schondel, C. (1993). Research note: An evaluation of juvenile sexual offender treatment. *Crime and Delinquency, 39,* 543–553.

Lewis, A. (1999). *Cultural diversity in sexual abuser treatment: Issues and approaches.* Brandon, VT: Safer Society Press.

Lightfoot, L. O., & Barbaree, H. E. (1993). The relationship between substance use and abuse and sexual offending in adolescents. In H. E. Barbaree, W. L. Marshall, & S. M. Hudson (Eds.), *The juvenile sex offender* (pp. 203–224). New York: Guilford Press.

Maslach, C. (2003). Job burnout: New directions in research and intervention. *Current Directions in Psychological Science, 12,* 189–192.

McClelland, G. M., Teplin, L. A., & Abram, K. M. (2004). Detection and prevalence of substance abuse among juvenile detainees. *Juvenile Justice Bulletin.* Available online at www.ncjrs.org/pdffiles1/ojjdp/203934.pdf

McGrath, R. J., Cumming, G. F., & Burchard, B. L. (2003). *Current practices and trends in sexual abuser management: Safer Society 2002 nationwide survey.* Brandon VT: Safer Society Press.

Moody, E. E., Brissie, J., & Kim, J. (1994). Personality and background characteristics of adolescent sexual offenders. *Journal of Addictions and Offender Counseling, 14,* 38–48.

National Adolescent Perpetrator Network. (1993). The revised report from the National Task Force on Juvenile Sexual Offending. *Juvenile and Family Court Journal, 44,* 1–121.

National Institute of Mental Health. (2003). *Antidepressant medication for children and adolescents: Information for parents and caregivers.* Available online at www.nimh.nih.gov/healthinformation/antidepressant_child.cfm

Prentky, R. A., Harris, B., Frizzell, K., & Righthand, S. (2000) An actuarial procedure for assessing risk with juvenile sex offenders. *Sexual Abuse: A Journal of Research and Treatment, 12,* 71–93.

Prentky, R. A., & Righthand, S. (2003). *Juvenile Sexual Offender Assessment Protocol—II manual.* Unpublished manuscript.

Schechtman, Z. (2000). Bibliotherapy: An indirect approach to treatment of childhood aggression. *Child Psychiatry and Psychology, 30,* 39–53.

Smith, W. R., Monastersky, C., & Deisher, R. M. (1987). MMPI-based personality types among juvenile sexual offenders. *Journal of Clinical Psychology, 43,* 422–430.

Wasserman, G., Jensen, P., & Ko, S. (2003). Mental health assessments in juvenile justice: Report on the Consensus Conference. *Journal of the American Academy of Child and Adolescent Psychiatry, 42*(7), 751–761.

Weinrott, M. R. (1996). *Juvenile sexual aggression: A critical review* (Center Paper No. 005). Boulder, CO: University of Colorado, Center for the Study and Prevention of Violence.

Worling, J. R. (2001). Personality-based typology of adolescent male sexual offenders: Differences in recidivism rates, victim-selection characteristics, and personal victimization histories. *Sexual Abuse: A Journal of Research and Treatment, 13*, 149–166.

Worling, J. R., & Curwen, T. (2000). Adolescent sexual offender recidivism: Success of specialized treatment and implications for risk prediction. *Child Abuse and Neglect, 24*, 965–982.

Worling, J. R., & Curwen, T. (2001). *The ERASOR: Estimate of Risk of Adolescent Sexual Offense Recidivism, Version 2.0.* Toronto, Ontario, Canada: Ontario Ministry of Community and Social Services, Thistletown Regional Centre, SAFE-T Program.

Zakireh, B. (2000). Residential and outpatient adolescent sexual and non-sexual offenders: History, sexual adjustment, clinical, cognitive, and demographic characteristics. *Dissertation Abstracts International: Section B: The Sciences and Engineering, 61*(2-B), 1102.

CHAPTER 14

A Reevaluation of Relapse Prevention with Adolescents Who Sexually Offend
A Good-Lives Model

Jo Thakker
Tony Ward
Patrick Tidmarsh

Although juvenile sexual offending is becoming an increasingly popular focus for research, it nonetheless remains an area in need of greater investigative emphasis (e.g., Miner, 2002). As in many areas of applied psychology, individuals treating juveniles who sexually offend have typically applied adult models and approaches to this group with little or no modification (Jones, 2003). For example, Jones (2003) notes that clinical practice with juveniles who sexually offend has usually utilized adult conceptualizations with insufficient acknowledgment of the role of developmental factors. Though such an approach is often a good starting point, it can have the disadvantage of obscuring important differences between the two populations. Thus it has become apparent that children and young people who engage in sexually abusive behaviors need to have interventions designed to fit their developmental needs. In addition, family, caregiver, and community contexts should be taken into account, with appropriate therapeutic and risk management strategies. Furthermore, relapse prevention and follow-up frameworks need to address the family, community, and developmental contexts into which the young person is returning.

To date, research has identified a number of important differences between juveniles who sexually offend and adult sex offenders. For instance, studies indicate that the distinction between rapists and child sexual abusers that is often applied to adult sex offenders is less appropriate in relation to juveniles who sexually offend (Jones, 2003). Also, evidence suggests that compared with adults, adolescents' sexual preferences show a lesser association with their offense histories (Hunter & Lexier, 1998). In other words, their offense types are less likely to reflect their sexual preferences. Similarly, other research has shown that, in general, adolescents do not have established, well-developed patterns of sexual interest and sexual arousal (Trivits & Reppucci, 2002).

This is not surprising given that adolescence is often a time of experimentation and rapid change. One would accordingly expect that in adolescents, sexual offending would be less indicative of long-term ingrained tendencies. Research indicates that young men have a propensity to engage in a range of risk-taking behaviors (Nell, 2002), including behaviors that may be illegal. One of the key psychological mechanisms underlying this tendency appears to be "sensation seeking," which is defined by Zuckerman (1994) as "the seeking of varied, novel, complex, and intense sensations and experiences, and the willingness to take physical, social, legal, and financial risks for the sake of such experiences" (p. 27). What this example highlights is that adolescence is a developmental stage with a range of attendant propensities and inclinations. Accordingly, patterns of offending during this period do not necessarily reflect enduring behavioral tendencies but may rather be indicative of more transient developmental processes.

In regard to recidivism, recent research suggests that variables that have been identified as predictors of reoffending in adults may not apply to adolescents (Miner, 2002). Similarly, Trivits and Reppucci (2002) note that, whereas in adults recidivism has been found to be associated with specific victim characteristics—such as gender and degree of familiarity—this has not been found to be the case with young offenders.

The fact that adolescence is a time of transition is fundamental to the development of clinical intervention approaches, as it highlights the need for such approaches to be both early and effective. Research demonstrates that approximately 50% of adult sex offenders report an onset of offending prior to the age of 18 years (Gray & Pithers, 1993). Therefore, it may be assumed that if sexual offending is recognized and successfully treated early, then the development of chronic patterns of adult offending will be less likely. Hence the unstable and transitive nature of adolescence may be seen as a window of opportunity through which one may have a significant positive impact on young sex offenders' lives.

The core of childhood and adolescence is the development of the self (Keenan, 2002). It is a time dominated by learning, in which each stage offers opportunities for the development of all aspects of the adult self (Collins & Kuczaj, 1991). In treatment terms, this offers an opportunity for an adolescent to change his conception of himself from that of a developing sexual offender to someone trying to live a different kind of life (Ward, 2002). To saddle adolescents with the notion that their offending "self" is so fully formed that they will need to "control" it for the rest of their lives (i.e., to focus primarily on risk management) seems almost to defeat the purpose of treatment before it starts. Treatment is about *change*, about *development*. Bukowski, Sippola, and Brender (1993) argue that the development of sexuality, including "abnormal" behaviors, is a synthesis of self, other, and society, developed through experience and context. The context and experiences of treatment should therefore reflect the needs of adolescents in addressing the process of change and "self"-development. Treatment and theoretical terminology that focuses exclusively on risk and on offending limits the capacity to focus on that which is positive and possible. For example, description of adolescents as "sex offenders" already presumes an identity developed around offending. Although this may be an accurate depiction of current risk and the potential for continued offending, it runs counter to the therapeutic goal of helping young people to develop an identity apart from sexual offending. Such fundamental terminology directs young people toward the assumption of an offending identity at the very time in which the "context and experience" should reflect the possibility of profound and lifelong self-change.

The terminology we use to describe offending should accurately reflect the needs and experience of adolescence. Labeling the adolescent as a "sex offender" during a key developmental phase would seem counterproductive. We suggest that the terminology of "adolescents who sexually offend" more accurately reflects the developmental phase in which the sexual offending behavior takes place, while allowing young people to continue the process of self-discovery and identity development in a more positive context.

In this chapter we propose that the risk–need perspective, on which traditional relapse prevention (RP) is based, has a number of shortcomings that limit its applicability as both a treatment model and a model for risk management. The focus on risk factors is a necessary but not sufficient treatment goal. Instead, we contend that the risk–need approach should be grounded in the "good-lives" model (e.g., Ward, 2002; Ward & Mann, 2004). Targeting risk factors alone will not give

therapists the guidance to effectively treat sex offenders and will not sufficiently motivate offenders to change the ways in which they meet their
human needs. In short, our position is that the good-lives model grounds
or underpins the risk–need principles and provides an explanation of
why criminogenic needs (i.e., dynamic risk factors) are problematic for
the person and society and why they also account for their interrelation-
ships.

To develop our argument, we first outline the risk–need-based
relapse prevention approach, including its origins. Second, we describe a
self-regulation model of relapse prevention that expands on earlier
notions of what relapse is and how it unfolds. We then present the good-
lives model, followed by a discussion of how this can be integrated with
the risk management perspective. And last, we present a model of RP for
young people who offend based on an integration of the good-lives and
risk management approaches. We would like to acknowledge the pioneering work by Haaven (Haaven & Coleman, 2000), Freeman-Longo
(Freeman-Longo, 2001), and Ellerby (Ellerby, Bedard, & Chartrand,
2002) and their colleagues in the development of more constructive
ways of working with sexual offending.

Relapse Prevention and Sexual Offending

Relapse prevention (RP) was initially developed as a way of conceptualizing and managing the maintenance stage of substance-related treatment (Marlatt, 1985). This development grew out of the recognition
that although substantial gains were often made during cognitive-
behavioral treatment of drug and alcohol problems, these gains were not
maintained following the cessation of treatment. The RP approach outlined a systematic means of identifying and targeting the factors that
contributed to relapse. Subsequently, RP was applied to sexual offending
(Pithers, Marques, Gibat, & Marlatt, 1983), and over the past two
decades it has had a significant impact on the way that sex offender
treatment is conceptualized and implemented (Laws, 1989). For example, a considerable proportion of—if not most—sex-offender treatment
programs throughout the world currently incorporate a relapse prevention component (Ward & Mann, 2004).

RP rests on the assumption that sexual offending results from a
complex process that unfolds over time (Gray & Pithers, 1993). The initial model of this process as outlined by Pithers (1990) differed little
from its original depiction in the substance abuse field; it presents
relapse as a linear process in which the offender moves through a series
of steps in a specified order. Following the occurrence of seemingly

unimportant decisions (SUDS), the offender enters a high-risk situation. If he or she is unable to cope with this situation, a lapse occurs—for example, viewing pornography—followed by the abstinence violation effect (AVE). The AVE includes a number of phenomena, such as internal attributions and the problem of immediate gratification. The latter simply refers to the alluring and powerful nature of the presence of the possibility of immediate reward. If an offender is able to cope with these cognitive and affective experiences, then relapse is avoided. However, if there is no adaptive coping response, then a relapse occurs. The premise underlying this model is that relapse does not occur spontaneously but, rather, follows a pattern of interconnected thoughts, emotions, and behaviors that occur in a predictable linear fashion.

The RP model also includes the delineation of a range of risk factors that are grouped under three main headings: predisposing, precipitating, and perpetuating factors (Gray & Pithers, 1993). As outlined by Gray and Pithers in their discussion of RP for juveniles who sexually offend, predisposing risk factors include such phenomena as early physical and sexual abuse and chaos within the familial environment. Precipitating risk factors include sexual fantasies, poor impulse control, and opportunities to offend. And perpetuating risk factors refer to phenomena such as sexual gratification and offense-promoting cognitions. The key idea behind this identification and classification of risk factors is that if such factors are understood, they can then be addressed therapeutically, thereby reducing the chance of relapse. The goal of the clinician is not simply to explain how the offending behavior developed but, rather, to explain how it is maintained, as it is the more proximal contributory variables that are the focus of RP. In light of program outcome evaluations, this would seem a wise approach. For example, as noted by Eldridge (1998), treatment is more efficacious when it incorporates current life events and situations rather than looking to the past to make sense of an individual's behavior, as might be encouraged by some other treatment approaches.

In explaining the role of RP in the area of sex offender treatment, Gray and Pithers (1993) propose that it has three primary functions. First, it is used as a means of promoting internal self-management. Second, it is used as a way of supervising offenders' self-management. And third, it is used as an underlying theoretical framework upon which the treatment approach is based. It is therein apparent that the role of RP has broadened from its original conceptualization. Whereas initially it had a predominantly posttreatment focus, its principles and related practices are now integrated within treatment proper. For example, Gray and Pithers (1993, p. 315) state that "RP thus permits the integration of distinct treatment approaches for specific behavioral excesses and deficits within a single comprehensive therapeutic framework." And that "treatment within the RP model becomes an individualized program tailored to meet each client's unique needs comprehensively."

As with adults, the typical approach to RP with adolescents who offend involves the use of a group, as group therapy has a number of significant advantages. For instance, a group context facilitates the breaking down of patterns of deceit and secrecy that are often involved in sexual offending, and offenders within the group can challenge each others' beliefs and attitudes toward offending. Also important is the support and encouragement that they can give one another as they go through the treatment process (Towl & Crighton, 1996). This is particularly important, as admitting details of their offenses can be very challenging for young men. Perhaps most important, being treated alongside other young men provides opportunities for them to learn from each other. Even though their presence in the group is a result of previous offending, each group member, nonetheless, has various strengths and abilities that can contribute to the rehabilitation of other group members. For example, one individual may be a particularly good communicator, and he could serve as a model for other group members who have difficulty with verbal expression.

The Self-Regulation Model of Relapse Prevention

As a model of treatment and maintenance, the traditional RP model has a number of identified shortcomings (for systematic critiques, see Hanson, 1996; Ward & Hudson, 1996). First, both Marlatt's original RP theory (Marlatt & Gordon, 1985) and Pithers et al.'s (1983) adaptation for sex offenders rely on diverse theoretical sources that have not been well integrated. Second, the original model does not cover all the possible pathways to a reoffense. The three pathways to high-risk situations all reflect skill deficits and ignore situations in which individuals deliberately "use or abuse," as is the case with appetitively driven behavior. And finally, the adaptation of the RP model for sex offenders (Pithers et al., 1983) further delimits the scope of the theory, as it focuses predominantly on the covert route.

The self-regulatory model (Ward & Hudson 1998, 2000; Ward, Hudson, & Keenan, 1998) was developed out of our previous work on modeling offending processes. Our original descriptive model of the offense chain allowed for different offense patterns, planned and unplanned sexually deviant behavior, and positive and negative affective pathways and incorporates offender's perceptions of relationships (Ward, Louden, Hudson, & Marshall, 1995). The self-regulation model

(Ward & Hudson, 1998; Ward, Hudson, & Keenan, 1998) both broadens the scope further and provides a more elegant theoretical formulation of the offense and relapse process.

Self-regulation does not just include the inhibition of behavior, affect, or cognitions but can also include enhancement of these aspects of functioning. For example, anxiety about an examination may be a motivator for studying. Goals, desired states or situations, are central to self-regulation theory and can vary in level of abstractness and type—such as avoidance versus approach goals (Cochran & Tesser, 1996). Goals are also related to affect insofar as ongoing monitoring involves an evaluation of the likelihood of goal attainment, with positive affective states arising from anticipated goal attainment and negative states from perceived goal frustration (Carver & Scheier, 1990).

The self-regulation model of relapse prevention has four alternative pathways based on two types of goals (avoidant vs. approach) and three types of regulation strategies and has nine phases (which closely follow Pithers's original model). The *avoidant–passive* pathway most closely resembles the original sex-offender adaptation of the relapse prevention picture; in other words, the covert route (Pithers, 1990). Life circumstances create negative affect and overload coping skills, leading to deviant sexual desire, but the awareness of harm and/or significant fear of consequences generates restraint. Covert planning, such as seemingly unimportant decisions, together with a deficient level of skills, leads to a high-risk situation arising (i.e., the presence of a potential victim). A lapse (giving in and adopting an approach goal—the problem of immediate gratification) and subsequent relapse follows (with the abstinence violation effect in response to negative postoffense evaluations).

The *avoidant–active* pathway partially resembles Marlatt's second route to relapse, as outlined in the original model (Marlatt & Gordon, 1985). Life events directly, rather than covertly, lead to the development of a high-risk situation. In our terms, however, it is the influence of flawed self-regulation strategies (misregulation) that drive this process. Misplaced short-term emphasis on affect regulation and paradoxical strategies with contradictory effects (e.g., masturbating to deviant sexual fantasies to "drain" off sexual desire) lead to misregulation, despite active efforts on the part of the offender (Baumeister & Heatherton, 1996). There is still a commitment to restraint, as the overall goal is one of avoidance. However, paradoxically, the strategies used to restrain serve to actually enhance the possibility that, once in a high-risk situation, the young man will experience a loss of control and therefore adopt a short-term approach goal—in other words a lapse.

The *approach–automatic* pathway is the first that reflects approach goals, and to some extent it resembles Marlatt's final pathway in which high-risk situations are encountered by genuine chance as opposed to covert planning. Goals and the associated strategies are unlikely to be under direct attentional control, at least initially, with only rudimentary planning being evident. The notion of planned impulsivity (Pithers, 1990) captures the essence of this pathway; that is, the desire for offensive sex is acknowledged at a quite general level, but the relevant overlearned scripts are only enacted when opportunity presents itself. Thus the offense often appears as if "out of the blue" and additionally occurs over what is often a remarkably short time frame. This reflects underregulation. Postoffense evaluations are typically positive, with the negative attitudes toward women and a sense of sexual entitlement being reinforced. Thus the probability of future offending is usually strengthened.

Finally, the *approach–explicit* pathway involves intact self-regulation and explicit goals with respect to sexual offending. If any restraint is evident, it is likely to be at the level of grooming to avoid "rejection," which is quite similar to the restraint exercised by adults in their appropriate dating behaviors, or the avoidance of social sanctions, for example, getting caught. System-level goals (higher level or more abstract goals), such as being emotionally intimate with someone, have become linked with abusive or offensive sexual behaviors. As such, the initiating events are as likely to be positive as they are negative. If negative, then this may reflect explicit needs, such as wanting to be close or "in love" and being aware that this is not yet the case; that is, goal–current situation discrepancy.

We propose that the self-regulatory model of RP overcomes a significant number of the problems outlined here. In brief, the model allows for multiple pathways, which attends to the concern about scope and also increases the degree of flexibility. Second, it helps clarify where and when the processes that mediate the transition points in the offense chain might occur. Third, it knits together some of the diverse theoretical sources involved in relapse prevention and adds some new material. Finally, the model is open-ended, as it has the capacity to be modified in light of both empirical and theoretical developments.

That the self-regulation model increases the scope and flexibility of the original conceptualization of relapse means that it is likely to be more useful with young people who offend. That it has multiple pathways means it is more likely to include the diversity of offending styles seen in young people who offend (Jones, 2003). Also, perhaps most important, it encourages the examination of an underlying skill—self-regulation—that appears to play an important role in the offense process, thereby creating an avenue for intervention. Relatedly, it should be noted that the purpose of this model is simply to allow for the identification of self-regulation problems so that these can be targeted in treatment. It is not aimed at placing individuals in categories that are representative of any lifelong tendencies. This is particularly important in relation to young people who offend, as any one individual may have various self-regulation issues that change in different circumstances and also over time. Therefore, this model is merely a useful way of conceptualizing self-regulation dysfunction in specific instances and should not be used to draw rigid conclusions about ongoing future behavior.

Taking a More Positive Approach

The emergence of a risk–need perspective and its attendant relapse prevention model of sex-offender treatment have provided the field with a theoretical framework and a map with which to guide clinicians, policy makers, and correctional authorities. However, alongside these strengths, there are a number of difficulties that place constraints on the model's capacity to guide and structure effective treatment. The majority of these difficulties revolve around the issue of offender responsivity and motivation to change. Specifically, if treatment revolves around past offending and risk, then the offenders involved will be exposed to a significant amount of very negative messages.

Another major drawback of the risk–need approach is that it is essentially concerned with removing risk, as opposed to promoting more positive and constructive behaviors. In other words, it focuses on removing what is "bad" rather than encouraging that which is "good," so that offenders may be left with absences or gaps in their lives. For example, most programs outline their treatment strategies in rather negative terms; the focus is often on the *elimination* of maladaptive attitudes, the *reduction* of cognitive distortions, the *extinction* of deviant sexual interests, and the generation of a list of people, activities, and places to *avoid* (i.e., relapse prevention). What may not be addressed is the need to understand the goods associated with the commission of an offense and the requirement to ensure that these goods are met in other, more socially acceptable and genuinely satisfying ways (Ward & Mann, 2004).

Analogous to this point is the idea of a doctor treating only the symptoms of a condition rather than the underlying disease that is causing the symptoms. Similarly, it may be theorized that a risk of reoffending arises only because certain "goods" are not being attained; therefore, in order to deal effectively with the risk, it is necessary to determine what goods are missing and to identify the specific problems associated with the attainment of these primary goods. If only the risk factors involved are attended to, it is possible that the underlying reason for offending will continue, thereby increasing the likelihood that, even if risk factors are controlled, they may still emerge at some later time, due to the fact that the underlying etiological factors have not been adequately addressed. Similarly, if a doctor treats only the presenting symptoms, there may well be short-term relief; however, if the underlying disease process is not targeted, then the symptoms are likely to recur.

In light of the problems with the risk–need approach and recent trends toward a more positive approach, we propose (e.g., Ward, 2002; Ward & Mann, 2004; Ward & Stewart, 2003) that a good-lives model provides a comprehensive framework for the conceptualization and instigation of sex-offender treatment. The key aim arising from this model is to equip individuals with the necessary *internal* and *external* conditions (capabilities) to secure primary human goods in socially acceptable and personally meaningful ways. (Note that the term "good lives" and the basic ideas associated with the model have been developed from the excellent work of Kekes, 1989.) The core idea is that all meaningful human actions reflect attempts to achieve primary human goods (Emmons, 1999).

Primary goods are actions, states of affairs, characteristics, experiences, and states of mind that are viewed as intrinsically beneficial to human beings and are therefore sought for their own sake rather than as means to some more fundamental ends (Deci & Ryan, 2000; Emmons, 1996, 1999; Schmuck & Sheldon, 2001). Primary goods emerge out of basic needs, whereas instrumental or secondary goods provide concrete ways of securing these goods, for example, certain types of work, relationships, or language ability. The nature of the primary goods sought by individuals and their weightings are formed in specific cultural contexts and represent individuals' interpretations of interpersonal and social events. This knowledge is clearly influenced by culturally derived beliefs, values, and norms (D'Andrade, 1995). The underlying metaphor is that of a complex, dynamic system wherein the way that individuals seek specific human goods affects the other goods sought, the environment, and, ultimately, the quality of their lives.

A careful review of research findings and theories in a number of different disciplines indicates a considerable level of agreement concerning the basic or primary goods that are sought by human beings and that are thereby essential ingredients of a "good" life. This includes the primary human goods noted in psychological and social science research (Cummins, 1996; Emmons, 1999), evolutionary theory (Arnhart, 1998), practical ethics (Murphy, 2001), and philosophical anthropology (Nussbaum, 2000; Rescher, 1990). Based on this work, we propose that there are at least nine primary human goods: life (including healthy living and functioning), knowledge, excellence in play and work (including mastery experiences), excellence in agency (i.e., autonomy and self-directedness), inner peace (i.e., freedom from emotional turmoil and stress), friendship (including intimate, romantic, and family relationships), community, spirituality (in the broad sense of finding meaning and purpose in life), happiness, and creativity.

In the case of criminal behavior, the problem resides in the *means* used to secure goods, a lack of *scope* within a good-lives plan, the presence of *conflict* among goals (goods sought), or the lack of the necessary *capacities* to form and adjust a plan to changing circumstances (e.g., impulsive decision making). For example, an offender might seek the primary human goods of intimacy and mastery in a sexual relationship with a child. Clearly, this is an inappropriate way of seeking these valued states and is unlikely to result in higher levels of well-being. A primary aim of therapy would be to identify the types of relationships an offender finds satisfying (providing they are socially acceptable) and to equip him with the necessary internal (skills) and external conditions to increase his chances of establishing these relationships. Secondary goods provide ways of achieving primary human goods. For example, an individual may find meaning and purpose in life (primary good) from his or her involvement with an animal welfare organization (secondary good).

The possibility of constructing and translating conceptions of good lives into actions and concrete ways of living depends crucially on the possession of internal (skills and capabilities) and external (opportunities and supports) conditions. For example, self-regulation is an internal capability that may play an important role in constructing a good life, and therefore treatment may need to include a component that teaches this particular skill. Also, treatment needs to include external support systems and should be consistent with opportunities that are actually available. In other words, it should be realistic and take into account the individual's strengths and weaknesses and external constraints.

Arguably one of the advantages of an approach centered on the idea of good lives is that it allows for a more positive therapeutic setting, which would in turn facilitate the development of a sound therapeutic alliance. It has been noted that the quality of the therapeutic alliance is pivotal to the success of treatment both in adults (Ackerman & Hilsenroth, 2003) and in children and adolescents (Eltz, Shirk, & Sarlin, 1995). As determined by Ackerman and his colleagues, a number of therapist characteristics have been found to be particularly important to the development of a good alliance—for example, friendliness, warmth, and openness. In addition, Marshall et al. (2003) have concluded that increasing sexual offenders' self-esteem, working collaboratively with offenders in developing treatment goals, cultivating therapist features such as displays of empathy and warmth, and giving encouragement and rewards for progress facilitate the change process in sex offenders.

Thus the good-lives model encourages a more positive and constructive focus and thereby provides more opportunities for the therapist to display characteristics that are conducive to the development of a good therapeutic alliance. This may be particularly important when working with young people, as many adolescents who sexually offend come from abusive backgrounds (Flitton & Brager, 2002). Evidence suggests that children and adolescents who have been exposed to physical and sexual abuse are more likely to have interpersonal difficulties (Eltz et al., 1995). In particular, as found by Eltz and colleagues, they have a tendency to display excessive vigilance and to have difficulty placing their trust in others. This is important because research on adults has found that the capacity for establishing relationships is fundamental to the development of a good therapeutic alliance (Eltz et al., 1995). Hence, arguably, the therapist working with young people who offend may have to work harder at establishing a strong alliance.

The Risk–Need and Good-Lives Models

We propose that the key theoretical perspective that guides treatment should be that of human well-being (i.e., good lives), rather than of risk management or relapse prevention. A conceptualization of human well-being will specify the various goods (e.g., intimacy, health, autonomy, creativity, knowledge, etc.) that are naturally sought by human beings and the circumstances and conditions necessary to secure these goods. However, we suggest also that the risk–need approach to offender treatment could usefully be embedded within a good-lives model. This means that the focus of therapy should be on instilling the capabilities to achieve human goods in ways that are socially acceptable and personally meaningful and satisfying. Treatment should proceed on the assumption that effective treatment requires the acquisition of competencies and external supports and opportunities to lead different kinds of lives.

This does not mean that the concept of risk is irrelevant and that offenders should not avoid certain activities (e.g., working with children, for a child molester). It simply means that the therapeutic emphasis would be on understanding what primary goods have been sought in sexual offenses and on designing a way of living that addresses those goods in ways that are personally satisfying, that take account of a person's strengths and interests, and, most important, that are socially acceptable and do not place the individual concerned at risk for reoffending.

The idea that criminogenic needs or dynamic risk factors are internal or external obstacles that frustrate or block the acquisition of human goods provides a useful way of integrating the two approaches. From the perspective of the good-lives model, treatment should focus first on identifying the various obstacles that prevent offenders from living balanced and fulfilling lives, and then seek to equip them with the skills, beliefs, values, and supports needed to counteract their influence. In other words, criminogenic needs (dynamic risk factors) signal that a person's ability to secure human goods in socially acceptable and personally fulfilling ways is impaired (was never present) or is compromised (was present but is not now). Criminogenic needs function as markers that a problem exists in the way that an individual is seeking primary human goods, a problem that is directly related to his or her acting in an antisocial way. Thus different types of risk factors are likely to be related to distinct clusters of primary human goods. For example, the presence of deviant sexual interests indicates that some of the necessary internal and external conditions required for healthy sexuality and relationships are missing or distorted in some way.

Good Lives and Juveniles Who Sexually Offend

As noted by researchers (e.g., Flitton & Brager, 2002), the average juvenile who sexually offends is not necessarily motivated by sexual factors. Rather, the offending may be precipitated by feelings of hurt or anger or thoughts of revenge. More generally, what is important is that sexual offending is often associated with the experience of strong negative emotion (as outlined in RP theory), which the offender has difficulty managing. Hence self-regulation may be seen to play a crucial role in sexual offending. It is perhaps particularly important in the case of adolescents who offend, as adolescence is a period in life that, for many, is dominated by the experience of intense emotion, due in part to the presence of hormonal changes (Newberger, 1999). It is as if experiences, especially interpersonal ones, are magnified, so that they take on greater significance and result in greater emotional impact. In this sense, adolescence is likely to be a time during which self-regulation skills are still developing but the burden placed on those skills is particularly onerous. Hence adolescence may be seen as a time when an individual will be particularly likely to have self-regulation difficulties.

What this highlights is that working with adolescents requires an understanding of how developmental issues may affect their offending behavior. To some extent their offending needs to be understood in relation to the particular developmental context in which it took place. As outlined earlier, many of the assumptions applied to adult sex offenders do not apply to young people who offend. Specifically, it appears that sexual offending in younger individuals is less likely to indicate ingrained tendencies. Therefore, the need to provide a therapeutic environment in which new ways of being may be developed is particularly important in this population.

As mentioned earlier, one of the primary difficulties with the risk–need-focused RP approach is that it is essentially negative. The RP theory, dominated as it is by notions of suppression and control, lacks hopefulness for adolescents, condemning them to an apparent lifetime of struggle. RP presupposes a dominant and aberrant sexuality, a formed construct that may leave little concept of any possible transformation. It involves the use of a range of negative terms, and it is centered on the notion of avoidance. This is likely to be particularly problematic for young people who offend because adolescence is a stage during which the self is still developing. In fact, some researchers propose that the development of the self is at the heart of adolescence (e.g., Keenan, 2002). Therefore, it is imperative that intervention promotes the development of a positive sense of self; otherwise, there is a risk of creating further problems for the young person through the persistence of a negative self-perception. Such a perception would be problematic not just in relation to offending but in all aspects of the individual's life.

Outline of Treatment

In Figure 14.1 we provide an outline of how RP would be conceptualized according to a "good-lives" framework. This is intended primarily as a general guide for the way in which the RP component of treatment might progress, but it may also be used as a framework for the development of an individualized RP plan. Note that this model is consistent with the aforementioned work already being done by Mann and her colleagues (Mann, Webster, Schofield, & Marshall, 2002).

To begin with, it is important to identify the various risk factors involved in the young person's offending, and as detailed by Gray and Pithers (1993) these are divided into predisposing, precipitating, and perpetuating risk factors. Obviously, this would form an important part of the clinician's formulation of the individual's sexual offending behavior, in that the identification of these factors goes some way toward telling the story of why the offending took place. Based on these risk factors it is then possible to create a model of the offense process. The perpetuating factors that increase risk should include the "goods" to which young people would otherwise aspire had offending not become the dominant factor in their lives. What perpetuates the offending behavior

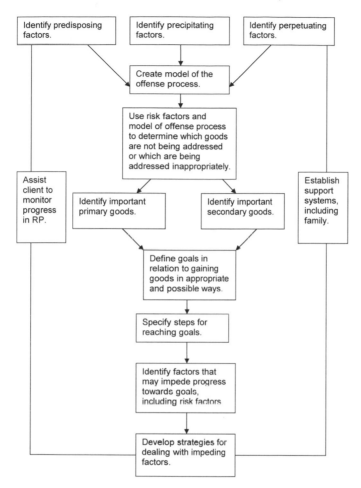

FIGURE 14.1. RP conceptualization based on good-lives and risk management approaches.

is not only the negative pattern of behavior that has formed but also the lack of a more positive construction. Both elements play a critical role in perpetuating the offending and must therefore inform the construct of any treatment interventions.

This part of the RP process is important because it conveys to the offender that there are various events in their lives that contributed to their offending and, relatedly, that the offending did not simply occur "out of the blue," as well as conveying the message that the overall goal of treatment is to prevent further offending through the construction of that which is "good." Though individuals need to be encouraged to take responsibility for their offending, it is also useful for them to have the opportunity to make sense of it and to see how various individual and environmental characteristics may have facilitated a particular course of action. Also, they may not understand that the offending process unfolded over time, often involving a number of associated events and decisions. The aim is to encourage responsibility taking in a supportive manner, to encourage and reward disclosure, to challenge where necessary, and to demonstrate through the therapeutic alliance that regardless of what they have done they are still valuable human beings who have the ability to change.

Next, as shown in the model, risk factors and the offense process are used to determine which goods are not being addressed or satisfied or which are being met inappropriately. For example, a young male offender may have the following identified risks:

1. Predisposing—Lack of primary caregiver and chaotic home environment resulting in emotional neglect and poor attachment.
2. Precipitating—Recent death of sibling and argument with girlfriend.
3. Perpetuating—Social isolation, beliefs of entitlement in relation to women, limited knowledge about sexual functioning, difficulty in coping with strong negative emotion and boredom, lack of goals, lack of positive self-identity.

Taken together, these risk factors highlight a number of important issues that relate to primary human goods. The more distal factors related to family background point to the primary good of relatedness and suggest that due to early life experiences this young man may not have been exposed to the love and affection that are required for good emotional development. Furthermore, he may not have been given the opportunities to develop the skills required to have successful close relationships. Also relevant here is the presence of social isolation under perpetuating factors. The precipitating event of an argument with his girlfriend also relates to this human good insofar as it may indicate that he has limited experience in dealing with interpersonal difficulties. Note, however, that it is not that this event per se is indicative of this, but rather it contributed to his offending. His difficulty managing this argument may be linked to problems achieving the primary good of inner peace (i.e., freedom from emotional turmoil and stress).

This precipitating factor (of interpersonal conflict) is also connected to the good of agency, along with the other precipitant involving loss. Agency essentially refers to autonomy and self-directedness and involves the ability to manage oneself in a controlled and reasoned manner. Specifically, the preceding scenario indicates that this young man may at times have difficulty with self-control and self-regulation and may therefore be vulnerable to responding quite impulsively.

His beliefs about women and his lack of understanding about sexual functioning relate to the goods of knowledge and life (which include healthy living and optimal physical functioning). If he has had few opportunities in which to practice and develop interpersonal skills, then he is likely to be lacking in relevant knowledge about sexuality and may also be more likely to harbor inappropriate beliefs about women. Moreover, his socially impoverished background may have afforded him limited opportunities to observe positive and successful interpersonal relations, again making it more likely that his knowledge about women may not be accurate.

At this point in the RP process, it is also important to identify any other goods that are not directly related to the offending but that are considered to be important nonetheless in terms of the individual's overall well-being. For example, the good of creativity may not be highlighted by any of the risk factors but may be mentioned by the client as being important. For instance, the young man in this example may state that he has always wanted to pursue his dream of learning to play a musical instrument but that he has never been given the opportunity. In this way, goods identified as being in need of attention through treatment are not only those that relate to identified risks but also others that are seen as important to the individual's general level of life satisfaction. A satisfying life is likely also to be a safe and offense-free life.

The next stage in this RP approach is to clarify, through the preceding analysis, the primary and secondary goods that are considered to be important and to define goals that are considered essential in achieving them. For example, in the preceding example, the primary goods of friendship, agency, knowledge, and creativity are identified as being important, and these will delineate the areas that treatment should cover. For instance, working toward the basic good of friendship may include the goals of gaining social skills and developing conflict resolution skills. And the good of agency may involve the goal of developing good self-regulation, including, in particular, the regulation of emotion.

Following this, it is useful to specify the steps required for reaching goals. For instance, if attending a tertiary institution is a specified goal, steps involved might include gathering information or talking to parents about possible financial support. From the perspective of the good-lives model, a plan is only feasible if it has been formed with an individual's future living circumstances, supports, opportunities, and internal capabilities (values, beliefs, skills, abilities) clearly in mind. This part of the intervention may also involve the consolidation of skills acquired (or partially developed) during treatment proper, as these are likely to be important in terms of working toward certain goals. Also, more generally, RP should build on previous therapeutic work so that it becomes a seamless part of the overall treatment package.

The last two steps in the process involve the identification of factors that may impede progress and the development of strategies to deal with them. For example, there may be financial constraints or difficulties in the home environment. Accordingly, it is important to develop ways of managing these factors in order to maximize the individual's chances of reaching the goals that have been delineated. This is particularly important for young people, as they may be dependent on others in terms of their ability to create an optimal home environment in which to work toward their goals. The previously identified risk factors are also relevant here insofar as they may recur and therefore impede the person's progress.

As indicated in Figure 14.1, support systems are seen as playing a significant role throughout the entire treatment process. As emphasized by Gray and Pithers (1993) in their discussion of RP with young people who offend, it is essential that family are informed and involved so that they can provide support. However, we propose that the focus should be on encouraging the young person who offends to work toward his or her goals rather than simply being alert to and reporting the presence of risk factors or risky behaviors. Although the latter has a role to play in the management of future risk, it should not be the predominant approach, as it has the potential to disrupt family relationships and contribute to an overly negative familial environment.

Also important to the efficacy of RP are ongoing monitoring and evaluation. This component requires not only that the therapist monitor the progress of young people who offend but also that therapists encourage and instruct offenders to monitor their own progress. This is a particularly important skill in relation to goal setting, as the skill of self-monitoring is crucial to the ability to organize oneself and direct oneself toward specific targets.

The primary aim of this approach is to provide an overarching good-lives conceptualization within which the traditional aims of RP can still be realized. Though many of the tasks and details of this part of treatment remain the same, from a theoretical perspective the entire process is turned on its head. Rather than attempting to eliminate certain risks or behaviors, the focus is on setting goals and moving toward them. And it is theorized that this reconceptualization is especially advantageous when working with young people who offend. Also important is that the model is flexible and not overly prescriptive, as it must be able to meet a wide range of individual needs. It is essentially a guiding framework that sets the direction and proposes how risk may still be included within the good-lives model.

Summary and Conclusions

As detailed in this chapter, over the past decade there have been a range of significant changes in the way that RP is conceptualized and applied, both generally and also in relation to young people who sexually offend. In particular, there is growing acknowledgment that the risk–need model in which it is embedded has a range of disadvantages as an overarching treatment approach. Most important, it places treatment within a negative framework that focuses on removing deficits or problems rather than on building positive behavioral alternatives. This in turn has the disadvantage of encouraging offenders to examine their problems and weaknesses without adequate attention being paid to their strengths or their positive future goals. Such an approach is particularly problematic for young people who offend, as they may be still struggling with issues of self and identity, and encouraging this sort of negative approach may further increase any negative self-perceptions and self-esteem problems.

The good-lives model provides a useful theoretical framework around which a more positive treatment approach can be built, as illustrated by our proposed model. Also, it is able to incorporate the risk–need approach so that risk prevention can remain an important target. The aim is not to supersede the risk–need perspective but to embed it within a more positive framework so that risk is dealt with through the instigation of positive changes. This is based on the idea that if a person has a good and satisfying life, he or she will be less inclined to offend. Therapists in this case should include in their approach a focus on filling the gap that the removal of offending behavior has left in the young person's life.

Naturally, the concept of RP remains an important part of the risk–need perspective and therefore also an important component of treatment. Adolescents can learn much from the RP model, especially about their own vulnerabilities and the sorts of processes that lead to sexual offending. We argue, however, that the self-regulation model of RP provides a more effective conceptual tool than the original model, as it allows for alternative pathways and also, through its inclusion of the concept of self-regulation, provides more immediate treatment goals. Also, as proposed earlier, self-regulation may be a particularly important for young people who offend; hence, this model may have specific benefits in this population.

Obviously more research is needed in the area of juvenile offending in order to fully understand its etiology and to provide optimal treatment. However, it is hoped that a move toward a more positive approach will improve the efficacy of treatment and thereby reduce the risk of further offending.

References

Ackerman, S. J., & Hilsenroth, M. J. (2003). A review of therapist characteristics and techniques positively impacting the therapeutic alliance. *Clinical Psychology Review, 23,* 1–33.

Arnhart, L. (1998). *Darwinian natural right: The biological ethics of human nature.* Albany, NY: State University of New York Press.

Baumeister, R. F., & Heatherton, T. F. (1996). Self-regulation failure: An overview. *Psychological Inquiry, 7,* 1–15.

Bukowski, W. M., Sippola, L., & Brender, W. (1993). Where does sexuality come from? Normative sexuality from a developmental perspective. In H. E. Barbaree, W. L. Marshall, & S. M. Hudson (Eds.), *The juvenile sex offender* (pp. 84–103). New York: Guilford Press.

Carver, C. S., & Scheier, M. F. (1990). Principles of self-regulation: Action and emotion. In E. T. Higgins & R. M. Sorrentino (Eds.), *Handbook of motivation and cognition, Vol. 2: Foundations of social behavior* (pp. 3–52). New York: Guilford Press.

Cochran, W., & Tesser, A. (1996). The "what the hell" effect: Some effects of goal proximity and goal framing on performance. In L. L. Martin & A. Tesser (Eds.), *Striving and feeling: Interactions among goals, affect, and self-regulation* (pp. 99–120). New York: Erlbaum.

Collins, W. A., & Kuczaj, S. A. (1991). *Developmental psychology: Childhood and adolescence.* New York: Macmillan.

Cummins, R. A. (1996). The domains of life satisfaction: An attempt to order chaos. *Social Indicators Research, 38,* 303–328.

D'Andrade, R. (1995). *The development of cognitive anthropology.* Cambridge, UK: Cambridge University Press.

Deci, E. L., & Ryan, R. M. (2000). The "what" and "why" of goal pursuits: Human needs and the self-determination of behavior. *Psychological Inquiry, 11,* 227–268.

Eldridge, H. (1998). *Therapist guide for maintaining change: Relapse prevention for adult male perpetrators of child sexual abuse.* Thousand Oaks, CA: Sage.

Ellerby, L., Bedard, J., & Chartrand, S. (2002). Holism, wellness, and spirituality: Moving from relapse prevention to healing. In D. R. Laws, S. M. Hudson, & T. Ward (Eds.), *Remaking relapse prevention with sex offenders: A sourcebook* (pp. 427–452). Thousand Oaks, CA: Sage.

Eltz, M. J., Shirk, S. R., & Sarlin, N. (1995). Alliance formation and treatment outcome among maltreated adolescents. *Child Abuse and Neglect, 19,* 419–431.

Emmons, R. A. (1996). Striving and feeling: Personal goals and subjective well-being. In P.M. Gollwitzer & J. A. Bargh (Eds.), *The psychology of action: Linking cognition and motivation to behavior* (pp. 313–337). New York: Guilford Press.

Emmons, R. A. (1999). *The psychology of ultimate concerns: Motivation and spirituality in personality.* New York: Guilford Press.

Flitton, A. R., & Brager, R. C. (2002). Juvenile sex offenders: Assessment and treatment. In R. G. Ribner (Ed.), *Handbook of juvenile forensic psychology* (pp. 343–363). San Francisco: Wiley.

Freeman-Longo, R. E. (2001). *Paths to wellness: A holistic approach and guide for personal recovery.* Holyoke, MA: NEARI Press.

Gray, A., & Pithers, W. D. (1993). Relapse prevention with sexually aggressive adolescents and children: Expanding treatment and supervision. In H. E. Barbaree, W. L. Marshall & S. M. Hudson (Eds.), *The juvenile sex offender* (pp. 289–319). New York: Guilford Press.

Haaven, J. L., & Coleman, E. M. (2000). Treatment of the developmentally disabled sex offender. In D. R. Laws, S. M. Hudson, & T. Ward (Eds.), *Remaking relapse prevention with sex offenders: A sourcebook* (pp. 369–388). Thousand Oaks, CA: Sage.

Hanson, R. K. (1996). Evaluating the contribution of relapse prevention theory to the treatment of sexual offenders. *Sexual Abuse: A Journal of Research and Treatment, 8,* 201–208.

Hunter, J. A., & Lexier, L. J. (1998). Ethical and legal issues in the assessment and treatment of juvenile sex offenders. *Child Maltreatment, 3,* 339–348.

Jones, R. (2003). Research and practice with adolescent offenders: Dilemmas and directions. In T. Ward, D. R. Laws, & S. M. Hudson (Eds.), *Sexual deviance: Issues and controversies* (pp. 190–206). Thousand Oaks, CA: Sage.

Keenan, T. (2002). *An introduction to child development.* London: Sage.

Kekes, J. (1989). *Moral tradition and individuality.* Princeton, NJ: Princeton University Press.

Laws, D.R. (1989). *Relapse prevention with sex offenders.* New York: Guilford Press.

Mann, R. E., Webster, S. D., Schofield, C., & Marshall, W. L. (2002). Approach versus avoidance goals in relapse prevention with sexual offenders. *Sexual Abuse: A Journal of Research and Treatment, 16,* 65–75.

Marlatt, G. A. (1985). Relapse prevention: Theoretical rationale and overview of the model. In G. A. Marlatt & J. R. Gordon (Eds.), *Relapse prevention: Maintenance strategies in the treatment of addictive behaviors* (pp. 3–70). New York: Guilford Press.

Marlatt, G. A., & Gordon, J. R. (Eds.). (1985). *Relapse prevention: Maintenance strategies in the treatment of addictive behaviors.* New York: Guilford Press.

Marshall, W. L., Fernandez, Y. M., Serran, G. A., Mulloy, R., Thornton, D.,

Mann, R. E., et al. (2003). Process variables in the treatment of sexual offenders. *Aggression and Violent Behavior, 8*, 205–234.

Miner, M. H. (2002). Factors associated with recidivism in juveniles: An analysis of serious juvenile sex offenders. *Journal of Research in Crime and Delinquency, 39*, 421–436.

Murphy, M. C. (2001). *Natural law and practical rationality.* New York: Cambridge University Press.

Nell, V. (2002). Why young men drive dangerously: Implications for injury prevention. *Current Directions in Psychological Science, 11*, 75–79.

Newberger, E. H. (1999). *The men they will become: The nature and nurture of male character.* Reading, MA: Perseus Books.

Nussbaum, M. C. (2000). *Women and human development: The capabilities approach.* New York: Cambridge University Press.

Pithers, W. D. (1990). Relapse prevention with sexual aggressors: A method for maintaining therapeutic gain and enhancing external supervision. In W. L. Marshall, D. R. Laws, & H. E. Barbaree (Eds.), *Handbook of sexual assault: Issues, theories and treatment of the offender* (pp. 343–361). New York: Plenum Press.

Pithers, W. D., Marques, J. K., Gibat, C. C., & Marlatt, G. A. (1983). Relapse prevention with sexual aggressors: A self-control model of treatment and maintenance of change. In J. G. Greer & I. R. Stuart (Eds.), *The sexual aggressor: Current perspectives on treatment* (pp. 214–234). New York: Van Nostrand Reinhold.

Rescher, N. (1990). *Human interests: Reflections on philosophical anthropology.* Stanford, CA: Stanford University Press.

Schmuck, P., & Sheldon, K. M. (Eds.). (2001). *Life goals and well-being.* Toronto, Ontario, Canada: Hogrefe & Huber.

Towl, G. J., & Crighton, D. A. (1996). *The handbook of psychology for forensic practitioners.* London: Routledge.

Trivits, L. C., & Reppucci, D. (2002). Application of Megan's Law to juveniles. *American Psychologist, 57*, 690–704.

Ward, T. (2002). Good lives and the rehabilitation of sex offenders: Problems and promises. *Aggression and Violent Behavior, 7*, 1–17.

Ward, T., & Hudson, S. M. (1996). Relapse prevention: A critical analysis. *Sexual Abuse: A Journal of Research and Treatment, 8*, 177–200.

Ward, T., & Hudson, S. M. (1998). A model of the relapse process in sexual offenders. *Journal of Interpersonal Violence, 13*, 400–425.

Ward, T., & Hudson, S. M. (2000). A self-regulation model of relapse prevention. In D. R. Laws, S. M. Hudson, & T. Ward (Eds.), *Remaking relapse prevention with sex offenders: A sourcebook* (pp. 79–101). Thousand Oaks, CA: Sage.

Ward, T., Hudson, S. M., & Keenan, T. (1998). A self-regulation model of the offense process. *Sexual Abuse: A Journal of Research and Treatment, 10*, 141–157.

Ward, T., Louden, K., Hudson, S. M., & Marshall, W. L. (1995). A descriptive model of the offense chain in child molesters. *Journal of Interpersonal Violence, 10,* 453–473.

Ward, T., & Mann, R. (2004). Good lives and the rehabilitation of sex offenders: A positive approach to treatment. In A. Linley & J. Stephen (Eds.), *Positive practice in psychology* (pp. 598–617). Chichester, UK: Wiley.

Ward, T., & Stewart, C. A. (2003). Good lives and the rehabilitation of sexual offenders. In T. Ward, D. R. Laws, & S. M. Hudson (Eds.), *Sexual deviance: Issues and controversies* (pp. 21–44). Thousand Oaks, CA: Sage.

Zuckerman, M. (1994). *Behavioral expressions and biosocial bases of sensation seeking.* Cambridge, UK: Cambridge University Press.

CHAPTER 15

Disposition and Treatment of Juvenile Sex Offenders from the Perspective of Restorative Justice

Mary P. Koss
Karen Bachar
C. Quince Hopkins

Juveniles under age 18 represent 16% of all arrests for forcible rape and 17% of arrests for other sexual offenses (Righthand & Welch, 2001). Juvenile sex offending includes a wide range of acts such as exhibitionism, voyeurism, child molestation, and rape (Abel, Osborn, & Twigg, 1993). Because the juvenile justice system is the avenue by which these youths enter specialized sex-offender treatment, providers can benefit from familiarity with its processes. In our brief overview, we highlight the eroding of distinctions between juvenile and adult justice due to increased focus on punishment and the lack of involvement or underutilization of direct victims and families in the disposition of cases. We then introduce restorative justice theory, describe methods designed to operationalize it, and present empirical data that support the claim that these methods, compared with traditional juvenile justice, improve responsiveness to victims, increase perceptions of fairness among all participants, and lead to better objective outcomes. Restorative justice methods may be implemented at any stage of the justice process, including precharging and postconviction. A short history of restorative justice and a brief summary of its principal methods is included, as well as a social science analysis of the value of face-to-face shared emotion and the apology process. Next, we briefly review multiple systems therapies for juvenile sex offenders, noting that they are the methods with the strongest empirical validation. However, we fault them for lack of attention to victims and for failure to promote apology and reparations. We conclude with a proposal for how restorative methods could be integrated into multiple system approaches and highlight some of the features that catalyze the primary aims of sex-offender treatment.

Disposition of Cases within Juvenile Justice Systems

Historically, juvenile justice has downplayed sanctioning and has chosen to develop individualized treatment plans that attempt to focus on the best interests of the child (e.g., Melton, 1989). Many jurisdictions in the United States and Canada, however, have more recently converted to the "get tough on crime" zeitgeist (Wilson, Huculak & McWhinnie, 2002, p. 363). In contrast, in the United Kingdom, the Crime and Disorder Act of 1998 reaffirmed that youth justice is aimed toward prevention (cited in Mirsky, 2003a, 2003b). However, the introduction of policies including mandatory and determinate sentencing, procedures to ease transfer to adult court, and expanded prosecutorial roles that were intended to reduce inconsistency have instead resulted in an expansion of punitiveness (McAllair, 1993). These initiatives blur the distinctions between juvenile and adult jurisdiction and are incompatible with the rationale that a separate justice system is needed to recognize the developmental status and rehabilitative objectives of youthful offenders (Feld, 1990). Many citizens and stakeholders in the justice system believe that highly punitive and restrictive sanctions best express disapproval of behavior, denounce crime, and provide deserved consequences for the offender. One result of this philosophy is a significant increase in residential placements for youths charged with misdemeanors and first offenders in some large states (Bazemore & McLeod, 2002).

Increasing reliance on the most restrictive sanctions may be diverting funding once available to support community-based offender services and victim services into the building of larger and more secure detention facilities (Cullen & Wright, 1995). One strategy used to respond to dwindling rehabilitative resources is to give offenders several opportunities ("bites of the apple") by which little (dismissed charges, probation supervision) is done to hold perpetrators accountable until their repeat offending overtaxes the patience of the system (Bazemore & McLeod, 2002). Advocates of system reform warn that the current system fails to hold most offenders accountable and sends a message that juvenile crime isn't a big deal (Bazemore & McLeod, 2002). Abel and colleagues caution that, "If an individual begins to engage in such behaviors [sexual offending] and is not subject to intervention and/or negative consequences for such actions, he will be reinforced by the innate positive reinforcers of the sexual act. These inherent positive reinforcers include, but are not limited to, the pleasure of orgasm, the pleasure of stress reduction, and the feeling of power the individual may feel over another person" (Abel et al., 1993, p. 15).

In the juvenile justice system, offenders, their parents, and victims are relegated to a passive role or excluded (McGarrell, 2001; Small & Kimbrough-Melton, 2002). Many states have passed legislation requiring juvenile courts to offer victims most of the same rights they have in adult court (Torbert et al., 1997). However, juvenile court judges who participated in focus groups expressed concern that victims were not "clients" of the juvenile justice system and were hesitant even to admit victim impact statements (Bazemore & Leip, 2000). This point may be moot because there is no evidence that making an impact statement leads victims to experience greater satisfaction with justice or with disposition of their cases (Davis & Smith, 1994). And raising victims' expectations may also backfire when they see that their input had no influence (Erez & Roeger, 1995).

Many victims of youth crime are unsatisfied with their experience with the system. For example, in one large outcome study almost half of all victims whose crimes were adjudicated by traditional juvenile justice methods rated their court experience as unsatisfactory and unfair (McCold & Wachtel, 2002). Strang (2002) described the experiences of victims of juvenile offenders throughout Western criminal justice systems as consisting of lack of attention to questions of restitution and repair of the harm, neglect of emotional reactions such as fear and anger, routine lack of communication about court dates and the progress of the case, exclusion from decision making, and no participating role. Juvenile justice systems do little to address the stigmatizing impact on families when a member is labeled a sex offender, and the potential of families to resolve problems is largely ignored. Victims and families may think that law enforcement and prosecution should address the wrongs done to them and facilitate repair of damage, but they learn from bitter experience that police, prosecutors, and the courts each consider them to be outside their area of responsibility (Strang, 2002).

Restorative Justice Defined

Restorative justice philosophy differs from retributive justice primarily in how harm and accountability are conceptualized. From the restorative justice perspective, "Crime is a violation of people and relationships. It creates obligations to make things right. Justice involves the victims, the offender, and the community in a search for solutions which [sic] promote repair, reconciliation, and reassurance" (Zehr, 1990, p. 181). Restorative justice emphasizes less punitive, less costly, and less stigmatizing methods of accountability and involves victims and the community in the sanctioning process. A shift to restorative models could meet the needs of communities to confront offenders and hold them accountable, convey the message that delinquent behavior is unacceptable, denounce delinquent behavior without relying on punishment or incarceration, and promote responsibility for the crime. In contrast, retributive justice sees crime as a violation against the state, interprets accountability to mean punishment, and does little to encourage the offender to take responsibility for his actions. Also relevant here is the concept of therapeutic jurisprudence (Zehr, 1990). Therapeutic jurisprudence emphasizes "the law's impact on emotional life and psychological well-being" and identifies therapeutic or antitherapeutic aspects of the legal process on the offender (Wexler, 1998, p. 317; Wexler, 1991). Restorative justice is differentiated by its broader definition of who is harmed by crime and whom the antitherapeutic aspects of traditional justice affect, including within its perspective the victim, offender, and community.

It is informative to examine the history of restorative concepts. Strang (2002) writes that throughout most of human existence there were no criminal justice institutions, and people turned to their relatives for score settling. Compensation and restitution were the dominant models of resolution, although their success was reinforced by the threat of blood feuding. In Saxon England the offender was required to make a payment to the lord or king for negotiating settlement with the victim's family. By the seventh century these arrangements were formalized, and a role for the church was added. Between 700 and 1066 A.D. the share paid to lords and bishops increased. By the late 12th century, the monarchy had grown strong enough that the king was able to impose a judicial system that forbade private settlement and replaced the needs of victims with the interests of the state. From this point forward, the Crown and not victims and their families was the recipient of compensation. Victims did retain the right (and expense) of bringing prosecution, but it soon became clear that many perpetrators escaped prosecution because their victims lacked the resources to press their cases. In response, offices of public prosecution were established in the United Kingdom in 1879, removing from victims any meaningful role in or control of decision making in their cases. This arrangement was soon replicated throughout all common-law countries with British traditions of jurisprudence.

In the past 50 years, the justice systems in these countries have vac-
illated between retributive and rehabilitative emphasis and found neither
satisfactory (Braithwaite, 1999). Most recently, criminal justice practice
has emphasized harsh punishment. Revival of the idea of direct reparations can be traced to Margery Fry's 1951 book, *Arms of the Law*.
The reemergence of restorative philosophy grew from experience with
victim–offender mediation (Schneider, 1985), the victim's rights movements, the rise of neighborhood-level justice, and new thinking on equity
in human relationships that characterized several social movements,
including efforts directed at women's equality, peace, and social justice
(Messmer & Otto, 1992; Pepinsky & Quinney, 1991). Hudson (2002)
argues that restorative justice is better for carrying out the traditional
functions of criminal justice—retribution, rehabilitation/reintegration,
and individual and public protection. She writes that it is not just that
restorative justice is better than lack of justice, but that it is *effective* justice in the sense of reducing reoffending and in demonstrating strong disapproval for behavior that is beyond social tolerance.

From the restorative perspective, crime causes both *material
harm*—lost or damaged property or monetary losses, damage to business
or public spaces—and *personal/relational harm*—physical injury, anxiety, anger, or depression, fractured relationships, weakened social bonds,
increased fear, and diminished sense of community (Karp, 2001). Likewise, there are two types of repair of harm. *Material reparation* results
from a negotiated agreement between the victim and the offender,
whereas *symbolic reparation* is the result of direct communication and
involves social rituals of respect, courtesy, apology, and forgiveness
(Schiff, 1998). The direct stakeholders in these harms are victims,
offenders, and their communities of care—those who have emotional
connections to the parties, including parents, other family members,
teachers, employers, and others (McCold & Wachtel, 2002). The indirect stakeholders live nearby or are officials of government, religious,
social, or business organizations. The restorative justice perspective
argues that those directly harmed should have decision-making authority on the resolution of the crime. The aims of restorative justice are
empowerment of victims, acceptance of responsibility of offenders,
repair of harm, strengthening the social bonds of victims and offenders
to their community, reduction of offending, and more cohesive, peaceful
communities within the constraints of due process and proportionality
(Hudson, 2002). A core value of restorative justice is that there should
be a balance or parity among the victims, offenders, and the community,
which constitute the three "customers" of the criminal justice system
(Bazemore & Umbreit, 1995, p. 304).

Restorative justice programs aim to improve victim experience and outcomes by utilizing participatory methods, providing opportunity to receive answers to questions such as why they were victimized, promoting restoration of material and emotional losses, reducing fear of the offender, and increasing perceptions of a fair participation process (Daly, 2002). The success of sanctions from the victim's perspective depends on the extent of involvement, the degree of reparation, and the perception of fairness of process and outcomes (Bazemore & McLeod, 2002). For the community, success is reflected by information that indicates justice has been served, that offenders have been denounced and held accountable, and that a sense of community healing has begun (Yazzie, 1994). From a psychological perspective, apology may be the process that creates the therapeutic outcomes experienced by victim, offender, and community as a result of restorative methods.

Apology and Restorative Justice Process

There is little discussion of apology in the criminology literature, a fact that is attributed to the field's dominant retributive paradigm and to the fact that, until recently, offenders have had no avenues to speak directly to victims (Strang, 2002). Concessions, justifications, excuses, and refusals are all various types of accounts (Gonzales, Haugen, & Manning, 1994). Apologies are differentiated from these by serving purposes for which no other forms of account taking are sufficient (Abel, 1998; Goffman, 1971; Tavuchis, 1991; for a review see Petrucci, 2002). Apologies are conceptualized as a speech act composed of three core elements: (1) acknowledgment of the legitimacy of the violated rule; (2) admission of fault and responsibility; and (3) expression of genuine regret and remorse for the harm done followed by acceptance or rejection by the injured party (Tavuchis, 1991; Petrucci, 2002). Apologies require that the offender accept the wrongdoing as part of him- or herself, and from that realization flow the sorrow and regret that are the heart of the process. Experimental social psychology data demonstrate a linear relationship between the number of core elements in an apology and progressively lessened blame and sanctions for the offender (Scher & Darley, 1997).

Apologies serve multiple functions, including: (1) acknowledging the importance of the rule that has been broken; (2) accepting responsibility and recognizing the capacity to change future behavior; (3) restoring identity of the perpetrator by expressing regret; (4) reducing victims' feelings of anger and blameworthiness toward the offender; and (5) resolving the conflict by reaching a mutual resolution and equalizing the power imbalance created by victimization (original sources documented in Petrucci, 2002). An apology is a ritual that must be offered and accepted. Reconciliation depends on both actions. Victims' ability to accept or reject the apology contributes to reempowering them (Abel, 1998). The evidence suggests that most often victims will accept apologies, however (Bennett & Dewberry, 1994; Bennett & Earwaker, 1994). Victims' primary gain from apology is the opportunity to be relieved of the anger and bitterness that results from having their emotional hurt acknowledged. Anger in victims was dissipated when the offender was seen as responsible (Bennett & Earwaker, 1994). In restorative justice proceedings in which apology does not occur, the level of tension in the room remains high, and participants leave feeling dissatisfied (Retzinger & Scheff, 1996).

None of the restorative approaches include in their agenda a specific process that is intended to elicit apologies; however, they frequently occur spontaneously. In one conferencing evaluation, 96% of victims said that offenders apologized during the conference, and 88% of victims perceived that the offender seemed sorry for what he did (McCold & Wachtel, 1998). Strang (2002) reported that the percentage of victims who received an apology in Reintegrative Shaming Experiments (RISE) was 72% for cases receiving restorative justice processing, compared with 19% in court. And restorative justice participants were more likely to perceive that the apology was sincere (77%) compared with victims whose cases were tried in traditional court (41%). Daly (2002) examined the processing of juvenile sexual assault cases in the South Australia Juvenile Justice Program. Sexual assault had the lowest rate of conviction of the crimes she examined (33% for sex crimes, 65% for burglary, 62% for assault, 89% for driving offenses). Thus restorative justice offered victims much greater odds of receiving acknowledgment of the harm they had experienced and the potential for apology from offenders. In contrast, the likelihood of going away from traditional court retraumatized is very high in the context of the low conviction rate that was observed, coupled with the iatrogenic aspects of court process. Among offenders who participated in the victim–offender mediation model of restorative justice, 9 of 10 listed apologizing to the victim as one of the four most important issues to be dealt with in the process (Umbreit & Greenwood, 1999). Interviews conducted within 90 days from completion of the restorative intervention demonstrated that apology was an important element not only for victims (80%) but even more so for offenders (91%). Apology was the most frequent reason chosen by perpetrators for participating, and afterward virtually 100% of offenders felt it was "important" or "very important" (Fercello & Umbreit, 1998).

It is possible that the process of apologizing sets in motion cognitive changes that are important in governing future offending behavior. For example, recognizing the rule, acknowledging that the rule was broken, accepting responsibility for having broken the rule, and understanding the consequences of that act on the victim and others may reduce the likelihood of future offending. In New Zealand, youthful offenders who did not apologize during a family conference were three times more likely to reoffend after 3 years of follow-up than youths who apologized (Morris & Maxwell, 1997). Because this evidence is correlational, it cannot support the conclusion that making apologies is a determinant of subsequent offender behavior. What the data do suggest is the potential that risk assessment might be enhanced by considering whether a youth took advantage of the opportunity to apologize when it was available.

Restorative Justice in Action

Many programs differ in the extent to which they successfully operationalize the principle and achieve the goals of restorative justice. *Mostly restorative programs* involve victims and offenders but typically exclude the community, such as victim–offender reconciliation and victim–offender mediation programs (McCold & Wachtel, 2002). Victim offender reconciliation programs originated in Kitchener, Ontario, Canada, in 1974 on the basis of Mennonite church traditions (Strang, 2002). Victim–offender mediation is similar, with more emphasis placed on reparation, but this method often lacks a face-to-face meeting. *Fully restorative programs* involve all three sets of stakeholders, including victims, offenders, and their communities of care, such as sentencing circles and family group or community conferencing (McCold & Wachtel, 2002). Sentencing circles arose in Canada in 1992 in the Yukon Territory and the Province of Saskatchewan in both rural and urban settings as a response of First Nations people to crime (Wilson et al., 2002). These programs have been criticized on several grounds, including reliance on court processes and personnel (LaPrairie, 1995).

Many experts consider the conferencing approach to be the most developmentally advanced form of restorative justice and best at implementing its principles. Family group conferencing was established as the primary mechanism for youth crime in New Zealand in 1989, in response to reassessment of the implications of the Treaty of Waitangi for present-day relations between whites and Maori. Restorative conferencing was judged to be more similar to indigenous approaches to justice than traditional jurisprudence based on British traditions. Conferences were introduced to Australia in Wagga, New South Wales (1991), and in Canberra, ACT (1993). In the United States, restorative conferencing grew out of concerns about the effectiveness of incapacitation, punishment, and individual treatment provided in diversion programs, probation services, and community corrections units (Bazemore & Umbreit, 2001). Today, the method is in widespread use for resolving juvenile crime in Australia (Daly, 2001; Sherman, Strang, & Woods, 2000); Canada (Stuart, 2001; Bonta & Wallace-Capretta, 1998); Europe (Walgrave, 1999, Weitekamp, 1999; Young & Hoyle, 2004; Miers, 2001); New Zealand (Morris & Maxwell, 2001); and the United States (Umbreit, 2001; McCold & Wachtel, 1998). One recent survey identified 773 programs in the United States (Schiff & Bazemore, 2002). These programs ranged from demonstration projects to systemwide initiatives. In several states (California, Massachusetts, Arkansas, Vermont, and Delaware) more than 50% of counties have restorative conferencing programs (Schiff & Bazemore, 2002). Half or more of the communities in the United Kingdom are using or considering family group conferencing. In New Zealand, family group conferencing is a right under the Children, Young Persons and Their Families Act (1989; cited in Daly, 2002).

Family and community conferencing programs operate under varied names and differ in terms of operational details. One representative family model, family group decision making, was implemented by Pennell and Burford (2000) in Newfoundland and Labrador, Canada, to address families in which children were being abused. The average conference had 13 participants, including 2 of 13 who were professionals. There were five stages of work with the family, beginning with referral. The second stage involved planning for the conference and included identifying the people who should attend. The third stage was the actual conference, which lasted on average 5.5 hours. The conference began with an opening suitable to the cultural group represented (prayer, greeting); then the coordinator reviewed the conference's purposes, process, and ground rules. Next, service providers gave information, including reports covering the reasons for referral and the concerns that needed to be addressed by the family in formulating their plan. Other guest speakers included representatives from treatment programs and general education on addictions and the harm of witnessing violence. After providing the information, the professionals left the room. Once the group developed its plan, the family recalled the coordinator and the protective service workers. Together they reviewed the plan and set up mechanisms to ensure compliance and monitoring. In the fourth stage, the referring agency reviewed and approved the plans. The fifth stage involved implementation of the plan, including counseling, addiction treatment, in-home supports, child-care arrangements, transportation assistance, material aid, and recreation and leisure activities. Families who had a conference demonstrated just half the rate of child-protection events during follow-up compared with matched cases that received traditional case management.

Community conferencing or family conferencing often takes place under the auspices of the law enforcement system as opposed to social services, although conference coordinators may or may not be police officers. Depending on the approach adopted, the coordinator may or may not read from a script or follow a standard order. The agenda generally has the coordinator or coordinators greeting the group and explaining the ground rules. Then the perpetrator is asked to tell the group what he or she did. Next, the victim is asked to respond, telling how these acts affected him or her, followed by an invitation to friends and family to describe the impact of the victimization on them. The family of the perpetrator is also asked to describe the impact they have experienced, as there is often a stigmatization attached to having a family member involved in offending. Once the impact has been thoroughly aired, the perpetrator is asked to respond to what he has heard; at this point, many spontaneously apologize, although that is not required. The conference participants then turn their attention to developing a plan to make reparations to the victim, rehabilitate the offender, and undertake steps that will strengthen community bonds and make amends for the harm caused to the fabric of relationships.

Many question, when hearing these methods described, whether victims would want any further contact with the offender. The British crime survey of 1984 found that half of respondents would have accepted a chance to meet their offender personally and discuss restitution and an additional 20% would have liked to reach agreement without a meeting (cited in Strang, 2002). A Minnesota study showed that three fourths of victims wanted a chance to speak directly to the offender (Umbreit, 1989). Only 6% of victims in New Zealand said they did not want to attend a conference (Maxwell & Morris, 1996), although programmatic features may influence the actual rate of victim participation achieved.

There have been numerous empirical evaluations of conferencing for juvenile crime. For example, McCold and Wachtel (1998) report a random assignment experiment and found that 97% of conferenced victims said they experienced fairness, compared with 79% of the control group and 73% of those who declined conferencing and also received traditional processing. Similar figures were reported for feelings that the offender had been adequately held accountable. The Reintegrative Shaming Experiments (RISE) in Australia (Strang, Barnes, Braithwaite, & Sherman, 1999) consisted of several study arms addressing different crime categories. In the arm involving violent crime by offenders under age 30, 845 offenders were randomly assigned to participate in either court or conference. All of the satisfaction and fairness ratings favored the conference process. For example, victims were much more likely to be kept informed of their cases in conference (79%) compared with court (14%). Daly (2002) focused on cases that involved sexual assault by juveniles and examined 23 offenders in detail. The cases predominately involved serious indecent assaults. Offenders were 11–18 years old, and all but four cases involved victims who were brothers, sisters, cousins, family friends, or school acquaintances. Except for offenders who lived in rural areas, all offenders attended a sex-offender treatment program as part of the plan developed at the conference; in all, 20 of 23 offenders fully completed their plans.

McGarrell (2001) reports on evaluation of the Indianapolis Restorative Justice Experiment. Cases were randomly assigned to traditional juvenile court processing or to conferencing. Victim satisfaction was more than 90% after conferences, compared with 68% following traditional process. Conferences produced 13.5% less recidivism at 6 months, and youths were significantly more likely to complete their programs. At 12 months, rearrest rates were 30% (conferences) versus 42% (court).

A recent secondary analysis of 41 published evaluations of juvenile justice programs classified them as nonrestorative, partly, mostly, or fully restorative justice (McCold & Wachtel, 2002). To recall, fully restorative programs involve victims, offenders, and family/community in a face-to-face intervention. In terms of victim satisfaction, 9 of the top 10 programs were fully restorative, and 9 of the bottom 10 were nonrestorative. Mean satisfaction was 91% for conferencing (fully restorative), 82% for victim–offender mediation (partly restorative), and 56% for traditional justice (nonrestorative). Satisfaction was highly related to perceptions of fairness ($r = .815$). Both victims and offenders rated fully restorative programs as more fair. Seven of nine fully restorative programs showed less than 15% difference in satisfaction among the ratings of victims, offenders, and family and community members, reflecting successful achievement of a balanced approach. On average, victims and offenders rated programs that included their community of care as more fair and satisfying than both traditional justice and those programs that involved the victim but excluded their community of care.

Therapeutic Intervention with Juvenile Sex Offenders

Community-based treatment has been operationally defined as consisting of group therapy (typically social skills and anger management training, sex education, confrontation, cognitive restructuring involving correction of distortions that feed sex offending, strengthening impulse control, teaching empathy, and coaching in relapse prevention techniques) supplemented by individual therapy (Hunter & Longo, 2004). Individual treatment often results in little family involvement and limited attention to social and environmental causes in the community. Hunter and colleagues (Hunter, Gilbertson, Vedros, & Morton, 2003) suggest that community-based interventions can be improved by developing treatment plans that are tailored to the operative determinants in an individual case, enhancing coordination between community and institutional providers, and involving probation and parole in decision making (e.g., clinical treatment planning, delivery of intervention services to youths and their families, assessing readiness for release to the community, and in aftercare and placement assignments), and by using social-ecological interventions such as multisystemic treatment (MST).

MST is the only individual counseling approach that has been validated with chronic juvenile sex offenders (Henggeler, Schoenwald, Borduin, Rowland, & Cunningham, 1998; Borduin, Henggeler, Blaske, & Stein, 1990). Other community-based interventions have shown positive, but less substantial, evidence of efficacy (Lipsey & Wilson, 1998). MST addresses multiple determinants of serious antisocial behavior. Its overriding goal is to empower parents with skills and resources to support positive behavior in the youth and to likewise empower youths with skills and resources to cope with the problems that characterize their homes (Borduin & Schaeffer, 2001). Parent interventions target barriers to effective parenting, such as drug abuse or marital violence, establishing effective communication lines between parents and teachers, and restructuring after-school hours to promote academic success. Interventions at the individual level redress social-skill and problem-solving deficits with the aim of fostering peer friendship and dating, social-perspective-taking skills, and positive changes in belief systems or attitudes that contribute to offending. Other multiple-system approaches include Wraparound Milwaukee (Gilbertson, Storm, & Fischer, 2001) and the Norfolk Juvenile Sex Offender Program (Hunter et al., 2003). The Norfolk program includes individual therapy, family therapy, in-home services, sex-offender treatment groups, parents' and caretakers' groups, and relapse prevention, combined with intensive supervision two to four times per week face to face, risk adjusted. Graduated sanctions address noncompliant behavior.

Multiple-systems approaches focus on some of the same concepts common in the juvenile delinquency literature. For example, *social capital* references the norms and networks that people living in community use to solve problems rather than looking to outside support (Rose & Clear, 1998). Social capital is the set of social skills and resources needed to bring about and maintain positive community life (Putnam, 2000). Social capital enables social control; it is the essence of what enables groups to enforce norms. *Social support* consists of the affective and material resources provided through intimate relationships or through macro-level social institutions. Lack of social support is considered a neglected cause of crime (Cullen, Wright, & Chamlin, 1999). In contrast, bonds to conventional institutions and supportive adults are important in preventing crime in the first place and in facilitating the transition from criminal to conventional lifestyles (Hirschi, 1969; Elliott, 1994). The punishment paradigm tends to focus on a "kinds of people" analysis, and criminologists consider it important to focus on the social characteristics of collectivities that foster violence and crime (Sampson & Wilson, 1995, p. 54). From this perspective, MST is an advance over earlier therapeutic approaches for sex offenders.

Integrating Restorative Concepts into Multisystemic Treatment

Restorative justice proponents stand with advocates of rehabilitation and treatment in affirming the need to respond to the range of needs that are related to offending, using a variety of evidence-based interventions aimed at asset building and reintegration. However, an examination of MST from the perspective of restorative justice identifies several paradigm differences. Specifically, current therapeutic approaches (1) typically exclude victims who also cannot count on reparation, assistance, or acknowledgment even from offenders who successfully complete treatment; (2) privilege the voices of mental health experts and, to a lesser extent, criminal justice authorities in formulating treatment plans; (3) underutilize neighbors and family members other than legal guardians for their perspectives on meeting sanctioning, rehabilitation, and public safety objectives; (4) expect the community to bond with perpetrators without attention to the psychological processes that need to occur for people to move beyond fear, anger, and bitterness; and (5) cast offenders in a passive role with few opportunities to make amends for their behavior (see Bazemore & Umbreit, 1995; Petrunick, 2002).

    Restorative methods may be incorporated at any stage from predisposition to postconviction. We assert that multiple-system approaches and restorative methods are very compatible and that merging them could address some of the perennial challenges of sex-offender treatment. If restorative justice programs are not available as a preconviction option in one's area, treatment providers or probation and supervision personnel can plan and hold family group or community conferences after conviction. Conferences offer a forum for victims and community to air the impact of the act, to denounce violations of norms, and to provide social support and validation of the victim. Conferences permit offenders to hear how their behavior has affected others, to feel remorse and perhaps apologize, and to receive social support for taking concrete steps toward restoring themselves to the good graces of those closest to them. Finally, conferences provide a forum for all participants to collaborate in the development of a program that restores the losses of the victim, enumerates the amends that are demanded by the community, and stipulates the therapeutic regimen for offenders. The community, as well as the victim, has the right to demand that the person responsible for the harm agree to participate in the rehabilitation program that is recommended (Carlen, 1989, cited in Karp, 2001). However, restorative justice should never utilize a process that relies exclusively on victims and community members to assist the offender in achieving rehabilitation (Umbreit, Coates, & Kalanj, 1994). It is the essence of the restorative philosophy that the gains must be balanced among the participants.

Treatment planning for sex offenders typically occurs after a period of information gathering and assessment, and decisions about the components to assign in a given case are usually made by mental health professionals, sometimes with input from probation personnel. A review of conferencing protocols reveals several alternative procedures by which professionals could place their designated treatment design into the plan developed by conference participants. The remedies that might result from typical case conferences may be highly similar to those that emerge on a typical MST plan. The difference is in the process of decision making. It may be easier for offenders to accept measures recommended by those closest to them and by those they have harmed, rather than those imposed upon them by state authority. Use of the written plan that is the product of a conference is consistent with recommendations that sex-offender treatment should involve highly structured written contracts (Morenz & Becker, 1995).

The plans developed by a community conference can be broader and more culturally sensitive than what the formal mental health system could impose. Perhaps the offender needs a chaperone at family gatherings. If so, one of the participants can volunteer to receive training. Maybe the family feels that the youth could gain from strengthening spiritual ties. If so, the plan can stipulate religious activities or time with the clergy. Or the group may believe that Western medicine would be most effective if paired with a traditional healing ceremony. When parental problems such as alcohol abuse are identified that interfere with compliance, conference participants can troubleshoot practical solutions, such as who might be available for transportation or child care to facilitate attendance at treatment programs. Lastly, when the victim, offender, family, and friends share a language different from English, conferencing approaches allow them to use the primary language, the one in which emotions are easier to express and more deeply experienced.

The sex-offender-treatment literature notes several long-standing challenges, including involving family, dealing with denial, developing empathy, correcting cognitive distortions, and developing the motivation for relapse prevention. The conference process could catalyze success in each of these areas. The conferencing process clearly goes beyond the strategies in existing literature for involving family members, such as providing written information on cognitive distortions, educational videotapes of abusers discussing their relapse process, literature on the recovery process of sexual abuse victims, referral to treatment groups for adult survivors of sexual abuse, opportunity to be included in occasional adolescent group therapy sessions, support groups for parents, and attention to concerns of the siblings (e.g., Gray & Pithers, 1993). A concrete example of how restorative methods have been used to build social resources and increase emotional bonds is the circles-of-support approach being implemented by the Mennonite Central Committee of Ontario (Cesaroni, 2001). This program is a response to the negative consequences of community notification on sex offenders who have been released from prison after serving their full sentence, and who therefore receive no probation or community reintegration services. Instead of reacting with fear over a sex offender coming to live in their community, this group forms a circle of support around the perpetrator consisting of people who can assist him in locating employment, educational, and residential options and offer continuing social support. When citizens are enmeshed in mutual ties of empathy, trust, and obligation, they are more insulated from crime (Chamlin & Cochran, 1997).

Generally, the first stage in motivating youths to change sexual behavior is helping them accept responsibility for what they have done and develop empathy with the victim (Becker & Hunter, 1997). Under traditional juvenile court process, this step is difficult because of legal defense strategies to maintain innocence, because of parental disbelief, and because no opportunity exists for the victim to voice the impact of the crime directly to the offender. Among the participants in the Norfolk Program (Hunter et al., 2003), the majority acknowledged some or all of the sexual offenses for which they were convicted (88%) and took partial or total responsibility (93%). Nevertheless, minimizing or denying perpetration of sexual abuse are common and considered problematic (National Adolescent Perpetrator Network, 1993, as cited in Righthand & Welch, 2001). So serious is the problem of denial that some programs refuse to accept youths who are unmoving in their stance toward personal responsibility (Barbaree & Cortoni, 1993). Denial of responsibility is also a major predictor of treatment outcome—75% of those who evidenced no denial of their offense completed treatment successfully, compared with 25% among juveniles with complete denial (Hunter & Figueredo, 1999). Cognitive distortions are also a concern. These include blaming the victim, a factor that is associated with heightened risk of reoffending (Schram, Milloy, & Rowe, 1991). Finally, lack of empathy has been identified as an important factor in failures of relapse prevention measures (Gray & Pithers, 1993). "Without the dedication derived from the empathy for sexual abuse victims developed in treatment, RP [relapse prevention] risks becoming an intellectual exercise that educates offenders about what they need to do to avoid reoffending but that finds offenders lacking in the motivation to use this knowledge" (Gray & Pithers, 1993, p. 299).

These problematic issues in therapy track very closely to the aims that restorative sanctions were designed to accomplish. Restorative sanctions aim for *cognitive and emotional changes*—to promote the offender's understanding of the consequences of his or her act, to encourage feelings of remorse, and ideally to develop empathy—and *behavioral acts*—repayment of victims, community service, other acts of reparation, rebuilding bonds to the community, and reduction of reoffending (Bazemore & McLeod, 2002). The previous discussion highlights the processes that are put into play by bringing victim, offender, family, and community together face to face. Conferences harness strong social forces with the aim of decreasing denial, increasing empathy, and reframing cognitions. The conferencing format promotes recognition that a rule was broken, that the offender was the one who broke the rule, and that the act harmed others, and it also creates a safe setting in which offenders can safely experience the remorse and regret that flows from acknowledging the harm done. In the case of sexual assault crimes, the emotional intensity of conferences is noted to be higher than for other juvenile crimes (Daly, 2002).

To put our belief in the value of stakeholder involvement and face-to-face dialogue to empirical test, we are currently implementing RESTORE, a restorative-justice-based alternative adjudication process for date and acquaintance rape and other selected sexual offenses in Pima County, Arizona, that is funded by the Centers for Disease Control and Prevention. For reasons of safety in this demonstration program, we are limiting our participants to offenders over age 18 years who offended against adults. We work in partnership with sex-offender evaluators and treatment providers. This program uses a community conference approach and then supervises the responsible party for a period of

12 months, during which he or she carries out the written plan generated in the conference to which he or she has agreed. We look forward to reporting the results of this intervention as they become available.

Summary and Conclusions

Restorative justice views crime as harm for which the person responsible must be held accountable by a victim-driven, community-based process. This chapter examines juvenile justice processes in Canada and the United States and identifies trends toward more intense punishment, routine lack of attention to victim needs, and underutilization of the family. When cases are referred to therapeutic options, MST has the strongest empirical success record. However, these approaches also pay scant attention to healing the impact of crime on victims and family members. Incorporating restorative justice principles could strengthen sex-offender treatment by involving the direct victims and fostering shared emotion and through acknowledgment of wrongdoing, apology, and reparation. These practices enhance the likelihood that victims are satisfied they have received fair justice, strengthen social control within the community, reduce recidivism, and enhance the benefits to offenders by promoting cognitive reframing, empathy, restoration of self-esteem, and community reintegration.

References

Abel, G. G., Osborn, C. A., & Twigg, D. A. (1993). Sexual assault through the life span: Adult offenders with juvenile histories. In H. E. Barbaree, W. L. Marshall, & S. M. Hudson (Eds.), *The juvenile sex offender* (pp. 104–117). New York: Guilford Press.

Abel, R. (1998). *Speaking respect, respecting speech*. Chicago, IL: University of Chicago Press.

Barbaree, H. E., & Cortoni, F. A. (1993). Treatment of the juvenile sex offender within the criminal justice and mental health systems. In H. E. Barbaree, W. L. Marshall, & S. M. Hudson (Eds.) *The juvenile sex offender* (pp. 243–263). New York: Guilford Press.

Bazemore, S. G., & Leip, L. (2000). Victim participation in the new juvenile court: Tracking judicial attitudes toward restorative justice reforms. *Justice System Journal, 21*(2), 199–226.

Bazemore, S. G., & McLeod, C. (2002). Restorative justice and the future of diversion and informal social control. In E. G. M. Weitekamp & H. J.

Kerner (Eds.), *Restorative justice: Theoretical foundations* (pp. 143–176). Devon, UK: Willan.

Bazemore, S. G., & Umbreit, M. (1995). Rethinking the sanctioning function in juvenile court: Retributive or restorative responses to youth crime. *Crime and Delinquency, 41*(3), 296–316.

Bazemore, S. G., & Umbreit, M. (2001, February). A comparison of four restorative conferencing models. *Juvenile Justice Bulletin*, pp. 1–19.

Becker, J. V., & Hunter, J. A. (1997). Understanding and treating child and adolescent sexual offenders. *Advances in Clinical Child Psychology, 19,* 177–197.

Bennett, M., & Dewberry, C. (1994). I've said I'm sorry, haven't I? A study of the identity implications and constraints that apologies create for their recipients. *Current Psychology: Developmental, Learning, Personality, Social, 13,* 10–20.

Bennett, M., & Earwaker, D. (1994). Victim's responses to apologies: The effects of offender responsibility and offense severity. *Journal of Social Psychology, 134,* 457–464.

Bonta, J., & Wallace-Capretta, S. (1998). *Restorative justice: An evaluation of the restorative resolutions project.* Ottawa, Ontario, Canada: Department of the Solicitor General of Canada.

Borduin, C. M., Henggeler, S. W., Blaske, D. M., & Stein, R. J. (1990). Multisystemic treatment of adolescent sexual offenders. *International Journal of Offender Therapy and Comparative Criminology, 34*(2), 105–113.

Borduin, C. M., & Schaeffer, C. M. (2001). Multisystemic treatment of juvenile sexual offenders: A progress report. *Journal of Psychology and Human Sexuality, 13*(3&4), 25–42.

Braithwaite, J. (1999). Restorative justice: Assessing optimistic and pessimistic accounts. *Crime and Justice: A Review of Research, 25,* 1–127.

Cesaroni, C. (2001). Releasing sex offenders into the community through circles of support: A means of reintegrating the worst of the worst. *Journal of Offender Rehabilitation, 34*(2), 85–98.

Chamlin, M. B., & Cochran, J. K. (1997). Social altruism and crime. *Criminology, 35*(2), 203–227.

Cullen, F. T., & Wright, J. P. (1995). The future of corrections. In B. Maguire & P. Radosh (Eds.), *The past, present, and future of American criminal justice* (pp. 198–219). New York: General Hall.

Cullen, F. T., Wright, J. P., & Chamlin, M. B. (1999). Social support and social reform: A progressive crime control agenda. *Crime and Delinquency, 45,* 188–207.

Daly, K. (2001). Conferencing in Australia and New Zealand: Variations, research findings and prospects. In A. Morris and G. Maxwell (Eds.), *Restorative justice for juveniles: Conferencing, mediation and circles* (pp. 59–89). Oxford, UK: Hart.

Daly, K. (2002). Sexual assaults and restorative justice. In H. Strang & J. Braithwaite (Eds.), *Restorative justice and family violence* (pp. 62–88). Cambridge, UK: Cambridge University Press.

Davis, R., & Smith, B. (1994). Victim impact statements and victim satisfaction: An unfulfilled promise? *Journal of Criminal Justice, 22*(1), 1–12.

Elliott, D. (1994). Serious violent offenders: Onset, developmental course, and termination. *Criminology, 32*(1), 1–21.

Erez, E., & Roeger, L. (1995). The effects of victim impact statements on sentencing patterns and outcomes: The Australian experience. *Journal of Criminal Justice, 23*(4), 363–375.

Feld, B. (1990). The punitive juvenile court and the quality of procedural justice: Disjunctions between rhetoric and reality. *Crime and Delinquency, 36,* 443–464.

Fercello, C., & Umbreit, M. (1998, November 25). *Client evaluation of family group conferencing in 12 sites in 1st Judicial District of Minnesota.* St. Paul: University of Minnesota, Center for Restorative Justice and Mediation.

Fry, M. (1951). *Arms of the law.* London: Gollancz.

Gilbertson, S. A., Storm, H., & Fischer, E. (2001, November). *Evaluating the families of juvenile sex offenders in Milwaukee County, Wisconsin.* Poster session presented at the annual meeting of the Association for the Treatment of Sexual Abusers, San Antonio, TX.

Goffman, E. (1971). *Relations in public: Microstudies of the public order.* New York: Basic Books.

Gonzales, M. H., Haugen, J. A., & Manning, D. J. (1994). Victims as "narrative critics": Factors influencing rejoinders and evaluative responses to offenders' accounts. *Personality and Social Psychology Bulletin, 20,* 691–704.

Gray, A. S., & Pithers, W. D. (1993). Relapse prevention with sexually aggressive adolescents and children: Expanding treatment and supervision. In H. E. Barbaree, W. L. Marshall, & S. M. Hudson (Eds.), *The juvenile sex offender* (pp. 289–319). New York: Guilford Press.

Henggeler, S. W., Schoenwald, S. K., Borduin, C. M., Rowland, M. D., & Cunningham, P. B. (1998). *Multisystemic treatment of antisocial behavior in children and adolescents.* New York: Guilford Press.

Hirschi, T. (1969). *Causes of delinquency.* Berkeley, CA: University of California Press.

Hudson, B. (2002). Restorative justice and gendered violence: Diversion or effective justice. *British Journal of Criminology, 42,* 616–634.

Hunter, J. A., & Figueredo, A. J. (1999). Factors associated with treatment compliance in a population of juvenile sexual offenders. *Sexual Abuse: A Journal of Research and Treatment, 11*(1), 49–67.

Hunter, J. A., Gilbertson, S. A., Vedros, D., & Morton, M. (2003). Strengthening community-based programming for juvenile sexual offenders: Key concepts and paradigm shifts. *Journal of Child Maltreatment, 9*(2), 177–189.

Hunter, J. A., & Longo, R. (2004). Relapse prevention with juvenile sexual abusers: A holistic and integrated approach. In G. O'Reilly, W. L. Marshall, A. Carr, & R. Beckett (Eds.), *Handbook of clinical intervention with young people who sexually abuse* (pp. 297–314). New York: Taylor & Francis.

Karp, D. R. (2001). Harm and repair: Observing restorative justice in Vermont. *Justice Quarterly, 18*(4), 727–757.

LaPrairie, C. (1995, December). Altering course: New directions in criminal justice and corrections: Sentencing circles and family group conferences. *Australian and New Zealand Journal of Criminology,* 78–99.

Lipsey, M. W., & Wilson, D. B. (1998). Effective intervention for serious juvenile offenders: A synthesis of research. In R. Loeber & D. P. Farrington (Eds.), *Serious and violent juvenile offenders* (pp. 313–345). Thousand Oaks, CA: Sage.

Maxwell, G., & Morris, A. (1996). Research on family group conferences with young offenders in New Zealand. In J. Hudson, A. Morris, G. Maxwell, & B. Galaway (Eds.), *Family group conferences: Perspectives on policy and practice* (pp. 88–110). Monsey, NY: Criminal Justice Press.

McAllair, D. (1993). Reaffirming rehabilitation in juvenile justice. *Youth and Society, 25,* 104–125.

McCold, P., & Wachtel, B. (1998). *Restorative policing experiment: The Bethlehem Pennsylvanian Police Family Group Conferencing Project.* Pipersville, PA: Community Service Foundation.

McCold, P., & Wachtel, T. (2002). Restorative justice theory validation. In E. G. M. Weitekamp & H. J. Kerner (Eds.), *Restorative justice: Theoretical foundations* (pp. 110–142). Devon, UK: Willan.

McGarrell, E. F. (2001) *Restorative justice conference as an early response to young offenders* (NCJ No. 187769). Washington, DC: U.S. Department of Justice, Office of Juvenile Justice and Delinquency Prevention.

Melton, G. B. (1989). Taking Gault seriously: Toward a new juvenile court. *Nebraska Law Review, 68,* 146–181.

Messmer, H. E., & Otto, H. U. (Eds.). (1992). *Restorative justice on trial: Pitfalls and potentials of victim offender mediation: International research perspectives.* Norwell, MA: Kluwer Academic.

Miers, D. (2001). *An international review of restorative justice* (Crime Reduction Research Series, Paper 10). London: Home Office.

Mirsky, L. (2003a, February 20). Family group conferencing worldwide: Part 1. *Restorative Practices E Forum.* Retrieved February 27, 2003, from www.restorativepractices.org

Mirsky, L. (2003b, April 3). Family group conferencing worldwide: Part 2. *Restorative Practices E Forum.* Retrieved February 27, 2003, from www.restorativepractices.org

Morenz, B., & Becker, J. V. (1995). The treatment of youthful offenders. *Applied and Preventive Psychology, 4*(4), 247–256.

Morris, A., & Maxwell, G. (1997). Reforming juvenile justice: The New Zealand experiment. *Prison Journal, 77,* 125–134.

Morris, A., & Maxwell, G. (Eds.). (2001). *Restorative justice for juveniles: Conferencing, mediation and circles.* Oxford, UK: Hart.

Pennell, J., & Burford, G. (2000). Family group decision-making: Protecting children and women. *Child Welfare, 79*(2), 131–158.

Pepinsky, H. E., & Quinney, R. (Eds.). (1991). *Criminology as peacemaking.* Bloomington: Indiana University Press.

Petrucci, C. J. (2002). Apology in the criminal justice setting: Evidence for including apology as an additional component in the legal system. *Behavioral Sciences and the Law, 20,* 337–362.

Petrunik, M. (2002). Managing unacceptable risk: Sex offenders, community response, and social policy in the United States and Canada. *International Journal of Offender Therapy and Comparative Criminology, 46,* 483–511.

Putnam, R. (2000). *Bowling alone: The collapse and revival of American community.* New York: Simon & Shuster.

Retzinger, S., & Scheff, T. (1996). Strategy for community conferences: Emotions and social bonds. In B. Galaway & J. Hudson (Eds.), *Restorative justice: International perspectives* (pp. 316–318). Monsey, NY: Criminal Justice Press.

Righthand, S., & Welch, C. (2001). *Juveniles who have sexually offended* (NCJ No. 184739). Washington, DC: U.S. Department of Justice, Office of Juvenile Justice and Delinquency.

Rose, D., & Clear, T. (1998). Incarceration, social capital and crime: Implications for social disorganization theory. *Criminology, 36*(3), 471–479.

Sampson, R. J., & Wilson, J. (1995). *Toward a theory of race, crime, and urban inequality.* In J. Hagan & R. D. Peterson (Eds.), *Crime and urban inequality* (pp. 37–54). Stanford, CA: Stanford University Press.

Scher, S. J., & Darley, J. M. (1997). How effective are the things people say to apologize? Effects of the realization of the apology speech act. *Journal of Psycholinguist Research, 26,* 127–140.

Schiff, M. (1998). Restorative justice intervention for juvenile offenders: A research agenda for the next decade. *Western Criminology Review, 1*(1). Retrieved October 14, 2000, from wrc.sonoma.edu/vlnl/schiff.html

Schiff, M., & Bazemore, S. G. (2002). Restorative conferencing for juveniles in the United States: Prevalence, process, and practice. In E. G. M. Weitekamp & H. J. Kerner (Eds.), *Restorative justice: Theoretical foundations* (pp. 177–203). Devon, UK: Willan.

Schneider, A. (Ed.). (1985). *Guide to juvenile restitution.* Washington, DC: U.S. Department of Justice, Office of Juvenile Justice and Delinquency Prevention.

Schram, D. D., Milloy, C. D., & Rowe, W. E. (1991). *Juvenile sex offenders: A follow-up study of reoffense behavior.* Olympia, WA: Washington State Institute for Public Policy, Urban Policy Research, and Cambie Group International.

Sherman, L., Strang, H., & Woods, D. J. (2000). *Recidivism patterns in the Canberra reintegrative shaming experiments.* Canberra: Australian National University.

Small, M.A., & Kimbrough-Melton, R. (2002). Rethinking justice. *Behavioral Sciences and the Law, 20,* 309–315.

Strang, H. (2002). *Repair or revenge: Victims and restorative justice.* Oxford, UK: Clarendon Press.

Strang, H., Barnes, G. C., Braithwaite, J., & Sherman, L. W. (1999). *Experiments in restorative policing: A progress report on the Canberra reintegrative shaming experiments (RISE)*. Canberra: Australian National University.

Stuart, B. (2001). Guiding principles for designing peacemaking circles. In S. G. Bazemore & M. Schiff (Eds.), *Restorative community justice: Repairing harm and transforming communities* (pp. 219–241). Cincinnati, OH: Anderson.

Tavuchis, N. (1991). *Mea culpa: A sociology of apology and reconciliation*. Stanford, CA: Stanford University Press.

Torbert, P., Gable, R., Hurst, H., Montgomery, I., Szymanski, L., & Thomas, D. (1997). *State responses to serious and violent juvenile crime* (OJJDP Research Report). Pittsburgh, PA: National Center for Juvenile Justice.

Umbreit, M. S. (1989). Crime victims seeking fairness, not revenge: Toward restorative justice. *Federal Probation, 53*(3), 52–57.

Umbreit, M. S. (2001). *The handbook of victim–offender mediation*. San Francisco: Jossey-Bass.

Umbreit, M., Coates, R., & Kalanj, B. (1994). *Victim meets offender: The impact of restorative justice and mediation*. Monsey, NY: Criminal Justice Press.

Umbreit, M. S., & Greenwood, J. (1999). National survey of victim–offender mediation programs in the United States. *Mediation Quarterly, 16*, 235–251.

Walgrave, L. (1999). Community service as a cornerstone. In L. Walgrave & S. G. Bazemore (Eds.), *Restorative juvenile justice: Repairing harm of youth crime* (pp. 129–154). Monsey, NY: Criminal Justice Press.

Weitekamp, E. (1999). The history of restorative justice. In L. Walgrave & S. G. Bazemore (Eds.), *Restorative juvenile justice: Repairing harm of youth crime* (pp. 75–102). Monsey, NY: Criminal Justice Press.

Wexler, D. B. (1991). An introduction of therapeutic jurisprudence. In D. B. Wexler & B. J. Winick (Eds.), *Essays in therapeutic jurisprudence* (pp. ix–xiv). Durham, NC: Carolina Academic Press.

Wexler, D. B. (1998). Therapeutic jurisprudence forum: Practicing therapeutic jurisprudence: Psycholegal soft spots and strategies. *Revista Juridica Universidad de Puerto Rico, 67*, 317–342.

Wilson, R. J., Huculak, B., & McWhinnie, A. (2002). Restorative justice innovations in Canada. *Behavioral Sciences and the Law, 20*, 363–380.

Yazzie, R. (1994). Life comes from it: Navajo justice concepts. *New Mexico Law Review, 24*, 175–190.

Young, R., & Hoyle, C. (2004). New improved police led restorative justice? Action research and the Thames Valley police initiative. In A. von Hirsch, A. Bottoms, J. Roberts, K. Roach, & M. Schiff (Eds.), *Restorative justice and criminal justice: Competing or reconcilable paradigms*. Oxford, UK: Hart.

Zehr, H. (1990). *Changing lenses: A new focus for crime and justice*. Scottsdale, PA: Herald Press.

CHAPTER 16

Pharmacological Treatment of the Juvenile Sex Offender

John M. W. Bradford
Paul Fedoroff

Adolescence is a unique time for intervention in deviant sexual behavior. Sexually deviant behavior starts in adolescence, close to the onset of puberty, with deviant sexual fantasies. Although it has been said previously that the paraphilias are mostly a problem of male behavior, this has been disputed more recently, at least as far as pedophilia is concerned. It is becoming clear that females abuse children at a significant rate and that the incidence and prevalence of pedophilia among females is higher than was first thought (Bradford, Curry, & Fedoroff, 2004).

Deviant sexual behavior in adolescence starts with the development of deviant sexual fantasy, which then becomes associated with masturbation and stays chiefly at this level throughout adolescence in the majority of cases. The acting out of deviant sexual behavior starts most often in late adolescence and early adulthood (Abel, Mittelman, & Becker, 1985). This means that there is a unique opportunity during this time frame of early adolescence (12 or 13 years of age) up until late adolescence (17 or 18 years of age), during which the treatment of deviant sexual behavior could occur before it reaches the stage of acting out. This, by definition, would be a primary prevention strategy. If such intervention is accepted and carried out on a large scale, it potentially can have a dramatic impact on the incidence of the sexual abuse of children. Pedophilia would be held to the stage of deviant sexual fantasy and urges while preventing sexually acting-out behavior against children.

Abel et al. (1985), in a classic study, reported that 42% of all male paraphiliacs exhibited deviant sexual arousal by age 15, and 57% by age 19. Homosexual pedophilia had the earliest onset, with 53% reporting deviant arousal by age 15 and 74% by age 18. This means that the presence of paraphilias in adolescence can be documented by a detailed sexual-behaviors assessment, including sexual arousal tests. As these tests provide objective evaluations of deviant sexual arousal, this means that the presence of paraphilias in early adolescence can be reliably diagnosed. Objective evaluation is important, as self-report in adolescence is problematic. This procedure would allow the diagnosis by objective testing of paraphilias and particularly serious sexual deviations such as pedophilia.

Although an argument can be made that the degree of intrusiveness of sexual arousal tests using a penile tumescence technique in adolescents would contraindicate this type of evaluation, this argument needs to be considered against the serious consequences of not making a diagnosis and the effects it could have on the sexual abuse of children. Further, visual reaction time, as opposed to penile tumescence testing, is less intrusive and provides an objective measure of deviant sexual interests. It can also be used as a large-scale screening tool with adolescents (Abel, Jordan, Hand, Holland, & Phipps, 2001). If large-scale screening of adolescents is feasible, then large-scale treatment intervention is also feasible and can have a dramatic impact on the incidence of child sexual abuse through the early treatment of pedophilia. This in turn can have a dramatic impact on the costs associated with the treatment of victims, as well as associated costs of the prosecution and incarceration of the adolescent offender. Treating sexually deviant behavior in adolescence, therefore, should be a priority. There are well-accepted psychological methods of treatment for the adolescent sexual offender, but pharmacological treatments have lagged behind in the treatment of sexual deviation in adolescence. Because of advances in the pharmacological treatments of the paraphilias, some pharmacological agents can be used safely with adolescents and are likely to play an increasing role in the treatment of adolescent sexual offenders. This unique opportunity for primary prevention based on early treatment intervention is not being taken on a wide scale. This is unfortunate, and leaders in the field need to approach this in unison. This type of intervention needs to become part of a larger debate on public and social policy.

Hormones and Sexual Behavior

In the prepubertal years, the plasma levels of various sex hormones are low. This specifically applies to the gonadotropins and androgens. With the onset of puberty, secretion of adrenal androgens, dehydroepiandrosterone and androstenedione increases. Onset usually occurs at about 10 years of age, antedating the maturation of the hypothalamic–pituitary–gonadal axis (Bancroft, 1989). Some of the early sex differentiation seen in adolescence is driven by adrenal androgens; specifically, this includes the growth spurt and the development of axillary hair and pubic hair. During the prepubertal period, the gonadotropins and the androgens produced by the testes are at low levels; due partly to the increased sensitivity of androgen receptors in the hypothalamus. The exact hormonal changes at puberty are not fully understood. Changes in the sensitivity of androgen receptors lead to the hypothalamic–pituitary axis responding with increased secretion of gonadotropins. The gonadotropin-luteinizing hormone (LH) is secreted at a higher level than follicle-stimulating hormone (FSH). Over time the levels increase and are sustained 24 hours a day. The increase in gonadotropins is secondary to the release of luteinizing hormone-releasing hormone (LHRH) from the hypothalamus. The actual role of some of these polypeptide hormones, such as prolactin, is not absolutely clear. Puberty is regarded as being delayed if onset does not occur prior to age 15. The development of secondary sex characteristics accompanies puberty, and these hormonal changes are dependent on the levels of these hormones. The growth spurt is variable and occurs anywhere from 10.5 years to 16 years of age. Considerable individual variability occurs both in the onset and progress of these changes, and this variability has to be carefully taken into account in the assessment and treatment of adolescent sex offenders.

Although a full discussion of the effects of hormones on human sexual behavior is beyond the scope of this chapter, some principles need to be reviewed. Sexual behavior in most subprimates is predominantly under hormonal control. Females are sexually active only at certain times of the hormonal cycle known as estrus. In males, sexual behavior is very androgen dependent, specifically testosterone dependent, regardless of the species (Bancroft, 1989). With the greater biological development of the species, sexual behavior has become less directly determined by hormonal factors and more influenced by other factors, such as social learning and environment. Many of the findings in research on subprimates are relevant to human sexual behavior. For example, following castration, a predictable decline in male sexual behavior occurs that is similar to what is seen in human sexual behavior. Sexual drive, sexual fantasies, and copulation decrease in humans. In animal research, ejaculation disappears first, then intromission, and eventually mounting; with androgen replacement, these behaviors are restored in reverse order (Bancroft, 1989). Although the sexual decline generated by castration is predictable, the rate of decline varies from individual to individual and from species to species (Bancroft, 1989). Further, if the prepubertal androgen rise does not occur, then adult patterns of sexual behavior do not occur. If, however, the androgen surge occurs later on, the adult patterns of behavior will occur. Actions of androgens in male animals take place in the limbic system (especially the anterior hypothalamus), the spinal cord, and the penis. The role of hormones in male human sexuality is still controversial; however, evidence of the influence of hormones is well established in the hormonal replacement treatment of hypogonadal man, and the effects of antiandrogens and exogenous androgens are established in eugonadal man. These studies show that androgen levels affect sexual interest, erections, sexual fantasies, and sexual behavior (Bancroft, 1989).

With the increasing use of selective serotonin reuptake inhibitors (SSRIs), both in adults and adolescents, physicians have become increasingly aware of the side effects of these drugs, particularly on sexual behavior. Although these drugs are mostly used for the treatment of depression, obsessive–compulsive disorder, panic disorder, and other conditions, the increasing knowledge of their side-effects on sexual behavior has made the use of SSRIs in the treatment of sexually deviant behavior more acceptable. The neurobiology and neuropharmacology of sexual behavior is also becoming increasingly understood because of advances in recent years (Bradford, 2001). There has been significant research on serotonin (5-HT) receptors, as well as on the action of serotonin itself in the brain. This research has come largely as a result of 5-HT being involved in the neurobiology of many psychiatric disorders. This involvement is seen specifically in mood disorders but also in schizophrenia and some other psychiatric disorders. Although the etiology of these disorders is not understood, pharmacological interventions that affect the levels of 5-HT in the brain are effective treatments in many of these conditions (Bradford, 2001).

The response of a group of psychiatric conditions to drugs that modulate 5-HT levels in the brain has led to speculation that a group of disorders could be classified as obsessive–compulsive spectrum disorders (Bradford, 1999; Hollender et al., 1996). Some of the diagnostic characteristics of these disorders as outlined in DSM-IV (American Psychiatric Association, 1994) and DSM-IV-TR (American Psychiatric Association, 2000) are similar. There is no agreement as to whether sexual deviation or paraphilias should be incorporated in obsessive–compulsive spectrum disorders, but they do clearly have features in common with these disorders. Obsessive–compulsive spectrum disorders include obsessive–compulsive disorder, eating disorders, somatoform disorders, impulse-control disorders, and also disorders such as Tourette's disorder.

As the therapeutic spectrum for SSRIs has increased, it has also led to research that maps out the 5-HT receptor subtypes (Kennet, 2000). Most of the SSRIs are nonspecific and act on many of the receptor subtypes (Kennet, 2000). There are four main subgroups of 5-HT receptors that have been identified, specifically 5-HT_1, 5-HT_2, 5-HT_3, and 5-HT_4 (Kennet, 2000). Molecular biological techniques have broken these down into further receptor subtypes. Pharmacological research is establishing selective ligands for the various receptor subtypes, which in time will result in pharmacological agents that are specific agonists and antagonists for the receptor subtypes. Some of the receptor subtypes are specific for sexual behavior, and this research will further elucidate which receptor subtypes affect behavior, including sexual disorders as well as general psychiatric disorders.

The neurobiology of hypersexuality has shown that certain parts of the brain can effect disinhibition of sexual behavior (Stein, Hugo, Oosthuizen, Hawkridge, & van Heerden, 2000). The scientific literature contains many references to disinhibited sexual behavior caused by brain lesions, including frontal lobe lesions. In the same context, sexually deviant behavior has been reported in a wide variety of neuropsychiatric conditions, including temporal lobe epilepsy, postencephalitic syndromes, septal lesions, Tourette's disorder, frontal lobe lesions, cerebral tumors in various anatomical areas of the brain, bilateral temporal lobe lesions, and multiple sclerosis (Chow & Cummings, 1999). Brain lesions have resulted in both documented hyposexuality and hypersexuality (Chow & Cummings, 1999). Further, obsessive–compulsive disorder syndromes secondary to brain lesions, has been reported in the same neuroanatomical areas of the brain where sexual disorders have been documented as having been caused by brain lesions (Chow & Cummings, 1999). Some studies show Tourette's disorder and obsessive–compulsive disorder are associated neuroanatomically with the corticostriatal circuit of the brain (Stein et al. 2000; Chow & Cummings, 1999; Comings, 1987). Comorbidity between paraphilic and hypersexual behavior and Tourette's disorder has also been documented (Kerbeshian & Burd, 1991). Copralalia and copropraxia are diagnostic criteria for Tourette's disorder, and they often have a sexual component (Kerbeshian & Burd, 1991).

Research has also found that sexual symptoms decrease with treatment with SSRIs and with drugs that block dopamine (Stein et al., 2000). These observations support a relationship between sexually deviant behavior, compulsive sexual behavior, Tourette's disorder, and obsessive–compulsive disorder and some underlying neurobiological abnormality. The results also support the inclusion of the paraphilias in the obsessive–compulsive spectrum disorders. It is also significant that obsessive–compulsive disorder and Tourette's disorder are both present during adolescence.

The research also supports the use of the SSRIs in the treatment of the paraphilias and compulsive sexual behavior, or nonparaphilic hypersexuality. SSRIs have been used extensively in the treatment of psychiatric conditions since the early 1990s. Therefore, the common and less frequent side effects have been well documented. SSRIs can induce hyperprolactinemia, sexual dysfunction, extrapyramidal symptoms, galactorrhea, and gynecomastia, as well as a number of other side effects such as cognitive dysfunction (Damsa et al., 2004). The documented side effects created an opportunity to use the side-effect profile for therapeutic purposes in treating sexual disorders. Hyperprolactinemia is caused by hypothalamic stimulation of the release of prolactin, without going into the neurobiological mechanisms involved. An increase in prolactin causes a decrease in sexual behavior. Further, the sexual side effects of the SSRIs have been explained by other mechanisms of action, including dopaminergic inhibition, anticholinergic effects, and the inhibition of nitric oxide synthetase. The role of SSRIs in dopaminergic inhibition is supported by the observation that dopaminergic agonists can reverse the ejaculatory dysfunction that is secondary to SSRI treatment (Damsa et al., 2004). Further, other pharmacological agents have been used to prevent SSRI-induced sexual side effects, including serotonin receptor antagonists, adrenergic receptor antagonists, and dopaminergic agents. This usage supports the idea that various neurotransmitter systems are involved in sexual behavior, and this knowledge can be used to modify human sexual behavior. Unfortunately, there have not been a high number of human clinical studies in this area; such studies would be helpful in understanding more fully the neurobiological mechanisms involved (Damsa et al., 2004). The research also demonstrates that the SSRIs have sexual side effects similar to those of antiandrogens. Antiandrogens have been used to treat deviant sexual behavior on the basis of its side effects since 1971 (Bradford, 2000). As outlined later in this chapter, the SSRIs can be used in the treatment of paraphilic behavior in adolescents with less concern for side effects compared with antiandrogens. This means that the SSRIs are the pharmacological agent of first choice in the treatment of paraphilias in adolescents, as well as the first line of pharmacological treatment in adults.

More recently, the neurochemistry of sexual behavior has been studied, and it is clear that central serotonin metabolism also has a significant effect on sexual behavior (Greenberg & Bradford, 1997). Decreased central serotonin levels in experimental animals are associated with an increase in sexual drive. By contrast, increased serotonin levels reduce sexual drive. In humans the role of serotonin in sexual behavior is extremely complex, and, in addition, a variety of serotonin receptors are present (Bradford, 1999; Greenberg & Bradford, 1997).

Pharmacological Treatment

There are three main types of pharmacological treatment:

1. The selective serotonin reuptake inhibitors (SSRIs). The most common SSRIs used are sertraline, fluoxetine, and, to a lesser extent, paroxetine.
2. The antiandrogens and hormonal agents. In Canada, cyproterone acetate is most commonly used, and medroxyprogesterone acetate is mostly used in the United States.
3. The luteinizing hormone-releasing hormone agonists, including leuprolide acetate, goserelin acetate, and triptorelin acetate. Leuprolide acetate and goserelin acetate are available in North America. Triptorelin acetate is not available at this time but is likely to become available in the near future.

Bradford (2000) put forward an algorithm for the pharmacological treatment of the paraphilias. This is based on an enhanced classification of the severity of paraphilias used in DSM-III-R (American Psychiatric Association, 1987). The classification of severity comprises the following four categories: (1) mild, (2) moderate, (3) severe, and (4) catastrophic. The full version of this classification has been published elsewhere (Bradford, 2000). In brief, only paraphilic fantasy is present in mild cases, but this would include all of the "hands-off" paraphilias such as exhibitionism, voyeurism, and fetishism. Moderate cases would include "hands-on" paraphilias such as pedophilia would be included provided the number of victims was low and the level of intrusive sexual behavior was limited to fondling. Severe cases include "hands-on" paraphilias such as pedophilia with a larger number of victims and evidence of intrusive sexual behavior beyond fondling. Catastrophic cases include cases in which sexual sadism is the defining feature. The risk of serious physical violence associated with sexually violent behavior would be of serious concern.

The algorithm encompasses six levels of pharmacological treatment corresponding to the different levels of severity of the paraphilia. The aim of pharmacological treatment, regardless of the level of severity, is to suppress or eliminate deviant sexual fantasies; to eliminate deviant sexual urges and behavior; and ultimately to reduce the risk of future victimization by reducing sexual offender recidivism. The algorithm follows:

- Level 1: Cognitive-behaviorial treatment and relapse prevention treatment would always be given, regardless of the severity of the paraphilia.
- Level 2: Pharmacological treatment would start with SSRIs and is indicated in most cases of mild paraphilias.
- Level 3: If SSRIs are not effective in 4–6 weeks at adequate dosage levels, then a small dose of an antiandrogen would be added (e.g., sertraline 200 mg daily and 50 mg of medroxyprogesterone acetate daily). This would be used in mild and moderate paraphilias.
- Level 4: Full antiandrogen treatment or hormonal treatment given orally (e.g., 50–300 mg of medroxyprogesterone acetate per day or 50–300 mg of cyproterone acetate per day). This would be used in moderate cases and some cases of severe paraphilias.
- Level 5: Full antiandrogen treatment or hormonal treatment given intramuscularly (e.g., 300 mg of medroxyprogesterone acetate given intramuscularly per week or 200 mg of cyproterone acetate given intramuscularly every 2 weeks). This would be used in severe cases of paraphilias.
- Level 6: Complete androgen suppression and sex-drive suppression by giving cyproterone intramuscularly (e.g., cyproterone acetate 200 to 400 mg intramuscularly given weekly or a luteinizing hormone-releasing hormone agonist). This is for severe cases of paraphilia and is the only treatment in catastrophic cases (Bradford, 2000).

The levels of severity of mild, moderate, severe, and catastrophic cases would determine what level of the treatment algorithm would be used. Typically mild cases would receive treatment at level 1 or 2 of the algorithm. Moderate to severe paraphilias would start or include levels 1 and 2 but most likely would need level 3 intervention and, in severe cases, levels 4 and 5. Cases classified as catastrophic would go directly for treatment at level 6. With adolescent sexual offenders, concerns over the use of hormonal or antiandrogen drugs would mean that levels 1 and 2 and possibly 3 would be the treatment range used. It would be only in exceptional circumstances that levels 4, 5, and 6 would even be considered and should only be done by psychiatrists well versed in the pharmacological treatment of sexual deviation with antiandrogens and LHRH agonists and only in consultation with a pediatric endocrinologist. Our position is that, if any type of antiandrogen or hormonal treatment is considered, it should be used only for a short duration to get very serious and dangerous sexual behavior under control. Once that has happened, it is most likely that SSRIs would be sufficient for the maintenance of control of the seriously deviant behavior.

The Aims of Pharmacological Treatment

The aims of treatment at all levels of severity would be the same, as follows:

1. To suppress and eliminate deviant sexual fantasies.
2. To eliminate deviant sexual urges and behaviors.
3. To reduce the risk of further victimization through a reduction in sexual offender recidivism as a result of the impact of the first two aims of treatment.

This treatment algorithm would have the following effects on sexual behavior:

1. Suppression of deviant sexual fantasies, urges, and behaviors, with a minor impact on sexual drive occurring at levels 1 and 2.
2. Suppression of deviant sexual fantasies, urges, and behaviors, with a moderate reduction in sexual drive. Normophilic behavior will occur but at a low level. This effect will be seen at levels 2 and 3, but it is dose dependent.
3. Suppression of deviant sexual fantasies, urges, and behaviors, with a severe reduction of sexual drive so that normophilic behavior occurs but at a very low level. This effect would be seen at levels 4 and 5.
4. The complete suppression of sexual drive with no paraphilic or normophilic sexual behavior, creating an asexual individual. This effect would be seen at level 6.

This algorithm can be used only if the treating psychiatrist has a full understanding of the pharmacology of the various agents used in the treatment and is assured that there are no contraindications from a general medical standpoint for the use of these pharmacological agents. It is strongly recommended that consultation with an endocrinologist be considered with adults, it is an absolute requirement with adolescents in any consideration of an antiandrogen or hormonal treatment.

The Selective Serotonin Reuptake Inhibitors

The SSRIs have been the most recent pharmacological agents used in the treatment of sexual disorders, including sexual deviation (Greenberg & Bradford, 1997). The earliest indication of the usefulness of SSRIs in the treatment of deviant sexual behavior was a case report by Bianchi (1990). He reported on the successful treatment of a man with exhibitionism using fluoxetine hydrochloride. The patient subjectively reported a reduction in deviant urges and deviant sexual fantasy (Bianchi, 1990). Other case reports soon followed (Perilstein, Lipper, & Friedman, 1991; Lorefice, 1991; Emmanuel, Lydiard, & Ballenger, 1991). Kafka (1991) treated four patients complaining of nondeviant hypersexuality with fluoxetine hydrochloride and reported significant reductions in sexual drive. He also reported on three cases of sexual deviation treated with fluoxetine hydrochloride that showed considerable improvement. Kafka and Prentky (1992b) completed an outpatient study ($n = 16$) in which half of the patients showed sexual deviance and the other half showed nondeviant hypersexuality. Over a 3-month period, all of the patients improved on an average daily dose of 39 mg of fluoxetine hydrochloride. Stein and colleagues (1992) treated five paraphilic males and reported that none of them had shown any decrease in deviant sexual behavior when treated with fluoxetine hydrochloride. Coleman, Cesnik, Moore, and Dwyer (1992) completed a retrospective study of 13 paraphilic males and reported improvement in all aspects of sexually deviant behavior when treated with fluoxetine hydrochloride. Kafka (1994) reported on an open clinical trial of men suffering from both paraphilia ($n = 13$) and nonparaphilic hypersexuality ($n = 11$) and reported significant reductions in deviant sexual fantasies, urges, masturbation, and sexual behavior in general. The SSRI used in this study was sertraline. About half of the participants responded to sertraline. The nonresponders were treated with fluoxetine hydrochloride, and about two thirds showed clinical improvement. The duration of treatment was approximately 18 weeks, and the average dosage of sertraline used was approximately 100 mg per day. The average dose of fluoxetine hydrochloride for the treatment of the nonresponders was 51.1 mg per day.

Bradford, Greenberg, Gojer, Martindale, and Goldberg (1995) reported on a 12-week open-label dose-titrated study of pedophilia ($n = 20$) using sertraline. The mean effective dosage of sertraline was 131 mg per day. Eight-six percent of patients completed the study, and no patients were discontinued due to an inadequate treatment response. Overall, the severity of the pedophilia rated by the physicians in the study decreased dramatically over the duration of the study; this was a statistically significant decrease. Eighty-six percent of patients were rated as responders in the study. Various deviant and nondeviant sexual behaviors were significantly reduced over the duration of the study. In contrast, heterosexual coitus with adult females actually showed a small increase during the study. This increase in nondeviant sexual behavior in admitted pedophiles when treated with sertraline was seen as a highly desirable outcome. With pedophiles, anything that can generate sexual interest in adults is clearly a significant treatment response. Physiological measures of sexual arousal showed decreases in pedophilic arousal and improved or maintained normophilic arousal or arousal to adults. This paralleled the self-reported finding of an increase in heterosexual intercourse. Although this was an open-label study, it did show evidence of improvement or maintenance of normophilic behavior in known pedophiles.

This finding is similar to one reported in a study of the antiandrogen cyproterone acetate. Greenberg, Bradford, Curry, and O'Rourke (1996) completed a retrospective study of treatment with three different SSRIs (fluoxetine hydrochloride, sertraline hydrochloride, and fluvoxamine hydrochloride) in a sample of sexually deviant males ($n = 58$). The aim of the study was to see whether the three different SSRIs were equally effective in treatment effect on deviant sexual behavior. The study showed them to be equally effective. Sexual fantasies were markedly reduced by all three medications. Greenberg and Bradford (1997) completed a retrospective study of paraphilic males ($n = 95$) treated with SSRIs. A control group ($n = 104$) received only psychological treatment over a 12-week period. The frequency and severity of paraphilic fantasies were significantly reduced in the sample treated with SSRIs compared with the control group treated only with psychological treatment.

Determining the treatment effectiveness of SSRIs in sexually deviant behavior still requires the completion of double-blind treatment studies. This need is offset in part by studies on the neurobiology of 5-HT in animal sexual and other behavior. SSRIs have a significant impact on human sexual behavior, as is well documented in clinical studies reporting these side effects to SSRI treatment. The SSRIs are recommended as the primary pharmacological treatment of choice for adolescent sexual offenders as per level 2 of the algorithm. As already outlined, in by far the majority of cases of adolescent sex offenders, the pharmacological treatment should remain at level 2 of the algorithm. The algorithm was developed for the treatment of adult sexual offenders, and this needs to be taken into consideration with adolescent sexual offenders. This means, in practical terms, that regardless of the classification of severity, SSRIs are the treatment of choice and need to be used at adequate dosage levels for an extended period of time prior to any decision on their effectiveness. As outlined in the algorithm, this treatment needs to be combined with the most up-to-date cognitive behavioral treatment for the paraphilias.

Antidepressants and Suicidality

Recently, the safety of SSRIs and serotonin–norepinephrine reuptake inhibitors (SNRIs) has been seriously questioned because of reports that they could increase aggressive and suicidal behaviors. The increase in suicidality was defined as the emergence or worsening of suicidal thoughts, behaviors, and attempts (Lam & Kennedy, 2005). In general, there is less evidence that the use of antidepressants for the treatment of depression in adolescents and children is beneficial when compared with the evidence of the same medications used for the same indications in adults. Initially, studies showed that SSRIs were beneficial compared with placebo in the treatment of major depressive disorder in adolescents and children; however, of 15 random controlled trials funded by pharmaceutical companies, only six were published. A review of the unpublished studies revealed that most of the new antidepressants, including SSRIs and SNRIs (citalopram, paroxetine, sertraline, and venlafaxine), were found to be no better than placebo in relieving the symptoms of depression. Only fluoxetine was consistently found to be superior to placebo in two studies. The risk of suicidality was identified as a serious issue in a meta-analysis of these studies (Whittington et al., 2004).

The U.S. Food and Drug Administration (FDA) issued a public health advisory on October 15, 2004, addressing the issue of suicidality in children and adolescents being treated with antidepressants (U.S. Food and Drug Administration, 2004). In the statement, the FDA directed the manufacturers of antidepressant drugs to revise the labeling of their products to include an expanded warning statement to alert health care providers to the increased risk of suicidality in children and adolescents being treated with these agents. In addition, manufacturers were to include information about the results of studies of children and adolescents receiving these drugs. The FDA also directed drug manufacturers to include a guide for patients receiving the drugs to inform them about the risks associated with the medications and advise them about precautions that they can take. These labeling changes came from recommendations made to the FDA following a joint meeting of the Psychopharmacological Drugs Advisory Committee and the Pediatric Drugs Advisory Committee on September 13 and 14, 2004. The risk of suicidality for these drugs was identified in a combined analysis of short-term placebo-controlled trials of nine antidepressant drugs, including the SSRIs, in children and adolescents with major depressive disorder, obsessive-compulsive disorder, and other psychiatric disorders. The joint committees reviewed a total of 24 trials involving 4,400 patients. An analysis showed an increased risk of suicidality during the first few months of treatment with these medications. An analysis of the average risk of suicidality was 4%, twice the placebo risk of 2%; no actual suicides occurred in the patient sample. It was quite clear, however, that the FDA determined the following:

- The risk of suicidal thinking and behavior in children and adolescents with major depressive disorder and other psychiatric disorders is increased in children and adolescents receiving antidepressants.
- A physician considering prescribing antidepressants to children and adolescents for any clinical indication must balance this risk of increased suicidality against the clinical need of the antidepressant.
- Any adolescents or children treated with antidepressants must be closely observed clinically for suicidality or any other changes in behavior.
- Patients' families need to be clearly advised as to the risks associated with the drugs. They also need to be advised to observe their children closely for any behavioral changes or suicidality and to notify their health care provider immediately if such changes occur.
- A statement regarding whether a particular drug is approved for any pediatric indications needs to be made and those indications need to be discussed (U.S. Food and Drug Administration, 2004).

When considering the full range of antidepressants, it is important to note that only fluoxetine is approved for use in treating major depressive disorder in pediatric patients, but fluoxetine, sertraline, fluvoxamine, and clomipramine are approved for the treatment of obsessive–compulsive disorder in pediatric patients. None of the antidepressants discussed here are approved for any other psychiatric indications in children or adolescents (U.S. Food and Drug Administration, 2004).

Hormonal Agents

Historically, estrogens were used for sexual drive reduction (Foote, 1944; Golla & Hodge, 1949; Symmers, 1968; Whittaker, 1959). According to the clinical reports, this was a successful treatment, with the side effects of nausea, vomiting, and feminization limiting its use. Medroxyprogesterone acetate (MPA) has been the most important form of hormonal agent used in the United States. The first study was done by Heller, Laidlaw, Harvey, and Nelson (1959). Since then a number of clinical studies have been completed (Berlin & Meinecke, 1981; Cooper, Sandhu, & Losztyn, 1992; Gagne, 1981; Gottesman & Schubert, 1993; Kiersch, 1990; Langevin et al., 1979; Meyer, Collier, & Emery, 1992; Money, 1970; Money, Wiedeking, Walker, & Gain, 1976; Walker & Meyer, 1981; Wiedeking, Money, & Walker, 1979; Wincze, Bansal, & Malamud, 1986).

The mechanism of action of MPA is through the induction of testosterone-a-reductase in the liver. This increases the metabolic clearance of testosterone, and plasma testosterone is reduced. In addition, it has a progestinic effect, which results in a reduction of the secretion of gonadotropins. It does not compete with androgen receptors at a receptor level and therefore by definition is not a true antiandrogen (Southren, Gordon, Vittek, & Altman, 1977). Treatment with MPA results in a number of side effects. These include weight gain, decreased sperm production, a hyperinsulinar response to a glucose load that leads to potential problems with diabetes mellitus, headaches, deep vein thrombosis, hot flashes, nausea, and vomiting, all of which can be managed medically (Walker & Meyer, 1981; Gagne, 1981; Berlin & Meinecke, 1981). At the same time a significant impact on sexual behavior was observed, including a reduction in sex drive, sexual fantasy, and sexual activity (Walker & Meyer, 1981; Gagne, 1981; Berlin & Meinecke, 1981).

The clinical studies of MPA are mostly open trials, starting with the work of Money (1970, 1972). These were followed by other clinical studies (Wiedeking et al., 1979; Langevin et al. 1979). Two early open clinical studies of most importance were those of Berlin and Meinecke (1981) and Gagne (1981). Both studies showed that MPA was an effective treatment provided the participants complied. There tended to be a significant relapse rate if treatment was discontinued. Wincze et al. (1986) used MPA in a single-case experimental design with three pedophiles. They included a double-blind procedure. The results showed that self-reported arousal outside of a laboratory setting was unreliable; however, within a laboratory setting, significant reduction in arousal to erotic stimuli was noted, and this result was statistically significant compared with the placebo phase. Nocturnal penile tumescence was reduced in all cases. Kiersch (1990) completed a 64-week follow-up study of eight patients treated with MPA. MPA was given as 400 mg weekly depot injections for 16 weeks, alternating with saline injections for a crossover period of 16 weeks. The results were variable, but problems with the design of the study may be responsible for the variable results. Meyer et al. (1992) studied 40 men (mostly pedophiles) treated with MPA and group and individual therapy. The treatment was 400 mg a week by depot injection for 6 months through 12 years. A control group of 21 treatment refusers were also studied. They were treated with psychotherapy over the same follow-up period. In the pharmacological treatment group, 18% reoffended while on MPA, and 35% reoffended after MPA was discontinued. This compared with 58% in the control group. The risk factors for reoffense were documented as raised baseline testosterone levels, head injury, and alcohol and substance abuse. Gottesman and Schubert (1993) used a low-dose oral MPA treatment regimen for the paraphilias. They used 60 mg of MPA a day for 15 months in an open trial involving 7 participants. This treatment regimen resulted in significant drops in plasma testosterone levels when compared with baseline, and a positive outcome was reported with significant reductions in paraphilic fantasies.

MPA can be used as an intervention according to the treatment algorithm at levels 3, 4, and 5. MPA is certainly not a frontline treatment for adolescent sexual offenders. If used, it should be at level 3, combined with an SSRI for a relatively short time. In late adolescence, from 18 years of age onward, it could be used as defined in the algorithm.

LHRH Agonists

LHRH agonists have a very specific treatment role in the paraphilias in that they produce a pharmacological "castration." The use of a pharmacological "castration" in an adolescent sexual offender would be an extremely rare event, other than with a highly sadistic individual of 18 years or older. Given that, the review of these pharmacological agents is brief.

The hypothalamic–pituitary axis is overstimulated by the LHRH agonists and is exhausted. Following the exhaustion of the axis, there is a significant inhibition of gonadotropin secretion. LHRH agonists that have a prolonged action are the pharmacological agents that were described by Bradford (1985) when they were just being developed as potential treatments for sexual deviation. These pharmacological agents are principally used for treatment of prostate cancer. The aim of treatment in prostate cancer is the complete reduction or elimination of testosterone, which drives the cancer growth. They have been shown to be very effective in clinical studies of prostate cancer treatment. Clearly, with such a significant effect on plasma testosterone, it is not surprising that they could be used as a pharmacological castration agent. Since that time, there have only been a few open clinical studies on the use of LHRH agonists in treatment of sexual deviation. Rousseau, Dupont, Labrie, and Couture (1988) reported on the changes in sexual behavior in prostate cancer patients treated with flutamide (a nonsteroidal antiandrogen), up to 750 mg per day in divided dosages, and surgical castration. Another group of patients in the same study who did not undergo surgical castration were treated with flutamide but were also treated with an LHRH agonist, LHRH ethylamide, administered subcutaneously at 500 mcg for the first month and 250 mcg in ongoing treatment. The pretreatment sexual functioning of the patients was compared with posttreatment sexual activity. In the pretreatment phase, 80% of the patients were sexually active and had sexual intercourse at least once a week, and 50% were able to achieve erections generated by sexual fantasy. These 50% also never had any erectile difficulties. Posttreatment, more than 70% of patients had a major decrease in sexual interest, with sexual intercourse and sexual activity maintained in only 20% of cases, and about 60% of cases unable to achieve an erection by sexual fantasy. This showed that the LHRH agonist and surgical castration had a significant impact on all aspects of sexual behavior, and this result was related to the reduction of plasma testosterone. Dickey (1992) reported on a single case study of successful treatment of a paraphilia with leuprolide acetate. Thibaut, Cordier, and Kuhn (1993) reported on the treatment of six males with paraphilia treated with triptorelin, 3.75 mg per month intramuscularly. All of the men had paraphilias; most were pedophiles, and a third had failed other oral antiandrogen treatment, although treatment compliance was suspect. The patients were treated with triptorelin, 3.75 mg per month, concurrently with cyproterone (CPA), 200 mg a day for 5.5 months. In 5 of the 6 patients the deviant sexual behavior was markedly decreased without significant side effects in a follow-up period ranging from 7 months to 3 years. One patient interrupted treatment after 12 months and relapsed 2–3 months later. The most important study to date with LHRH agonists in the treatment of sexual deviation was by Rosler and Witztum (1998). This was an uncontrolled open study of the treatment of 30 men with a mean age of 32 years who suffered from longstanding severe sexual deviation. Twenty-five of the 30 men suffered from pedophilia. They were treated with monthly injections of 3.75 mg of triptorelin and supportive psychotherapy for a follow-up period of 8 to 42 months. The treatment outcome was evaluated monthly by questionnaires. All of the men showed a decrease in the number of deviant sexual fantasies and urges. Quantitatively during therapy, this was reduced to zero. There was also a significant decrease in the number of deviant sexual interests—also to zero—while they were receiving triptorelin. These effects were observed for at least 1 year in all of the men ($n = 24$) who continued treatment for a year. The plasma testosterone levels fell to castration levels. With the triptorelin treatment, side effects were erectile failure, hot flashes, and some decrease in bone mineral density.

LHRH analogues, specifically leuprolide acetate, triptorelin (not available in the United States and Canada), and goserilin acetate, are treatments that can be used at level 6 of the treatment algorithm. We would not recommend LHRH agonists for treatment of paraphilias in anyone less than 18 years of age.

Antiandrogen

Cyproterone acetate (CPA) has antiandrogenic, antigonadotropic, and also progestinic effects, and has a principal mode of action at the androgen receptors throughout the body. Its mode of action here is that it blocks intracellular testosterone uptake and the intracellular metabolism of the androgen (Bradford, 1983; Neumann, 1977). The effects of this medication are largely dose dependent. Sexual behavior decreases because of a reduction of plasma testosterone, as well as the receptor blockade. Side effects decrease sexual behavior, including erections, masturbation, sexual intercourse, and deviant sexual behavior (Bradford, 1983; Neumann & Schleusener, 1980). CPA has very strong progestational action; it is 100 times stronger than progesterone in the Kleiberg test (Schering, 1983). It is designated as an antiandrogen, as it clearly acts at the level of the androgen receptor. Cyproterone and flutamide (a nonsteroidal true antiandrogen) have no antigonadotropic effects. It is the acetate radical that gives CPA the progestational action that is seen. CPA blocks or reduces LHRH secretion (Neumann & Schleusener, 1980). The full antigonadotropic effect of CPA is only seen in females, as in males the antiandrogen and antigonadotropic effects balance out. The specific mode of action of CPA is competitive inhibition of testosterone and dihydrotestosterone at the androgen receptors. CPA is 100% bioavailable orally with a plasma half life of 38 HR ± 5 hours, and in the intramuscular depot form it reaches maximum plasma levels in 82 hours (Schering, 1983).

The theoretical risks of CPA treatment are very similar to those with MPA, although unlikely to occur at the dosage levels that are used to treat paraphilias. There is a possibility of liver dysfunction and adrenal suppression (Cremonocini, Viginati, & Libroia, 1976). It is also clear that long-term treatment with CPA can lead to osteoporosis and osteopenia in certain individuals (Grasswick & Bradford, 2003). CPA is also the most widely studied pharmacological agent in the treatment of the paraphilias.

The first clinical studies were done in Germany in 1971 by Laschet and Laschet (1971), who treated more than 100 sexually deviant men. The participants were mostly exhibitionists and pedophiles, as well as sadists, and about half were sexual offenders. The duration of treatment in an open clinical trial varied from 6 months to longer than 4 years. In 80% of cases, CPA at 100 mg a day eliminated sexual drive, erections, and orgasms, whereas at 50 mg a day, a reduced libido was noted, but erections were possible, and reduced but ongoing sexual behavior could occur. CPA was also administered intramuscularly at 300 mg biweekly; about 20% of exhibitionists showed a complete elimination of all deviant sexual behavior even after treatment was discontinued. The undesirable side effects reported in this study were fatigue, transient depression, weight gain (20% of cases), and some form of feminization, including slight gynecomastia. Laschet and Laschet (1975) reported on 300 men treated for up to 8 years with an excellent response. Minimal side effects in long-term management were reported. Davies (1974) and Bancroft, Tennent, Loucas, and Cass (1974) completed studies with positive treatment results and few side effects. Cooper (1981), Cooper, Ismail, Phanjoo, and Love (1972), and Ott and Hoffet (1968) showed that CPA was an effective treatment agent in reducing deviant sexual behavior. The largest group of sexually deviant men ever studied in pharmacological treatment was examined by Mothes, Lehnert, Samimi, and Ufer (1971). Laschet and Laschet (1975) reported on 200 patients, with a duration of treatment from 2 months to 8 years, treated with 50 to 100 mg daily of CPA given orally and intramuscular CPA given weekly or biweekly in dosages between 300 and 600 mg. They found that treatment was very successful. In 80% of the cases on the oral dose, deviant sexual behavior was reduced, with an associated decrease in sexual drive. The side effects in the first 2 months were fatigue, hypersomnia, depression, negative nitrogen balance, and weight gain. At about 3 months, the nitrogen balance had returned to normal, and calcium and phosphate metabolism normalized. About 8 months into treatment, about 20% of cases showed signs of feminization, with some gynecomastia and a reduction in body hair. Twenty-five patients were followed for up to 5 years after the discontinuation of CPA and showed no evidence of any recurrence of sexually deviant behavior. A double-blind placebo-crossover study was completed by Bradford and Pawlak (1993a). A similar study of the effects of CPA on the sexual arousal of pedophiles in treatment with CPA was also completed (Bradford & Pawlak, 1993b). A single-case study, with repeated measures of the successful treatment, of a homicidal sadistic homosexual pedophile with very serious brain damage treated with CPA was also reported (Bradford & Pawlak, 1987). It was also noted in the single-case study that CPA had a differential effect on the sexual arousal patterns. What was observed was that the sadistic and pedophilic arousal was suppressed at a higher rate than the arousal to consenting sex with adults. This meant that CPA had a treatment effect of normalizing the sexual arousal patterns. In the study on the sexual arousal patterns of pedophiles (Bradford & Pawlak, 1993b), this normalizing of the sexual arousal pattern was seen in the larger sample, thereby confirming that this appeared to be a treatment effect. In the double-blind placebo-crossover study of 19 participants, mostly pedophiles, a positive treatment effect compared with placebo was noted. The sample was mostly made up of sexual-offender recidivists with an average of 2.5 previous sexual-offense convictions per participants. CPA was administered orally in 3-month active treatment phases with a crossover placebo design. During the active treatment phases, a reduction of sexual arousal responses occurred that did not quite reach statistical significance. Self-report measures of arousal were all significantly reduced. Psychopathology measured by rating scales showed significant reductions, and self-reported sexual activity was also significantly reduced. Other objective measures of sexuality, including fantasies and masturbation, were all significantly decreased by CPA (Bradford & Pawlak, 1993a).

Further, CPA is the one pharmacological intervention that has been subjected to research into treatment outcome and recidivism. Eight studies have shown that CPA is effective in reducing posttreatment recidivism rates (Horn, 1972; Fahndrich, 1974; Davies, 1974; Appelt & Floru, 1974; Jost, 1975; Baron & Unger, 1977). All of these studies showed posttreatment recidivism rates that were significantly reduced, with the pretreatment rate and recidivism ranging from 50% to 100% and the posttreatment rate being 0% in follow-up periods ranging from 1 to 5 years. In only one study was there a 16.7% recidivism rate in a 1.5 year follow-up period on 6 patients (Appelt & Floru, 1974).

Summary and Conclusions

The pharmacological treatment of sexual deviation using SSRIs, antiandrogens, or hormonal treatments has a sound scientific basis in the understanding of the mechanisms of action of the pharmacological agents. This is likely to increase as further work on 5-HT receptors and subreceptors continues. In fact, it is this work that is most likely going to unravel the specific sexual behaviors that are all controlled by 5-HT. The efficacy of the antiandrogens in reducing sexual offense recidivism is based on the large surgical castration studies that were completed in Europe, which also have long periods of community follow-up. The scientific observation that CPA has a differential effect on sexual-arousal pattern in the direction of normalization is of significant scientific interest and supports a positive treatment outcome effect with CPA. Similar results have been seen with the SSRI sertraline. If this finding holds up with further replication, it is a very positive scientific finding and worthy of considerable optimism for pharmacological treatment in the future. This would be a highly desirable result of treatment for sexual offenders.

The use of pharmacological agents to treat adolescent sexual offenders is limited because of the potential hormonal effects from the antiandrogens and hormonal agents. The discovery that the SSRIs can be effective treatment agents and the existence of pharmacological agents that can be used relatively safely with adolescents means that these drugs are the primary pharmacological treatments in this age group. Clearly, further research is necessary in the whole area, but specifically into the

SSRIs. Hopefully the increased use of SSRIs in the treatment of juvenile sexual offenders will have an impact at a primary prevention level in the future, thereby drastically reducing the victimization of women and children by sexually deviant adolescents.

It should be noted that, at this time, all medications used for the treatment of sexual deviation are prescribed off-label. This means that a formal indication for the use of SSRIs, SNRIs, antiandrogens, or hormonal agents in the treatment of sexual deviation is not currently recognized by the FDA or equivalent regulatory agencies in the United Kingdom, Canada, or most other Western nations. In order to obtain a formal (i.e., government-approved) indication for any pharmacological agent requires the pharmaceutical company to conduct randomized controlled studies in a clinical sample of patients—adults or children—suffering from the psychiatric disorder. This process is funded by the pharmaceutical companies and is an extremely expensive exercise. In general, the pharmaceutical industry is not motivated to develop an indication for the treatment of sexual deviation either in adults or adolescents for the SSRIs, antiandrogens, and hormonal agents, which means that, for the time being, the use of these medications is going to remain off-label (Bradford 1998). Given the public health advisory from the FDA and other international agencies for the use of these medications in adolescents and children, even for psychiatric disorders for which a formal indication has been approved, any off-label use of these drugs must be approached with extreme caution. This situation also highlights a significant scientific problem that occurs when the pharmaceutical industries in most Western countries are responsible for developing indications for their own products: Only indications that fit within the general corporate policies will be investigated and promoted, while others—ones that do not fit corporate policy—are not pursued. Simply put, the pharmaceutical industry is not interested in promoting pharmacological agents specifically for the treatment of sexual deviation and pedophilia. This means that if any progress is to be made in the pharmacological treatment of sexual deviation, government agencies such as the FDA and the Surgeon General in the United States and the equivalent agencies in Canada and Europe would have to breach this gap to support the random controlled clinical trials necessary to develop a formal indication. As this has never happened, it has been left to practitioners and academic researchers to continue promoting the pharmacological treatment of sexual deviation in adults and adolescents.

Unfortunately, research support for the scientific investigation of the pharmacological treatment of sexual deviation has been very poor. The pharmaceutical industry, which traditionally supports pharmacological research, appears reluctant to support research into the treatment of sexual deviation. This is understandable from a public relations stand-point; however, government funding agencies also have not supported this work to any great extent. This means that this type of research has been very difficult to do and extremely difficult to fund. In addition, significant ethical barriers exist in completing double-blind placebo pharmacological treatment studies in sexually deviant men. Pharmacological treatment is an effective treatment that needs to be combined with a cognitive-behavioral approach and, specifically, relapse-prevention treatment. There clearly is a role for government funding agencies to look at pharmacological treatment in positive terms and to support further research into the pharmacological treatment of juvenile, as well as adult, sexual offenders.

References

Abel, G. G., Jordan, A., Hand, C. G., Holland, L. A., & Phipps, A. (2001). Classification models of child molesters utilizing the Abel Assessment for sexual interest. *Child Abuse and Neglect: The International Journal, 25*, 703–718.

Abel, G. G., Mittelman, M. S., & Becker, J. V. (1985). Sexual offenders: Results of assessment and recommendations for treatment. In M. H. Ben-Aron, S. J. Hucker, & C. D. Webster (Eds.), *Clinical criminology: The assessment and treatment of criminal behaviour* (pp. 191–206) Toronto, Ontario, Canada: M and M Graphics.

American Psychiatric Association. (1987). *Diagnostic and statistical manual of mental disorders* (3rd ed., rev.). Washington, DC: Author.

Appelt, M., & Floru, L. (1974). The effect on sexuality of cyproterone acetate. *International Pharmacopsychiatry, 9*, 61–76.

Bancroft, J. (1989). The biological basis of human sexuality. In J. Bancroft (Ed.), *Human sexuality and its problems* (pp. 12–127) Edinburgh, UK: Church Livingstone.

Bancroft, J., Tennent, G., Loucas, K., & Cass, J. (1974). The control of deviant sexual behavior by drugs: 1. Behavioural changes following oestragens and antiandrogens. *British Journal of Psychiatry, 125*, 310–315.

Baron, D., & Unger, H. (1977). A clinical trial of cyproterone acetate for sexual deviancy. *New Zealand Medical Journal, 85*, 366–369.

Berlin, F. S., & Meinecke, C. F. (1981). Treatment of sex offenders with antiandrogenic medication: Conceptualization, review of treatment modalities and preliminary findings. *American Journal of Psychiatry, 138*(5), 601–607.

Bianchi, M. D. (1990). Fluoxetine treatment of exhibitionism [Letter to the editor]. *American Journal of Psychiatry, 147*(8), 1089–1990.

Bradford, J. M. W. (1983). Research in sex offenders. In R. L. Sadoff (Ed.), *The psychiatric clinics of North America* (pp. 715–733). Philadelphia: Saunders.

Bradford, J. M. W. (1994). Can pedophilia be treated? *Harvard Mental Health Letter, 10*(8),

Bradford, J. M. W. (1999). The paraphilias, obsessive compulsive spectrum disorder and the treatment of sexually deviant behavior. *Psychiatric Quarterly, 70*(3), 209–220.

Bradford, J. M. W. (2000). The treatment of sexual deviation using a pharmacological approach. *Journal of Sex Research, 3,* 248–257.

Bradford, J. M. W. (2001). The neurobiology, neuropharmacology and pharmacological treatment of the paraphilias and compulsive sexual behavior. *Canadian Journal of Psychiatry, 46,* 26–34.

Bradford, J. M. W., Curry, S., & Fedoroff, P. (2004). *Reports of childhood sexual abuse perpetrated by females in a sample of male offenders.* Manuscript submitted for publication.

Bradford, J. M. W., Greenberg, D., Gojer, J., Martindale, J. J., & Goldberg, M. (1995). *Sertraline in the treatment of pedophilia: An open label study.* New Research Program Abstracts NR 441; APA MTA, Florida, May 24, 1995.

Bradford, J. M. W., & Pawlak, A. (1987). Sadistic homosexual pedophilia: Treatment with cyproterone acetate. A single case study. *Canadian Journal of Psychiatry, 32,* 22–31.

Bradford, J. M. W., & Pawlak, A. (1993a). Double-blind placebo-crossover study of cyproterone acetate in the treatment of the paraphilias. *Archives of Sexual Behavior, 22*(5), 383–402.

Bradford, J. M. W., & Pawlak, A. (1993b). Effects of cyproterone acetate on sexual arousal patterns of pedophiles. *Archives of Sexual Behavior, 22*(6), 629–641.

Chow, T. W., & Cummings, J. L. (1999). Neuropsychiatry: Clinical assessment and approach to diagnosis. In B. J. Sadock & V. A. Sadock (Eds.), *Comprehensive textbook of psychiatry* (7th ed., pp. 221–41). Baltimore: Lippincott, Williams and Wilkins.

Coleman, E., Cesnik, J., Moore, A. M., & Dwyer, S. M. (1992). An exploratory study of the role of psychotropic medications in treatment of sexual offenders. *Journal of Offender Rehabilitation, 18,* 75–88.

Comings, D. E. (1987). A controlled study of Tourette syndrome: VII. Summary: A common genetic disorder causing disinhibition of the limbic system. *American Journal of Human Genetics, 41,* 839–866.

Cooper, A. J. (1981). A placebo controlled study of the antiandrogen cyproterone acetate in deviant hypersexuality. *Comprehensive Psychiatry, 22,* 458–464.

Cooper, A. J., Ismail, A. A., Phanjoo, A. L., & Love, D. L. (1972). Antiandrogen (cyproterone acetate) therapy in deviant hypersexuality. *British Journal of Psychiatry, 120,* 59–63.

Cooper, A. J., Sandhu, S., & Losztyn, S. (1992). A double-blind placebo controlled trial of medroxyprogesterone acetate and cyproterone acetate with seven pedophiles. *Canadian Journal of Psychiatry, 37,* 687–693.

Cremonocini, C., Viginati, E., & Libroia, A. (1976). Treatment of hirsutism and acne in women with two combinations of cyproterone acetate and ethinyloestradiol. *Acta European Fertility, 7,* 299–314.

Damsa, M. D., Bumb, A., Bianchi-Demicheli, F., Vidailhet, P., Sterck, R., Andreoli, A., et al. (2004). "Dopamine-dependent" side effects of selective serotonin reuptake inhibitors: A clinical review. *Journal of Clinical Psychiatry, 65,* 1064–1068.

Davies, T. D. (1974). Cyproterone acetate for male hypersexuality. *Journal of International Medical Research, 2,* 159–163.

Dickey, R. (1992). The management of a case of treatment-resistant paraphilia with a long-acting LHRH agonist. *Canadian Journal of Psychiatry, 37,* 567–569.

Emmanuel, N. P., Lydiard, R. B., & Ballenger, J. C. (1991). Fluoxetine treatment of voyeurism. *American Journal of Psychiatry, 148,* 950.

Fahndrich, E. (1974). Cyproterone acetate in the treatment of sexual deviation in men. *Deutsche-Medizinische Wochenschrift, 99,* 234–242.

Foote, R. M. (1944). Diethylstilboestrol in the management of psychopathological states in males. *Journal of Nervous and Mental Disease, 99,* 928–935.

Gagne, P. (1981). Treatment of sex offenders with medroxyprogesterone acetate. *American Journal of Psychiatry, 138*(5), 644–646.

Golla, F. L., & Hodge, S. R. (1949). Hormone treatment of sexual offenders. *Lancet, 1,* 1006–1007.

Gottesman, H. G., & Schubert, D. S. (1993). Low-dose oral medroxyprogesterone acetate in the management of the paraphilias. *Journal of Clinical Psychiatry, 54*(5), 182–188.

Grasswick, L. J., & Bradford, J. M. W. (2003). Osteoporosis associated with the treatment of paraphilias: A clinical review of seven case reports. *Journal of Forensic Science, 48*(4), 1–7.

Greenberg, D. M., & Bradford, J. M. W. (1997). Treatment of the paraphilic disorders: A review of the role of the selective serotonin reuptake inhibitors. *Sexual Abuse: A Journal of Research and Treatment, 9,* 349–361.

Greenberg, D. M., Bradford, J. M. W., Curry, S., & O'Rourke, A. (1996). A comparison of treatment of paraphilias with three serotonin reuptake inhibitors: A retrospective study. *Bulletin of the American Academy of Psychiatry and the Law, 24,* 525–532.

Heller, C., Laidlaw, W., Harvey, H., & Nelson, W. (1959). Effects of progestational compounds on the reproductive processes of the human male. *Annals of the New York Academy of Science, 71,* 649–655.

Hollender, E., Kwon, J. H., Stein, D. J., Broatch, J., Rowland, C. T., & Himelein, C. A. (1996). Obsessive-compulsive and spectrum disorder: Overview and quality of life issues. *Journal of Clinical Psychiatry, 57*(8), 3–6.

Horn, J. A. (1972). The treatment of sexual deviation with the antiandrogen cyproterone acetate 1971 to 1975. *Der Informiette Arzt, 3,* 303–309.

Jost, F. (1975). Zur Behandlung abnormen sexual verhaltnas mit dem antiandrogen cyproteronacetat [Treatment of abnormal sexual behavior with the antiandrogen cyproterone acetate]. *Der Informiette Arzt, 3,* 303–309.

Kafka, M. P. (1991). Successful treatment of paraphilic coercive disorder (a rapist) with fluoxetine hydrochloride. *British Journal of Psychiatry, 158,* 844–847.

Kafka, M. P. (1994). Sertraline pharmacotherapy for paraphilias and paraphilia-related disorders: An open trial. *Annals of Clinical Psychiatry, 6,* 189–195.

Kafka, M. P., & Prentky, R. (1992). Fluoxetine treatment of nonparaphilic sexual addictions and paraphilias in men. *Journal of Clinical Psychiatry, 53,* 351–358.

Kerbeshian, J., & Burd, L. (1991). Tourette syndrome and recurrent paraphilic masturbatory fantasy. *Canadian Journal of Psychiatry, 36,* 155–157.

Kiersch, T. A. (1990). Treatment of sex offenders with Depo-provera. *Bulletin of the American Academy of Psychiatry and Law, 18*(2), 179–187.

Lam R. W., & Kennedy S. H. (2005). Prescribing antidepressants for depression in 2005: Recent concerns and recommendations [Canadian Psychiatric Association Position Statement]. *Canadian Journal of Psychiatry, 49*(12), 1–6.

Langevin, R., Paitich, D., Hucker, S., Newman, S., Ramsay, G., Pope, S., Geller, G., & Anderson, C. (1979). The effect of assertiveness training, provera and sex of therapist in the treatment of genital exhibitionism. *Journal of Behavioral Therapy and Experimental Psychiatry, 10,* 275–282.

Laschet, U., & Laschet, L. (1971). Psychopharmacotherapy of sex offenders with cyproterone acetate. *Pharmakopsychiatrie Neuropsychopharmakologic, 4,* 99–104.

Laschet, U., & Laschet, L. (1975). Antiandrogens in the treatment of sexual deviations of men. *Journal of Steroid Biochemistry, 6,* 821–826.

Lorefice, L. S. (1991). Fluoxetine treatment of a fetish [Letter to the editor]. *Journal of Clinical Psychiatry, 52*(1), 436–437.

Meyer, W. J., Collier, C., & Emory, E. (1992). Depo provera treatment for sex offending behavior: An evaluation of outcome. *Bulletin of the American Academy of Psychiatry and Law, 20*(3), 249–259.

Money, J. (1970). Use of androgen depleting hormone in the treatment of male sex offenders. *Journal of Sex Research, 6,* 165–172.

Money, J. (1972). The therapeutic use of androgen-depleting hormone. *International Psychiatry Clinics, 8,* 165–174.

Money, J. M., Wiedeking, C., Walker, P. A., & Gain, D. (1976). Combined antiandrogen and counseling program for treatment of 46, XY and 47, XYY sex offenders. In E. Sachar (Ed.), *Hormones, behavior and psychopathology* (pp. 195–120) New York: Raven Press.

Mothes, C., Lehnert, J., Samimi, F., & Ufer, J. (1971). Schering symposium uber sexual deviationen und ihre medikamentose Behandlung [Schering symposium on sexual deviation and its medical treatment]. *Life Sciences Monograph, 2,* 65.

Neumann, F. (1977). Pharmacology and potential use of cyproterone acetate. *Hormone and Metabolic Research, 9,* 1–13.

Neumann, F., & Schleusener, A. (1980). Pharmacology of cyproterone acetate with special reference to the skin. In R. Vokoer & D. Fanta (Eds.), *The pharmacology of cyproterone acetate, combined antiandrogen–estrogen therapy in dermatology.* Proceedings of Dianne Symposium, Brussels, 19–51.

Ott, F., & Hoffet, H. (1968) The influence of antiandrogens on libido, potency and testicular function. *Schweiz Medizin Wochenschrift, 98,* 1812.

Perilstein, R. D., Lipper, S., & Friedman, L. J. (1991). Three cases of paraphilias responsive to fluoxetine treatment. *Journal of Clinical Psychiatry, 52,* 169–170.

Rosler, A., & Witztum, E. (1998). Treatment of men with paraphilia with a long acting analogue of gonadotropin-releasing hormone. *New England Journal of Medicine, 338,* 416–465.

Schering, A. G. (1983). *Androcur.* Berlin, Germany: Berlin/Bergkamen.

Southren, A. L., Gordon, G. G., Vittek, J., & Altman, K. (1977). Effect of progestagens on androgen metabolism. In L. Martini & M. Motta (Eds.), *Androgens and antiandrogens* (pp. 263–279), New York: Raven Press.

Stein, D. J., Hollander, E., Anthony, D. T., Schneider, F. R., Fallon, B. A, & Liebowitz, M. R. (1992). Serotonergic medications for sexual obsessions, sexual addictions and paraphilias. *Journal of Clinical Psychiatry, 53,* 267–271.

Stein, D. J., Hugo, F., Oosthuizen, P., Hawkridge, S. M., & van Heerden, B. (2000). Neuropsychiatry of hypersexuality. *CNS Spectrums, 5,* 36–46.

Symmers W. S. C. (1968). Carcinoma of the breast in transsexual individuals after surgical and hormonal interference with primary and secondary sex characteristics. *British Medical Journal, 2,* 3–8.

Thibaut, F., Cordier, B., & Kuhn, J. M. (1993). Effect of a long-lasting gonadotrophin hormone-releasing hormone agonist in sex cases of severe male paraphilia. *Acta Psychiatrica Scandinavica, 87*(6), 445–50.

U.S. Food and Drug Administration, Center for Drug Evaluation and Research, Department of Health and Human Services. (2004, October 15). *Public Health Advisory.*

Walker, P. A., & Meyer, W. J. (1981). Medroxyprogesterone acetate treatment for paraphiliac sex offenders. In J. R. Hays, T. K. Roberts, & K. S. Solway (Eds.), *Violence and the violent individual* (pp. 353–373). New York: SP Medical and Scientific Books.

Whittaker, L. H. (1959). Estrogens and psychosexual disorders. *Medical Journal of Australia, 2,* 547–549.

Whittington, C. J., Kendall, T., Fonagy, P., Cottrell, D., Cotgrove, A., & Boddington, E. (2004). Selective serotonin reuptake inhibitors in childhood depression: A systematic review of published versus unpublished data. *Lancet, 363,* 1341–1345.

Wiedeking, C., Money, J., & Walker, P. A. (1979). Follow-up of 11 XYY males with impulsive and/or sex-offending behavior. *Psychological Medicine, 9,* 287–292.

Wincze, W. P., Bansal, S., & Malamud, M. (1986). Effects of medroxyprogesterone acetate on subjective arousal, arousal to erotic stimulation and nocturnal penile tumescence in male sex offenders. *Archives of Sexual Behavior, 15,* 293–305.

Index